DISPUTI)RLD
T

Any experienced lawyer knows that cases are most often won or lost on procedural grounds; yet procedural issues are often considered too technical for proper treatment in legal literature. In this extensively revised new edition of Palmeter and Mavroidis' authoritative book on WTO dispute settlement, the authors discuss all WTO dispute settlement provisions and their interpretation in WTO jurisprudence. All the decisions of panels and the Appellate Body are discussed, from the inception of the WTO in 1995 until the end of May 2003. Although the book contains considerable technical expertise, it is at the same time written for accessibility to a wide readership. This volume – an essential tool for practitioners, diplomats and government lawyers – is a comprehensive study of compulsory third party adjudication in international law.

DAVID PALMETER is a partner in the law firm of Sidley Austin Brown & Wood LLP, and a long-time advisor of governments and interested private parties in WTO dispute settlement proceedings. From 1994 to 1998 he was liaison for the International Bar Association to GATT, the WTO and UNCTAD. He is a regular lecturer on WTO law at numerous universities, and is the author of *The WTO as a Legal System.*

PETROS C. MAVROIDIS is Professor of Law at Columbia Law School, New York, and the University of Neuchâtel, Switzerland. He previously taught at the European University Institute, Florence and was with the GATT/WTO Legal Service from 1992 to 1996. He is currently chief co-reporter of the American Law Institute for the project on "Principles of WTO Law."

DISPUTE SETTLEMENT IN THE WORLD TRADE ORGANIZATION

Practice and Procedure

Second Edition

DAVID PALMETER AND PETROS C. MAVROIDIS

CAMBRIDGE
UNIVERSITY PRESS

PUBLISHED BY THE PRESS SYNDICATE OF THE UNIVERSITY OF CAMBRIDGE
The Pitt Building, Trumpington Street, Cambridge, United Kingdom

CAMBRIDGE UNIVERSITY PRESS
The Edinburgh Building, Cambridge, CB2 2RU, UK
40 West 20th Street, New York, NY 10011–4211, USA
477 Williamstown Road, Port Melbourne, VIC 3207, Australia
Ruiz de Alarcón 13, 28014 Madrid, Spain
Dock House, The Waterfront, Cape Town 8001, South Africa

http://www.cambridge.org

First edition published by Kluwer Law International 1999

Second edition first published by Cambridge University Press 2004

Printed in the United Kingdom at the University Press, Cambridge

Typeface Minion 10.75/12.75 pt. *System* LaTeX 2ε [TB]

A catalogue record for this book is available from the British Library

Library of Congress Cataloguing in Publication data
Palmeter, N. David.
Dispute settlement in the World Trade Organization: practice and procedure / David Palmeter
and Petros C. Mavroidis. – 2nd ed.
p. cm.
Includes bibliographical references and index.
ISBN 0 521 82311 0 (hardback) – ISBN 0 521 53003 2 (paperback)
1. World Trade Organization. 2. Tariff – Law and legislation. 3. Foreign trade regulation.
4. Dispute resolution (Law) I. Mavroidis, Petros C. II. Title.
K4610.P35 2004
382′.92 – dc22 2003049548

ISBN 0 521 82311 0 hardback
ISBN 0 521 53003 2 paperback

Legal progress is often secreted
in the interstices of legal procedure.

– Oliver Wendell Holmes, Jr.

CONTENTS

PREFACE

This is a work for practitioners – for diplomats, government officials and lawyers – who prepare and present cases to dispute settlement panels of the World Trade Organization (WTO) and its Appellate Body, and for private practitioners who advise or represent governments and private clients with an interest in the outcomes of these proceedings. It grew from the experience of its authors, a private practitioner who has advised and represented governments and private parties under both the WTO and its predecessor, the General Agreement on Tariffs and Trade (GATT), and a former official of the Legal Affairs Division of both GATT and the WTO, who advised numerous panels.

The book attempts to address the kinds of procedural questions that confront practitioners in the very practical world of dispute settlement. While it relies heavily on panel and Appellate Body jurisprudence, it also describes the informal practices and WTO "ways of doing things" that have evolved, both to facilitate the dispute settlement process and to contend with the lacunae in the legal texts that time has exposed. From time to time we do comment critically on the decisions of panels and the Appellate Body, but this is not the focus of the book. Scholars increasingly are producing critical and analytical procedural literature, to which we refer at appropriate points in the text and list in the bibliography.

The first edition of this work, which appeared in 1999, contained extended annexes setting forth the text of the *Understanding on Rules and Procedures Governing the Settlement of Disputes* and the relevant dispute settlement provisions of other WTO agreements. For this edition, we concluded that the widespread availability of those documents makes their further reproduction here unnecessary. They may be found at the WTO's web site, www.wto.org, and are published in a convenient volume by the WTO and Cambridge University Press in The WTO Dispute Settlement Procedures, now in its second edition.

Chapter 3 of this volume is a now highly revised version of an article, *The WTO Legal System: Sources of Law*, that first appeared in volume 92 of the AMERICAN JOURNAL OF INTERNATIONAL LAW, © The American Society of International Law, which has kindly consented to its use here.

For their assistance in answering questions, furnishing documents, or reading and commenting on early versions of the text, we thank: Guy Evans, Todd J. Friedbacher, Reto Malacrida, Niall P. Meagher, Julia Pain, Yves Renouf, Celso de Tarso Pereira, Arun Venkataraman, Joelle Vuillemenot, Hannu Wager, Jasper-Martijn Wauters, Rhian-Mary Wood-Richards, and Werner Zdouc. Special thanks to Laurie Hieta, who read every word and checked every footnote, a task that called for courage above and beyond the call of duty.

1

Overview

§ 1.01 The ITO, the GATT, and the WTO

[1] Bretton Woods and the Havana Charter

Even as World War II was being fought, allied leaders began to plan for the post-war world which, they hoped, would not be characterized by the economic isolationism that had marked the pre-war years. Many believed that this contributed in no small way to the deepening of the Great Depression and the onset of war. In a 1941 speech entitled "Post-War Commercial Policy," United States Undersecretary of State Sumner Wells said:

> Nations have more often than not undertaken economic discriminations and raised up trade barriers with complete disregard for the damaging effects on the trade and livelihood of other peoples, and ironically enough, with similar disregard for the harmful resultant effects upon their own export trade.
>
> The resultant misery, bewilderment, and resentment, together with other equally pernicious contributing causes, paved the way for the rise of those very dictatorships which have plunged almost the entire world into war.[1]

These economic concerns eventually led to the famed July 1944 conference at Bretton Woods, New Hampshire, and the resulting "Bretton Woods organizations," the International Bank for Reconstruction and Development (commonly known as the World Bank) and the International Monetary Fund. Probably because Bretton Woods was attended only by representatives of finance ministries and not by representatives of trade ministries, an agreement covering trade was not negotiated there. A

[1] US Dep't. of State, Pub. No. 1660, Commercial Policy Series 71 (1941), *quoted* in John H. Jackson, World Trade and the Law of GATT 38 (Bobbs-Merrill, 1969).

trade agreement was very much in the minds of allied economic leaders, however, and in early December 1945, the United States issued a proposal for an International Trade Organization, the ITO. But it was not the time for such an ambitious proposal. To the contrary, almost five years later to the day, on December 6, 1950, the United States Department of State announced that the ITO was dead, killed by the United States Congress, which – eerily reminiscent of the United States Senate's treatment of the Treaty of Versailles and the League of Nations – refused to approve it.[2] Still, all was not lost. An odd portion of the ITO, in an odd way, survived. It was known as the General Agreement on Tariffs and Trade, or GATT, and it lasted for nearly half a century, for 47 years. On January 1, 1995, it was replaced by the World Trade Organization, the WTO, an entity broader both in its reach and in its effectiveness, but which is not at all what the ITO was intended to be.

[2] The negotiation of GATT

The ITO was ambitious, certainly too ambitious for the United States Congress and perhaps, with the advantage of hindsight, too ambitious by almost any reasonable standard. It was negotiated over a two-year period, from 1946 through 1948, at a series of meetings in London, New York, Geneva, and finally at a United Nations Conference on Trade and Employment in Havana, which produced the "Havana Charter for an International Trade Organization." As the conference name suggests, the ITO encompassed not only trade policy, but also employment policy. In addition, it covered commodity agreements, economic development, and restrictive business practices.

While the more ambitious provisions of the ITO were being negotiated, however, governments were interested in relaxing tariffs and other trade restrictions more rapidly. A Drafting Committee, under the sponsorship of the Preparatory Committee charged with drafting the ITO charter,

[2] This section draws heavily on Richard N. Gardner, Sterling-Dollar Diplomacy in Current Perspective: The Origins and Prospects of Our International Economic Order (Columbia Univ. Press ed., 1980); Robert E. Hudec, The GATT Legal System and World Trade Diplomacy (2d ed., Butterworth, 1990); Jackson, *supra* note 1; and on the World Trade Organization, Analytical Index, Guide to GATT Law and Practice (1995). In addition, John Jackson, The World Trading System (2d ed., MIT Press, 1997) provides an excellent history and description of the world trading system.

meeting in January and February 1947 at Lake Success, New York, produced a full draft of the GATT. From April through October 1947, the members of the Preparatory Committee conducted a round of tariff negotiations in the course of their ITO work at the European Office of the United Nations in Geneva. This became the first of GATT's eventual eight rounds of negotiations. It produced the "Geneva Final Act," consisting of the Lake Success text of GATT and the schedules of tariff commitments made by the 25 governments taking part.[3] It also included a "Protocol of Provisional Application" or "PPA," a measure intended to be a temporary expedient, but which ended up being fundamental to GATT for its 47-year existence.

[3] The Protocol of Provisional Application (PPA)

The broad scope of the ITO called for changes in the laws of many signatory governments and, consequently, eventual legislative approval under their various constitutional systems before it could become effective. Some governments did not want to wait until that process was completed and, accordingly, at the end of October 1947, eight of them agreed to apply GATT provisionally as of January 1, 1948.[4] Under the terms of the PPA, the eight undertook to apply Parts I and III of GATT fully, and to apply Part II only "to the fullest extent not inconsistent with existing legislation."[5] Part I contained just two articles, dealing with non-discrimination among competing foreign suppliers (most-favored-nation, or MFN) and the schedule of tariff rates just negotiated. Part III contained articles dealing, for the most part, with administrative matters. The substantive heart of GATT, Part II, consisted of Articles III through XXIII. These included provisions covering national treatment; antidumping and countervailing duties; valuation of imports for customs purposes; marks of origin; import and export quotas and limitations; restrictions on imports for balance of payments purposes; exchange arrangements; subsidies; state trading enterprises; governmental assistance to economic development; emergency action on imports of particular products; exceptions to GATT

[3] Final Act Adopted at the Conclusion of the Second Session of the Preparatory Committee of the United Nations Conference on Trade and Employment, UN Sales No. 1947.II/10; 55 UNTS 187 (1947).

[4] The eight were: Australia, Belgium, Canada, France, Luxembourg, the Netherlands, the United Kingdom, and the United States.

[5] 55 UNTS 308, 1 (a) and (b) (1947).

obligations, including exceptions necessary to protect human, plant, and animal life, health, and safety; and exceptions for national security purposes. Part II thus provides the necessary market access complement to Part I.

Together, Parts I and II set out the basic policy agreed to in GATT for trade liberalization. It is a policy that is based on: (i) preference for tariff protection to other forms of protection, such as quantitative restrictions or quotas; (ii) following on this, abolition (in principle, but not always in practice) of all quotas; (iii) application of quotas only exceptionally and only with multilateral permission; (iv) most-favored-nation (MFN) treatment, granted in principle to all GATT parties, subject to specific, narrowly-drawn exceptions; and (v) national treatment granted to all products of GATT parties that have lawfully cleared customs.

The application of Part II only to the extent that its articles were consistent with existing legislation created what became known as the "grandfather rights."[6] Consequently, parties with these grandfather rights were allowed to continue applying GATT-inconsistent measures notwithstanding their obligations under the General Agreement. Article XXIX:2 of GATT shows how temporary this was intended to be. It provides, "Part II of this Agreement shall be suspended on the day on which the Havana Charter comes into force." This was expected to occur within a fairly short time, so that inconsistent domestic legislation was not expected to be long-lived. But because the Havana Charter never came into force, GATT, for its entire 47 years, was applied on a "provisional" basis.

[4] GATT's 47 "provisional" years

Between the October 1947 issuance of the Protocol of Provisional Application and its effectiveness on January 1, 1948, most of the other countries participating in the Geneva tariff negotiations also agreed to apply the Protocol. The 1947 Geneva negotiations were followed by seven additional negotiations, called "rounds," each of which involved more participants as additional countries acceded to the General Agreement and the current Doha Development Round under the WTO:

[6] An example would be the US countervailing duty law, which did not require a determination of material injury, as called for by Article VI in Part II of GATT, until the United States agreed to include such a requirement for signatories to the so-called 1979 Tokyo Round Subsidies Code or for other countries that entered into comparable bilateral agreements with the United States.

Round[7]	*Dates*	*Number of Parties*[8]
Geneva	1947	19
Annecy	1949	27
Torquay	1950	33
Geneva	1956	36
Dillon	1960–61	43
Kennedy	1962–67	74
Tokyo	1973–79	85
Uruguay	1986–94	128
Doha	2001–	146

All of the rounds through the 1960–61 Dillon Round dealt with tariff cuts. In the Kennedy Round, a first, relatively unsuccessful attempt was made to deal with so-called "non-tariff barriers," or NTBs. As tariffs were progressively cut, NTBs became more prominent as trade barriers. A Kennedy Round Antidumping Code and an agreement dealing with a highly protectionist US method of valuing certain chemicals and footwear for customs purposes were not accepted by the US Congress on the stated grounds that in reaching these agreements, the US negotiators had exceeded their mandate.[9]

This experience soured many trading partners of the United States, who found themselves having to negotiate twice: first with the US negotiators and then with the Congress. If NTBs were to be dealt with in future negotiations, another way had to be found. Another way was found that took into account the need of US trading partners to know that a package put together with US negotiators would not be taken apart by the Congress, and the constitutional need of the United States to refer to Congress all

[7] The first four rounds are named for the place where they were held: Geneva; Annecy, France; and Torquay, England. The Dillon Round and the Kennedy Round were named after the United States Under Secretary of State, C. Douglas Dillon, and President John F. Kennedy, respectively, who were instrumental in starting the rounds. The Tokyo and Uruguay Rounds were named after the city and the country, respectively, where trade ministers agreed to launch the rounds, as was the Doha Development Round.

[8] Computations of the total number of parties vary from source to source, because some of the original 1947 group subsequently withdrew from GATT (*e.g.*, China, Czechoslovakia) and because countries that acceded to GATT during the course of a round would be counted at the end, but not at the beginning. Counts of participants in GATT activities may vary too depending on how the European Union is accounted for – as a single entity or as individual Members.

[9] *See* Russell Long, *United States Law and the International Antidumping Code*, 3 INT'L LAWYER 464 (1969).

agreements requiring statutory change, which was the case with most measures dealing with NTBs. The solution was the so-called "fast-track procedure" first included in the Trade Act of 1974.[10] Under this procedure, the Congress agreed that a bill implementing a negotiated agreement would not be amendable on the floor of either House of Congress, would not be stalled in Committee, and would receive a straight "yes or no" vote within a stated time period.

This provision permitted the Tokyo Round negotiations to go forward, and led to the adoption of a wide variety of side-agreements or "codes" dealing with non-tariff issues:

1. Agreement on Implementation of Article VI of the General Agreement on Tariffs and Trade (Antidumping Code)
2. Agreement on Interpretation and Application of Articles VI, XVI and XXIII of the General Agreement on Tariffs and Trade (Subsidies Code)
3. Agreement on Import Licensing Procedures
4. Agreement on Trade in Civil Aircraft
5. Agreement on Technical Barriers to Trade
6. Agreement on Implementation of Article VII of the General Agreement on Tariffs and Trade and Protocol to the Agreement (Customs Valuation Code)
7. Agreement on Government Procurement

The Tokyo Round negotiations were the most extensive ever undertaken, but the 1986–1994 Uruguay Round was even more extensive in both its reach and its results. Before turning to a discussion of the Uruguay Round, however, we shall review briefly the evolution of dispute settlement under GATT, particularly as it evolved after the Tokyo Round. As we shall see, dispute settlement was one of the major goals of the Uruguay Round negotiators, and one of their major accomplishments.

[5] GATT dispute settlement[11]

Early dispute settlement in GATT reflected its diplomatic roots. In fact, the process initially was referred to as "conciliation," not as dispute

[10] Pub. Law 93-618, 88 Stat. 1978.

[11] This section draws heavily on Robert E. Hudec's outstanding two-volume history of GATT dispute settlement, THE GATT LEGAL SYSTEM AND WORLD TRADE DIPLOMACY, *supra* note 2, and ENFORCING INTERNATIONAL TRADE LAW: THE EVOLUTION OF THE MODERN GATT LEGAL SYSTEM (Butterworth, 1993) (hereafter ENFORCING INTERNATIONAL TRADE LAW).

settlement. It all began with a complaint in the summer of 1948 by the Netherlands against Cuba which presented the question: Does the most-favored-nation obligation of Article I apply to consular taxes? The matter was referred to the chairman, who ruled that Article I did apply. From these early beginnings of rulings by the chairman, disputes later came to be referred to working parties, consisting of the complaining party, the party complained against, and any others that had an interest. Eventually, the parties directly involved were dropped, and a three- or five-member panel process was adopted, using neutral panelists rather than representatives of parties with an interest in the issue. The term "panel" came from the term "panel of experts" – a term, Robert E. Hudec has noted, that was "coined long before GATT to describe an *ad hoc* group of government experts (rather than policy officials) convened to render an expert opinion about some technical question that is capable of being answered objectively. The term thus connoted objective decisions based on expertise rather than political representation of one's government."[12] Most of the advocates before panels and most of the panelists themselves – the "judges" – were diplomats, not lawyers. Not surprisingly, therefore, "legal rulings were drafted with an elusive diplomatic vagueness."[13] The goal of the process was more to reach a solution mutually agreeable to the parties than to render a decision in a legal dispute.[14]

GATT dispute settlement was characterized as well by the fact that its procedural rules were very limited, largely because it was anticipated that the ITO rules soon would apply. The ITO Charter contained detailed dispute settlement rules that included a provision for the reference of questions to the International Court of Justice, the ICJ. The only dispute settlement rules in GATT, based on two of the proposed ITO rules, were GATT Articles XXII and XXIII, dealing, respectively, with consultations and with "nullification and impairment," a phrase that was basic to the jurisprudence of GATT and now is basic to the jurisprudence of the WTO.

By themselves, the consultation provisions of Article XXII have no direct consequences. Article XXII:1 simply requires each contracting party to afford other parties adequate opportunity for consultation with respect to any matter affecting the operation of the Agreement. Article XXII:2

[12] Robert E. Hudec, *The Role of the GATT Secretariat in the Evolution of the WTO Dispute Settlement Procedure*, in Bhagwati & Hirsch (Eds), THE URUGUAY ROUND AND BEYOND: ESSAYS IN HONOUR OF ARTHUR DUNKEL (Springer, 1998).

[13] Hudec, ENFORCING INTERNATIONAL TRADE LAW, *supra* note 11, at 12.

[14] *See*, William J. Davey, *Dispute Settlement in GATT*, 11 FORDHAM INTERNATIONAL LAW JOURNAL 51, 65 (1987).

authorizes the CONTRACTING PARTIES acting jointly, at the request of a contracting party, to consult with other parties on matters which were not resolved through Article XXII:1 consultations.[15] Eventually, these consultations became a basis for the generation of GATT's dispute settlement process, which was grounded in Article XXIII.

Article XXIII:1 provided that if any contracting party considered that any benefit directly or indirectly accruing to it under the Agreement was being nullified or impaired by another party, it could make written representations or proposals to that other party. If this did not lead to a satisfactory adjustment, the complaining party was authorized by Article XXIII:2 to refer the matter to the CONTRACTING PARTIES, who were required to investigate and make recommendations. In an appropriate case, Article XXIII:2 permitted the CONTRACTING PARTIES to authorize the complaining party to suspend the application of tariff concessions or other GATT obligations to the party found to be acting inconsistently with its obligations under the Agreement.

Neither article contained any specific procedures.[16] These evolved over time. Some formality was added at the conclusion of the Tokyo Round with the adoption of the *Understanding on Notification, Consultation, Dispute Settlement and Surveillance of 28 November 1979*, which included an annex setting out an *Agreed Description of the Customary Practice of the GATT in the Field of Dispute Settlement.* This *Description* noted, in part, that:

> Panels set up their own working procedures. The practice for the panels has been to hold two or three formal meetings with the parties concerned. The panel invited the parties to present their views either in writing and/or orally in the presence of each other. The panel can question both parties on any matter which it considers relevant to the dispute. Panels have also heard the views of any contracting party having a substantial interest in the matter, which is not directly party to the dispute, but which has expressed in the Council a desire to present its views. Written memoranda submitted to the panel have been considered confidential, but are made available to the parties to the dispute. Panels often consult with and seek information from

[15] The term CONTRACTING PARTIES in upper case letters was the GATT convention for referring to joint action by all of the parties to the Agreement. Since GATT was an agreement, not an organization, GATT itself could not act. In lower case, the term referred to individual signatories.

[16] An early decision by the CONTRACTING PARTIES held that consultations under Article XXII:1 would be considered as fulfilling the consultation requirements of Article XXIII:1. BISD 9S/20.

> any relevant source they deem appropriate and they sometimes consult experts to obtain their technical opinion on certain aspects of the matter. Panels may seek advice or assistance from the secretariat in its capacity as guardian of the General Agreement, especially on historical or procedural aspects. The secretariat provides the secretary and technical services for panels.[17]

Three years later, acting at a Ministerial Conference, the CONTRACTING PARTIES reaffirmed the 1979 Understanding and added more detail, including a requirement that, "The contracting party to which such a recommendation [i.e., to bring a challenged measure into conformity with GATT] has been addressed, shall report within a reasonable specified period on action taken or on its reasons for not implementing the recommendation or ruling by the CONTRACTING PARTIES."[18] Further minor steps were taken in a *Decision on Dispute Settlement Procedures* on November 30, 1984.[19]

Dispute settlement under GATT was handicapped, however, by the requirement of Article XXIII that all matters be decided, and all action be approved, by the CONTRACTING PARTIES. GATT, in legal form, was a contract – a multi-party contract – and any decision to amend, modify, or interpret that contract required the consent of all of the parties.[20] In practice, this meant that the losing party in a dispute settlement proceeding not only could refuse to agree, and therefore "block" the adoption of an adverse report, it could even refuse to agree to the very establishment of a panel, thereby avoiding even the embarrassment of a panel proceeding.

Adverse GATT panel reports indeed were blocked by losing parties. In fact, parties who anticipated losing sometimes even blocked the establishment of a panel. It is a tribute to the system and the degree to which the parties valued it that blocking of both the establishment of panels and the adoption of their reports did not occur more often than they did. In fact, Prof. Hudec's study shows that from 1947 to 1992, the losing party eventually accepted the results of an adverse panel report in approximately 90 percent of the cases.[21] Still, blocking was a problem and seemed to be occurring with increasing frequency in the 1980s. A significant step toward

[17] *Agreed Description of the Customary Practice of the GATT in the Field of Dispute Settlement* (Article XXIII:2), BISD 26S/215, 217, ¶ 6 (iv).

[18] BISD 29S/13, 15, ¶ (viii).

[19] BISD 31S/9.

[20] In the absence of a specific rule providing otherwise, Article 40 of the *Vienna Convention on the Law of Treaties* requires unanimity among the contracting states.

[21] Hudec, ENFORCING INTERNATIONAL TRADE LAW, *supra* note 11, at 278.

reducing the blockage – at least at the stage of establishing a panel – was taken with the adoption of the "Montreal Rules." These grew out of a December 1988 Ministerial meeting in that Canadian city to review the progress of the Uruguay Round and to reap an "early harvest" of any completed results of the Round. Following further consideration in early 1989 in Geneva, the Montreal Rules were adopted by the CONTRACTING PARTIES in April of that year.[22] They formed the basis of what eventually became the *WTO's Understanding on Rules and Procedures Governing the Settlement of Disputes.*

The CONTRACTING PARTIES agreed to apply the Montreal Rules "on a trial basis from 1 May 1989 to the end of the Uruguay Round in respect of complaints brought during that period under Article XXII or XXIII."[23] The most significant portions of the rules were those that placed time limits on consultations and that provided further for the automatic establishment of a panel. Parties to which a request for consultations had been made under either Article XXII:1 or XXIII:1 would be required to reply to that request within 10 days, and to agree to enter into consultations in good faith in no less than 30 days. In the absence of an agreement to consult and the holding of timely consultations, the complaining party could proceed directly to request the establishment of a panel.[24] If consultations failed to settle the dispute within 60 days of the request, the complaining party then could request the establishment of a panel.[25]

Most significantly, in GATT's all-too-typically indirect language, the Montreal Rules provided that, "[i]f the complaining party so requests, a decision to establish a panel or a working party shall be taken at the latest at the Council meeting following that at which the request first appeared as an item on the Council's regular agenda, unless at that meeting the Council decides otherwise."[26] This meant that a panel would be established, without fail, at the second meeting of the GATT Council after the request was put on the agenda, unless the Council decided otherwise. For the Council to decide "otherwise" under GATT's process of decision by consensus, however, all parties – including the complaining party – would have to decide "otherwise." In other words, the system had changed from one that required consensus – "positive consensus" – to establish a panel to a system of "negative consensus" – a system that required consensus not to establish a panel.

[22] *Improvements to the GATT Dispute Settlement Rules and Procedures*, Decision of 12 April 1989, BISD 36S/61 (hereafter "Montreal Rules").

[23] *Id.* ¶ A.3. [24] *Id.* ¶ C.1. [25] *Id.* ¶ C.2. [26] *Id.* ¶ F.(a).

These changes were adopted on a permanent basis in the WTO. Other significant provisions of the Montreal Rules that eventually found their way into the WTO, in identical or similar form, dealt with the terms of reference for panels, the composition of panels, procedures for multiple complaints and for third party participation, and time limits. Specific rules were included, too, on the sensitive topic of adoption of panel reports, which made blocking somewhat more embarrassing diplomatically, but did not eliminate the practice. Elimination of the power of the losing party unilaterally to block adoption of a report had to await the completion of the Uruguay Round and the establishment of the World Trade Organization.

§ 1.02 The Uruguay Round

The Uruguay Round was the largest, most far-reaching, longest, and most contentious round of multilateral trade negotiations ever undertaken. It began in September of 1986, the end of the Southern Hemisphere's winter, in a driving wind, under a gray sky, with an off-season meeting of GATT Ministers in the Uruguayan resort city of Punta del Este. It concluded nearly eight years later, in the warm April sunshine of Marrakesh, Morocco. "Few trading caravans can have viewed this beautiful city with as much pleasure – and as much relief – as ours does," GATT Director-General Peter Sutherland told the representatives of 124 Uruguay Round participants assembled to sign the *Marrakesh Agreement Establishing the World Trade Organization.* "But then very few trading caravans were on the road for more than seven years, and none carried such a priceless cargo."[27]

The Uruguay Round grew largely out of the unfinished business of the Tokyo Round which, despite its achievements, was viewed by many as incomplete. The Tokyo Round had largely solved the structural problems of dealing with non-tariff barriers, but parties were not required to agree to its codes dealing with dumping, subsidies, government procurement and the like. These agreements bound only those parties that adhered to them, creating what many called "GATT *a la carte.*" Agriculture, the perennial problem of international trade, had been left all but untouched, and nothing had been done about trade in counterfeit goods, a new concern of the industrialized countries, particularly of the United States.

[27] GATT Focus, May 1994, No. 107 *Special Issue* at 2.

These and other concerns led to a November 1982 meeting of GATT Ministers in Geneva, called primarily by the United States in the hope of launching a new round of multilateral negotiations. The effort failed, but not completely. Attempts to find a basis for further negotiations continued through the early 1980s, and these led eventually to the decision to meet in September 1986 in Punta del Este.

The Punta del Este Declaration, issued by the Ministers at the close of the conference, outlined the agenda for the negotiations and stated, with undue optimism, that they would be concluded within four years. The negotiations, as noted, took nearly twice as long. In the process, the negotiating agenda, not surprisingly, changed in important ways. As it was, however, the Punta del Este agenda was far-reaching.

The major portion of the agenda concerned trade in goods, GATT's traditional subject. In addition to tariff liberalization, the Punta del Este agenda called for negotiations on non-tariff measures, tropical and natural resource-based products, textiles and clothing, agriculture, safeguards (provisions that allow countries temporarily to protect domestic industries injured by import competition), subsidies, and dispute settlement. Particularly noteworthy was the inclusion on the agenda of a broadened version of the counterfeit goods item: "Trade-related aspects of intellectual property rights, including trade in counterfeit goods," and a further item covering trade-related investment measures. These led eventually to WTO agreements in each area, the Agreement on Trade-Related Aspects of Intellectual Property Rights (TRIPS) and the Agreement on Trade-Related Investment Measures (TRIMS). Finally, Part II of the agenda called for negotiations on trade in services, leading to the WTO's General Agreement on Trade in Services (GATS).

The course of the Uruguay Round negotiations, as Peter Sutherland's Marrakesh remarks suggest, was long and tortuous.[28] Deadlines were set, missed, set again, and missed again. The most likely Round-breaker, as

[28] The history of the Uruguay Round has been told in a number of works. John Croome, Reshaping the World Trading System: A History of the Uruguay Round (World Trade Organization, 1995) is the most comprehensive; Hugo Paemen & Alexandra Bensch, From the GATT to the WTO: The European Community in the Uruguay Round (Leuven University Press, 1995) offers a European perspective; Ernest H. Preeg, Traders in a Brave New World: The Uruguay Round and the Future of the International Trading System (Chicago, 1995) offers a United States perspective; and Jeffrey J. Schott, The Uruguay Round: An Assessment (Institute for International Economics, 1994) is an early evaluation of the results from an economic and policy perspective.

the headlines of the times suggested, was agriculture, but agriculture was not alone. Industries interested in the use of antidumping laws against imported goods had their own demands, which almost sank the Round at the last minute.[29] But success finally came, and on December 15, 1993, negotiations were formally ended. The world's press congratulated the negotiators, but much work remained, including the monumental clerical and administrative task of putting the agreements into consistent form, and preparing for Marrakesh and the formal signing. When it all was done, the world had a new World Trade Organization.

§ 1.03 The World Trade Organization

The World Trade Organization officially was established on January 1, 1995, as the successor to GATT and as the legal and institutional foundation of the international trading system. It was formally created by the *Marrakesh Agreement Establishing the World Trade Organization* ("*WTO Agreement*"), signed by the Ministers the previous April. Unlike GATT, the WTO is an organization, not just an agreement. It is on an official par with the Bretton Woods organizations, the World Bank and the International Monetary Fund.[30]

Attached to the *WTO Agreement* are four annexes which contain the substance of the organization. Annex 1, with three subparts, is its substantive core. The first subpart, Annex 1A, contains 13 separate agreements covering trade in goods:

1. General Agreement on Tariffs and Trade 1994
2. Agreement on Agriculture
3. Agreement on the Application of Sanitary and Phytosanitary Measures
4. Agreement on Textiles and Clothing
5. Agreement on Technical Barriers to Trade
6. Agreement on Trade-Related Investment Measures
7. Agreement on Implementation of Article VI of the General Agreement on Tariffs and Trade 1994 (Antidumping Agreement)

[29] Ernst-Ulrich Petersmann, *The Dispute Settlement System of the World Trade Organization and the Evolution of the GATT Dispute Settlement System Since 1948*, 31 COMMON MARKET LAW REVIEW 1157, 1204, 1224 (1994).

[30] The WTO is described in detail in Bernard Hoekman & Michel Kostecki, THE POLITICAL ECONOMY OF THE WORLD TRADING SYSTEM: FROM GATT TO THE WTO (Oxford, 1995); *see* also, Patrick Messerlin, LA NOUVELLE OMC (Dunod, 1995).

8. Agreement on Implementation of Article VII of the General Agreement on Tariffs and Trade 1994 (Customs Valuation Agreement)
9. Agreement on Preshipment Inspection
10. Agreement on Rules of Origin
11. Agreement on Import Licensing Procedures
12. Agreement on Subsidies and Countervailing Measures
13. Agreement on Safeguards

The first of the 13 agreements, the General Agreement on Tariffs and Trade 1994, known as GATT 1994, contains the text of the original GATT, now known as GATT 1947, its "acquis" or the decisions of the GATT CONTRACTING PARTIES, six separate interpretative Understandings, and an implementing protocol signed at Marrakesh. Along with its annexes, GATT 1994 comprises the WTO's rules governing trade in goods. The next two subparts of Annex 1 cover the important new trade areas: GATS, in Annex 1B, and TRIPS in Annex 1C.

Annex 2 to the *WTO Agreement* consists of the *Understanding on Rules and Procedures Governing the Settlement of Disputes*, which is the subject of this volume. Annex 3 contains the Trade Policy Review Mechanism, by which the WTO Secretariat conducts regular studies of the trade policies of its Members, while Annex 4 contains the text of two plurilateral agreements, the only a la carte aspects of the WTO that Members may join or not, as they wish. These are the *Agreement on Trade in Civil Aircraft* and the *Agreement on Government Procurement.*[31]

The WTO is governed by a Ministerial Conference that meets at least every two years to review its performance and establish policy. On a day-to-day basis, the WTO is governed by its General Council and several subsidiary bodies, principally by separate Councils for Goods, for Services, and for TRIPS. In addition, there are committees for 12 of the 13 multilateral goods agreements and for the two plurilateral agreements. (The *Agreement on Preshipment Inspection* does not provide for a committee.)

The WTO has established a number of other committees dealing with areas of substantive and negotiating interest, such as trade and the environment, trade and development, and regional trade agreements. In addition, a number of substantive negotiation groups, dealing with such topics as telecommunications, financial services, and maritime services, were established by the GATS Council. Of particular relevance to this

[31] Two other plurilateral agreements, the *International Dairy Agreement* and the *International Bovine Meat Agreement*, were terminated as of 1 January 1998. WT/L/251, 17 December 1997, and WT/L/252, 16 December 1997.

study is one of the most important of the new bodies created by the *WTO Agreement* – the Dispute Settlement Body.

§ 1.04 The Dispute Settlement Body

The Dispute Settlement Body (DSB) consists of representatives of every WTO Member. It was created during the Uruguay Round to deal with disputes arising under any of the WTO agreements; it does so in accordance with the provisions of the *Understanding on Rules and Procedures Governing the Settlement of Disputes*, the "Dispute Settlement Understanding" or "DSU." The DSB has the authority to establish dispute settlement panels, to adopt panel and Appellate Body reports, to maintain surveillance of the implementation of the rulings and recommendations it adopts, and to authorize the suspension of concessions and other obligations under the covered WTO agreements, if its rulings and recommendations are not acted upon by Members in a timely fashion.

The DSB meets "as often as necessary to carry out its functions,"[32] normally monthly, but it also may meet at special sessions at the request of a Member. Its decisions are taken by consensus, which is deemed to have resulted if no Member present at the DSB meeting when a decision is taken formally objects.[33] It is presided over by a chairman, usually the head of one of the permanent missions to Geneva of one of its Members.

The DSB is more than the vehicle by which panels are established and reports adopted and implemented; it also serves as the forum where matters of dispute are discussed. While it has the legal authority not to establish a panel or not to adopt a report, this power is more illusory than real because the DSB operates on the "negative" consensus principle, the opposite of GATT's positive consensus principle. Under the WTO, as under GATT after the Montreal Rules became effective, panels will be established automatically, *unless* there is consensus to the contrary. Unlike under GATT, however, under the WTO reports also will be adopted automatically *unless* there is consensus to the contrary. Since consensus requires the approval of the complaining party and the prevailing party, those parties, not the DSB, normally will have the effective last word on these crucial topics.

[32] DSU Article 2.3.

[33] A WTO body "shall be deemed to have decided by consensus on a matter submitted for its consideration, if no Member, present at the meeting when the decision is taken, formally objects to the proposed decision." *WTO Agreement* Article IX, note 1.

§ 1.05 The Dispute Settlement Understanding

The Dispute Settlement Understanding or DSU, with 27 sections totalling 143 paragraphs and four appendices, is perhaps the most significant achievement of the Uruguay Round negotiations. Unique in public international law, it confers compulsory jurisdiction on the DSB for purposes of resolving disputes. In the words of Article 3.2 of the DSU, "The dispute settlement system of the WTO is a central element in providing security and predictability to the multilateral trading system."

The DSU sets out the basic institutional and jurisdictional scope of WTO dispute settlement. Its four appendices specify the agreements covered by the Understanding; itemize special or additional dispute settlement rules and procedures contained in covered agreements; outline working procedures and a suggested timetable for panels; and set out the rules and procedures that apply to any expert review groups that may be established by panels, in accordance with DSU Article 13.2. The specialized dispute settlement requirements listed in Appendix 2 of the DSU require particular attention. To the extent that there is a difference between the DSU and the special or additional rules and procedures, the latter prevail.[34]

Article 17 of the DSU provides for the establishment of a standing Appellate Body which has published its own "Working Procedures for Appellate Review." The Appellate Body is discussed in Chapter 6.

[34] *See* Chapter 5.

2

Jurisdiction

§ 2.01 Overview

Neither the Dispute Settlement Understanding nor any of the WTO agreements contains an article, comparable to Article 36 of the *Statute of the International Court of Justice*, explicitly setting forth the jurisdiction of the Dispute Settlement Body, panels, or the Appellate Body. However, a number of articles in the DSU treat jurisdictional issues, without explicitly using the term. These include: Article 1, which specifies the coverage and application of the DSU; Article 2, establishing the Dispute Settlement Body to administer the DSU; Article 3.1, in which Members affirm their adherence to the principles for the management of disputes previously applied under Articles XXII and XXIII of GATT 1947; Article 6, providing for the establishment of dispute settlement panels; Article 7, specifying the terms of reference for panels; Article 17.6, limiting jurisdiction of the Appellate Body to issues of law covered in a panel report and legal interpretations developed by a panel; and Article 17.13, authorizing the Appellate Body to uphold, modify or reverse legal findings and conclusions of panels. Perhaps the most notable structural distinction between the International Court of Justice (ICJ) and the WTO with regard to jurisdiction is not the DSU's lack of an explicit article dealing with the subject, but the fact that, with the DSU, the WTO system enjoys compulsory jurisdiction, something the ICJ does not possess. The extent of a panel's jurisdiction, however, is dependent upon the subject matter of the dispute, *ratione materiae*, and the parties to the dispute, *ratione personae*. The basic document, in any dispute, is that setting forth the terms of reference.[1]

[1] *See* generally, Bernhard Jansen, *Scope of Jurisdiction in GATT/WTO Dispute Settlement: Consultations and Panel Requests* in Friedl Weiss (Ed) IMPROVING WTO DISPUTE SETTLEMENT PROCEDURES: ISSUES AND LESSONS FROM THE PRACTICE OF OTHER INTERNATIONAL COURTS AND TRIBUNALS 45 (Cameron May, 2001).

§ 2.02 Terms of reference

[1] Rationale for terms of reference

The terms of reference of a panel are important for two basic reasons: (1) they fulfill an important due process objective by giving the respondent and interested third parties sufficient information concerning the claims at issue in the dispute to allow them to respond to the complainant's case; and (2) they establish the jurisdiction of the panel by defining the precise claims at issue in the dispute.[2]

[2] Parallelism between consultations and terms of reference

The terms of reference are determined by the complaining party's request for the establishment of a panel.[3] The scope of the request for consultations, as well as the actual consultations (which might, in fact, go beyond what was included in the request), in turn, affect the scope of the request for the establishment of a panel which, as noted in the following section, is incorporated into the terms of reference. However, because the consultations themselves may lead the parties to a new appreciation of the nature of their dispute, there need not necessarily be an exact parallel between the request for consultations and the request for the establishment of a panel. One panel has stated that the "matter" on which consultations are requested may not necessarily be the same "matter" for which a panel is requested because facts that are established during the consultations may shape the substance and scope of subsequent panel proceedings.[4] The Appellate Body has said that "lack of prior consultations is not a defect that, by its very nature, deprives a panel of its authority to deal with and dispose of a matter."[5]

[2] Appellate Body Report, *Brazil – Measures Affecting Desiccated Coconut*, WT/DS22/AB/R, adopted 20 March 1997, DSR 1997:I, 167, 186, § VI.

[3] Panel Report, *Canada – Measures Affecting the Export of Civilian Aircraft*, WT/DS70/R, adopted 20 August 1999, as upheld by the Appellate Body Report, WT/DS70/AB/R, DSR 1999:IV, 1443, ¶ 9.12.

[4] *Id.* citing Appellate Body Report, *India – Patent Protection for Pharmaceutical and Agricultural Chemical Products*, WT/DS50/AB/R, adopted 16 January 1998, DSR 1998:I, 9. *See* also, §§ 4.02, 4.04.

[5] Appellate Body Report, *Mexico – Anti-Dumping Investigation of High Fructose Corn Syrup (HFCS) from the United States – Recourse to Article 21.5 of the DSU by the United States*, WT/DS132/AB/RW, adopted 21 November 2001, ¶ 54.

[3] *Standard terms of reference*

Under the standard terms of reference, contained in Article 7 of the DSU, panels are directed:

> To examine, in light of the relevant provisions in (name of covered agreement(s) cited by the parties to the dispute), the matter referred to the DSB by (name of party) in document . . . and to make such findings as will assist the DSB in making recommendations or in giving rulings provided for in that/those agreement(s).

The ellipses in Article 7 indicate where the document number given to the complainant's request for the establishment of a panel will appear in the terms of reference. In its request, the complaining party will have referred to the particular agreements at issue and also to the relevant provisions of those agreements.[6]

[4] *Non ultra petita*

The aim of the dispute settlement mechanism is to secure a positive resolution of disputes.[7] Accordingly, panels address only claims that are put before them, either by the complaining party through its request for the establishment of a panel, which is incorporated into the terms of reference, or by the defending party.[8] Thus, it has been said that it is not for a panel to examine on its own initiative the exceptions to WTO obligations provided by Article XX of GATT unless they have been invoked by a party.[9]

However, in *US – Offset Act (Byrd Amendment)*, the Panel explicitly decided to consider a claim under Article 15 of the Antidumping Agreement, concerning special and differential treatment for developing countries, even though there was no reference to that article in the panel requests.[10] The Panel noted Article 12.11 of the DSU, which requires

[6] The specificity required of these requests is discussed in § 4.04. [7] *DSU* Art. 3.7

[8] Panel Report, *Brazil – Export Financing Programme for Aircraft – Recourse by Canada to Article 21.5 of the DSU*, WT/DS46/RW, adopted 4 August 2000, as modified by the Appellate Body Report, WT/DS46/AB/RW, DSR 2000:IX, 4093, note 17.

[9] Panel Report, *European Communities – Measures Affecting Asbestos and Asbestos-Containing Products*, WT/DS135/R and Add.1, adopted 5 April 2001, as modified by the Appellate Body Report, WT/DS135/AB/R, note 115.

[10] Panel Report, *United States – Continued Dumping and Subsidy Offset Act of 2000*, WT/DS217/R, WT/DS234/R, adopted 27 January 2003, as modified by the Appellate Body Report, WT/DS217/AB/R, WT/DS234/AB/R, ¶ 7.87.

that panels "explicitly indicate the form in which account has been taken of relevant provisions on differential and more-favourable treatment for developing country Members . . . which have been raised by the developing country Member in the course of the dispute settlement procedures." It concluded that Article 12.11 required it to consider the Article 15 claim, even though the claim was not referred to in the requests for the establishment of a panel, since Article 15 "has been raised by developing country Members in the present proceedings."[11] Having agreed to consider the claim, however, the Panel proceeded to dismiss it on the merits.[12]

The terms of reference may be used to preclude inquiry into matters that are raised in defense of a challenged measure. In *Japan – Alcoholic Beverages II*, the Panel declined to consider arguments put forward in its defense by Japan concerning the taxation systems of other countries: "The Panel noted that its terms of reference were strictly confined to the Japanese legislation. The Panel could not, therefore, consider the domestic taxation systems of other countries since they lie outside its terms of reference."[13] In other circumstances, however, the legislation of other Members might be put forward by a party as factual evidence with relevance to the question of a reasonable interpretation of a WTO requirement. This might occur, for example, with regard to antidumping legislation implementing the *Agreement on Implementation of Article VI of GATT 1994*, or with regard to legislation implementing some aspect of GATS or TRIPS.

[5] The obligation of panels to consider all issues referred to in the terms of reference

Panels are required to consider everything within their terms of reference. Thus, also in *Japan – Alcoholic Beverages II*, the Panel was asked to consider whether a wide variety of specifically named alcoholic beverages were "like products" or "directly competitive or substitutable" products within the meaning of Article III of GATT 1994. Included in one of the requests for the establishment of a panel was the category "all other distilled spirits and liquers falling within HS heading 2208." The Panel's conclusions did not explicitly incorporate this "all other" category, an omission the Appellate

[11] *Id.* [12] *Id.* ¶ 7.88.

[13] Panel Report, *Japan – Taxes on Alcoholic Beverages*, WT/DS8/R, WT/DS10/R, WT/DS11/R, adopted 1 November 1996, as modified by the Appellate Body Report, WT/DS8/AB/R, WT/DS10/AB/R, WT/DS11/AB/R, DSR 1996:I, 125, ¶ 6.26.

Body considered to be an error of law.[14] However, when a complaining party fails to raise, at any point in the proceedings, specific arguments against a measure, or submit any factual or scientific evidence against the measure, the panel may consider the measure outside the scope of the dispute, even though "technically" within the terms of reference.[15]

[6] Parallelism between the terms of reference and submissions to a panel

Inclusion of a claim in submissions to a panel is not enough to cure failure to include the claim in the request for the establishment of a panel and thus to bring it within the panel's terms of reference.[16] Further, a claim based on a loan not identified in the request for the establishment of a panel is not within the terms of reference even if it is one aspect of the program which is the subject of the request.[17] When Article XXIII of GATT is not mentioned in a request for the establishment of a panel as a legal basis for the complaint, but only as a legal ground to obtain the establishment of a panel, and the panel request does not refer to the non-violation provision of Article XXIII:1(b), a non-violation complaint falls outside the terms of reference.[18]

§ 2.03 Jurisdiction *Ratione Materiae*

[1] Covered agreements

The Dispute Settlement Understanding applies to disputes brought pursuant to its consultation and dispute settlement provisions concerning the "covered agreements" which are listed in its Appendix 1. These are: the

[14] Appellate Body Report, *Japan – Taxes on Alcoholic Beverages*, WT/DS8/AB/R, WT/DS10/AB/R, WT/DS11/AB/R, adopted 1 November 1996, DSR 1996:I, 97, 118, § H.2(a).

[15] Panel Report, *EC – Measures Concerning Meat and Meat Products (Hormones) – Complaint by the United States*, WT/DS26/R/USA, adopted 13 February 1998, as modified by the Appellate Body Report, WT/DS26/AB/R, WT/DS48/AB/R, DSR 1998:III, 699, 925, ¶ 8.17.

[16] Panel Report, *United States – Definitive Safeguard Measures on Imports of Circular Welded Quality Line Pipe from Korea*, WT/DS202/R, adopted 8 March 2002, as modified by the Appellate Body Report, WT/DS202/AB/R, ¶ 7.125.

[17] Panel Report, *Indonesia – Certain Measures Affecting the Automobile Industry*, WT/DS54/R, WT/DS55/R, WT/DS59/R, WT/DS64/R and Corr.1, 2, 3 and 4, adopted 23 July 1998, DSR 1998:VI, 2201, ¶ 14.3.

[18] Panel Report, *Australia – Measures Affecting Importation of Salmon*, WT/DS18/R and Corr.1, adopted 6 November 1998, as modified by the Appellate Body Report, WT/DS18/AB/R, DSR 1998:VIII, 3407, ¶ 8.21.

Agreement Establishing the World Trade Organization; the 13 individual multilateral agreements on trade in goods; GATS; TRIPS; and the two plurilateral agreements.[19] The DSU encompasses "measures affecting the operation of any covered agreement taken within the territory" of a Member, including, as discussed in § 2.04 [2] below, measures taken by regional or local governments.[20] It does not extend to other matters.[21] Claims that do not refer to a covered agreement do not fall within a panel's terms of reference.[22]

[2] Conflicts among agreements

A number of WTO agreements contain special or additional rules governing disputes. In the event of conflict in these rules in cases involving two or more covered agreements (other than the DSU), Article 1.2 calls upon the parties themselves to attempt to agree on the rules and procedures to apply in the conduct of the dispute settlement proceeding. If they are unable to do so within 20 days of the establishment of the panel, the Chairman of the DSB shall, within 10 days of a request to do so by either party, and in consultation with the parties, determine the rules and procedures to be followed. The DSB Chairman should be guided by the principle that special or additional rules and procedures should be used where possible, with the DSU rules and procedures being used where necessary to avoid conflict.[23]

[3] Simultaneous application of different agreements

Obligations can and do exist simultaneously under different WTO agreements, including, for example, GATT 1994 and the General Agreement on Trade in Services.[24] As one panel stated:

[19] DSU Art. 1.1. [20] DSU Art. 4.2.

[21] In GATT Panel Report, *Canada – Administration of the Foreign Investment Review Act*, BISD 30S/140, adopted 7 February 1984, at 141, ¶ 1.4, the GATT Council confirmed that "the panel would be limited in its activities and findings to within the four corners of GATT."

[22] Panel Report, *Canada – Export Credits and Loan Guarantees for Regional Aircraft*, WT/DS222/R and Corr.1, adopted 19 February 2002, ¶ 7.49.

[23] DSU Art. 1.2.

[24] Appellate Body Report, *European Communities – Regime for the Importation, Sale and Distribution of Bananas*, WT/DS27/AB/R, adopted 25 September 1997, DSR 1997:II, 591, 680, ¶ 222; Panel Report, *Canada – Certain Measures Concerning Periodicals*, WT/DS31/R and Corr.1, adopted 30 July 1997, as modified by the Appellate Body Report,

> [I]f we were to find the scope of the GATS and that of GATT to be mutually exclusive, in other words, if we were to find that a measure considered to fall within the scope of one agreement could not at the same time fall within the scope of the other, the value of members' obligations and commitments would be undermined and the object and purpose of both agreements would be frustrated. Obligations could be circumvented by the adoption of measures under one agreement with indirect effects on trade covered by the other without the possibility of any legal recourse.[25]

If different components of the same administrative measure are covered by more than one WTO Agreement, it is within the competence of a panel to determine which applies. Panels are not obliged to base their decision solely on the arguments of the parties.[26]

[4] Non-application between particular Members

The WTO Agreement provides that the DSU, the 13 multilateral agreements on trade in goods, GATS, and TRIPS "shall not apply as between any Member and any other Member if either of the Members, at the time either becomes a Member, does not consent to such application."[27] This provision conforms to Article XXXV of GATT 1947, which was widely invoked, particularly against Japan when it acceded to GATT in 1955. At present, there are only two outstanding invocations of Article XIII: the United States, with respect to Moldova,[28] and El Salvador, with respect to China.[29]

[5] The DSU and the competence of other WTO bodies

Dispute settlement procedures are available for disputes relating to any matters concerning balance-of-payments, notwithstanding the competence of the WTO General Council and the Balance of Payments Committee, under Article XVIII:12 of GATT 1994 and the *Understanding*

WT/DS31/AB/R, DSR 1997:1, 481, 576, ¶ 5.17; Appellate Body Report, *Canada – Certain Measures Concerning Periodicals*, WT/DS31/AB/R, adopted 30 July 1997, DSR 1997:1, 449, 465, § IV.

[25] Panel Report, *European Communities – Regime for the Importation, Sale and Distribution of Bananas – Complaint by the United States*, WT/DS27/R/USA, adopted 25 September 1997, as modified by the Appellate Body Report, WT/DS27/AB/R, DSR 1997:II, 943, 1037, ¶ 7.283.

[26] Panel Report, *EC – Asbestos, supra* note 9, ¶ 8.32 and note 24.

[27] Art. XIII:1.

[28] WT/L/395.

[29] WT/L/429.

on Balance-of-Payments Provisions of the General Agreement on Tariffs and Trade 1994, to deal with those issues.[30] Further, panels have authority to examine measures adopted at the formation of customs unions, notwithstanding GATT Article XXIV or the *Understanding on the Interpretation of Article XXIV of the General Agreement on Tariffs and Trade 1994.*[31]

[6] The "matter" before the Panel

A complaining party refers a "matter" to the Dispute Settlement Body, and this becomes the subject of a panel's terms of reference.[32] A "matter" consists of two elements: (1) the *measure* at issue, such as a law or regulation, and (2) the legal basis in a covered agreement of the complainant's claim.[33] "Taken together, the 'measure' and the 'claims' made concerning that measure constitute the 'matter referred to the DSB,' which forms the basis for a panel's terms of reference."[34] The word "matter" has the same meaning in Article 17 of the *Agreement on Implementation of Article VI of the General Agreement on Tariffs and Trade 1994* (the Antidumping Agreement) as it has in Article 7 of the DSU.[35] The "measure" that is part of the "matter" must, of course, be a governmental measure.[36]

[7] Measures changed during proceedings

Under GATT, when a challenged measure was changed or amended during the course of a proceeding, the practice of panels depended upon whether the parties agreed to consideration of the measure as amended. In *United States – Section 337 of the Tariff Act of 1930*, the law was amended after

[30] Appellate Body Report, *India – Quantitative Restrictions on Imports of Agricultural, Textile and Industrial Products*, WT/DS90/AB/R, adopted 22 September 1999, DSR 1999:IV, 1763, ¶ 88.

[31] Panel Report, *Turkey – Restrictions on Imports of Textile and Clothing Products*), WT/DS34/R, adopted 19 November 1999, as modified by the Appellate Body Report, WT/DS34/AB/R, DSR 1999:VI, 2363, ¶ 9.51.

[32] *DSU* Art. 7.1.

[33] Appellate Body Report, *Guatemala – Anti-Dumping Investigation Regarding Portland Cement from Mexico*, WT/DS60/AB/R, adopted 25 November 1998, DSR 1998:IX, 3797, ¶ 72.

[34] *Id.* ¶ 73. [35] *Id.* ¶ 76.

[36] Panel Report, *European Communities – Measures Affecting the Importation of Certain Poultry Products*, WT/DS69/R, adopted 23 July 1998, as modified by the Appellate Body Report, WT/DS69/AB/R, DSR 1998:V, 2089, ¶ 272.

the Panel was established. The Panel based its report on the version of the law in effect at the time that it was established.[37] In *Tuna II*, the complainants requested a pause in the proceedings so that they could assess recent changes in the relevant United States legislation. The Panel agreed to this request and, subsequently, the United States agreed to the complainants' request for additional consultations, explicitly reserving the question whether these were supplementary consultations or initial consultations under a new dispute settlement proceeding. The parties eventually reached an understanding on the newly-enacted provisions of the legislation that could be considered by the Panel, and the matter went forward. In the end, however, the United States blocked adoption of the report.[38]

The practice has continued in the WTO. In *India – Autos*, the measure at issue was changed during the course of the dispute.[39] The Panel concluded that its jurisdiction extended to the measures as they existed at the time of the request for the establishment of a panel.[40] New measures that have been taken after the beginning of panel proceedings, it held, were not within its terms of reference.[41] The Panel went on to state that "it may need to consider whether these developments affect the continued relevance . . . of any findings and conclusions it might make as to the consistency of the measures as at the date of its establishment."[42] It further stated that its "ability to make meaningful recommendations to the DSB under Article 19.1 of the DSU may be affected if any changes in the measures had occurred which would affect the continued existence of any violations that might be identified as at the date of establishment."[43] The potential relevance of the changes in the measure to a compliance panel "does not in any way diminish this Panel's obligation to comply with its express mandate from the DSB to consider the measures before it."[44]

Similarly, in *Chile – Price Band System*, when faced with a changed measure, the Panel held that it could assess the relevance of the change only after determining the extent of Chile's obligations under the provisions

[37] BISD 36S/345, 383, adopted 7 November 1989, ¶ 5.2. *See*, David Palmeter, *Section 337 and the WTO Agreements – Still in Violation?*, 20 WORLD COMPETITION 27 (No. 1, September 1996).

[38] GATT Panel Report, *United States – Restrictions on Imports of Tuna*, DS33/1, 10 June 1994, unadopted, 33 I.L.M. 839 (1994).

[39] Panel Report, *India – Measures Affecting the Automotive Sector*, WT/DS146/R, WT/DS175/R and Corr.1, adopted 5 April 2002 after appeal withdrawn.

[40] *Id.* ¶ 7.22. [41] *Id.* ¶ 8.20. [42] *Id.* ¶ 7.30. [43] *Id.* [44] *Id.* ¶ 7.149.

of the agreements cited in the panel request.[45] "We would be acting in a manner inconsistent with our duties under Article 11 of the DSU if we were to refrain from making findings for the sole reason that Chile amended the challenged measure at a late stage of the proceedings."[46]

[8] Change in legal justification for a measure

When a defending party changes the legal justification for its challenged measure, it may force the complaining party to reinstitute consultations. In *Norway – Textiles,* Hong Kong requested consultations after unilateral import restrictions were imposed by Norway. When the consultations proved unsuccessful, Hong Kong requested the establishment of a panel. The following month, Norway invoked GATT Article XIX to justify the measure, and, because the legal basis for Norway's action had changed, Hong Kong sought new consultations. A panel eventually was established to review Norway's Article XIX justification.[47]

While a change in the legal justification for a challenged measure could result in a similar interruption of proceedings under the DSU, the DSU's time constraints, supervised by the DSB, make it unlikely that the resulting delay would approximate the year-long delay in the dispute between Norway and Hong Kong.

In *Argentina – Footwear and Textiles,* the initial measure was revoked and another measure was substituted as justification for the restriction. This case is discussed in the following section.

[9] Measures no longer in effect

The fact that a measure has been withdrawn does not prevent it from being ruled upon by a panel, provided the measure is within the panel's terms of reference. In *US – Wool Shirts and Blouses,* the import restriction that was the subject of the dispute was withdrawn after the Panel had submitted its interim report to the parties, but before the final report was issued. The Panel decided to continue to consider the matter:

[45] Panel Report, *Chile – Price Band System and Safeguard Measures Relating to Certain Agricultural Products,* WT/DS207/R, adopted 23 October 2002, as modified by the Appellate Body Report, WT/DS207/AB/R, ¶ 7.7.

[46] *Id.*

[47] GATT Panel Report, *Norway – Restrictions on Imports of Certain Textile Products,* BISD 27S/119, adopted 18 June 1980, ¶ 5.

> In the absence of an agreement between the parties to terminate the proceedings, we think it is appropriate to issue our final report regarding the matter set out in the terms of reference of this Panel in order to comply with our mandate . . . notwithstanding the withdrawal of the US restraint.[48]

In *Argentina – Footwear and Textiles*, the United States challenged a series of specific duties imposed by Argentina, on the ground that they violated the rates bound under Article II of GATT 1994. Argentina revoked the measure imposing the specific duties after circulation of the request for the establishment of a panel, but before the panel was established by the DSB.[49] On the day the measure was revoked, Argentina re-imposed the same duties as a provisional safeguard measure.[50] Even though the same specific duties were referred to in its terms of reference, the Panel declined to consider the revoked measure, quoting from the Appellate Body's opinion in *US – Wool Shirts and Blouses*:

> The aim of dispute settlement is not 'to encourage either panels or the Appellate Body to "make law" by clarifying existing provisions of the WTO Agreement outside the context of resolving a particular dispute. A panel need only address those claims which must be addressed in order to resolve the matter in issue in the dispute.'[51]

However, when a safeguard measure simply was extended in *Chile – Price Band System*, the Panel ruled on the initial measure, observing:

> Article 19.1 DSU does not prevent us from making *findings* regarding the consistency of an expired provisional safeguard measure, if we were to consider that the making of such findings is necessary "to secure a positive solution" to the dispute. We would not, however, formulate *recommendations* with regard to those measures.[52]

GATT cases reached similar results. In *US – Tuna from Canada*, restrictions on imports imposed pursuant to a provision of the Fishery Conservation and Management Act were challenged. During the course of the

[48] Panel Report, *United States – Measure Affecting Imports of Woven Wool Shirts and Blouses from India*, WT/DS33/R, adopted 23 May 1997, as upheld by the Appellate Body Report, WT/DS33/AB/R, DSR 1997:I, 343, ¶ 6.2.

[49] Panel Report, *Argentina – Measures Affecting Imports of Footwear, Textiles, Apparel and Other Items*, WT/DS56/R, adopted 22 April 1998, as modified by the Appellate Body Report, WT/DS56/AB/R, DSR 1998:III, 1033, 1147, ¶ 6.4.

[50] *Id.* ¶ 6.5.

[51] *Id.* ¶ 6.13, 1150 quoting Appellate Body Report, *US – Wool Shirts and Blouses, supra* note 48, at 19, DSR 1150.

[52] Panel Report, *Chile – Price Band System, supra* note 45, ¶ 7.124.

proceedings, the restrictions were lifted, but the provision of law under which they were imposed remained in effect. At a meeting of the Panel held to determine the appropriate course of action, Canada argued that the Panel should go forward because the law requiring restrictions remained in place and, accordingly, the possibility of further embargoes remained. The United States stated that it doubted the necessity of proceeding since the restriction had been eliminated, but said that it would cooperate should the Panel decide to continue. The proceeding went forward.[53]

The Panel concluded that the temporary embargo was inconsistent with GATT Article XI, even though it had expired, but the Panel made no finding with regard to the underlying, mandatory law that was its legal basis.[54] Presumably, the Panel reasoned that even if the law was consistent with GATT requirements, specific action requiring particular findings could be inconsistent, and that this phenomenon could recur. In these circumstances, if the Panel had declined to consider the measure because it was no longer in effect, it might be re-imposed in a process that could continue *ad infinitum*. The same reasoning may have motivated the Panels in two cases involving five month-long restrictions imposed on imports of apples, which expired after the Panels were established, but before they issued their reports. In both cases, the Panels found in favor of the complainant, and in neither case was the issue of the termination of the measures discussed.[55]

[10] Review of measures taken to comply with rulings and recommendations of the DSB

Members whose measures have been found not to be consistent with WTO obligations are called upon to bring those measures into conformity.[56] Where there is disagreement between the parties as to whether this has been done, this disagreement in turn is subject to dispute settlement,

[53] GATT Panel Report, *United States – Prohibition of Imports of Tuna and Tuna Products from Canada*, BISD 29S/91, adopted 22 February 1982, ¶¶ 2.2, 2.8, and 4.8. In GATT Panel Report, *EEC – Measures on Animal Feed Proteins*, the challenged restriction came into effect in April 1976 and was terminated the following October. BISD 25S/49, adopted 14 March 1978, ¶ 2.4. The panel issued a complete report on the merits. It does not appear that the question of the measure's termination was argued.

[54] *Id.* at 109, ¶ 4.15.

[55] GATT Panel Report, *EEC – Restrictions on Imports of Apples from Chile*, BISD 27S/98, adopted 10 November 1980; GATT Panel Report, *European Economic Community – Restrictions on Imports of Dessert Apples, Complaint by Chile*, BISD 36S/93, adopted 22 June 1989.

[56] DSU Art. 19.1. Under Art. 4.7 and Art. 7.8 of the *Agreement on Subsidies and Countervailing Measures*, Members are called upon to "withdraw the [prohibited] subsidy" and to "remove the adverse effects or . . . withdraw the [actionable] subsidy," respectively. *See* § 7.08.

before the original panel if possible.[57] The role of the review panel is to "render a decision 'where there is disagreement' as to the existence or consistency with a covered agreement of measures taken to comply with the recommendations and rulings of the DSB."[58] For discussion of the scope of Article 21.5 review and the mandate of "compliance" panels, see §7.06.

§ 2.04 Jurisdiction *Ratione Personae*

[1] Non-Members

The WTO's obligations extend only to Member governments, those that have acceded to the *WTO Agreement*. "Only Members may become parties to a dispute of which a panel may be seized, and only Members 'having a substantial interest in a matter before a panel' may become third parties in the proceedings before that panel."[59] Non-members may neither take advantage of the WTO, nor are they subject to its requirements. In this regard, the WTO's judicial organs differ from the ICJ where non-members of the United Nations may be parties as applicant, respondent, and perhaps as intervenor.[60] Under GATT, however, contracting parties brought disputes on behalf of non-member territories for which they had international responsibility at the time. For example, the United Kingdom initiated dispute settlement proceedings against Norway on behalf of Hong Kong, while the Netherlands did so against the United States on behalf of the Netherlands Antilles.[61]

Issues of WTO applicability may arise when political developments call into question the continued existence of a Member government. Under GATT, for example, the European Community refused to proceed with a panel established at the request of Yugoslavia on the ground that the succession of the Socialist Federal Republic of Yugoslavia by the Federal Republic of Yugoslavia, consisting of Serbia and Montenegro, called into question Yugoslavia's status as a contracting party.[62]

[57] DSU Art. 21.5.

[58] Panel Report, *Brazil – Aircraft (Article 21.5 – Canada)*, *supra* note 8, note 17.

[59] Appellate Body Report, *United States – Import Prohibition of Certain Shrimp and Shrimp Products*, WT/DS58/AB/R, adopted 6 November 1998, DSR 1998:VII, 2755, ¶ 101; *see* also, *Turkey – Textiles, supra* note 31, ¶ 9.41.

[60] Shabtai Rosenne, The World Court 31 (5th ed., Martinus Nijhoff, 1995).

[61] *Norway – Textiles, supra* note 47; and *Tuna II, supra* note 38. Hong Kong subsequently became a GATT contracting party and is now a Member of the WTO.

[62] GATT Council Minutes 256, at 32.

[2] Regional and local government measures

With one exception, the DSU itself does not refer specifically to measures taken by regional (*e.g.*, state or provincial) or local governments. That exception is contained in a footnote to Article 4.2 of the DSU. Article 4.2 simply requires each Member "to accord sympathetic consideration to and afford adequate opportunity for consultation regarding any representations made by another Member concerning measures affecting the operation of any covered agreement taken within the territory of the former." The footnote, at the end of that sentence, specifies:

> Where the provisions of any other covered agreement concerning measures taken by regional or local governments or authorities within the territory of a Member contain provisions different from the provisions of this paragraph, the provisions of such other covered agreement shall prevail.

While the footnote deals only with conflicts between another agreement and Article 4 of the DSU, and seems simply to re-enforce, redundantly, the general requirements of Article 1.2 of the DSU for regional and local measures, it is clear that the obligations under both GATT 1994, encompassing goods, and GATS, encompassing services, extend to the actions of regional and local governments.

Article XXIV:12 of GATT 1994 provides explicitly that: "Each contracting party shall take such reasonable measures as may be available to it to ensure observance of the provisions of this Agreement by the regional and local governments and authorities within its territories." This provision was cited by the Panel in *Canada – Dairy* in considering the extent to which the Canadian Government was involved in supporting the dairy industry:

> Canada is a federal state with a federal government and ten provincial governments. Regulatory jurisdiction over trade in dairy products is divided between the federal government and the provinces. The federal government has constitutional authority over interprovincial and international trade. All other aspects of production and sale of milk are under provincial jurisdiction. Both the Canadian federal government and provincial governments are "governments" for purposes of Article 9.1(a) [of the *Agreement on Agriculture*].[63]

[63] Panel Report, *Canada – Measures Affecting the Importation of Milk and the Exportation of Dairy Products*, WT/DS103/R, WT/DS113/R, adopted 27 October 1999, as modified by the Appellate Body Report, WT/DS103/AB/R, WT/DS113/AB/R, DSR 1999:VI, 2097, ¶ 7.73.

The *Understanding on the Interpretation of Article XXIV of the General Agreement on Tariffs and Trade 1994*, which is part of GATT 1994, makes the point clearly:

> Each Member is fully responsible under GATT 1994 for the observance of all provisions of GATT 1994, and shall take such reasonable measures as may be available to it to ensure such observance by regional and local governments and authorities within its territory.[64]

The *Understanding* goes on to make clear that if the "reasonable measures available" to the Member are not sufficient to remove an inconsistent regional or local measure, the Member remains responsible: "The provisions relating to compensation and suspension of concessions or other obligations apply in cases where it has not been possible to secure such observance."[65]

GATS, by its terms, applies only to "measures by Members affecting trade in services."[66] However, it defines the phrase "measures by Members" to mean measures taken by "central, regional or local governments and authorities."[67] TRIPS, however, does not refer to measures taken by regional or local governments, presumably because governments at these levels do not customarily regulate intellectual property rights in a manner inconsistent with the requirements of the national government. The national treatment article of TRIPS does require Members to "accord to nationals of other Members treatment no less favourable than that it accords to its own nationals."[68] Moreover, TRIPS requires Members to meet the standards of the major international intellectual property conventions, including the Paris Convention (1967) and the Berne Convention (1971). In almost identical language, both conventions require parties to adopt measures necessary to ensure the convention's application, and to be in a position, under domestic law, to give effect to its provisions.[69] This requirement also would seem to make the national governmental parties to the conventions responsible for any measures taken by regional and local authorities within their territories.

64 *Understanding on the Interpretation of Article XXIV*, ¶ 13.

65 *Id.* ¶ 14. 66 GATS Art. I:1.

67 *Id.* Art. I:3(a)(i). It also includes measures taken by "non-governmental bodies in the exercise of powers delegated by central, regional or local governments or authorities." Art. I:3(a)(i).

68 TRIPS Art. 3.1.

69 Paris Convention for the Protection of Industrial Property, Art. 25; Berne Convention for the Protection of Literary and Artistic Works, Art. 36.

[3] Application of customary international law to WTO Members

Article 3.2 of the DSU specifies that the WTO texts are to be interpreted in accordance with the customary rules of interpretation of public international law. One panel has suggested, however, that at least in the context of a non-violation complaint, panels have jurisdiction to apply substantive rules of customary international law to WTO Members.

In *Korea – Procurement*, the Panel took note of the DSU's requirement that WTO agreements be interpreted in accordance with customary rules of interpretation of public international law, but then said in a footnote, that "we can see no basis here for an *a contrario* implication that rules of international law *other than* rules of interpretation do *not* apply."[70] It then went on to say, with regard to the rules of interpretation, that "the relationship of the WTO Agreements to customary international law is broader than this [*i.e.*, the rules of interpretation]. Customary international law applies generally to the economic relations between the WTO Members. Such international law applies to the extent that the WTO treaty agreements do not 'contract out' from it."[71]

The Panel then went on to "apply" Article 48 of the *Vienna Convention* relating to error in treaty formation in the context of a claim of non-violation nullification or impairment under Article XXII:2 of the *Agreement on Government Procurement*.[72] It found that Article 48 was a codification of customary international law, but it did not conclude that Article 48 is a customary rule of interpretation. In the end, however, the Panel concluded that the complainant had not established non-violation nullification or impairment.[73] Consequently, the Panel's discussion is *obiter dicta*.

No doubt the customary rules of international law, other than the rules of interpretation, apply generally to WTO Members in the same way that they apply to all nations. But to say this is not to say that WTO panels necessarily have jurisdiction to apply those rules to WTO Members. The Panel in *Korea – Procurement*, however, could be interpreted as stating that panels may use substantive customary international law as a standard by which to determine whether non-violation nullification or impairment has occurred, *i.e.*, that Members may assume that other Members will comply with customary international law, and the failure of a Member to

[70] Panel Report, *Korea – Measures Affecting Government Procurement*, WT/DS163/R, adopted 19 June 2000, DSR 2000:VI, 3541, ¶ 7.96 and footnote 753 (emphasis added). *See* also, § 3.04.

[71] *Id.* [72] *Id.* ¶ 7.123. [73] *Id.* ¶ 8.2.

do so provides grounds for a non-violation complaint. The Panel did not address how this theory would fit with the text of Article XXII:2 of the *Government Procurement Agreement* which refers, in relevant part, to "any measure, whether or not it conflicts with provisions of this Agreement."[74] Since the report was not appealed, the views of the Appellate Body on this subject are not known.

§ 2.05 Standing (*Locus Standi*)

[1] Requirement of a legal interest

A measure inconsistent with a WTO obligation could prevent another Member from even developing an economic interest in a particular area of trade. Thus, WTO rules in principle are not concerned with actual trade, but rather with competitive opportunities. Article XXIII:1 of GATT 1994, accordingly, provides that a Member may challenge measures whenever it considers "that any benefit accruing to it directly or indirectly . . . is being nullified or impaired or that the attainment of any objective of the Agreement is being impeded."

Based in part on the language of Article XXIII:1, the Appellate Body affirmed the finding of the Panel in *Bananas* that it is not necessary that a Member have a "legal interest" as a prerequisite to initiating dispute settlement.[75] The Appellate Body noted that the United States, though not an exporter of bananas, was a producer and a potential exporter. Moreover, "[t]he internal market of the United States for bananas could be affected by the EC banana regime, in particular, by the effects of that regime on world supplies and world prices of bananas."[76] It should be noted that the Appellate Body concluded that, "Taken together, these reasons are sufficient justification for the United States to have brought its claim." However, it added, "[t]his does not mean, though, that one or more of the factors we have noted in this case would necessarily be dispositive in another case."[77]

The term "legal" interest was used in *Bananas* to mean "economic" interest, in the sense of an existing economic interest. However, as noted above, WTO benefits may be nullified or impaired even without an existing economic interest. This was confirmed by a later panel in *Korea – Dairy*,

[74] This is, of course, the same language that appears in the relevant text of Article XXIII(1)(b) of GATT 1994, which applies to non-violation complaints generally.

[75] *EC – Bananas III*, *supra* note 24, ¶ 132. [76] *Id.* ¶ 136. [77] *Id.* ¶ 138.

which held that, "under the DSU there is no requirement that parties have an economic interest."[78]

This was reinforced by the decision of the Appellate Body in *United States – Section 211*, where the measure was successfully attacked by the European Communities on the ground that it violated the national treatment rights of Cuban nationals under the TRIPS Agreement. The EC argued:

> [B]oth Sections . . . violate the national treatment obligation under the *TRIPS Agreement* and the *Paris Convention (1967)* because they provide less favourable treatment to *Cuban* nationals who are original owners than to United States nationals who are original owners.[79]

The argument was challenged on the merits by the United States, but not on the jurisdictional grounds of lack of economic or legal interest. The Appellate Body agreed with the argument, and found a denial of national treatment.[80]

[2] Exhaustion of local remedies

In *Guatemala – Cement II*, where Mexico challenged the imposition of antidumping measures, the Panel stated, "Whether Mexico chose not to pursue its rights under Guatemalan law is of no concern to us, as this would not affect its rights under the WTO Agreements."[81] A similar argument was made in *United States – Safeguard Measures on Imports of Lamb*,[82] with a similar result:

> Arguments before national competent authorities may be influenced by, and focused on, the requirements of the national laws, regulations and procedures. On the other hand, dispute settlement proceedings brought

78 Panel Report, *Korea – Definitive Safeguard Measure on Imports of Certain Dairy Products*, WT/DS98/R and Corr.1, adopted 12 January 2000, as modified by the Appellate Body Report, WT/DS98/AB/R, DSR 2000:I, 49, ¶ 7.13.

79 Appellate Body Report, *United States – Section 211 Omnibus Appropriations Act of 1998*, WT/DS176/AB/R, adopted 1 February 2002, ¶ 275.

80 *Id.* ¶ 296.

81 Panel Report, *Guatemala – Definitive Anti-Dumping Measures on Grey Portland Cement from Mexico*, WT/DS156/R, adopted 17 November 2000, DSR 2000:XI, 5295, ¶ 8.83.

82 Appellate Body Report, *United States – Safeguard Measures on Imports of Fresh, Chilled or Frozen Lamb Meat from New Zealand and Australia*, WT/DS177/AB/R, WT/DS178/AB/R, adopted 16 May 2001.

> under the DSU concerning safeguard measures imposed under the *Agreement on Safeguards* may involve arguments that were not submitted to the competent authorities by the interested parties.[83]

Nevertheless, the Appellate Body said, "WTO Members cannot improperly withhold arguments from competent authorities with a view to raising those arguments later before a panel."[84]

The general rule under GATT appears to be that the doctrine of exhaustion of local remedies by private parties did not apply.[85] In most contexts, this makes sense. GATT was, and the WTO agreements are, government-to-government agreements involving products and services, not agreements between private parties *per se*, although private parties often have a profound interest in the obligations that other governments owe their government. The failure of private parties to exhaust local remedies, therefore, should not have a bearing on whether one government has acted in a manner inconsistent with its obligations to another government. This approach is consistent with the International Law Commission's recent draft report on State Responsibility.[86]

However, a number of the WTO agreements, including GATS and TRIPS, include legal substantive and procedural obligations directly applicable to private parties. Arguably, a Member should not be able to complain that another is denying substantive rights if that other Member provides the required procedural channels for the enforcement and redress of those substantive rights and the relief afforded by these channels has not been utilized by those complaining of the substantive issue.[87]

[3] Participation by amicus curiae

The question of participation by *amicus curiae* in WTO disputes has been and remains highly controversial. As the situation has evolved, it appears that panels, and the Appellate Body, may accept submissions by *amicus*

[83] *Id.* ¶ 113. [84] *Id.* ¶ 115.

[85] GATT Panel Report, *United States – Imposition of Anti-Dumping Duties on Imports of Fresh and Chilled Atlantic Salmon from Norway*, BISD 41S/229, adopted 27 April 1994, ¶¶ 347–35.

[86] UN GA Doc. A/CN.4/L.528/Add.2 of 16 July 1996, Art. 22.

[87] *See*, Rutsel Silvestre J. Martha, *World Trade Dispute Settlement and the Exhaustion of Local Remedies Rule*, 30 Journal of World Trade 107 (No. 4, August 1996).

curiae, subject to considerations of due process, but that they may not formally request them – at least not without significant objection by a large number of Members.[88]

The *amicus* saga began when two environmental organizations filed briefs with the Panel in *US – Shrimp*.[89] Although these briefs were served upon the parties and acknowledged by the Panel, the Panel declined to take them into consideration.[90] It reasoned that while, under Article 13 of the DSU, it had the authority to seek information from any source, it had not sought information from the organizations submitting the briefs. The Panel stated, "Accepting non-requested information from non-governmental sources, would be, in our opinion, incompatible with the provisions of the DSU as currently applied."[91] However, the Panel noted that if any of the parties wished to put forward all or parts of the *amicus* briefs as their own documents, the Panel would be willing to accept them as such. The United States, accordingly, designated a portion of one of the briefs as an annex to its second submission to the Panel.[92]

The United States appealed the Panel's conclusion that it could not accept non-requested submissions from non-governmental organizations, and the Appellate Body reversed. It first noted that only WTO Members had the right to participate in proceedings. With respect to non-Members, it said, panels had discretion to accept their submissions or not. Based on this distinction between the obligation of WTO adjudicating bodies to accept submissions from WTO Members (provided, of course, that the relevant paragraphs of the DSU have been complied with) and their discretion to accept submissions from other sources, the Appellate Body went on to state:

> . . . we do not believe that the word 'seek' must necessarily be read, as apparently the Panel read it, in too literal a manner. That the Panel's reading of the word 'seek' is unnecessarily formal and technical in nature becomes clear should an 'individual or body' first ask a panel for permission to file a statement or a brief. In such an event, the panel may decline to grant the

88 For a discussion of the treatment of *amicus curiae* briefs by WTO adjudicating bodies, *see* Petros C. Mavroidis, *Amicus Curiae Briefs before the WTO: Much Ado About Nothing* in Armin von Bogdandy, Petros C. Mavroidis & Yves Meny (Eds) EUROPEAN INTEGRATION AND INTERNATIONAL CO-ORDINATION: STUDIES IN TRANSNATIONAL ECONOMIC LAW IN HONOUR OF CLAUS-DIETER EHLERMANN (Kluwer, Leiden 2002).

89 Panel Report, *United States – Import Prohibition of Certain Shrimp and Shrimp Products*, WT/DS58/R and Corr.1, adopted 6 November 1998, as modified by the Appellate Body Report, WT/DS58/AB/R, DSR 1998:VII, 2821.

90 *Id.* ¶ 3.129. 91 *Id.* ¶ 7.8. 92 *Id.*

> leave requested. . . . In the present context, authority to *seek* information is not properly equated with a *prohibition* on accepting information which has been submitted without having been requested by a panel. A panel has the discretionary authority either to accept and consider or to reject information and advice submitted to it, *whether requested by a panel or not.*[93]

But this was not the end of the story. *Amicus* briefs and how to handle them within the WTO context have continued to haunt the deliberations at the DSB and the General Council.

The issue returned in *United States – Lead and Bismuth II.*[94] There the Panel declined to review an unsolicited *amicus* brief because it was submitted belatedly in the proceedings. In the Panel's view, acceptance would have denied the parties an adequate opportunity to respond.[95] This denial was not appealed by the parties (and the non-party could not appeal). However, when the United States appealed on the merits, two non-parties filed *amicus* briefs with the Appellate Body. The European Communities argued that *amicus* briefs are inadmissible in appellate proceedings. Article 13, the EC contended, applies only to panels and further, is limited to factual information and technical advice, not legal arguments.[96]

The EC's argument was not accepted. While neither the DSU nor the Appellate Body's *Working Procedures* provides for *amicus* submissions, the Appellate Body said neither explicitly prohibits them:

> Individuals and organizations, which are not Members of the WTO, have no legal *right* to make submissions to or to be heard by the Appellate Body. The Appellate Body has no legal *duty* to accept or consider unsolicited *amicus curiae* briefs submitted by individuals or organizations, not Members of the WTO. The Appellate Body has a legal *duty* to accept and consider *only* submissions from WTO Members which are parties or third parties in a particular dispute.[97]

[93] Appellate Body Report, *US – Shrimp, supra* note 59, ¶¶ 107 and 108 (italics in the original).

[94] Panel Report, *United States – Imposition of Countervailing Duties on Certain Hot-Rolled Lead and Bismuth Carbon Steel Products Originating in the United Kingdom*, WT/DS138/R and Corr.2, adopted 7 June 2000, as upheld by the Appellate Body Report, WT/DS138/AB/R, DSR 2000:VI, 2631.

[95] *Id.* ¶ 6.3.

[96] Appellate Body Report, *United States – Imposition of Countervailing Duties on Certain Hot-Rolled Lead and Bismuth Carbon Steel Products Originating in the United Kingdom*, WT/DS138/AB/R, adopted 7 June 2000, DSR 2000:V, 2601, ¶ 36.

[97] *Id.* ¶ 41 (emphasis in original).

However, it added that "we have the legal authority under the DSU to accept and consider *amicus curiae* briefs in an appeal in which we find it pertinent and useful to do so."[98] As it happened, the Appellate Body found it unnecessary to take the two submissions into account in reaching its decision.[99]

In *Australia – Salmon (Article 21.5 – Canada)*, the Panel accepted unsolicited information in the form of a letter from "Concerned Fishermen and Processors," which, in its view, was "relevant to its procedures."[100] It cited Article 13.1 of the DSU as its authority.[101] It also quoted the Appellate Body's language, noted above, in *US – Shrimp*.[102] In *EC – Asbestos*, the Panel received five *amicus* briefs, four initially and one after the Panel's Interim Report had been circulated to the parties.[103] The defendant incorporated two of them in its brief and urged the Panel to dismiss the other two briefs originally submitted to it. The complainant requested the Panel to dismiss all four briefs originally submitted to it. The Panel accepted the two briefs that the defendant had incorporated into its own submission. The fifth, "submitted at a stage in the procedure when it could no longer be taken into account," was not accepted.[104] The Panel transmitted the fifth submission to the parties for their information along with its decision not to accept it, and also informed them that the same decision would apply to any submissions received from non-governmental organizations subsequently.[105]

When the *Asbestos* report was appealed, the Appellate Body anticipated a large number of *amicus* submissions. After consultations with the parties and third parties to the dispute, citing Rule 16(1) of the *Working Procedures for Appellate Review*, the Appellate Body proposed an additional procedure to deal with the anticipated submissions.[106] In its communication to the DSB, the Appellate Body stated that its initiative was not a new working procedure drawn up pursuant to Article 17.9 of the DSU, but was adopted for the purposes of the *Asbestos* appeal only. The Additional Procedures laid out a series of procedural requirements for *amicus curiae*.

[98] *Id.* ¶ 42. [99] *Id.*

[100] Panel Report, *Australia – Measures Affecting Importation of Salmon – Recourse to Article 21.5 of the DSU by Canada*, WT/DS18/RW, adopted 20 March 2000, DSR 2000:IV, 2035, ¶ 7.8.

[101] *Id.* [102] *Id.* ¶ 7.9. [103] *EC – Asbestos*, *supra* note 9, ¶¶ 8.12–8.13.

[104] *Id.* ¶ 8.14. [105] *Id.*

[106] *EC – Asbestos*, Communication from the Appellate Body, WT/DS135/9, 8 November 2000.

This initiative met strenuous objection. Egypt, on behalf of the Informal Group of Developing Countries, requested a special meeting of the General Council to discuss the Communication.[107] Egypt said the decision to adopt an additional procedure "went far beyond the Appellate Body's mandate and powers."[108] "Uruguay viewed with great concern the appearance and mass circulation outside the WTO of the Appellate Body communication establishing the additional procedure for the submission of written briefs from persons or institutions that were neither parties nor third parties in a particular dispute at the appeal stage."[109] Hong Kong, China expressed concern that the "decision could create an impossible burden on developing country Members, and indeed any Member, who may wish to comment on and respond to any briefs submitted but would be limited by time and resources constraints."[110] India said, "The Appellate Body had unfortunately ignored the overwhelming sentiment of Members against acceptance of unsolicited *amicus curiae* briefs."[111] "Brazil expected that when exercising the discretionary authority granted in Article 17.9 of the DSU, the Appellate Body would use the consultation provision of that same Article whenever it faced an issue that could be either substantive in nature, or otherwise had systemic implications."[112]

Numerous other Members spoke, most of them critical. In support of the Communication, the United States said that "the Appellate Body had adopted procedures to manage this issue in a fair, legal and orderly manner, taking into account the interests of members of civil society in having their views considered, the interests of the parties and third parties in being able to review and respond to any *amicus* submissions, and the interests of all in resolving the dispute."[113] In its Report, the Appellate Body did not refer to the meeting of the General Council, but noted that it received 11 applications for leave to file an *amicus* brief. Each application was denied without further explanation.[114]

[107] A detailed report of the meeting is contained in, General Council, Minutes of Meeting held in the Centre William Rappard on 22 November 2000, WT/GC/M/60, 23 January 2001.

[108] *Id.* ¶ 10. [109] *Id.* ¶ 5. [110] *Id.* ¶ 27.

[111] *Id.* ¶ 31. [112] *Id.* ¶ 47. [113] *Id.* ¶ 74.

[114] Appellate Body Report, *European Communities – Measures Affecting Asbestos and Asbestos-Containing Products*, WT/DS135/AB/R, adopted 5 April 2001, ¶ 56. *See* also, Geert Z. Zonnekeyn, *The Appellate Body's Communication on Amicus Curiae Briefs in the Asbestos Case*, 35 Journal of World Trade 553 (No. 3, June 2001). Robert Howse & Reinhard Quick, *Trade, Environment and the Role of NGOs* (separate contributions under the same title), 4 Journal of World Intellectual Property 277, 281 (No. 4, March 2001).

§ 2.06 Review of jurisdictional claims

[1] Challenge to jurisdiction by parties

In *US – 1916 Act*, the United States appealed the Panel's finding that it had jurisdiction to consider certain claims.[115] The European Communities argued that an objection to a panel's jurisdiction, not raised until the interim review stage of a panel's proceeding, should be rejected as untimely.[116] The Appellate Body rejected the EC's argument, stating that while issues of jurisdiction should be raised as early as possible in the proceedings, "some issues of jurisdiction may be of such a nature that they have to be addressed by the Panel at any time."[117]

[2] Ex officio *review of jurisdiction*

"[I]t is a widely accepted rule that an international tribunal is entitled to consider the issue of its own jurisdiction on its own initiative, and to satisfy itself that it has jurisdiction in any case that comes before it."[118] This includes a WTO panel which has the "competence of its competence" and may determine whether a given claim can be addressed irrespective of the positions of the parties.[119] Indeed, a panel has the responsibility to determine its own jurisdiction,[120] and cannot simply ignore issues which "go to the root" of that jurisdiction.[121]

While the panel's jurisdiction will be limited by the terms of reference, and while it may not go beyond them to consider whether the measures or actions complained of are inconsistent with other agreements or other provisions of the agreements cited,[122] a panel has the responsibility to determine its jurisdiction, and "the scope of its terms of reference is an essential part of this determination."[123]

[115] Appellate Body Report, *United States – Anti-Dumping Act of 1916*, WT/DS136/AB/R, WT/DS162/AB/R, adopted 26 September 2000, DSR 2000:X, 4793, ¶ 52.

[116] *Id.* ¶ 53. [117] *Id.* ¶ 54.

[118] Appellate Body Report, *US – 1916 Act*, *supra* note 115, note 30.

[119] Panel Report, *United States – Anti-Dumping Act of 1916 – Complaint by the European Communities*, WT/DS136/R and Corr.1, adopted 26 September 2000, as upheld by the Appellate Body Report, WT/DS136/AB/R, WTDS162/AB/R, DSR 2000:X, 4593, ¶ 6.72.

[120] Panel Report, *United States – Import Prohibition of Certain Shrimp and Shrimp Products – Recourse to Article 21.5 of the DSU by Malaysia*, WT/DS58/RW, adopted 21 November 2001, as upheld by the Appellate Body Report, WT/DS58/AB/RW, ¶ 5.6.

[121] Appellate Body Report, *Mexico – Corn Syrup (Article 21.5 US)*, *supra* note 5, ¶ 64.

[122] Panel Report, *Japan – Alcoholic Beverages II*, *supra* note 13, ¶ 6.5.

[123] *US – Shrimp (Article 21.5 – Malaysia)*, *supra* note 120, ¶ 5.6.

The power of WTO tribunals to consider jurisdictional issues extends to the Appellate Body, which has held that it has the authority to consider claims that a panel has exceeded its terms of reference even if that claim was not made in the Notice of Appeal.[124]

[3] Res judicata

The Panel in *India – Autos* was the first to address in a report the question of whether *res judicata* exists in the WTO.[125] The Panel noted that this question "is of systemic importance," adding that "it is certainly true that certain widely recognized principles of international law have been found to be applicable in WTO dispute settlement, particularly concerning fundamental procedural matters."[126] The Panel also noted that the DSU does not directly address the issue.[127] "[F]or *res judicata* to have any possible role in WTO dispute settlement," the Panel said, "there should, at the very least, be in essence identity between the matter previously ruled on and that submitted to the subsequent panel."[128] Further, "the question to determine is whether a particular issue was ruled on and decided upon, and not merely whether the implementation of a previous ruling may have practical implications for particular measures in the later dispute."[129] After reviewing the respective matters, the Panel concluded that *res judicata* did not apply in that dispute. "The Panel does not seek to rule on whether the doctrine could potentially apply to WTO dispute settlement."[130]

In discussing the issue, the Panel noted that in a previous case, India had mentioned *res judicata*, but the issue there was successive complaints involving different Members.[131] In *Canada – Aircraft Credits and Guarantees*, the Panel asked the parties whether *res judicata* was applicable to the case. Neither party urged that *res judicata* controlled the dispute, and the Panel did not refer to the principle in its Report.[132]

[124] Appellate Body Report, *United States – Continued Dumping and Subsidy Offset Act of 2000*, WT/DS217/AB/R, WT/DS234/AB/R, adopted 27 January 2003, ¶ 208.

[125] *Supra* note 39. [126] *Id.* ¶ 7.57. [127] *Id.* ¶ 7.58. [128] *Id.* ¶ 7.66.

[129] *Id.* ¶ 7.94. [130] *Id.* ¶ 7.103.

[131] *Id.* note 331, referring to Panel Report, *India – Patent Protection for Pharmaceutical and Agricultural Chemical Products – Complaint by the European Communities*, WT/DS79/R, adopted 22 September 1998, DSR 1998:VI, 2661, ¶ 4.2.

[132] Panel Report, *Canada – Export Credits and Loan Guarantees for Regional Aircraft*, WT/DS222/R and Corr.1, adopted 19 February 2002, Annex A-9, p. 74 (response of Brazil) and Annex B-7, p. 57 (response of Canada).

Perhaps the first panel actually to apply the doctrine of *res judicata* did not use the term. In *EC – Bed Linen (Article 21.5 – India)*, the EC raised "novel and difficult issues concerning the scope of a panel's mandate under Article 21.5 of the DSU."[133] In the original investigation, India claimed, *inter alia*, that, during the antidumping proceeding, the EC had not properly evaluated "other factors" causing injury. This claim was dismissed by the Panel, which found that India had not presented a *prima facie* case in support of the claim.[134] India did not appeal the Panel's conclusion on the point, but, before a subsequent compliance panel, India again argued that the EC, in taking measures to comply with the recommendations and rulings of the DSB that had emerged from the original proceeding, again failed properly to consider "other factors." In the Article 21.5 Panel's words, "India is not challenging aspects of the EC determination that it raised, and could have pursued in the original dispute, but did not."[135]

In concluding that India's claim was not properly before it, the Panel reasoned that "the portions of the original Report of the Panel that are not appealed, together with the Appellate Body report resolving the issues appealed, must, in our view, be considered as the final resolution of the dispute, and must be treated as such by the parties, and by us, in this proceeding."[136]

The Appellate Body affirmed. After noting that DSU Article 17.14 provides that Appellate Body reports adopted by the DSB must be "unconditionally accepted by the parties to the dispute," it went on to state virtually the same thing, that "a panel finding which is not appealed, and which is included in a panel report *adopted* by the DSB, must be accepted by the parties as a *final* resolution to the dispute between them."[137]

Unlike *India – Autos*, *EC – Bed Linens* involved both the same issue and the same parties. This fits most definitions of *res judicata*.[138]

[133] Panel Report, *European Communities – Anti-Dumping Duties on Imports of Cotton-Type Bed Linen from India – Recourse to Article 21.5 of the DSU by India*, WT/DS141/RW, adopted 24 April 2003, as modified by the Appellate Body Report, WT/DS141/AB/RW, ¶ 6.37.

[134] *Id.* ¶ 6.41. [135] *Id.* ¶ 6.42. [136] *Id.* ¶ 6.51.

[137] Appellate Body Report, *European Communities – Anti-Dumping Duties on Imports of Cotton-Type Bed Linen from India – Recourse to Article 21.5 of the DSU by India*, WT/DS141/AB/RW, adopted 24 April 2003, ¶ 93.

[138] *See*, Panel Report, *India – Autos*, *supra* note 39: *res judicata* requires an identity between the matter previously ruled on and that submitted to a subsequent panel, as well as an identity of the parties.

[4] Estoppel

"Estoppel is premised on the view that where one party has been induced to act in reliance on the assurances of another party, in such a way that it would be prejudiced were the other party later to change its position, such a change in position is 'estopped,' that is precluded."[139] Thus, in *US – Steel Plate*, the Panel would not allow India to pursue a claim it had explicitly abandoned in its first written submission.[140] "The United States as the defending Member, and third parties participating in this proceeding, were justified in relying on India's statement that it was not pursuing this claim," the Panel said.[141] "[T]o allow a party to resurrect a claim it had explicitly stated . . . that it would not pursue would in the absence of significant adjustments in the Panel's procedures, deprive other Members participating in the dispute settlement proceeding of their full opportunities to defend their interests with respect to that claim."[142]

In *Mexico – Corn Syrup (Article 21.5 – US)*, again without using the word "estoppel," the Appellate Body held that failure to pursue an objection to the absence of consultations before the Dispute Settlement Body and the Panel effectively estops that party from arguing before the Appellate Body that the Panel was improperly established. In that case, an Article 21.5 review Panel had been established without consultations and without objection by Mexico until the appeal. "A Member that fails to raise its objections in a timely manner, notwithstanding one or more opportunities to do so," the Appellate Body said, "may be deemed to have waived its right to have a panel consider such objections."[143] The untimely raising of the issue was given by the Panel in *US – Lamb* as one of the reasons why it rejected a US request that the Panel find that the request for the establishment of the Panel was deficient.[144] Similarly, in *US – FSC*, without using the word "estoppel," the Appellate Body held that the United States,

[139] Panel Report, *Guatemala – Cement II*, *supra* note 81, ¶ 8.23. The Panel contrasted estoppel with "acquiescence" which it defined as "'qualified silence,' whereby silence in the face of events that call for a reaction of some sort may be interpreted as a presumed consent."

[140] Panel Report, *United States – Anti-Dumping and Countervailing Duty Measures on Steel Plate from India*, WT/DS206/R and Corr.1, adopted 29 July 2002, ¶ 7.29.

[141] *Id.* ¶ 7.26. [142] *Id.* ¶ 7.28.

[143] Appellate Body Report, *Mexico – Anti-Dumping Investigation of High Fructose Corn Syrup (HFCS) from the United States – Recourse to Article 21.5 of the DSU by the United States*, WT/DS132/AB/RW, adopted 21 November 2001, ¶ 50.

[144] Panel Report, *United States – Safeguard Measures on Imports of Fresh, Chilled or Frozen Lamb Meat from New Zealand and Australia*, WT/DS177/R, WT/DS178/R, adopted 16 May 2001, as modified by the Appellate Body Report, WT/DS177/AB/R, WT/DS178/AB/R, ¶ 5.32.

which engaged in three separate sets of consultations over a period of five months, could not subsequently raise the absence in the request for consultations of a "statement of available evidence," as called for by Article 4.1 of the *Agreement on Subsidies and Countervailing Measures.*[145]

When a Member raises its claims at an appropriate moment in WTO dispute settlement procedure, however, that Member is not estopped from bringing those claims because of its failure to protest before that time.[146] A Member also is not estopped from arguing that a measure notified under the *Agreement on Technical Barriers to Trade* is not a technical regulation. These notifications are made for reasons of transparency and do not have recognized legal effect.[147] Further, statements allegedly made during consultations do not estop a party, at least in the absence of showing a legitimate reliance and subsequent detriment.[148]

In GATT, the Panel in *US – Softwood Lumber*, without using the word "estoppel," effectively invoked the doctrine in the context of subsidies and countervailing measures.[149]

In *EC – Bed Linens (Article 21.5 – India)*, India argued that the EC was estopped from advocating before the Panel an interpretation of a provision of the Antidumping Agreement that differed from the interpretation given by the European Court of First Instance to an identical provision in the EC's municipal antidumping law.[150] The Panel rejected the argument, concluding that "'estoppel' based on national court decisions interpreting municipal law does not limit the decisions of WTO panels concerning covered agreements."[151]

Argentina, in *Argentina – Poultry*, argued that a previous proceeding before a Mercosur Ad Hoc Arbitral Tribunal estopped Brazil from pursuing an antidumping claim in the WTO.[152] The Panel quoted with approval the statement of a GATT Panel whose report was unadopted, that estoppel can only "result from the express, or in exceptional cases, implied consent of the complaining parties."[153] It found no such consent

[145] Appellate Body Report, *United States – Tax Treatment for "Foreign Sales Corporations,"* WT/DS108/AB/R, adopted 20 March 2000, ¶ 133. *See* § 5.09 [4].

[146] *Id.* ¶ 8.24. [147] Panel Report, *EC – Asbestos, supra* note 9, ¶ 8.60. [148] *Id.*

[149] GATT Panel Report, *United States – Measures Affecting Imports of Softwood Lumber from Canada*, BISD 40S/358, 480–486, adopted 27 October 1993, ¶¶ 308–325.

[150] *Supra* note 133, ¶ 6.89. [151] *Id.* ¶ 6.91.

[152] Panel Report, *Argentina – Definitive Anti-Dumping Duties on Poultry from Brazil*, WT/DS241/R, adopted 19 May 2003, ¶ 7.17.

[153] *Id.* ¶ 7.38, quoting GATT Panel Report, *EEC – Member States' Import Regimes for Bananas*, 3 June 1993, unadopted, DS32/R, ¶ 361.

in the case before it. "[T]he fact that Brazil chose not to invoke its WTO dispute settlement rights after previous Mercosur dispute settlement proceedings," the Panel said, "does not, in our view, mean that Brazil implicitly waived its rights under the DSU."[154] The Panel noted that in February 2002, Brazil signed the Mercosur Protocol of Olivos, which provides that once a party decides to bring a case under either Mercosur or WTO dispute settlement, the party may not begin a subsequent case regarding the same dispute before the other forum. However, that Protocol had not entered into force at the time the dispute was before the Panel.[155]

§ 2.07 Arbitration

An arbitration body established under Article 25.2 of the DSU held that, like any international tribunal, it, too, had the authority to consider issues of its jurisdiction on its own initiative.[156] The Arbitrators said that "their recognition of their jurisdiction in this case is not a unilateral extension of WTO jurisdiction, since it is dependent on the agreement of the parties to a dispute to have recourse to Article 25 of the DSU."[157] The Arbitrators noted that their jurisdiction was contained in the joint request for arbitration under Article 25.2.[158]

§ 2.08 Appellate jurisdiction

[1] General

The DSU establishes the jurisdiction of the Appellate Body. Article 17.6 provides that, "An appeal shall be limited to issues of law covered in the panel report and legal interpretations developed by the panel." Article 17.13 authorizes the Appellate Body to "uphold, modify or reverse the legal findings and conclusions of the panel." A panel's consideration and weighing of evidence relates to its assessment of the facts, and

154 *Id.* 155 *Id.*

156 Award of the Arbitrators, *United States – Section 110(5) of the US Copyright Act – Recourse to Arbitration under Article 25 of the DSU*, WT/DS160/ARB25/1, 9 November 2001, ¶ 2.1. *See* § 2.06 [2].

157 *Id.* ¶ 2.7, note 30.

158 *Id.* ¶ 1.6, referencing WT/DS160/15 (3 August 2001). For arbitration in the WTO, *see* § 5.15.

therefore falls outside the scope of appellate review.[159] This limitation of the Appellate Body's jurisdiction to questions of law has presented a degree of awkwardness when it considers the correct interpretation of the municipal law of a Member, ostensibly a question of fact, not law.

[2] Questions of municipal law[160]

It is a truism that, from the perspective of international law, domestic or municipal law is a question of fact. The Permanent Court of International Justice stated:

> From the standpoint of International Law and of the Court which is its organ, municipal laws are merely facts which express the will and constitute the activities of States, in the same manner as do legal decisions or administrative measures. The Court is certainly not called upon to interpret the Polish law as such; but there is nothing to prevent the Court's giving judgment on the question whether or not, in applying that law, Poland acted in conformity with its obligations towards Germany under the Geneva Convention.[161]

Many issues in international law generally, and by far most issues in WTO law in particular, involve questions of municipal law – a statute or a regulation, a "measure." Since international tribunals have no particular expertise in the laws of hundreds of states, they must, out of necessity, turn to experts. Still, the subject matter is "law" and international judges decide legal questions, and that, of necessity, involves deciding what the "facts" of a municipal legal question are – in a word, it involves "interpreting" municipal legal materials.

The question is more complicated in the WTO than in international law generally because the WTO legal system, with an Appellate Body, appears to have no international counterpart.[162] Even the ICJ is a court of original jurisdiction which decides both questions of fact and questions of law, and from which there is no appeal. Thus, the "fact/law distinction" ultimately is of limited importance in other international tribunals because those

[159] Appellate Body Report, *Australia – Measures Affecting Importation of Salmon*, WT/DS18/AB/R, adopted 6 November 1998, DSR 1998 VIII, 3327, ¶ 261; Appellate Body Report, *Japan – Measures Affecting Agricultural Products*, WT/DS76/AB/R, adopted 19 March 1999, DSR 1999:I, 277, ¶ 98.

[160] For discussion of what constitutes evidence of municipal law, *see* § 4.09 [9].

[161] *Certain German Interests in Polish Upper Silesia*, PCIJ Ser. A, no. 7, p. 19.

[162] *See* generally, David Palmeter, *The WTO as a Legal System*, 24 FORDHAM INTERNATIONAL LAW JOURNAL 444 (November-December 2000).

tribunals decide both.[163] It matters little whether those tribunals term a question one of law or one of fact. With the Appellate Body's jurisdiction confined to questions of law, however, the distinction takes on an importance not present elsewhere in international law.

The Appellate Body first confronted the problem in *India – Patents*, where it was argued that the Panel did not assess Indian law as a fact to be established, but rather as a law to be interpreted.[164] The Appellate Body disagreed. "Municipal law may serve as evidence of facts and may provide evidence of state practice," it said. "However, municipal law may also constitute evidence of compliance or non-compliance with international obligations."[165] After quoting from the opinion of the PCIJ in *German Interests in Polish Upper Silesia*,[166] it said that "the Panel was simply performing its task in determining whether [the measures] were in conformity with India's obligations,"[167] adding that "There was simply no way for the Panel to make this determination without engaging in an examination of Indian law."[168] Further, "To say that the Panel should have done otherwise would be to say that only India can assess whether Indian law is consistent with India's obligations under the *WTO Agreement*."[169]

In *US – Hot-Rolled Steel*, the Appellate Body was called upon to consider whether the so-called "captive production" provision of US antidumping law was, on its face, inconsistent with the Antidumping Agreement.[170] Citing *India – Patents*, it stated, "Although it is not the role of panels or the Appellate Body to interpret a Member's domestic legislation as such, it is permissible, indeed essential, to conduct a detailed examination of the legislation in assessing its consistency with WTO law."[171] It then went on to "observe," "further note," and "observe also" several aspects of the law,[172] and concluded that the provision did not "require" or "compel" a particular analysis.[173]

The question returned in another dispute involving the US, the *Section 211 Appropriations Act* case.[174] There the United States argued that the Appellate Body was bound by the Panel's conclusions about the meaning of the measure at issue, since that was a question of fact.[175] Again citing

[163] *See* generally, Richard B. Bilder, *The Fact/Law Distinction in International Adjudication* in Richard Lillich (Ed) FACT-FINDING BEFORE INTERNATIONAL TRIBUNALS 95 (Transnational, 1991).

[164] *Supra* note 4. [165] *Id.* ¶ 65. [166] *Supra* note 161.

[167] *Supra* note 4, ¶ 66. [168] *Id.* [169] *Id.*

[170] Appellate Body Report, *United States – Anti-Dumping Measures on Certain Hot-Rolled Steel Products from Japan*, WT/DS184/AB/R, adopted 23 August 2001.

[171] *Id.* ¶ 200. [172] *Id.* ¶ 203. [173] *Id.* ¶ 208.

[174] *US – Section 211 Appropriations Act*, *supra* note 79. [175] *Id.* ¶ 101.

India – Patents, the Appellate Body rejected the argument.[176] It held that an assessment of a municipal law for compliance with WTO obligations "is a legal characterization" by a panel, and "a panel's assessment of municipal law as to its consistency with WTO obligations is subject to appellate review."[177] "To address the legal issues raised in this appeal," the Appellate Body said, "we must . . . necessarily examine the Panel's *interpretation* of the meaning of Section 211 under United States law."[178]

[176] *Id.* ¶ 104. [177] *Id.* ¶ 105. [178] *Id.* ¶ 106 (emphasis added).

3

Sources of Law

§ 3.01 Overview

Modern discussions of the sources of international law usually begin with a reference to Article 38(1) of the Statute of the International Court of Justice which provides:

> The Court, whose function is to decide in accordance with international law such disputes as are submitted to it, shall apply:
>
> (a) international conventions, whether general or particular, establishing rules expressly recognized by the contesting states;
> (b) international custom as evidence of a general practice accepted as law;
> (c) the general principles of law accepted by civilized nations;
> (d) subject to the provisions of Article 59, judicial decisions and the teachings of the most highly qualified publicists of the various nations, as subsidiary means for the determination of rules of law.[1]

The *Marrakesh Agreement Establishing the World Trade Organization* – the WTO Agreement – is a "particular" international convention, within the meaning of Article 38(1)(a), as are the additional agreements and legal instruments dealing with trade in goods and services, as well as intellectual property rights, referred to in the Dispute Settlement Understanding as "covered agreements." Resolution of disputes concerning the substantive rights and obligations of Members of the WTO under the covered

[1] *See, e.g.*, Ian Brownlie, PRINCIPLES OF PUBLIC INTERNATIONAL LAW 3 (4th ed., Oxford, 1990); Barry E. Carter & Philip R. Trimble, INTERNATIONAL LAW 18 (2d ed., Little Brown, 1994); Rosalyn Higgins, PROBLEMS & PROCESS: INTERNATIONAL LAW AND HOW WE USE IT 17–18 (Oxford, 1994); Malcolm N. Shaw, INTERNATIONAL LAW 59 (Grotius, Cambridge, 1991); Lori F. Damrosch, Louis Henkin, Richard Pugh, Oscar Schachter, Hans Schmidt, INTERNATIONAL LAW, 503–517 (2d ed., West, 2002). Article 59 of the Statute, referred to in § 38(1)(d) provides simply that, "The decision of the Court has no binding force except between the parties and in respect of that particular case."

agreements, of course, is governed by the DSU. Thus, in the words of Article 38(1)(a), the rules of the DSU "are expressly recognized by the contesting states" that are parties to WTO dispute settlement procedures. The same is true of the special rules and procedures contained in several of the covered agreements.[2]

The fundamental source of law in the WTO is, therefore, the text of the relevant agreements themselves. All legal analysis begins there. In the words of the Appellate Body, "The proper interpretation of the Article is, first of all, a textual interpretation."[3] The texts, however, are only "first of all." They do not exhaust the sources of potentially relevant law. To the contrary, all of the subparagraphs of Article 38(1) are potential sources of law to be drawn on in WTO dispute settlement.[4] More specifically, prior practice under GATT, including reports of GATT dispute settlement panels; WTO practice, particularly reports of dispute settlement panels and the Appellate Body; custom; the teachings of highly qualified publicists; general principles of law; and other international agreements all contribute to the rapidly growing and increasingly important body of law known as "WTO Law."

While there is no explicit equivalent to Article 38(1) in the Dispute Settlement Understanding or any other of the WTO Agreements, its terms effectively are brought into WTO dispute settlement by Articles 3.2 and 7 of the DSU. Article 3.2 specifies that the purpose of dispute settlement is to "clarify the existing provisions" of the WTO Agreements "in accordance with customary rules of interpretation of public international law." Article 7 specifies that the terms of reference for panels shall be, "To examine, in the light of the relevant provisions in . . . the covered agreement(s) cited by the parties to the dispute the matter referred to the DSB" and to "address the relevant provisions in any covered agreement or agreements cited by the parties to the dispute."[5]

2 These are discussed in Chapter 5.

3 Appellate Body Report, *Japan – Taxes on Alcoholic Beverages*, WT/DS8/AB/R, WT/DS10/AB/R, WT/DS11/AB/R, adopted 1 November 1996, 19, DSR 1996:I, 97.

4 For differing views on this point, *see* Michael Lennard, *Navigating by the Stars: Interpreting the WTO Agreements*, 5 JOURNAL OF INTERNATIONAL ECONOMIC LAW 17, 36 (March 2002), and Gabrielle Marceau, *A Call for Coherence in International Law: Praises for the Prohibition against 'Clinical Isolation' in WTO Dispute Settlement*, 33 JOURNAL OF WORLD TRADE 87, 109 (No. 5, October 1999). For a view consistent with that taken here, *see* Joost Pauwelyn, *The Role of Public International Law in the WTO: How Far Can We Go?*, 95 AMERICAN JOURNAL OF INTERNATIONAL LAW 535, 561 (April 2001).

5 *See* generally, Lorand Bartels, *Applicable Law in WTO Dispute Settlement Proceedings*, 35 JOURNAL OF WORLD TRADE 499 (No. 3, June 2001).

§ 3.02 Covered agreements

The term "covered agreements" in Article 7 of the Dispute Settlement Understanding means all of the multilateral WTO Agreements annexed to the Marrakesh WTO Agreement. The DSU also is applicable to disputes between the parties to the two plurilateral agreements that also are part of the WTO.[6] These texts, as noted, are the starting point for dispute settlement proceedings, since Article 6.2 of the DSU requires that a request for the establishment of a panel identify the legal basis for the request.[7] The legal basis for a request would be the specific provisions of a particular agreement or agreements. Implicit in this requirement is a due process consideration of fair notice which has led the Appellate Body to observe, "it is incumbent upon a panel to examine the request for the establishment of the panel very carefully to ensure its compliance with both the letter and the spirit of Article 6.2 of the DSU."[8] The texts of several covered agreements explicitly refer to other international agreements which, in this sense, also may be considered to be "covered agreements."[9]

§ 3.03 Reports of prior panels and the Appellate Body

Other than the texts of the covered agreements themselves, no source of law is as important in WTO dispute settlement as are the reported decisions of prior dispute settlement tribunals. These include the reports of GATT panels as well as WTO panels and the Appellate Body. "Judicial decisions" are among the "subsidiary" sources for the determination of rules of international law specified in Article 38(1)(d) of the Statute of the ICJ. These "decisions" can be the decisions of the Court itself, as well as those of other tribunals.[10] Read together with Article 59 of the Statute, which confines the binding force of a decision of the Court to the parties, Article 38(1)(d) has produced a system of precedent under which the Court essentially refers to and considers its prior decisions, but is not legally required to follow them. As Judge Mohamed Shahabuddeen has

[6] *See* §§ 5.13 and 5.14.

[7] A claim that does not refer to a provision of a WTO agreement does not conform to Art. 6.2. Panel Report, *Canada – Export Credits and Loan Guarantees for Regional Aircraft*, WT/DS222/R and Corr.1, adopted 19 February 2002, ¶ 7.49.

[8] Appellate Body Report, *European Communities – Regime for the Importation, Sale and Distribution of Bananas*, WT/DS27/AB/R , adopted 25 September 1997, DSR 1997:II, 591, ¶ 142.

[9] *See* § 3.07 [1].

[10] *See, e.g.*, Brownlie, *supra* note 1, 19–24; § 3.08.

observed, however, the Court, "though having the power to depart from them, it will not lightly exercise that power."[11] Panel and Appellate Body reports are the "judicial decisions" of the WTO, which effectively duplicates this system. Of course, the World Court as well as WTO tribunals "apply" the law and do not "make" it so, in this strict sense, their decisions are not "sources" of law in the same sense in which treaty provisions are sources. A formalist might wish instead to refer to them as evidence – perhaps rather authoritative evidence – of what the law is, and, therefore, a "source" in the sense of where to look for evidence of the law. A realist would shrug, and move on.

[1] GATT practice

The issue whether GATT panels should follow the conclusions of previous panels that had dealt with the same issue was raised in *Tuna II*.[12] The Panel concluded:

> The EEC recognized that there was no *stare decisis* in the GATT, if only because there was no hierarchy between courts or arbitral bodies in the GATT. This was also the case for most international courts or tribunals. Nevertheless, such international courts and tribunals were always very careful about maintaining their own precedents and a certain coherence in their decisions. The GATT required such coherence in panel interpretations in order to provide stability within the international trading system.[13]

Although this report remains unadopted and hence, as discussed below,[14] is of limited legal value, it does reflect the willingness of panels in the GATT years to ensure that coherence would be preserved in case law. A significant point is the GATT Panel's reliance on the absence of a hierarchy "between courts or arbitral bodies in the GATT." With the advent of the Appellate Body, that portion of the Panel's reasoning no longer is relevant.[15]

[2] Adopted GATT Reports in the WTO

The WTO Agreement specifies that the WTO shall be guided by the decisions, procedures and customary practices followed by GATT 1947 and

[11] Mohamed Shahabuddeen, Precedent in the World Court 3 (Grotius, Cambridge, 1996).

[12] GATT Panel Report, *United States – Restrictions on Imports of Tuna*, DS33/1, 10 June 1994, unadopted, 33 I.L.M. 839 (1994).

[13] *Id.* ¶ 3.74 (emphasis in original). [14] *See* § 3.03 [3]. [15] *See* § 3.03 [5].

the bodies established in the framework of GATT 1947.[16] Implementing this requirement in the context of trade in goods, GATT 1994 specifies that the Agreement includes, *inter alia*, "decisions of the CONTRACTING PARTIES to GATT 1947."[17]

The question whether adopted GATT panel reports represent "decisions" of the CONTRACTING PARTIES to GATT 1947 arose in *Japan – Alcoholic Beverages II*.[18] Without referring explicitly to Article 38(1)(d) of the World Court Statute, the Panel effectively treated adopted reports as if they had the status of judicial decisions. Specifically, it determined that adopted reports are an integral part of GATT 1994 since they are "other decisions of the CONTRACTING PARTIES to GATT 1947" within the meaning of Article 1(b)(iv) of GATT 1994.[19] The Appellate Body disagreed, but in the end it is difficult to detect any practical difference resulting from the disagreement, which may have been largely semantic.

The Appellate Body held that a "decision" to adopt a panel report is not a "decision" within the meaning of Article 1(b)(iv). It did not say affirmatively what adopted reports are if they are not "decisions," other than to say that they are "an important part of the GATT *acquis*."[20] This is somewhat confusing, both because the legal source of this *acquis* is not specified and because, in its discussion of the issue, the Appellate Body itself refers to "a decision" and "decisions" to adopt panel reports.[21] The Appellate Body apparently was concerned that the Panel's conclusion could be interpreted as holding that adopted reports "constitute a definitive interpretation of the relevant provisions of GATT 1947."[22] A "definitive interpretation" presumably would be controlling and thus, on this theory, could amount to the importation of rigid *stare decisis* into the WTO, if not *sub rosa* amendment of its very texts. If this was the concern, it seems misplaced. The Panel treated adopted reports as "subsidiary" sources of WTO law, comparable in status to judicial decisions in the World Court. It did not say that adopted reports were controlling. Rather, it said that they "have to be taken into account by subsequent panels dealing with the same or a

[16] Art. XVI:1 (except as otherwise provided under the Agreement or the multilateral WTO Agreements).

[17] Art. 1(b)(iv).

[18] Panel Report, *Japan – Taxes on Alcoholic Beverages*, WT/DS8/R, WT/DS10/R, WT/DS11/R, adopted 1 November 1996, as modified by the Appellate Body Report, WT/DS8/AB/R, WT/DS10/AB/R, WT/DS11/AB/R, DSR 1996:I, 125.

[19] *Id.* ¶ 6.10.

[20] Appellate Body Report, *Japan – Alcoholic Beverages II*, *supra* note 3, at 15, DSR 108.

[21] *Id.* at 14, DSR 107.

[22] *Id.*

similar issue."[23] It specified, however, that, "it does not necessarily have to follow their reasoning or results."[24] Thus, in the Panel's view, an adopted report does not "constitute a definitive interpretation" of an agreement; it simply is a "decision" that has to be considered – but not necessarily followed – by a subsequent panel. The Panel effectively agreed with Judge Shahabuddeen's invocation of Shabtai Rosenne: "Precedents may be followed or discarded, but not disregarded."[25]

In its description of adopted reports, in any event, the Appellate Body came very close to saying the same thing. "[Adopted reports] are often considered by subsequent panels. They create legitimate expectations among WTO Members, and, therefore, should be taken into account where they are relevant to any dispute. However, they are not binding, except with respect to resolving the particular dispute between the parties to that dispute."[26]

This statement reads very much like Article 38(1)(d) of the Statute of the ICJ and its reference to "subsidiary" sources of international law. Indeed, in a footnote to this passage, the Appellate Body went on to draw a parallel to the practice of the World Court:

> It is worth noting that the Statute of the International Court of Justice has an explicit provision, Article 59, to the same effect. This has not inhibited the development by that Court (and its predecessor) of a body of case law in which considerable reliance on the value of previous decisions is readily discernible.[27]

[3] Unadopted GATT Reports in the WTO

The role of unadopted panel reports is something less, but they remain relevant. The Appellate Body agreed with the Panel in *Japan – Alcoholic Beverages II* that unadopted reports "have no legal status in either the GATT or the WTO system since they have not been endorsed through decisions by the Contracting Parties to GATT or WTO Members."[28]

[23] *See* Panel Report, *Japan – Alcoholic Beverages II, supra* note 18, ¶ 6.10. [24] *Id.*

[25] Shabtai Rosenne, THE LAW AND PRACTICE OF THE INTERNATIONAL COURT 56 (2d rev. ed. 1985), *quoted* in Shahabuddeen, *supra* note 11, at 131.

[26] Appellate Body Report, *Japan – Alcoholic Beverages II, supra* note 3, ¶ 6.10.

[27] *Id.* n. 30. *See* Malcolm N. Shaw, *A Practical Look at the International Court of Justice* in Malcolm Evans (Ed) REMEDIES IN INTERNATIONAL LAW: THE INSTITUTIONAL DILEMMA 13 (Hart Publishing, Oxford, 1998).

[28] *See supra* note 3, at 15, citing and quoting from the Panel Report in *Japan – Alcoholic Beverages II, supra* note 18, ¶ 6.10.

However, the Appellate Body also agreed that "a panel could nevertheless find useful guidance in the reasoning of an unadopted panel report that it considered to be relevant."[29]

In *US – Lamb*, the Panel noted the Appellate Body's statement as to the legal significance of GATT reports, and extensively discussed both adopted and unadopted GATT reports to support one of its findings.[30] Similarly, the Panel in *US – 1916 Act (Japan)* also looked to an unadopted GATT report for guidance.[31] In sum, within the parameters described by the Appellate Body as to their legal significance, WTO panels will look to unadopted GATT reports to support their legal conclusions if they find the reasoning in those reports persuasive.

In the end, it appears that the only difference between adopted and unadopted GATT panel reports is one of degree. Neither is binding; both can be persuasive. It is, perhaps, easier rhetorically for a WTO panel to dismiss an unadopted GATT report, but, given the fact that non-adoption more than likely means simply that the report was blocked by the losing party, and not that it was affirmatively rejected by the CONTRACTING PARTIES, even this might not always be the case.

[4] WTO Panel Reports

No case thus far has dealt explicitly with the legal significance of adopted WTO panel reports beyond their impact on the parties to a dispute.[32] However, the reasoning of the Appellate Body in *Japan – Alcoholic Beverages II* with regard to adopted GATT panel reports would seem to apply equally to adopted WTO panel reports.[33] Adopted WTO panel reports, like adopted GATT panel reports, "create legitimate expectations among

[29] *Id.* at 16.

[30] Panel Report, *United States – Safeguard Measures on Imports of Fresh, Chilled or Frozen Lamb Meat from New Zealand and Australia*, WT/DS/177/R, WT/DS178/R, adopted 16 May 2001, as modified by the Appellate Body Report, WT/DS177/AB/R, WT/DS178/AB/R, ¶¶ 7.78–7.100.

[31] Panel Report, *United States – Anti-Dumping Act of 1916 – Complaint by Japan*, WT/DS162/R and Add.1, adopted 26 September 2000, as upheld by the Appellate Body Report, WT/DS136/AB/R, WT/DS162/AB/R, DSR 2000:X, 4831, ¶ 6.189.

[32] *See*, Appellate Body Report, *European Communities – Anti-Dumping Duties on Imports of Cotton-Type Bed Linen from India – Recourse to Article 21.5 of the DSU by India*, WT/DS141/AB/RW, adopted 24 April 2003, ¶ 93: "[A] panel finding which is not appealed, and which is included in a panel report *adopted* by the DSB, must be accepted by the parties as a *final* resolution to the dispute between them." *See*, generally, *Res judicata*, § 2.06 [3].

[33] *See* § 3.03 [2].

WTO Members, and, therefore, should be taken into account where they are relevant to any dispute. However, they are not binding, except with respect to resolving the particular dispute between the parties to that dispute."[34] This is an effective statement of Article 59 of the Statute of the ICJ. A former member of the Appellate Body has explained that this is precisely how the dispute settlement system operates:

> It should be emphasized that the basis by which panels and the Appellate Body decide cases is substantially formulated on precedents. Indeed, the "common law" approach has become a predominant feature of WTO law although there is no formal "stare decisis" doctrine.[35]

Thus, the panel report on *India – Patents (EC)* stated that "panels are not *bound* by previous decisions of panels or the Appellate Body even if the subject-matter is the same. . . . However, . . . we will take into account the conclusions and reasoning in the Panel and Appellate Body reports in [an earlier dispute]. Moreover, in our examination we believe that we should give significant weight to both Article 3.2 of the DSU, which stresses the role of the WTO dispute settlement system in providing security and predictability to the multilateral trading system, and the need to avoid inconsistent rulings (which concern has been referred to by both parties)."[36]

Adopted reports have strong persuasive power and may be viewed as a form of non-binding precedent, comparable to the role played by *la jurisprudence* in the contemporary Civil Law of many countries, such as France, and comparable to the role played by decisions of courts at the same level in the United States. As a practical matter, parties will continue to cite prior reports to panels, and panels will continue to take them into account by adopting their reasoning – in effect, following precedent – unless panels conclude, for good and articulated reasons, that they should do otherwise.[37]

[34] *See supra* note 3.

[35] Mitsuo Matsushita, 5 SELECTED GATT/WTO PANEL REPORTS: SUMMARIES AND COMMENTARIES ix (Fair Trade Center, Tokyo, 1999).

[36] Panel Report, *India – Patent Protection for Pharmaceutical and Agricultural Chemical Products – Complaint by the European Communities*, WT/DS79/R, adopted 22 September 1998, DSR 1998:VI, 2661, ¶ 7.30 (emphasis in original).

[37] *Cf.* Malcolm N. Shaw, *A Practical Look at the International Court of Justice*, in Malcolm Evans (Ed) REMEDIES IN INTERNATIONAL LAW: THE INSTITUTIONAL DILEMMA (Hart Publishing, Oxford, 1999) at 13: "Although the decisions of the International Court bind only the parties in the instant case and for that case, it would be naïve to believe that such decisions are devoid of impact upon other States in similar situations."

The persuasive power of the prior reports rests not only on the reasoning they contain, important as this is, but also on the mere fact that once a dispute has been decided a certain way, subsequent panels are likely to follow even if they believe they might have decided the case otherwise had they been viewing the question in the first instance. Continuity and consistency are valuable attributes in any legal system: application of the same rules to the same factual issues, independent of the parties involved – treating like cases alike – is an important source of legitimacy for any adjudicator. It is particularly important for international adjudicators, who, unlike their municipal counterparts, lack a monopoly of enforcement power, and have only the power to persuade the addressees of their decisions that those decisions are correct.[38]

Thus, if a panel decides not to treat like cases alike by not following a prior report, the panel most certainly "should" – to use the words of the Appellate Body – address that report, which "create[d] legitimate expectations among WTO Members," and explain why it is not being followed. To do otherwise would call into serious question the very legitimacy of the process. In the words of one legal theorist, "the notion of formal justice requires that the justification of decisions in individual cases be always on the basis of universal propositions to which the judge is prepared to adhere as a basis for determining other like cases and deciding them in the like manner to the present one."[39]

Tribunals choose to follow previous cases not only for reasons of fairness and legitimacy, but also for reasons of efficiency: today's tribunal benefits from the work done yesterday on the same legal question; the wheel does not have to be re-invented. Finally, following precedent tends to make the law more certain and more clear, which also is of benefit to the legal system and those who take part in it.

The practical impact of the status of prior panel reports as persuasive but not binding is to put the burden on the party seeking a different interpretation to show the panel why it should depart from the reasoning and conclusions of its predecessor. Because, as the Appellate Body has said, adopted reports "create legitimate expectations," persuading a panel to depart from precedent can – and should – be difficult. It is not impossible, however, as can be seen from the statement of a GATT Panel declining to follow a previous panel in nearly identical circumstances, which is worth quoting at length:

[38] *See*, Thomas Frank, FAIRNESS IN INTERNATIONAL LAW AND INSTITUTIONS 26–46 (Clarendon Press, 1995).

[39] Neil MacCormick, LEGAL REASONING AND LEGAL THEORY 99 (Oxford, 1999).

> In considering the facts and arguments relating to Article XI in particular, the Panel took note of the fact that a previous Panel, in 1980, had reported on a complaint involving the same product and the same parties as the present matter and a similar set of GATT issues. The Panel noted carefully the arguments of the parties concerning the precedent value of this Panel's and other previous Panels' recommendations, and the arguments on the legitimate expectations of contracting parties arising out of the adoption of Panel reports. The Panel construed its terms of reference to mean that it was authorized to examine the matter referred to it by Chile in the light of all relevant provisions of the General Agreement and those related to its interpretation and implementation. It would take into account the 1980 Panel report and the legitimate expectations created by the adoption of this report, but also other GATT practices and Panel reports adopted by the Contracting Parties and the particular circumstances of this complaint. The Panel, therefore, did not feel it was legally bound by all the details and legal reasoning of the 1980 Panel report.[40]

The WTO Panel in *Japan – Alcoholic Beverages II* itself declined to follow the reasoning in two prior GATT panels, one unadopted, the other adopted. As to the unadopted report, the Panel said that it "was not persuaded by the reasoning," and, as to the adopted report, that it "decided not to follow the interpretation of the term 'like product' as it appears in Article III:2, first sentence, advanced by the 1992 *Malt Beverages* report in so far as it incorporates the aim-and-effect test" which it previously had discussed at length and dismissed.[41]

Each of these panels stated why it had decided not to follow the previously adopted reports. It is precisely this need to justify departures from prior cases that is the key for an international adjudicating body in its quest for legitimacy. Sir Gerald Fitzmaurice expressed a similar view with respect to the functioning of the World Court:

> It would seem that, although the Court is not obliged to decide . . . on the basis of previous decisions as such, what it can do is to take them fully into account in arriving at subsequent decisions, and that . . . it is mandatory for it to apply judicial decisions in the sense of employing them as part of the process whereby it arrives at its legal conclusions in the case.[42]

[40] GATT Panel Report, *European Economic Community – Restrictions on Imports of Dessert Apples, Complaint by Chile*, BISD 36S/93, adopted 22 June 1989, at 123–124, ¶ 12.1.

[41] Panel Report, *Japan – Alcoholic Beverages II*, *supra* note 18, ¶ 6.18, DSR 262.

[42] *See* Gerald Fitzmaurice, The Law and Procedure of the International Court of Justice 584 (Cambridge, 1986).

No doubt in part because prior panel reports are not legally binding, and perhaps in part because of GATT's diplomatic heritage, parties and panels use peculiar language in referring to earlier decisions. They "note" prior reports.[43] They "recall" them.[44] They "concur" with the reasoning of the prior panel.[45] In one of the early WTO panel reports, the panel quoted at length from another report and said, "We see great force in this argument."[46] Whatever word or words they use, however, panels are likely to "follow" the reports of previous panels unless those reports can be distinguished from the cases before them or unless the panels can be convinced that the previous panels were in error.[47]

Nevertheless, panels sometimes can seem to be trains passing in the night, as indicated by two reports arising out of the *Agreement on Textiles and Clothing* that were faced at the outset with the question of the appropriate standard of review. The first panel, *US – Underwear*, in a report dated 8 November 1996, found "great force" in the argument of a 1985 panel.[48] Two months later, the second panel, *US – Wool Shirts and Blouses*, in a report dated 6 January 1997, dismissed the same 1985 report, together with other reports cited by the parties:

> We do not consider that the reports cited by the parties are relevant to the present dispute . . . [they] were adopted many years ago . . . and they interpreted different agreements in different contexts . . . the ATC has

[43] *Id.* ¶ 6.11; Panel Report, *United States – Standards for Reformulated and Conventional Gasoline*, WT/DS2/R, adopted 20 May 1996, as modified by the Appellate Body Report, WT/DS2/AB/R, DSR 1996:I, 29, ¶ 6.11.

[44] *Id.* ¶¶ 6.10, 6.40; Panel Report, *Japan – Alcoholic Beverages II*, *supra* note 18, ¶ 6.19.

[45] Panel Report, *US – Gasoline*, *supra* note 43, ¶ 6.14.

[46] Panel Report, *United States – Restrictions on Imports of Cotton and Man-made Fibre Underwear*, WT/DS24/R, adopted 25 February 1997, as modified by the Appellate Body Report, WT/DS24/AB/R, DSR 1997:I, 31, ¶ 7.12 (referring to the GATT Panel Report, *New Zealand – Imports of Electrical Transformers from Finland*, BISD 32S/55, adopted 18 July 1985).

[47] This language suggests that the drafters of these reports were aware of comparable language in reports of the Permanent Court of International Justice. *See* Shahabuddeen, *supra* note 11, at 17. The phraseology continues in the World Court as evidenced by the recent *Case Concerning the Gabcíkovo-Nagymaros Project (Hungary/ Slovakia)*, 1997 ICJ No. 92 (Judgment of 25 September 1997): "The Court *recalls* that it has recently had occasion to stress . . ." (¶ 53); "The Court *recalls* that, in the *Fisheries Jurisdiction* case . . ." (¶ 104); "The Court will *recall* in this context that, as it said in the *North Sea Continental Shelf* case . . ." (¶ 141); but more authoritatively, "The Permanent Court of International Justice *stated* in its Judgment of 13 September 1928 in the case concerning the *Factory at Chorzow* . . ." (¶ 149) (emphasis added).

[48] *US – Underwear*, *supra* note 46, ¶¶ 7.11–12.

> instituted a new regime for textile products and the DSU has instituted new rules for panels.[49]

The *US – Wool Shirts and Blouses* Panel not only saw the prior reports very differently, but it did not even refer to the *US – Underwear* report and its consideration of the same question. Given the sizeable records in both cases, the fact that the nearly-contemporaneous proceedings overlapped to a considerable degree, and the time constraints on panels, this is not surprising. It is more than likely that the *US – Wool Shirts and Blouses* Panel was not even aware of the *US – Underwear* report at the time it prepared its own report.

The question of the degree to which factual findings (as opposed to legal conclusions) by a previous panel may be relevant to a later panel has not arisen often. Nevertheless, one of the early WTO panels had occasion to consider a purely factual conclusion reached by an earlier GATT panel. After quoting the factual finding of the previous panel, the WTO panel said, "Following its independent consideration of the factors mentioned in the 1987 Panel Report, the Panel agreed with this statement."[50] It went on to observe that the responding Member "offered no further convincing evidence that the conclusion reached by the 1987 Panel Report was wrong," making clear the otherwise always implicit burden on the party challenging a prior report, as to law or fact, to demonstrate its error.[51]

[5] Appellate Body Reports

As a formal matter, Appellate Body reports, like panel reports, bind only the parties to the particular dispute, and do not create binding precedent. Thus, the Panel in *India – Patents (EC)* no doubt was correct when it observed that "panels are not *bound* by previous decisions of . . . the Appellate Body."[52] Indeed, the text of any agreement is open to legal challenge regardless of how the Appellate Body previously may have interpreted it by virtue of the last sentence of Article 3.2 of the DSU which provides that, "Recommendations and rulings of the DSB cannot add to or diminish the rights and obligations provided in the covered agreements." If the recommendations and rulings of the DSB – which has the authority to

[49] Panel Report, *United States – Measure Affecting Imports of Woven Wool Shirts and Blouses from India*, WT/DS33/R, adopted 23 May 1997, as upheld by the Appellate Body Report, WT/DS33/AB/R and Corr.1, DSR 1997:I, 343, 431, ¶ 7.15.

[50] Panel Report, *Japan – Alcoholic Beverages II, supra* note 18, ¶ 6.22.

[51] *Id.*

[52] Panel Report, *India – Patents (EC), supra* note 36 (emphasis in original).

adopt or reject reports of panels or the Appellate Body – cannot add to or diminish the rights of Members under the agreements, *a fortiori*, those of panels or the Appellate Body cannot.

This having been said, however, it is clear that not very much has been said. The DSB cannot refuse to adopt a report absent consensus, and consensus requires at a minimum that the prevailing party not object.[53] Rarely will a party join in opposing the adoption of a report in its favor. The real question, therefore, is the extent to which panels and the Appellate Body itself treat Appellate Body reports as authoritative. The answer is clear: despite the statement of the *India – Patents (EC)* Panel, panels in fact follow the decisions of the Appellate Body in much the same way that a lower court follows the decisions of a higher court. This is a mandatory practice in some legal systems. In others, it occurs as a practical matter.[54] It also makes sense. A dispute settlement system with panels and subsequent appeals is a hierarchical system. "In a hierarchical system," Neil MacCormick has written, "only confusion and expense is caused by lower courts declining to follow precedents set by higher courts; so, standardly, the latter's decisions are binding on the former."[55] Given the fact that the Appellate Body, in practice, has the last word, it would also be futile for a panel simply to refuse to follow the Appellate Body's holding in a previous case. More likely, and perhaps more effectively, a panel would attempt to distinguish the case before it from the prior Appellate Body holding, and hope that the Appellate Body would find the distinction persuasive.

EC – Sardines is a rather typical example of a panel's following the Appellate Body.[56] One issue raised was whether a measure adopted before the 1 January 1995 effective date of the *Agreement on Technical Barriers to Trade* was subject to the requirements of that Agreement. The Panel referred to the Appellate Body's decision in *EC – Hormones*, where an analogous argument was made with regard to the *Agreement on Sanitary and Phytosanitary Measures*.[57] The Appellate Body affirmed the decision of the *Hormones* Panel that pre-1995 measures that did not cease to exist

53 DSU Art. 16.

54 *See, e.g.*, Rene David, FRENCH LAW: ITS STRUCTURE, SOURCES, AND METHODOLOGY 186 (Michael Kindred, trans.) (Louisiana State University Press, 1972).

55 MacCormick, *supra* note 39, 227.

56 Panel Report, *European Communities – Trade Description of Sardines*, WT/DS231/R and Corr.1, adopted 23 October 2002, as modified by the Appellate Body Report, WT/DS231/AB/R.

57 Appellate Body Report, *EC Measures Concerning Meat and Meat Products (Hormones)*, WT/DS26/AB/R, WT/DS48/AB/R, adopted 13 February 1998, DSR 1998:I, 135.

were subject to the Agreement, absent expression of a contrary intention in the Agreement itself.[58] The *Sardines* Panel stated:

> The factual aspect of the current dispute is not dissimilar to the one in hand in *EC – Hormones* in that, like the [pre-1995 measures at issue there] the EC Regulation is a "situation or measure that did not cease to exist" and the TBT Agreement does not reveal a contrary intention to limit the temporal application of the TBT Agreement to measures adopted after 1 January 1995.
>
> Therefore, Article 2.4 of the TBT Agreement applies to measures that were adopted before 1 January 1995 but which have not ceased to exist.[59]

The Appellate Body is more likely to follow its own prior decisions than panels are to follow the decisions of other panels. This is because the Appellate Body is effectively a standing judicial body; panels, by contrast, are composed of members who are chosen *ad hoc* and differ in composition from case to case. While only three of the seven members sit on any one "division" to hear a particular appeal,[60] the Appellate Body has chosen to operate on a "collegial" basis under which the division responsible for an appeal, while retaining full authority to decide, will exchange views with the other Members before finalizing its decision.[61] Consequently, Members of the Appellate Body, in confronting prior decisions, effectively are confronting their own decisions, or at least those of their close colleagues. This is seldom the case with panelists. Appellate Body Members, consequently, can be expected to have a stronger attachment to the reasoning and results of those decisions. "Once standing judicial bodies have come into existence," Judge Mohamed Shahabuddeen has observed, "they provide an additional mechanism for the further development of the law."[62]

An early example appears in the Appellate Body's second opinion, *Japan – Alcoholic Beverages II*, where it made two references to its first opinion, *US – Gasoline*, dealing with the subject of treaty interpretation: (1) "In *United States – Standards for Reformulated and Conventional Gasoline*, we stressed the need to achieve such clarification by reference to the

[58] *Id.* ¶ 128, DSR 182. [59] Panel Report, *EC – Sardines, supra* note 56, ¶¶ 7.59, 7.60.
[60] DSU Art. 17.1. [61] *See* § 6.04 [4].
[62] Shahabuddeen, *supra* note 11, at 45. The Secretariat serving panels provides some continuity and "institutional memory" to the extent that panelists wish to take advantage of their expertise, but members of the Secretariat, unlike panelists and Members of the Appellate Body, do not decide cases. On the rôle of the Secretariat, *see* § 4.08.

fundamental rule of treaty interpretation set out in Article 31 (1) of the *Vienna Convention*";[63] and (2) "In *United States – Standards for Reformulated and Conventional Gasoline*, we noted that. . . ."[64]

While the words "we stressed" and "we noted" are not the same, in a legal context, as "we held," there is an authoritative tone to them that suggests more than mere persuasion. The tone suggests that, in the view of the Appellate Body, those issues are closed. Subsequent statements confirm this analysis. For example, in *US – Shrimp (Article 21.5 – Malaysia)*, the Appellate Body concluded that its own reports form part of the WTO *acquis*:

> In this respect, we note that in our Report in *Japan – Taxes on Alcoholic Beverages*, we stated that:
>
> > Adopted panel reports are an important part of the GATT *acquis*. They are often considered by subsequent panels. They create legitimate expectations among WTO Members, and, therefore, should be taken into account where they are relevant to any dispute.
>
> This reasoning applies to adopted Appellate Body Reports as well. Thus, in taking into account the reasoning in an adopted Appellate Body Report – a Report, moreover, that was directly relevant to the Panel's disposition of the issues before it – the Panel did not err. The Panel was correct in using our findings as a tool for its own reasoning. Further, we see no indication that, in doing so, the Panel limited itself merely to examining the new measure from the perspective of the recommendations and rulings of the DSB.[65]

The extent to which the Appellate Body should depart from its own prior decisions presents it with something of a dilemma. On the one hand, stability in the law – and treating like cases alike – is served by declining to depart from prior decisions, even those that, in retrospect, may seem ill-advised, leaving it to the Members to change the text of an agreement should they believe the Appellate Body to be wrong. On the other hand, international legal institutions, like the WTO, lack legislatures and, as a consequence, international law notoriously lacks effective "rules of change."[66] One of the original members of the Appellate Body

[63] *See*, *supra* note 3, at 10–11 (emphasis added). [64] *Id.* at 13 (emphasis added).

[65] Appellate Body Report, *United States – Import Prohibition of Certain Shrimp and Shrimp Products*, WT/DS58/AB/R, adopted 6 November 1998, DSR 1998:VII, 2755, ¶¶ 108–109.

[66] *See* H. L. A. Hart, The Concept of Law 3, 95–96, 214 (2d ed., Oxford, 1994); David Palmeter, *The WTO as a Legal System*, 24 Fordham International Law Journal 444, 474–478 (November–December 2000).

stated, in an article published after his term ended, "I have been impressed by the imbalance between the strong (quasi-) judicial structure set up by the DSU and the inefficiency of the political decision-making process."[67]

Amending a WTO agreement is more like amending a written constitution than amending a statute.[68] This means that there is no practical way, apart from obtaining consensus or as part of a major round of trade negotiations, that Members can change the texts of a covered agreement – and thereby change the law – if many of them disagree with the Appellate Body. For all practical purposes, the word of the Appellate Body is likely to be the final word, at least for a very long time.

This effective power should lead to a greater willingness on the part of the Appellate Body to re-examine its prior holdings. The fact that the Appellate Body has the final word does not mean that it is infallible. It is, in substance if not in form, a court of last resort, and "courts of last resort have come to accept that they are not obliged to follow their previous decisions; within careful bounds, they may depart."[69] It is likely to be far better for the system for the Appellate Body to suffer occasional embarrassment than for the system to exist with the consequences of an erroneous decision.[70]

[67] Claus-Dieter Ehlermann, *Six Years on the Bench of the "World Trade Court" – Some Personal Experiences as a Member of the Appellate Body of the World Trade Organization*, 36 JOURNAL OF WORLD TRADE 605, 632 (No. 4, August 2002).

[68] There is a certain similarity between the rules for amendment of the WTO Agreement and those of the United States Constitution. Article X of the *Marrakesh Agreement Establishing the World Trade Organization* provides, *inter alia*, that two-thirds of the Members may propose an amendment that can be adopted by a three-fourths majority. Article V of the US Constitution provides for amendments proposed by a two-thirds vote of both Houses of Congress or by the legislatures of two-thirds of the States to become effective when approved by three-fourths of the States.

[69] *See* Shahabuddeen, *supra* note 11, at 238. The words of former U.S. Supreme Court Associate Justice Robert H. Jackson are relevant:

> Whenever decisions of one court are reviewed by another, a percentage of them are reversed. That reflects a difference in outlook normally found between personnel comprising different courts. However, reversal by a higher court is not proof that justice is thereby better done . . . We are not final because we are infallible, but we are infallible only because we are final."
>
> *Brown v. Allen*, 344 U.S. 443,540 (1953) (concurring).

[70] From 1946 to 1992, the US Supreme Court issued a total of 115 decisions overruling prior decisions – an average of 2.5 per year. Saul Brenner and Harold J. Spaeth, STARE INDECISIS: THE ALTERATION OF PRECEDENT ON THE SUPREME COURT, 1946–1992 23 (Cambridge, 1995).

§ 3.04 Custom

Customary international law plays a specific role in WTO dispute settlement by virtue of Article 3.2 of the Dispute Settlement Understanding, specifying that the purpose of dispute settlement is to clarify the provisions of the WTO Agreements "in accordance with customary rules of interpretation of public international law." In practice, Article 3.2 has led panels and the Appellate Body to Articles 31 and 32 of the *Vienna Convention on the Law of Treaties*, which have been held to codify customary international law on the subject.[71]

The issue of substantive – as opposed to procedural – custom first arose in *EC – Hormones*, where the question was whether the "precautionary principle" is part of customary international law.[72] The Panel stated that even if the precautionary principle were to be considered customary international law, it would not override explicit provisions of the WTO Agreements.[73] This conclusion was affirmed by the Appellate Body, which noted that the status of the precautionary principle in international law is itself the subject of debate.[74] The Appellate Body also stated that, while the precautionary principle might have crystallized into a general principle of customary international environmental law, it is less than clear whether it has been widely accepted as a principle of general or customary international law.[75] It is not clear from the opinion what the consequences would be if, in the view of the Appellate Body, the principle had been accepted as part of customary international environmental law, but not of customary international law generally.

In *Korea – Procurement*, the Panel stated that "the relationship of the WTO Agreements to customary international law is broader than" simply

[71] *See*, § 3.09 [1].

[72] Panel Report, *EC Measures Concerning Meat and Meat Products (Hormones) – Complaint by the United States*, WT/DS26/R/USA, DSR 1998:III, 699, ¶ 8.157, and Panel Report, *EC Measures Concerning Meat and Meat Products (Hormones) – Complaint by Canada*, WT/DS48/R/CAN, DSR 1998:II, 235, ¶ 8.160, both adopted 13 February 1998, as modified by the Appellate Body Report, WT/DS26/AB/R, WT/DS48/AB/R. The "precautionary principle" holds generally that, "Where there are threats of serious or irreversible damage, lack of full scientific certainty shall not be used as a reason for postponing cost-effective measures to prevent environmental degradation." Rio Declaration on Environment and Development, Article 15. *See, also*, Franck, *supra* note 38, at 370; Phillipe Sands, PRINCIPLES OF INTERNATIONAL ENVIRONMENTAL LAW, Vol. I at 208–13 (Manchester Univ. Press, 1995).

[73] *Id.*

[74] Appellate Body Report, *EC Measures Concerning Meat and Meat Products (Hormones)*, WT/DS26/AB/R, WT/DS48/AB/R, adopted 13 February 1998, DSR 1998:I, 135, 9, ¶ 123.

[75] *Id.*

the rules of interpretation.[76] At least in the context of non-violation complaints, the Panel said, "customary international law applies generally to the economic relations between WTO Members. Such international law applies to the extent that the WTO treaty agreements do not 'contract out' from it. To put it in another way, to the extent that there is no conflict or inconsistency, or an expression in a WTO covered agreement that implies differently, we are of the view that the customary rules of international law apply to the WTO treaties and to the process of treaty formation under the WTO."[77]

But the WTO, like GATT before it, is grounded in agreement, not in custom, and questions of custom, therefore, are likely to be infrequent.[78] Even GATT's first and most basic provision, the most-favored-nation clause (MFN), was not a codification of customary international law, nor did it establish a custom. To the contrary, GATT's MFN obligation extended only to other contracting parties, and contracting parties frequently denied MFN to non-parties. This remains true of the covered WTO agreements.

Article XVI:1 of the WTO Agreement, as stated earlier, specifies that "the WTO shall be guided by the decisions, procedures and customary practices followed by the CONTRACTING PARTIES to GATT 1947." It is doubtful that the "customary practices" referred to would be recognized as customary international law. Although the customary practices of GATT might meet some of the requirements of custom, it is doubtful that they were accepted by the parties to GATT or are viewed by the Members of the WTO "as law."[79]

§ 3.05 Teachings of the most highly qualified publicists

Sporadic references can be found in panel reports to the teachings and writings of highly qualified publicists in GATT law, but these references

[76] Panel Report, *Korea – Measures Affecting Government Procurement*, WT/DS163/R, adopted 19 June 2000, DSR 2000:VIII, 3541, ¶ 7.96. *See* also, § 2.04 [3].

[77] *Id.*

[78] "WTO dispute resolution panels and the Appellate Body are limited to the application of substantive WTO law and are not authorized to apply general substantive international law or other conventional international law." Joel P. Trachtman, *The Domain of WTO Dispute Resolution*, 40 HARVARD INTERNATIONAL LAW JOURNAL 333, 347–48 (Spring, 1999). The Panel in *Korea – Procurement* may be seen to disagree with this observation; however, that Report was not appealed. *See* also, Michael Lennard, *Navigating by the Stars: Interpreting the WTO Agreements, supra* note 4, 42–45.

[79] This is the *opinio juris* requirement, set out in Article 38(1)(b) of the Statute of the International Court of Justice.

were rare.[80] In large part, this reticence may stem from GATT's diplomatic heritage. What is now essentially a juridical system of dispute settlement began as a diplomatic system of "conciliation." Not only were diplomats less likely than lawyers even to be aware of, let alone to be influenced by, the writings of legal scholars, GATT diplomats for many years were decidedly averse to the very notion of turning conciliation into a legal proceeding.[81] The views of legal publicists, however highly qualified they might be, impressed few "old GATT hands."[82]

If legal scholars are more likely than diplomats to cite the writings of other legal scholars, one of the reasons for the relative absence of citation to scholarly writings in GATT reports was the relative absence of scholars among the panelists. While some academics served as panelists, for most of GATT's history the practice was not widespread. Academics, however, have served as WTO panelists with some frequency, and it is perhaps because of their presence that WTO reports often refer to the teachings of publicists. This began with some of the early reports,[83] and has continued.[84] The increasing presence of academics among panelists no doubt

[80] *See, e.g.*, GATT Panel Report, *United States – Measures Affecting Alcoholic and Malt Beverages*, BISD 39S/206, adopted 19 June 1992, at 285, citing the works of Profs. Robert E. Hudec and John H. Jackson.

[81] The history is recounted in R. E. Hudec's two volumes, THE GATT LEGAL SYSTEM AND WORLD TRADE DIPLOMACY (2d ed., Butterworth, 1990) and ENFORCING INTERNATIONAL TRADE LAW: THE EVOLUTION OF THE MODERN GATT LEGAL SYSTEM (Butterworth, 1993).

[82] This skeptical attitude toward law is apparent from the very title of a work by GATT's second Director General, OLIVER LONG: LAW AND ITS *LIMITATIONS* IN THE GATT MULTILATERAL TRADE SYSTEM (Martinus Nijhoff, 1985) (emphasis added).

[83] *See, e.g.*, Panel Report, *Argentina – Measures Affecting Imports of Footwear, Textiles, Apparel and Other Items*, WT/DS56/R, adopted 22 April 1998, as modified by the Appellate Body Report, WT/DS56/AB/R, DSR 1998:III, 1033, notes 176 (John H. Jackson), 184 (Keith Highet), and 185 (Mojtaba Kazazi); Appellate Body Report, *India – Patent Protection for Pharmaceutical and Agricultural Chemical Products*, WT/DS50/AB/R, adopted 16 January 1998, DSR 1998:I, 9, footnote 26 (F. Roessler and E.-U. Petersmann), footnote 28 (E.-U. Petersmann) and footnote 52 (I. Brownlie); Appellate Body Report, *EC – Hormones, supra* note 57, (P. Sands, J. Cameron, J. Abouchar, P. Birnie, A. Boyle, L. Gündling, A. de Mestral, and D. Bodansky).

[84] *See, e.g.*, Appellate Body Report, *Korea – Definitive Safeguard Measure on Imports of Certain Dairy Products*, WT/DS98/AB/R, adopted 12 January 2000, DSR 2000:I, 3, footnote 26 (M. Bronckers, M. Trebilcock, and R. Howse cited in the argument presented by the United States), footnote 44 (I. Brownlie, G. Fitzmaurice, A. McNair, I. Sinclair, M. O. Hudson, L. A. Podesta, and J. M. Ruda); Appellate Body Report, *United States – Section 211 Omnibus Appropriations Act of 1998*, WT/DS176/AB/R, adopted 1 February 2002, footnote 122 (D. Gervais); and Appellate Body Report, *United States – Tax Treatment for "Foreign Sales Corporations" – Recourse to Article 21.5 of the DSU by the European Communities*, WT/DS108/AB/RW, adopted 29 January 2002, footnote 119 (A. H. Qureshi and M. J. McIntyre), note 127 (A. H. Qureshi, B. J. Arnold, M. J McIntyre and J. Schuch).

also reflects recognition among diplomats and trade officials generally of the increasing importance of law to the trading system, an importance made clear by the very establishment of the Appellate Body. Confined to considering issues of law and legal interpretations of panel reports,[85] the Appellate Body, of necessity, brings a legal perspective to the process; and panels, advised by lawyers from the Secretariat (which was not the case for the first few decades of GATT), increasingly deal with complex issues of law.

§ 3.06 General principles of law

On occasion, GATT panels have invoked general principles of law in support of their reasoning, as have WTO panels and the Appellate Body. The principle that an exception to a general rule should be interpreted narrowly was utilized several times. The WTO Panel on *US – Underwear*, for example, concluded that the transitional safeguard mechanism of the *Agreement on Textiles and Clothing* is an exceptional measure and "should be interpreted narrowly."[86] However, the Appellate Body effectively repudiated this principle in *EC – Hormones*, where it said that the characterization of a treaty provision as an "exception" does not warrant an interpretation of the language of that provision other than in accordance with the normal rules of treaty interpretation.[87] In *US – Shrimp*, the Appellate Body observed that the chapeau of GATT Article XX is an expression of the principle of good faith which, as a general principle of international law, controls the exercise of rights by states.[88] Thus, the Appellate Body said, the principle of good faith encompasses the doctrine of *abus de droit*, the abusive exercise by a state of its rights.[89] In *Korea – Procurement*, the Panel referred to the public international law principles

[85] DSU Art. 17.6

[86] *Supra* note 46, ¶ 7.21 (citing several additional cases). *See* also, GATT Panel Report, *Canada – Import Restrictions on Ice Cream and Yoghurt*, BISD 36S/68, adopted 5 December 1989, ¶ 59: "The Panel recalled that . . . exceptions were to be treated narrowly," citing GATT Panel Report, *Japan – Restrictions on Imports of Certain Agricultural Products*, BISD 35S/163, adopted 22 March 1988, and GATT Panel Report, *EEC – Restrictions on Imports of Apples – Complaint by the United States*, BISD 36S/135, adopted 22 June 1989. This principle may no longer be applicable. *See* § 4.11 [5].

[87] Appellate Body Report, *EC – Hormones, supra* note 57, ¶ 104.

[88] Appellate Body Report, *US – Shrimp, supra* note 65, ¶ 158.

[89] *Id.* This principle was referred to by the Panel in *United States – Section 211 Omnibus Appropriations Act of 1998*, WT/DS176/R, adopted 1 February 2002, as modified by the Appellate Body Report, WT/DS176/AB/R, ¶ 8.57.

of good faith and error in the negotiation of treaty commitments.[90] The interpretive principle that readings which would result in reducing whole clauses or paragraphs of a text to "redundancy or inutility" must be avoided has been recognized several times by the Appellate Body.[91]

Articles 22.4 and 22.6 of the DSU, confining the level of suspension of concessions to the level of the nullification and impairment, are, of course, more than principle. They are the law of the agreement itself. It is worth noting, however, that these provisions conform to the principle of proportionality recognized by the World Court.[92]

§ 3.07 Other international agreements

Other international agreements are not "covered agreements" and do not, therefore, constitute – by themselves – authoritative sources of law in the WTO. However, other international agreements do play an important role in WTO dispute settlement. Panels and the Appellate Body have had occasion to consider international agreements referred to explicitly in the WTO Agreements, other multilateral agreements, and agreements between the parties to a dispute. Further, the WTO itself is a party to other international agreements.

[1] Agreements referred to in the WTO Agreements

The texts of several WTO agreements explicitly refer to other international agreements which may therefore serve as direct sources of law in WTO dispute settlement proceedings. These include the major international intellectual property conventions, the *Paris Convention* (1967), the *Berne Convention* (1971), the *Rome Convention*, and the *Treaty on Intellectual Property in Respect of Integrated Circuits*, as provided for in the TRIPS Agreement.[93] Thus, in *US – Section 211 Appropriations Act*, the Appellate Body observed that, "WTO Members, whether they are countries of the Paris Union or not, are obliged, under the WTO Agreement, to implement

[90] Panel Report, *Korea – Procurement, supra* note 76, ¶ 7.101.

[91] Appellate Body Reports, *United States – Standards for Reformulated and Conventional Gasoline*, WT/DS2/AB/R, adopted 20 May 1996, DSR 1996:I, 3, § III.B; *Japan – Alcoholic Beverages II, supra* note 3, at 12; *US – Underwear, supra* note 46, at 16.

[92] "[A]n important consideration is that the effects of a countermeasure must be commensurate with the injury suffered;" this is "the proportionality which is required by international law." *Case Concerning the Gabcíkovo-Nagymaros Project (Hungary/Slovakia), supra* note 47, ¶ 85. *See* ¶ 8.06 [1]. The principle of estoppel has also arisen in both GATT and WTO disputes. *See* ¶ 2.06 [4].

[93] TRIPS Art. I:3.

those provisions of the Paris Convention (1967) that are incorporated into the *TRIPS Agreement*."[94] The Panel in *Canada – Pharmaceutical Patents* went one step further.[95] It took into account the preparatory work of the *Berne Convention* to clarify the meaning of a condition laid down in a TRIPS Agreement provision it was called to interpret. In justifying its choice, the Panel noted that the text of the condition it was examining was drawn from the *Berne Convention*.[96]

The WTO *Agreement on Subsidies and Countervailing Measures* provides, somewhat indirectly, that the grant by governments of export credits in conformity with the provisions of the *Arrangement on Guidelines for Officially Supported Export Credits* of the Organization for Economic Cooperation and Development shall not be considered an export subsidy.[97] In *Canada – Aircraft (Article 21.5 – Brazil)*, the Panel held that it was required to interpret the text of the Arrangement since it is referred to in the SCM Agreement.[98] The Panel in *Canada – Aircraft Credits and Guarantees* also interpreted the terms of the Arrangement.[99] Article 2.4 of the *Agreement on Technical Barriers to Trade* requires Members to use "international standards" as the basis for their technical regulations. The Panel in *EC – Sardines* found that a standard of the Codex Alimentarius Commission of the UN was an international standard, within the meaning of Article 2.4, and interpreted the text of that standard.[100]

In *US – Section 110(5) Copyright Act*, the Panel considered the substantive legal status of the "minor exceptions doctrine" under the Berne

[94] Appellate Body Report, *United States – Section 211 Appropriations Act*, *supra* note 84, ¶ 125.

[95] Panel Report, *Canada – Patent Protection of Pharmaceutical Products*, WT/DS114/R, adopted 7 April 2000, DSR 2000:V, 2295. *See* also, § 3.09 [2].

[96] *Id.* ¶ 7.70.

[97] *Agreement on Subsidies and Countervailing Measures*, Annex I (k):

> . . . if a Member is a party to an international undertaking on official export credits to which at least twelve original Members to this Agreement are parties as of 1 January 1979 (or a successor undertaking which has been adopted by those original Members), or if in practice a Member applies the interest rates provisions of the relevant undertaking, an export credit practice which is in conformity with those provisions shall not be considered an export subsidy prohibited by this Agreement.

The "international undertaking" described is the OECD *Arrangement on Guidelines for Officially Supported Export Credits*.

[98] Panel Report, *Canada – Measures Affecting the Export of Civilian Aircraft – Recourse by Brazil to Article 21.5 of the DSU*, WT/DS70/RW, adopted 4 August 2000, as modified by the Appellate Body Report, WT/DS70/AB/RW, DSR 2000:IX, 4315.

[99] Panel Report, *Canada – Aircraft Credits and Guarantees, supra* note 7, ¶¶ 7.176, 7.234, 7.241.

[100] Panel Report, *EC – Sardines, supra* note 56, ¶¶ 7.67, 7.103.

Convention (1971).[101] The General Rapporteur to the Convention had presented a report on the doctrine which was adopted by the parties, but which was not inserted as an amendment to the Convention. The Panel held that adoption itself sufficed for it to consider the Rapporteur's report as subsequent agreement between the parties in accordance with Article 31.2(a) of the *Vienna Convention on the Law of Treaties.*[102]

The reference in Article 3.2 of the DSU to the "customary rules of interpretation of public international law" has been held by the Appellate Body to refer to Articles 31 and 32 of the Vienna Convention, whose provisions become a source of law insofar as they reflect customary international law.[103] Other provisions of the Vienna Convention may also provide law in WTO proceedings. For example, a WTO panel considered Article 28 of the Vienna Convention concerning non-retroactivity of treaties before concluding that it did not apply to the facts of the case.[104]

Some international agreements may be incorporated into the WTO even though not expressly referred to in a WTO text. This was the case when a waiver of specified obligations was granted by the GATT General Council and extended by the WTO General Council to the European Communities with respect to the Lomé Convention, which required the EC to extend preferential treatment to goods originating in certain African, Caribbean, and Pacific (ACP) countries.[105] The substantive question was: What was required by the Lomé Convention? The EC and the ACP countries argued that the Panel was not competent to answer that question. Rather, they contended, the Panel should defer to the interpretation advanced by the EC and the ACP countries who, as parties, were competent to answer it.[106]

The Panel disagreed. It noted that the EC and ACP countries initially had been granted a waiver by the GATT Contracting Parties to permit the preferential treatment. That waiver subsequently was adopted by the

[101] Panel Report, *United States – Section 110(5) of the US Copyright Act,* WT/DS160/R, adopted 27 July 2000, DSR 2000:VIII, 3769.

[102] *Id.* ¶ 6.53.

[103] *See* Appellate Body Report, *US – Gasoline, supra* note 91, and *infra,* § 3.09 [1].

[104] Panel Report, *EC – Hormones, supra* note 72, *Complaint by the United States* ¶¶ 8.24, 8.21, and *Complaint by Canada* ¶¶ 8.27, 8.28. Article 28 states that the provisions of a treaty normally do not bind a party in relation to any situation which ceased to exist before entry into force of the treaty.

[105] Panel Report, *European Communities – Regime for the Importation, Sale and Distribution of Bananas – Complaint by the United States,* WT/DS27/R/USA, adopted 25 September 1997, as modified by the Appellate Body Report, WT/DS27/AB/R, DSR 1997:II, 943.

[106] *Id.* ¶¶ 7.95, 7.97.

WTO. Clearly, therefore, the waiver itself was a WTO agreement, within the competence of a WTO panel. "Since the waiver applies to action 'necessary . . . to provide preferential treatment . . . as required by the relevant provisions of the Fourth Lomé Convention,' " the Panel said, "we must also determine what preferential treatment is required by the Lomé Convention."[107] The Appellate Body affirmed, observing, "To determine what is 'required' by the Lomé Convention, we must look first to the text of that Convention and identify provisions of it that are relevant to trade in bananas."[108]

Because the waiver effectively incorporated the Lomé Convention into a WTO agreement, the Panel's authority to interpret the waiver and, therefore, the Convention itself, parallels the authority that is likely to be claimed for the agreements explicitly referred to in the covered agreements, such as the intellectual property conventions. The report does not deal with the situation in which the international agreement at issue is not, at least implicitly, a WTO Agreement.

An as yet unresolved question is whether the rights and obligations brought into the WTO by these other agreements are only those that were in effect at the time the WTO Agreements became effective, or whether WTO rights and obligations change as these agreements change. Footnote 2 to the TRIPS Agreement states that references to the intellectual property conventions are to specific versions of those conventions.[109] Presumably, therefore, any rights and obligations negotiated later by the parties to the intellectual property conventions would not affect WTO rights and obligations and would not, therefore, be sources of WTO law. In this regard, the Panel in *Canada – Pharmaceutical Patents* stated that the TRIPS Agreement "incorporates certain provisions of the major

[107] *Id.* ¶ 7.97.

[108] Appellate Body Report, *EC – Bananas III*, *supra* note 8, ¶¶ 167, 169.

[109] The text of footnote 2 to the TRIPS Agreement in relevant *part* specifies:

> In this Agreement, "Paris Convention" refers to the Paris Convention for the Protection of Industrial Property; "Paris Convention (1967)" refers to the Stockholm Act of this Convention of 14 July 1967. "Berne Convention" refers to the Berne Convention for the Protection of Literary and Artistic Works: "Berne Convention (1971)" refers to the Paris Act of this Convention of 24 July 1971. "Rome Convention" refers to the International Convention for the Protection of Performers, Producers of Phonograms and Broadcasting Organizations, adopted at Rome on 26 October 1961. "Treaty on Intellectual Property in Respect of Integrated Circuits" (IPIC Treaty) refers to the Treaty on Intellectual Property in Respect of Integrated Circuits, adopted at Washington on 26 May 1989.

pre-existing international instruments on intellectual property."[110] In *US – Section 110(5) Copyright Act*, involving TRIPS and the Berne Convention, the Panel found that the WIPO Copy Right Treaty (WCT), adopted nearly two years after the effective date of TRIPS and the WTO, was relevant to the interpretation of terms in the Berne Convention.[111] The Panel noted that 127 countries participated in the diplomatic conference that led to the WCT, and that most of them were Members of the WTO and participated in the TRIPS negotiations.[112] "For these reasons," the Panel said, "it is relevant to seek contextual guidance also in the WCT when developing interpretations that avoid conflicts within the overall framework, except where these treaties explicitly contain different obligations."[113]

The second Article 21.5 Panel in *Brazil – Aircraft* determined that, for purposes of the SCM Agreement, the relevant version of the *OECD Arrangement* is the latest version, not the version that existed when the SCM Agreement became effective.[114] A similar issue arose before a panel established under the North American Free Trade Agreement. In considering a provision of NAFTA preserving the rights of the parties under GATT and agreements negotiated under GATT, the NAFTA Panel concluded that the particular reference at issue was not simply to GATT as it existed when the NAFTA provision came into effect, but to the GATT regime as it evolved, eventually, into the WTO.[115] The NAFTA Panel also noted that a reference in that agreement to customary international law was "a reference to an evolving system."[116]

[2] Other multilateral agreements

In addition to the *Vienna Convention on the Law of Treaties*, other multilateral international agreements have been looked at by WTO tribunals as indirect sources of law. Perhaps the most notable instance is the Report of the Appellate Body in *US – Shrimp*.[117] First, in interpreting the term "exhaustible natural resources" in Article XX(g) of GATT, the Appellate Body cited and quoted from the *United Nations Convention on the Law*

[110] *Supra* note 95, ¶ 7.14 (emphasis added).

[111] *Supra* note 101, ¶ 6.70. [112] *Id.* [113] *Id.*

[114] Panel Report, *Brazil – Export Financing Programme for Aircraft – Second Recourse by Canada to Article 21.5 of the DSU*, WT/DS46/RW/2, adopted 23 August 2001, ¶ 5.79.

[115] *In the Matter of Tariffs Applied by Canada to Certain U.S.-Origin Agricultural Products*, Final Report of the Arbitral Panel Established Pursuant to Article 2008 of the North American Free Trade Agreement, December 2, 1996.

[116] *Id.* ¶ 134. [117] Appellate Body Report, *US – Shrimp, supra* note 65.

of the Sea, the *Convention on Biological Diversity*, *Agenda 21*, the Resolution on Assistance to Developing Countries adopted in conjunction with the *Convention on Conservation of Migratory Species of Wild Animals*, and the *Convention on International Trade in Endangered Species of Wild Flora and Fauna*.[118] The Appellate Body referred to these agreements when faced with a question of interpretation of WTO treaty text. In this regard, Article 3.1 of the DSU requires WTO tribunals to utilize the rules of interpretation of customary international law in interpreting WTO treaty text.[119] But multilateral environmental treaties are not, in themselves, rules of *interpretation* of customary international law. The Appellate Body's resort to these agreements could not, therefore, be justified by Article 3.1. Nevertheless, the Appellate Body clearly found the use of similar or otherwise relevant terminology in these other agreements to be of evidentiary assistance in interpreting the WTO text before it.

However, not all of the Appellate Body's resort to other multilateral agreements in *US – Shrimp* was as directly related to interpretation. The Appellate Body, for example, noted the very existence of the *Inter-American Convention for the Protection and Conservation of Sea Turtles* as a fact bearing on the issue of discrimination.[120] It went on to observe that the WTO *Decision on Trade and the Environment* referred to both the *Rio Declaration on Environment and Development* and to *Agenda 21*, and found support in these agreements for the proposition that protection and conservation of highly migratory species require cooperative international efforts.[121] It further referred to and quoted from the *Convention on Biological Diversity* and the *Convention on the Conservation of Migratory Species of Wild Animals*.[122]

It certainly cannot be said that the Appellate Body directly found, much less applied, rules for the WTO in these agreements. Still the Appellate Body used the rules found in these agreements in a manner that differs markedly from the way in which it typically uses Articles 31 and 32 of the Vienna Convention. The use of the multilateral environmental agreements in *US – Shrimp* went to issues of substance, not just to issues of interpretation.[123]

Similarly, in *US – FSC*, the Appellate Body looked to a variety of bilateral and multilateral international agreements "to give meaning" to

[118] *Id.* ¶¶ 127–134. [119] *See* § 3.09 [1].
[120] Appellate Body Report, *US – Shrimp, supra* note 65, ¶ 167. [121] *Id.* ¶ 168. [122] *Id.*
[123] For a discussion of the difference between "rules" and "principles" that bears on this issue, *see*, Joel P. Trachtman, *The Domain of WTO Dispute Resolution, supra* note 78, at 350.

the term "foreign source income," which appears in footnote 59 to the *SCM Agreement*.[124] These included the *Model Tax Convention on Income and Capital* of the Organization for Economic Cooperation and Development, the United Nations *Double Taxation Convention between Developed and Developing Countries*, and the *Standard Agreement to Avoid Double Taxation between Member Countries and Other States Outside the Subregion* adopted by the Member States of the Andean Community and the Caribbean Community.[125]

This approach differs markedly from the approach under GATT. For example, in *Tuna II*, the United States argued that the *Convention on International Trade in Endangered Species* and a number of other bilateral and plurilateral agreements were relevant to the dispute between GATT parties who were parties to those agreements.[126] After noting, with a tone suggestive of less than whole-hearted approval, that "the parties based many of their arguments . . . on environmental and trade treaties," the Panel said that "it was first of all necessary to determine the extent to which these treaties were relevant to the interpretation of the text of the General Agreement."[127] The Panel concluded that they were not at all relevant, stating that, "the agreements cited by the parties to the dispute were bilateral or plurilateral agreements that were not concluded among the contracting parties to the General Agreement, and that they did not apply to the interpretation of the General Agreement or the application of its provisions."[128]

Finally, trade in textile and apparel products has, for many years, been subject to the Multifibre Agreement ("MFA"), a multilateral arrangement negotiated under GATT. A panel has stated that the MFA "is not an integral part of the WTO Agreement, and was not made 'in connexion with the conclusion of' this treaty.' "[129]

[3] Agreements between the parties

The WTO Agreement and its subsidiary agreements are among the many international regulatory agreements entered into by governments, particularly in the post-World War II era, to address economic, environmental,

[124] Appellate Body Report, *US – FSC (Article 21.5 – EC), supra* note 84. [125] *Id.* ¶ 141.
[126] *Supra* note 12, ¶¶ 3.14, 3.21–3.34. [127] *Id.* ¶ 5.18. [128] *Id.* ¶ 5.19.
[129] Panel Report, *United States – Transitional Safeguard Measure on Combed Cotton Yarn from Pakistan*, WT/DS192/R, adopted 5 November 2001, as modified by the Appellate Body Report, WT/DS192/AB/R, ¶ 7.74.

and social problems.[130] Many WTO Members are signatories to these agreements. Moreover, it seems likely that the number of regulatory agreements is likely to grow, particularly in the environmental field. This raises the question of the extent to which these agreements affect the rights and obligations of signatory WTO Members *vis-à-vis* each other and *vis-à-vis* other signatory WTO Members.

The issue began to appear in the early 1990s. One instance involved not a multilateral treaty, but a bilateral agreement between Canada and the European Community. In connection with negotiations in the early 1960s concerning Canada's exports of wheat to the EC under the Common Agricultural Policy, the parties entered into an agreement that would have extended the time limits within which Canada could challenge the EC's treatment of its wheat exports under Article XXVIII of GATT. Canada subsequently brought the challenge, but the EC objected that it was too late. The parties agreed to refer to arbitration the question of the timing of Canada's Article XXVIII complaint.

Before the arbitrator, the EC challenged Canada's right even to bring a claim based on a bilateral agreement under the multilateral procedures of GATT. The arbitrator disagreed:

> In principle a claim based on a bilateral agreement cannot be brought under the multilateral dispute settlement procedures of the GATT. An exception is warranted in this case given the close connection of this particular bilateral agreement with the GATT, the fact that the Agreement is consistent with the objectives of the GATT, and that both parties joined in requesting recourse to the GATT Arbitration procedures.[131]

A similar issue arose in a WTO panel's consideration of a dispute between Brazil and the Community involving exports of poultry products from Brazil to the EC.[132] Brazil argued that a bilateral "Oilseeds Agreement" between it and the Community applied to the resolution of the dispute. The EC did not explicitly object to consideration of the Oilseeds

[130] The apt phrase "international regulatory agreements" is taken from the subtitle of Abram Chayes & Antonia Handler Chayes, THE NEW SOVEREIGNTY: COMPLIANCE WITH INTERNATIONAL REGULATORY AGREEMENTS (Harvard, 1995).

[131] *Canada/European Communities Article XXVIII Rights, Award by the Arbitrator*, BISD 37S/80 at 84.

[132] Panel Report, *European Communities – Measures Affecting the Importation of Certain Poultry Products*, WT/DS69/R, adopted 23 July 1998, as modified by the Appellate Body Report, WT/DS69/AB/R, DSR 1998:V, 2089.

Agreement by the Panel, although the United States, as a third party, argued that it was not within the Panel's terms of reference.[133] However, noting that the Oilseeds Agreement had been negotiated within the framework of GATT Article XXVIII, and citing the *Canada/EC Wheat* arbitration, the Panel decided to consider the Oilseeds Agreement "to the extent relevant to the determination of the EC's obligations under the WTO agreements *vis-à-vis* Brazil."[134]

The Appellate Body found "no reversible error in the Panel's treatment" of the Oilseeds Agreement.[135] However, it described at length what the Oilseeds Agreement is *not*: as a bilateral agreement between Brazil and the European Communities, it is not a "covered agreement" within the meaning of Articles 1 and 2 of the DSU; it is not cited in an annex to the *WTO Agreement*; it is not among the legal instruments that entered into force under GATT 1947 that were made a part of GATT 1994; it does not constitute part of the "decisions, procedures and customary practices followed by the CONTRACTING PARTIES to GATT 1947" which, under Article XVI:1 of the WTO Agreement, are to guide the WTO.[136]

In the end, however, the Appellate Body reached a result not perceptibly different from that reached by the Panel. It recognized that the Oilseeds Agreement was negotiated within the framework of Article XXVIII of GATT and provided the basis for the tariff-rate quota that was at issue in the dispute. Accordingly, the Appellate Body stated, "the Oilseeds Agreement may serve as a *supplementary means* of interpretation."[137]

In *Turkey – Textiles*, a Panel concluded that a bilateral agreement between two WTO Members "does not alter the legal nature of the measure at issue or the applicability of the relevant GATT/WTO provisions."[138] The Panel went on to cite Article 41 of the *Vienna Convention on the Law of Treaties*, and hold that, even if the bilateral agreement required certain action of Turkey, "such requirement would not be sufficient to exempt

[133] *Id.* ¶ 197.

[134] *Id.* ¶ 2.02. The Panel also referred to the *Banana* Panel's consideration of the Lomé Convention. *See infra* note 88.

[135] Appellate Body Report, *European Communities – Measures Affecting the Importation of Certain Poultry Products*, WT/DS69/AB/R, adopted 23 July 1998, DSR 1998:V, 2031, ¶ 85.

[136] *Id.* ¶¶ 79–80. [137] *Id.* ¶ 83 (emphasis in original).

[138] Panel Report, *Turkey – Restrictions on Imports of Textile and Clothing Products*, WT/DS34/R, adopted 19 November 1999, as modified by the Appellate Body Report, WT/DS34/AB/R, DSR 1999:VI, 2363, ¶ 9.178.

Turkey from its obligations under the WTO Agreement."[139] In *US – FSC*, the Panel found that footnote 59 to the SCM Agreement, permitting Members to take measures (including agreements) to avoid double taxation of foreign source income, does not limit the right to resort to WTO dispute settlement.[140]

In *Argentina – Poultry*, Argentina argued that the Protocol of Olivos, negotiated under Mercosur, estopped Brazil from pursuing, in the WTO, an antidumping claim that had been subject to a previous Mercosur arbitration.[141] The Protocol provided that, if a party brings a dispute to either Mercosur or the WTO, it may not, subsequently, refer the same dispute to the other forum.[142] The Panel rejected Argentina's argument on the ground that the Protocol had not yet entered into force and, by its terms, did not apply to disputes, such as the poultry antidumping matter, that were decided under an earlier Mercosur protocol.[143]

[4] Agreements to which the WTO is a party

The WTO itself is a party to agreements with other organizations. Two of these involve the Bretton Woods organizations – the *Agreement between the International Monetary Fund and the World Trade Organization* and the *Agreement between the International Bank for Reconstruction and Development, the International Development Association and the World Trade Organization.*[144] The agreements are intended to strengthen the relationship between the WTO and the IMF and the World Bank. The Appellate Body has held that the agreement between the WTO and the IMF does

[139] *Id.* ¶ 9.182. Article 41 of the *Vienna Convention* deals with agreements to modify multilateral treaties between certain of the parties only.

[140] Panel Report, *United States – Tax Treatment for "Foreign Sales Corporations"*, WT/DS108/R, adopted 20 March 2000, as modified by the Appellate Body Report, WT/DS108/AB/R, DSR 2000:IV, 1677, ¶¶ 7.18–7.19.

[141] Panel Report, *Argentina – Definitive Anti-Dumping Duties on Poultry from Brazil*, WT/DS241/R, adopted 19 May 2003, ¶ 7.20.

[142] *Id.* ¶ 7.38 [143] *Id.*

[144] *See*, *WTO Agreements with the Fund and the Bank, Approved by the General Council at its meeting on 7, 8 and 13 November 1996*, WT/L/195 (18 November 1996). The WTO has also entered into an *Agreement between the World Intellectual Property Organization and the World Trade Organization*, 35 ILM 754 and an *Agreement between the World Trade Organization and the Office International des Épizooties*, WT/L/272, 8 July 1998. *See* also, § 5.05.

not modify, add to, or diminish the rights and obligations of Members under the WTO Agreement.[145]

§ 3.08 Decisions of other international tribunals

Panels and the Appellate Body frequently cite the decisions of other international tribunals, most notably the ICJ, to support their own decisions. For example, in its first report, *US – Gasoline*, the Appellate Body referred to decisions of the ICJ, the European Court of Human Rights, and the Inter-American Court of Human Rights as authority for its conclusion that Article 31 of the *Vienna Convention on the Law of Treaties* had attained the status of a rule of customary international law.[146] This practice has continued virtually without interruption. In a much later report, *US – Line Pipe*, for example, the Appellate Body cited a decision of the ICJ and a submission of the United States to the Arbitral Tribunal established by the Compromis of 11 July 1978 in the *Case Concerning the Air Services Agreement of 27 March 1946 (United States vs. France)* to support its conclusion that Article 51 of the International Law Commission's Draft Articles on Responsibility of States for Internationally Wrongful Acts sets out a recognized principle of customary international law.[147] In between, in *US – Shrimp*, the Appellate Body cited decisions of the ICJ to support its conclusion that Article XX(b) of GATT is not "static," but "evolutionary,"[148] and that the principle of *abus de droit* prohibits the abusive exercise by a state of its rights.[149]

In practice, if another international tribunal has dealt with an issue, a term, or a phrase that is relevant to the resolution of a WTO dispute, parties typically refer to the decisions of those tribunals to support their arguments, and panels and the Appellate Body use them to support their conclusions.

145 Appellate Body Report, *Argentina – Measures Affecting Imports of Footwear, Textiles, Apparel and Other Items*, WT/DS56/AB/R and Corr.1, adopted 22 April 1998, DSR 1998:III, 1003, ¶ 72.

146 Appellate Body Report, *US – Gasoline, supra* note 91, note 34.

147 Appellate Body Report, *United States – Definitive Safeguard Measures on Imports of Circular Welded Carbon Quality Line Pipe from Korea*, WT/DS202/AB/R, adopted 8 March 2002, footnotes 256 and 257.

148 Appellate Body Report, *US – Shrimp, supra* note 65, footnote 109.

149 *Id.* footnote 156.

§ 3.09 Interpretation of WTO law[150]

"There is as much freedom and latitude in the interpretation of laws as in their creation."

– Michel de Montaigne[151]

[1] The Vienna Convention on the Law of Treaties

Article 3.2 of the DSU requires panels and the Appellate Body to construe the provisions of WTO agreements in accordance with the customary rules of interpretation of public international law. Right from the start, in the WTO's first dispute settlement Report, the Panel looked to Article 31 of the Vienna Convention to implement Article 3.2 of the DSU.[152] The Appellate Body, in that first case, stated explicitly that the rule set out in Article 31 of the Convention "has attained the status of a rule of customary or general international law."[153] In its second report, the Appellate Body confirmed that Article 32 of the Convention had attained the same status.[154]

Article 31 of the Convention provides that a treaty shall be interpreted in accordance with the ordinary meaning of its terms, in their context and in light of the object and purpose of the treaty. Article 32 deals with supplemental means of interpretation, including the preparatory work of the treaty and the circumstances of its conclusion. Both articles have effectively become a fundamental part of WTO law. They reflect the principle of effective treaty interpretation, articulated by the Appellate Body in *US – Gasoline*, that "an interpreter is not free to adopt a reading that would result in reducing whole clauses or paragraphs of a treaty to redundancy or inutility."[155]

150 For an extensive discussion of this subject, *see* Michael Lennard, *Navigating by the Stars: Interpreting the WTO Agreements*, *supra* note 4. Also *see* Niall P. Meagher, *The Sound of Silence: Giving Meaning to Omissions in Provisions of the WTO Agreements*, 37 Journal of World Trade 417 (No. 2, April 2003).

151 *Of Experience* in Donald M. Frame (Ed) The Complete Essays of Montaigne 815 (Stanford, 1965).

152 Panel Report, *US – Gasoline, supra* note 43, ¶ 6.7.

153 Appellate Body Report, *US – Gasoline, supra* note 91, § III.B, p. 17.

154 Appellate Body Report, *Japan – Alcoholic Beverages II, supra* note 3, 11, DSR 104.

155 *See, supra* note 91. The principle is also referred to as *l'effet utile* or *ut res magis valeat quam pereat.*

[2] Travaux préparatoires

Article 32 of the *Vienna Convention on the Law of Treaties* has been referred to far less than Article 31, since panels and the Appellate Body frequently are able to resolve issues of interpretation through the text-context-object and purpose provisions of Article 31. Thus, in *India – Quantitative Restrictions*, the Panel declined to resort to supplementary means of interpretation, since "we find that the meaning resulting from the application of Article 31 is neither ambiguous nor obscure, and does not lead to a manifestly absurd or unreasonable result. We therefore do not need to consider the preparatory work as reflected in the negotiating history to determine the meaning of the terms."[156] Without expressly referring to Article 32, the Panel in *Canada – Pharmaceutical Patents*, examined the negotiating history of a provision of the TRIPS Agreement.[157] The Panel, however, decided to read the text literally.[158]

Resort has been made to preparatory work of the treaty, *travaux préparatoires*, when the issue has involved the specific negotiated commitments of a Member. In *Canada – Dairy*, the Appellate Body found the language of Canada's Schedule of Commitments under the *Agreement on Agriculture* was not clear on its face, and found it "appropriate, indeed necessary, in this case, to turn to 'supplementary means of interpretation' pursuant to Article 32 of the *Vienna Convention*."[159] Similarly, in *Korea – Procurement*, the Panel found ambiguity in a commitment under the *Agreement on Government Procurement*, and resorted to an examination of the negotiating history.[160] In *Korea – Various Measures on Beef*, on the other hand, the Schedule under consideration was interpreted without resort to supplemental means.[161]

156 Panel Report, *India – Quantitative Restrictions on Imports of Agricultural, Textile and Industrial Products*, WT/DS90, R, adopted 22 September 1999, as upheld by the Appellate Body Report, WT/DS90/AB/R, DSR 1999:V, 1799, ¶ 5.110,

157 Panel Report, *Canada – Pharmaceutical Patents*, *supra* note 95, ¶ 7.29.

158 *Id.* ¶ 7.31

159 Appellate Body Report, *Canada – Measures Affecting the Importation of Milk and the Exportation of Dairy Products*, WT/DS103/AB/R, WT/DS113/AB/R and Corr.1, adopted 27 October 1999, DSR 1999:V, 2057, ¶ 138.

160 Panel Report, *Korea – Measures Affecting Government Procurement*, WT/DS163/R, adopted 19 June 2000, DSR 2000:VIII, 3541, ¶ 7.74.

161 Appellate Body Report, *Korea – Measures Affecting Imports of Fresh, Chilled and Frozen Beef*, WT/DS161/AB/R, WT/DS169/AB/R, adopted 10 January 2001, ¶¶ 94–106.

[3] Use of dictionaries

The Appellate Body referred to a dictionary in its first report, and has done so repeatedly since.[162] Panel reports, too, are replete with dictionary definitions. Dictionary definitions are the first step in ascertaining the ordinary meaning of treaty terms that are in dispute. Nevertheless, dictionaries do not necessarily control. The Appellate Body has stated that "dictionary meanings leave many interpretive questions open."[163] In *US – Stainless Steel*, the Panel said, "We are cognizant, however, that dictionary definitions can only take the interpreter so far, and that in interpreting a provision of a treaty we must take into account both context and object and purpose."[164] In *US – Offset Act (Byrd Amendment)*, the Appellate Body said that, "dictionaries are important guides to, not dispositive statements of, definitions of words appearing in agreements and legal documents."[165]

[4] Lex specialis

The doctrine of *lex specialis*, which is not dealt with by the *Vienna Convention on the Law of Treaties*, was utilized by GATT panels and has continued in the WTO.[166]

In *EC – Bananas III*, the Appellate Body stated that the Panel should have applied the *Agreement on Import Licensing Procedures* before Article X:3(a) of GATT, since the Licensing Agreement "deals specifically, and in detail, with the administration of import licensing procedures."[167] This statement was cited by the Panel in *EC – Sardines* in support of its decision to examine a claim under the *Agreement on Technical Barriers to Trade* prior to examining it under Article III of GATT.[168] In *Indonesia – Autos*,

[162] Appellate Body Report, *US – Gasoline, supra,* note 91, at note 40.

[163] Appellate Body Report, *Canada – Measures Affecting the Export of Civilian Aircraft,* WT/DS70/AB/R, adopted 20 August 1999, DSR 1999:III, 1377, ¶ 153; Appellate Body Report, *United States – Tax Treatment for "Foreign Sales Corporations,"* WT/DS108/AB/R, adopted 20 March 2000, DSR 2000:III, 1619, ¶ 129; Appellate Body Report, *European Communities – Measures Affecting Asbestos and Asbestos-Containing Products,* WT/DS135/AB/R, adopted 5 April 2001, ¶ 92.

[164] Panel Report, *United States – Anti-Dumping Measures on Stainless Steel Plate in Coils and Stainless Steel Sheet and Strip from Korea,* WT/DS179/R, adopted 1 February 2001, ¶ 6.99.

[165] Appellate Body Report, *United States – Continued Dumping and Subsidy Offset Act of 2000,* WT/DS217/AB/R, WT/DS234/AB/R, adopted 27 January 2003, ¶ 248.

[166] *See generally,* Michael Lennard, *Navigating by the Stars: Interpreting the WTO Agreements, supra* note 4, 70–72.

[167] Appellate Body Report, *Bananas III, supra* note 8, ¶ 204.

[168] Panel Report, *EC – Sardines, supra* note 56, ¶¶ 7.15–7.19.

the Panel first examined the measure at issue under the more specific *Agreement on Trade Related Investment Measures* rather than under Article III of GATT.[169] The *Indonesia – Autos* Panel also observed that the *lex specialis* principle is inseparably linked to the question of conflict, and does not apply if two treaties deal with the same subject matter, but from different points of view, or when one provision is more far-reaching, but not inconsistent with another.[170]

[5] Principle of "contemporaneity"

In *US – Shrimp* the Appellate Body interpreted the term "exhaustible natural resources," in Article XX(g) of GATT, in accordance with the "evolutionary" principle of "contemporaneity."[171] The words "exhaustible natural resources," the Appellate Body said, "were actually crafted more than 50 years ago. They must be read by a treaty interpreter in the light of contemporary concerns of the community of nations about the protection and conservation of the environment."[172] Thus, despite the fact that the drafters of the term arguably intended to refer to finite resources, such as minerals, the Appellate Body did not explore the *travaux préparatoires*; rather, it observed that, "Textually, Article XX(g) is *not* limited to the conservation of 'mineral' or 'non-living' natural resources."[173] Accordingly, it said, "it is too late in the day to suppose that Article XX(g) of the GATT 1994 may be read as referring only to the conservation of exhaustible mineral or other non-living natural resources."[174]

The Appellate Body's conclusion in *US – Shrimp*, that the terms of Article XX(g) should be interpreted in light of their current meaning rather than their meaning at the time the treaty was concluded, is not universally accepted. Lassa Oppenheim's treatise asserts that, "a treaty's terms are normally to be interpreted on the basis of their meaning at the time the treaty was concluded, and in the light of the circumstances then prevailing."[175] Oppenheim goes on to state that "concepts embodied in a treaty may not be static but evolutionary," but whether the term "exhaustible natural resource" is such a "concept" would seem debatable.

[169] Panel Report, *Indonesia – Certain Measures Affecting the Automobile Industry*, WT/DS54/R, WT/DS55/R, WT/DS59/R, WT/DS64/R and Corr.1, 2, 3, and 4, adopted 23 July 1998, DSR 1998:VI, 2201, ¶ 14.63.

[170] *Id.* ¶ 14.28. [171] Appellate Body Report, *US – Shrimp, supra* note 65, ¶¶ 127–134.

[172] *Id.* ¶ 129. [173] *Id.* ¶ 128 (emphasis in original). [174] *Id.* ¶ 131.

[175] OPPENHEIM'S INTERNATIONAL LAW (Jennings & Watts, Eds) 1282 (9th ed., Longman, 1992) (citations omitted).

However, since the text of Article XX(g) itself, as the Appellate Body found, did not confine the term to "dead" as opposed to "living" natural resources, it certainly can be argued that the Appellate Body did not need to get into this question in the first place. Its usual Vienna Convention text-based approach would seem to have sufficed.[176]

[6] Principle of "effectiveness"

In *Argentina – Footwear (EC)*, the Appellate Body reversed the Panel's decision that the "express omission" in the *Agreement on Safeguards* of the "unforeseen circumstances" requirement of GATT Article XIX meant that the negotiators did not intend to require a finding of "unforeseen circumstances" in safeguard disputes.[177] The Panel's approach, the Appellate Body said, "failed to give meaning and legal effect to *all* the relevant terms of the *WTO Agreement*, contrary to the principle of effectiveness (*Ut res magis valeat quam pereat*) in the interpretation of treaties."[178] This decision was cited in *US – Line Pipe*, where the Panel said, "Just because some provisions of Article XIII are replicated in the Safeguards Agreement, that alone does not mean that the remaining provisions cease to be binding on Members."[179] In *Canada – Patent Term*, the Panel cited the Appellate Body's statement in *US – Gasoline*, and rejected an argument that would have reduced a portion of the TRIPS Agreement "to redundancy or inutility."[180]

[176] The argument of the complainants is set out in the Panel Report, *United States – Import Prohibition of Certain Shrimp and Shrimp Products*, WT/DS58/R and Corr.1, adopted 6 November 1998, as modified by the Appellate Body Report, WT/DS58/AB/R, DSR 1998:VII, 2821, ¶¶ 3.237–3.238.

[177] Appellate Body Report, *Argentina – Safeguard Measures on Imports of Footwear*, WT/DS121/AB/R, adopted 12 January 2000, DSR 2000:I, 515, ¶ 88.

[178] *Id.* (emphasis in original).

[179] Panel Report, *United States – Definitive Safeguard Measures on Imports of Circular Welded Carbon Quality Line Pipe from Korea*, WTDS202/R, adopted 8 March 2002, as modified by the Appellate Body Report, WT/DS202/AB/R, ¶ 7.44.

[180] Panel Report, *Canada – Term of Patent Protection*, WT/DS170/R, adopted 12 October 2000, as upheld by the Appellate Body Report, WT/DS170/AB/R, DSR 2000:XI, 5121, ¶¶ 6.48–6.50.

4

The Panel Process

§ 4.01 Overview

With the establishment of the WTO and adoption of the Dispute Settlement Understanding, resolution of international trade disputes has entered a new and, in the context of international trade law, a highly legalistic era. Under GATT, dispute settlement often was called "conciliation," a term reflecting GATT's diplomatic heritage and its indifference, if not hostility, to legalism. The early GATT process was very much a diplomatic process, seeking to reconcile the conflicting views of the parties, sometimes ending in stalemate if this could not be accomplished. Gradually, GATT dispute settlement became more legalistic in form, but it remained largely diplomatic and, in the view of many, of limited effectiveness, particularly because the losing party could prevent consensus and, therefore, could prevent adoption of an adverse report of a GATT dispute settlement panel. While this did not happen in most instances, it happened often enough to cause dissatisfaction and was an always present threat that, by itself, might have discouraged resort to dispute settlement.[1]

Under the WTO, the GATT consensus requirement is reversed: consensus in the WTO is required to reject, rather than to adopt, a report. This has resulted in a far more juridical system. Although the Dispute Settlement Body offers "good offices, conciliation and mediation" if the parties so desire, and although the WTO Members, acting collectively as the DSB, continue to have the last word as a formal matter, in a practical sense the last legal word really now lies with the panels and the Appellate Body. Thus, while panels and the Appellate Body are not courts, increasingly they bear a striking resemblance to courts, as can be seen from their reports themselves, particularly those of the Appellate Body.[2]

[1] *See* § 1.01 [5].

[2] *See*, David Palmeter, *The WTO Appellate Body's First Decision*, 9 LEIDEN JOURNAL OF INTERNATIONAL LAW 337, 356–358 (1996).

The legalization of the dispute settlement process led to the need for more formal rules of conduct for those involved in the process. The DSB, in 1996, responded with *Rules of Conduct for the Understanding on Rules and Procedures Governing the Settlement of Disputes.*[3]

§ 4.02 Good offices, conciliation and mediation

Good offices, conciliation or mediation ("mediation") may be requested by any party to a dispute at any time.[4] These proceedings, and the positions the parties take during them, are confidential and without prejudice to their rights in further proceedings.[5] If the parties agree, mediation efforts may continue while the panel process proceeds.[6] The Director-General may offer to mediate at any time during a dispute.[7] When mediation is entered into within 60 days of the request for consultations, the complaining party must allow a period of 60 days from the date of the consultation request before requesting a panel, unless the party complained against agrees that the effort has failed to settle the dispute.[8]

Formal mediation is rare, since the parties normally have exhausted all diplomatic efforts to resolve the matter prior to moving to the dispute settlement process. The first request to the WTO Director-General for mediation was not made until 10 October 2002, after the organization had been in existence for nearly eight years.[9]

The DSU also provides more specific procedures for good offices in disputes involving developing countries. These are discussed in § 5.03 [2]

§ 4.03 Consultations

[1] Purpose

Dispute settlement begins with a formal request for consultations.[10] In many instances, informal consultations may already have occurred between the Members concerned and the formal request is made only

[3] WT/DSB/RC/1, 11 December 1996. [4] DSU Art. 5.3. [5] DSU Art. 5.2.
[6] DSU Art. 5.5. [7] DSU Art. 5.6. [8] DSU Art. 5.4.
[9] *Request for Mediation by the Philippines, Thailand and the European Communities,* WT/GC/66, 16 October 2002.
[10] *See* William J. Davey, *WTO Dispute Settlement: Segregating the Useful Political Aspects and Avoiding "Over-Legalization,"* in Marco Bronckers and Reinhard Quick (Eds) NEW DIRECTIONS IN INTERNATIONAL ECONOMIC LAW: ESSAYS IN HONOR OF JOHN H. JACKSON 291 (Kluwer, 2000).

after the complaining Member concludes that the informal process has not been productive. The purpose of consultations is to enable the parties to gather relevant, and correct, information – both to assist them in reaching a mutually agreed solution or, failing that, to assist them in presenting accurate information to the panel.[11] Through consultations, the Appellate Body has observed, parties exchange information, assess the merits of their positions, and narrow the issues.[12]

[2] Form and content of the request

Requests for consultations should be in writing and a copy should be served on the DSB and to the relevant WTO Councils and Committees. The Councils are the Council for Trade in Goods, Council for Trade in Services, and Council for TRIPS. The Committees are those concerned with different substantive areas of the WTO agreements, such as the Committee on Anti-Dumping Practices, the Committee on Technical Barriers to Trade, and the Committee on Subsidies and Countervailing Measures. The request should specify the articles of the relevant WTO agreements under which consultations are sought. These normally would include Article 4 of the DSU, the corresponding provisions of other covered agreements, which are listed in footnote 4 to the DSU, and Article XXII or XXIII of GATT.

Article 4.5 requires that the complaining party "give the reasons for the request including identification of the measures at issue and an indication of the legal basis for the complaint." There is a necessary connection between the requirement of Article 4.5 and any subsequent request for the establishment of a panel. Article 6.2 requires that the request for establishment of a panel, *inter alia*, indicate whether consultations have been held and identify the specific measures at issue.[13] Certainly Article 4 contemplates that Members be given the opportunity to consult before a panel is established to consider a measure.

This raises the question whether there need be an exact identity between the measures identified in the request for consultations and those

[11] Panel Report, *Korea – Taxes on Alcoholic Beverages*, WT/DS75/R, WT/DS84/R, adopted 17 February 1999, as modified by the Appellate Body Report, WT/DS75/AB/R, WT/DS84/AB/R, DSR 1999:I, 44, ¶ 10.23.

[12] Appellate Body Report, *Mexico – Anti-Dumping Investigation of High Fructose Corn Syrup (HFCS) from the United States – Recourse to Article 21.5 of the DSU by the United States*, WT/DS132/AB/RW, adopted 21 November 2001, ¶ 54.

[13] *See* § 4.04.

identified in a subsequent request for the establishment of a panel. The issue first arose in *US – DRAMS*, where the United States asserted that a Member should be permitted to refer a claim to a panel if it was actually raised during consultations, even though it may not have been included in the written request for consultations.[14] The Panel, however, did not find it necessary to rule on the question.[15] In *Japan – Agricultural Products II*, the request for consultations used the phrase "including, but are not limited to" Articles 2, 4, 5 and 8. The Panel accepted the subsequent inclusion of Article 7 in the request for establishment of a panel, even though that article was not listed in the consultation request.[16]

A similar question arose in *Brazil – Aircraft*, where specific measures identified in the request for establishment post-dated the consultations.[17] The Panel held that the measures were properly included in the panel request and were properly before it because the "request for consultations related to the same general subject as the request for the establishment of a panel."[18] "One purpose of consultations," the Panel said, "is to 'clarify the facts of the situation,' and it can be expected that information obtained during the course of consultations may enable the complainant to focus the scope of the matter with respect to which it seeks establishment of a panel. Thus, to limit the scope of the panel proceedings to the identical matter with respect to which consultations were held could undermine the effectiveness of panel process."[19]

The Appellate Body agreed, holding that Articles 4 and 6 of the Dispute Settlement Understanding do not "require a *precise and exact identity* between the specific measures that were the subject of consultations and the specific measures identified in the request for the establishment of a panel."[20]

[14] Panel Report, *United States – Anti-Dumping Duty on Dynamic Random Access Memory Semiconductors (DRAMS) of One Megabit or Above from Korea*, WT/DS99/R, adopted 19 March 1999, DSR 1999:II, 521, ¶ 6.8. The United States made its statement in response to a question from the Panel. *Id.*

[15] *Id.*

[16] Panel Report, *Japan – Measures Affecting Agricultural Products*, WT/DS76/R, adopted 19 March 1999, as modified by the Appellate Body Report, WT/DS76/AB/R, DSR 1999:I, 315, ¶ 8.4. The result is not the same when the phrase is used in a request for the establishment of a panel. *See* § 4.04 [6].

[17] Panel Report, *Brazil – Export Financing Programme for Aircraft*, WT/DS46/R, adopted 20 August 1999, as modified by the Appellate Body Report, WT/DS46/AB/R, DSR 1999:III, 1221, ¶ 7.8.

[18] *Id.* [19] *Id.* ¶ 7.9.

[20] Appellate Body Report, *Brazil – Export Financing Programme for Aircraft*, WT/DS46/AB/R, adopted 20 August 1999, DSR 1999:III, 1161, ¶ 132.

A distinction between *US – DRAMS* and *Brazil – Aircraft* is that the former presented a situation in which consultations in fact were held about measures not identified in the consultation request, while in the latter it was conceded that consultations were not held with regard to the specific measures at all. However, in *Brazil – Aircraft*, both the Panel and the Appellate Body concluded that the measures in question were mere subsequent regulatory measures dealing with the underlying subsidies that were identified in the consultation request and were the subject of consultations.[21]

In *US – Certain EC Products*, the EC asked for consultations concerning a decision announced by the US on 3 March 1999 to impose increased bonding requirements on certain imports from the EC.[22] On 19 April, the US imposed 100 percent duties on some of those products that had entered the US after 3 March. Before the Panel, the EC "acknowledged that the 19 April action, *as such*, was not *formally* the subject of the consultations held on 21 April."[23] Accordingly, the Appellate Body upheld the conclusion of the Panel that the 19 April action did not fall within the Panel's terms of reference.[24] This conclusion appears consistent with *US – DRAMS* and *Brazil – Aircraft* in that, unlike the former case, the subsequent measure was not in fact the subject of consultations, and unlike the latter case, it was not considered to be a subsequent regulatory measure dealing with the underlying measure that was identified in the request and was the subject of consultations.

[3] Whether consultations occur

While Article 4 of the DSU provides for consultations, and requires that they be requested before a panel is requested under Article 6.2, Article 4.3 makes clear that, if the defending party declines to consult, a panel may be established without consultations. The Appellate Body relied in part on this fact in *Mexico – Corn Syrup (Article 21.5 – US)* when it found that Mexico effectively had waived any right to consultations it might have had.[25] In that case, an Article 21.5 review panel had been established by the DSB without prior consultations. Mexico did not object either at the time the Panel was established or before the Panel. It raised the issue for

[21] *Id.* and Panel Report, *Brazil – Aircraft*, *supra* note 17, ¶ 7.8.

[22] Appellate Body Report, *United States – Import Measures on Certain Products from the European Communities*, WT/DS165/AB/R, adopted 10 January 2001.

[23] *Id.* ¶ 70 (emphasis in original). [24] *Id.*

[25] Appellate Body Report, *supra* note 12.

the first time on appeal, arguing that Panel was obligated to address this defect *sua sponte*.[26] Since Article 6.2 envisions situations in which panels may be established without consultations, the Appellate Body found that "the lack of prior consultations is not a defect that, by its very nature, deprives a panel of its authority to deal with and dispose of a matter, and that, accordingly, such a defect is not one which a panel must examine even if both parties to the dispute remain silent thereon."[27] Accordingly, Mexico's appeal of the issue was dismissed.[28]

In *Brazil – Desiccated Coconut*, the complainant asked the Panel to find that Brazil's alleged refusal to hold consultations under Article XXIII:1 of GATT 1994 was inconsistent with its WTO obligations.[29] The Panel declined to do so, finding that, "there is nothing in the request for establishment of a panel that would lead to the conclusion that the requested panel would be asked to make any finding regarding Brazil's alleged failure to consult."[30]

[4] Adequacy of consultations

Neither the DSU nor WTO jurisprudence recognizes the concept of "adequacy" of consultations.[31] Consultations are confidential and take place without the involvement of the Dispute Settlement Body, the Panel, or the Secretariat, with no official records kept. A panel, therefore, is not in a position to know what in fact was discussed during consultations, and, therefore, is not in a position to resolve disputes between the parties on this point. Accordingly, what takes place in those consultations "is not the concern of a panel."[32] Its function is simply to ascertain that consultations were in fact held. "[T]here is nothing in the DSU that provides that a complainant cannot request a panel unless its case is adequately explained in consultations."[33]

[26] *Id.* ¶ 35. [27] *Id.* ¶ 64. [28] *Id.* ¶ 75.

[29] Panel Report, *Brazil – Measures Affecting Desiccated Coconut*, WT/DS22/R, adopted 20 March 1997, as upheld by the Appellate Body Report, WT/DS22/AB/R, DSR 1997:I, 189, ¶ 286.

[30] *Id.* ¶ 290. [31] Panel Report, *Korea – Alcoholic Beverages*, *supra* note 11, ¶ 10.19.

[32] *Id.*

[33] Panel Report, *European Communities – Regime for the Importation, Sale and Distribution of Bananas – Complaint by the United States*, WT/DS27/R/USA, adopted 25 September 1997, as modified by the Appellate Body Report, WT/DS27/AB/R, DSR 1997:II, 943, ¶ 7.20; Panel Report, *United States – Restrictions on Imports of Cotton and Man-Made Fibre Underwear*, WT/DS24/R, adopted 25 February 1997, as modified by the Appellate Body Report, WT/DS24/AB/R, DSR 1997:I, 31, 148, ¶ 7.61.

The Appellate Body has stated that all parties engaged in dispute settlement must be "fully forthcoming," and that, particularly in the consultation process, facts must be freely disclosed. Indeed, the Appellate Body has said, the demands of due process implicit in the DSU make full disclosure of facts during consultations especially important: "For the claims that are made and the facts that are established during consultations do much to shape the substance and the scope of subsequent panel proceedings. If, in the aftermath of consultations, any party believes that all the pertinent facts relating to a claim are, for any reason, not before the panel, then that party should ask the panel in that case to engage in additional fact-finding."[34] This rather clear statement has not resulted in significant immediate fact-finding. It may, however, have encouraged panels to use their Article 13 fact-finding powers more aggressively in later stages of the proceedings.

To the extent that discussions during consultations may have relevance later in the proceedings, parties often maintain a record of the topics discussed in the consultations. Written questions presented to the other party during consultations may serve this evidentiary purpose.[35]

[5] Confidentiality

Article 4.6 of the DSU requires that consultations be confidential and provides that they are without prejudice to the rights of a Member in any further proceedings. Thus, a Member's offer of compromise or adjustment of a particular measure would not constitute an admission that the measure is inconsistent with its WTO obligations. In *Korea – Alcoholic Beverages*, the Panel rejected the argument that the complainants breached the confidentiality requirements of Article 4.6 of the DSU by making reference in their submissions to information supplied by Korea during consultations.[36] Article 4.6 does require that information obtained not be disclosed to parties that were not involved in consultations, the Panel reasoned; however, consultations are part of the dispute

[34] Appellate Body Report, *India – Patent Protection for Pharmaceutical and Agricultural Chemical Products*, WT/DS50/AB/R, adopted 16 January 1998, DSR 1998:I, 9, ¶ 94. The duty of Members generally to provide evidence and information is discussed in § 4.09 [3], *infra*.

[35] Panel Report, *United States – Safeguard Measures on Imports of Fresh, Chilled or Frozen Lamb Meat from New Zealand and Australia*, WT/DS177/R, WT/DS178/R, adopted 16 May 2001, as modified by the Appellate Body Report, WT/DS177/AB/R, WT/DS178/AB/R, ¶¶ 5.36–5.40.

[36] *Supra* note 11, ¶¶ 10.20–10.23.

settlement process, as are panel proceedings, and they, too, are confidential. Therefore, the Panel said, "parties do not thereby breach any confidentiality by disclosing in those proceedings information acquired during the consultations."[37] Further, the Panel noted, "the very essence of consultations is to enable the parties [to] gather correct and relevant information, for purposes of assisting them in arriving at a mutually agreed solution, or failing which, to assist them in presenting accurate information to the panel. It would seriously hamper the dispute settlement process if the information acquired during consultations could not subsequently be used by any party in the ensuing proceedings."[38]

In *Australia – Automotive Leather II*, Australia requested the Panel to rule that information obtained by the United States in consultations conducted pursuant to an earlier request for consultations not be admissible before the Panel established pursuant to a second request.[39] The Panel disagreed, holding that the confidentiality provisions of Article 4.6 of the DSU do "not mean that facts and information developed in the course of consultations held pursuant to one request cannot be used in a panel proceeding concerning, as it does in this case, the same dispute, between the same parties, conducted pursuant to another, different request."[40]

Disclosure of information obtained by a party in consultations in its submissions to the panel necessarily would disclose that information to third parties that were not involved in consultations. The argument that this disclosure would violate the confidentiality of consultations was raised and rejected in *Mexico – Corn Syrup*.[41] The Panel noted that third parties participate in panel proceedings as a matter of right. The Panel said that "it would be anomalous" if a third party's exercise of this right "had the effect of limiting the evidence that could be relied upon" by the Panel, simply because the third party did not – or could not – participate in the consultations.[42] Third parties are subject to the same confidentiality requirements that apply to parties to a dispute, the Panel noted, in concluding that Article 4.6's confidentiality requirement is not violated

[37] *Id.* [38] *Id.*

[39] Panel Report, *Australia – Subsidies Provided to Producers and Exporters of Automotive Leather*, WT/DS126/R, adopted 16 June 1999, DSR 1999:III, 951, ¶ 9.31.

[40] *Id.* ¶ 9.32.

[41] Panel Report, *Mexico – Anti-Dumping Investigation of High Fructose Corn Syrup (HFCS) from the United States*, WT/DS132/R and Corr.1, adopted 24 February 2000, DSR 2000:III, 1345.

[42] *Id.* ¶ 7.41. Third parties may not join consultations under Article XXIII, and may join those under Article XXII only with the permission of the party requested to consult. *See, supra* § 4.03 [7].

by the inclusion of information obtained during consultations in submissions to panels that are made available to a third party, even if the third party did not participate in consultations.[43]

In *US – Lamb*, the complainants submitted written questions at consultations, and included them as exhibits in their submissions to the Panel.[44] The US neither confirmed nor contested that the questions were presented in consultations, but challenged "the admissibility and the relevance to panel proceedings of information from bilateral, confidential consultations – for which usually no neutral witnesses or written records exist – when ascertaining whether the specificity requirements stipulated by DSU Article 6.2 for *panel requests* are met."[45] The Panel did not accept this line of reasoning, stating that "we do not consider that the very purpose of consultations could be defeated if we were merely to take note of documentary evidence concerning the purely factual question of whether certain issues were raised during consultations."[46]

[6] Time elements

Members may request consultations with other Members at any time. The DSU admonishes, however, that, before bringing a case, a Member should consider whether action would be "fruitful."[47] Article 4.3 of the DSU requires a Member receiving a request for consultations to meet two deadlines: (1) it must respond to the request within 10 days of receipt; and (2) in that response, it must agree to consult within 30 days after receipt, or within a time frame mutually agreed. If the receiving Member does not respond within 10 days, or if it fails to consult within 30 days or within a period otherwise agreed, Article 4.3 provides that the Member requesting consultations may proceed immediately to request the DSB to establish a panel.

If consultations are held, but fail to settle a dispute within 60 days after receipt of the request for consultations, the complaining party may then request a panel.[48] A panel referred to this 60-day period in a case in which the parties did not consult because the responding party refused to do so. The Panel concluded that its only function was "to ascertain whether consultations were properly requested, in terms of the DSU, that the complainant was ready to consult with the defendant and that the 60

[43] *Id.* [44] Panel Report, *US – Lamb, supra* note 35, ¶ 5.36.
[45] *Id.* ¶ 5.39 (emphasis in original). [46] *Id.* ¶ 5.40. [47] DSU Art. 13.7.
[48] DSU Art. 4.7.

day period has lapsed before the establishment of a panel was requested by the complainant."[49] Presumably, however, in the face of an explicit refusal to agree to consult at all, the complainant could have moved sooner, even before the expiration of 10 days.

[7] Third parties

Because consultations are intended to resolve the dispute between the parties, the DSU provides only a limited role for third parties in the process. If the request is based on Article XXII of GATT, third parties with "a substantial trade interest" may notify the consulting Members and the DSB, within 10 days of the circulation of the initial request for consultations, of their desire to be joined in the consultations. They shall be joined unless the party to whom the original request for consultations was addressed objects. However, if the request for consultations is based on Article XXIII, third parties may not request to be joined. This distinction allows the requesting party to make the tactical decision as to whether it wants the presence, and presumably the support, of third parties. Of course, the responding party may veto the requests of any Member whose presence it thinks would be detrimental to its cause. In many cases, requesting parties have avoided the question entirely by using Article XXIII, presumably to keep "outsiders" out of the consultations.[50]

§ 4.04 Request for the establishment of a panel and terms of reference

[1] General

The complaining Member's request for the establishment of a panel is incorporated into the panel's terms of reference and, therefore, determines the subject matter jurisdiction of the panel.[51] It also fulfills the due process objective of notifying the responding party – and potential third parties – of the claims at issue.[52] Far more than the request for

[49] Panel Report, *Turkey – Restrictions on Imports of Textile and Clothing Products*, WT/DS34/R, adopted 19 November 1999, as modified by the Appellate Body Report, WT/DS34/AB/R, DSR 1999:VI , 2363, ¶ 9.24.

[50] DSU Art. 4.11.

[51] *See* William J. Davey, *WTO Dispute Settlement: Segregating the Useful Political Aspects and Avoiding "Over-Legalization," supra* note 10.

[52] Appellate Body Report, *Brazil – Measures Affecting Desiccated Coconut*, WT/DS22/AB/R, adopted 20 March 1997, DSR 1997:I, 167, 186, § VI, at 22–23.

consultations, the request for the establishment of a panel is a fundamental, jurisdictional document. Disagreements over the scope of terms of reference have figured importantly in WTO jurisprudence.

[2] Time elements

If the Member to which a request for consultations is made agrees within 10 days to consult within 30 days, and does so, the complaining Member may not ask for a panel until 60 days have elapsed from the date of the original request, unless the parties agree that further consultations would not be productive.[53] At the complaining party's request, a special meeting of the DSB shall be convened for this purpose within 15 days of the request, provided that at least 10 days' notice of the meeting is given.[54] An exception is provided in cases of urgency, including those which concern perishable goods. In these instances, DSU Article 4.8 provides that Members shall enter into consultations within 10 days of the receipt of the request for consultations, and the complaining Member may request a panel 20 days after the request, if consultations have not resolved the matter. The Panel, in turn, should attempt to issue its report to the parties within three months, half the time normally allowed.[55]

The text of Article 4.8 presumes agreement between the parties as to urgency. Of course, if there is agreement, then presumably consultations would be held within 10 days of receipt of the request and, if they do not resolve the matter, a panel request would be made, without objection, in 20 days, as Article 4.8 contemplates. However, Article 4.8 provides no mechanism for dealing with disagreement between the parties as to the question of urgency. The limited experience with claims of urgency suggests that agreement will not be frequent.

In *US – Automobiles from Japan*, Japan stated in its request for consultations that it regarded the matter as a case of urgency, and requested consultations within 10 days.[56] The United States, however, disagreed. At a meeting of the DSB held subsequent to the expiration of 10 days, Japan reiterated its claim, stating both that the claim presented important systemic issues and that, if the situation were not resolved quickly, dealer networks handling Japanese cars "would be adversely affected

[53] DSU Art. 4.7. [54] DSU footnote 5. [55] DSU Art. 12.8.

[56] *United States – Imposition of Import Duties on Automobiles from Japan Under Sections 301 and 304 of the Trade Act of 1974 – Request for Consultations from Japan*, WT/DS6/1, 22 May 1995.

and be forced to fire employees and face bankruptcy."[57] In expressing disagreement, the United States argued, *inter alia*, that neither the systemic nature of a claim nor its economic magnitude should be determinative of urgency. "Putting a dollar (or yen) value on disputes as a means to determine whether the matter was urgent, could inherently discriminate against smaller industries and economies," the US argued.[58] Further, if the economic or systemic importance of cases were to make them subject to the accelerated time limits of an "urgency" proceeding, they "would likely overwhelm the WTO dispute settlement system."[59]

In that dispute, consultations were held on 12 June 1995, 26 days after the 17 May request for consultations.[60] On 19 July 1995, the parties notified the DSB that they had settled the dispute.[61]

In *Romania – Wheat*, Hungary amended an initial request for consultations to invoke the "urgency" provisions of Article 4.8.[62] Consultations were held on the tenth day after the amended request, and the establishment of a panel was requested by Hungary 17 days later.[63] In justification of its claim of urgency, Hungary, at a subsequent DSB meeting, pointed to "the severe economic and trade losses caused to Hungarian farmers and exporters and the seasonal character of the measure."[64] Romania, however, stated that it "had never agreed and would not agree to Hungary's invocation of Article 4.8 of the DSU."[65] The United States, the only other Member to speak, expressed views in support of Romania.[66] Shortly thereafter, Romania terminated the measure, and Hungary withdrew its request for the establishment of a panel.[67]

[3] Form and content

Article 6.2 of the DSU sets out the formal requirements of a request for the establishment of a panel. First, the request shall be in writing. Second,

[57] Dispute Settlement Body, *Minutes of Meeting*, WT/DSB/M/5, 4 July 1995, ¶ 2.
[58] *Id.* [59] *Id.*
[60] *United States – Imposition of Import Duties on Automobiles from Japan Under Sections 301 and 304 of the Trade Act of 1974 – Communication by Japan*, WT/DS6/5, 27 June 1995.
[61] *Update of WTO Dispute Settlement Cases*, WT/DS/OV/13, 1 May 2003, § VII.A.2.
[62] *Romania – Import Prohibition on Wheat and Wheat Flour – Request for Consultations by Hungary, Addendum*, WT/DS240/1/Add.1, 28 November 2001.
[63] *Romania – Import Prohibition on Wheat and Wheat Flour – Request for the Establishment of a Panel by Hungary*, WT/DS240/2, 28 November 2001.
[64] Dispute Settlement Body, *Minutes of Meeting*, WT/DSB/M/115, 8 January 2002, ¶ 4.
[65] *Id.* ¶ 7. [66] *Id.* ¶ 9.
[67] *Romania – Import Prohibition on Wheat and Wheat Flour – Withdrawal of the Request for the Establishment of a Panel by Hungary*, WT/DS240/3, 7 January 2002.

it shall indicate whether consultations were held. Third, it shall identify the specific measures at issue. Fourth, it shall provide a brief summary of the legal basis of the complaint sufficient to present the problem clearly. Fifth, if special terms of reference are requested, the proposed text of the special terms must be set out in the request.

If consultations were held, it is customary, though not explicitly required, to state the date and place of consultations in the request. If consultations were not held because the Member complained against did not, within 10 days of the request, agree to consult within 30 days, as required by Article 4.3, the panel request should so state. Because this would be a rather unusual occurrence, the request should include as much detail as possible, including copies of any relevant correspondence.

Article 6.2 speaks of the "measure" at issue. The "measure" at issue is that taken by the Member that is subject to the complaint. A measure typically is a law or regulation, or an action that applies a law or regulation. Article 6.2 also requires that both the "measure at issue" and the "legal basis for the complaint" be identified in the panel request.[68] The legal basis for the complaint, or the "claim," together with the "measure" constitutes the "matter" before the panel that is referred to in the standard terms of reference set out in Article 7.1 of the DSU.[69] Factual findings requested in a panel request do not constitute a "matter."[70] There has been significant jurisprudence developed concerning the specificity required in a panel request for identification of both the measure and the claim.

[4] The specific measure at issue

In *Japan – Film*, Japan argued that eight measures, not contained in the panel request, were mentioned for the first time in the first written submission to the Panel by the United States.[71] The Panel stated that, "the requirements of Article 6.2 would be met in the case of a 'measure' that is subsidiary or so closely related to a 'measure' specifically identified, that the responding party can reasonably be found to have received adequate

[68] *Id.* ¶ 69.

[69] Appellate Body Report, *Guatemala – Anti-Dumping Investigation Regarding Portland Cement from Mexico*, WT/DS60/AB/R, adopted 25 November 1998, DSR 1998:IX, 3767, ¶ 75.

[70] Panel Report, *Canada – Export Credits and Loan Guarantees for Regional Aircraft*, WT/DS222/R and Corr.1, adopted 19 February 2002, ¶ 7.17.

[71] Panel Report, *Japan – Measures Affecting Consumer Photographic Film and Paper*, WT/DS44/R, adopted 22 April 1998, DSR 1998:IV, 1179, 1635, ¶ 10.2.

notice of the scope of the claims asserted by the complaining party."[72] Accordingly, the Panel concluded that three of the measures were closely related to measures specifically identified, and therefore were within its terms of reference, while the other five were not.[73] In *Indonesia – Autos*, the Panel determined that a loan, not identified in the panel request, was not within the terms of reference even if it was one aspect of the program which was the subject of the request.[74]

The panel request in *US – Steel Countervailing Duties* specified the statutory and regulatory basis of the US sunset review procedures for countervailing duty orders, both as such and as applied in the particular case.[75] The question was whether the specific aspects of the law dealing with the opportunity to submit evidence were within the terms of reference. The Panel concluded that they were not. To consider that specific claim to be within the terms of reference, the Panel said, "would mean that the general sentence 'certain aspects of the sunset review procedure which led to [the DOC decision not to revoke the CVDs on carbon steel]' put Members on notice that *any* aspect of US CVD law of relevance in the sunset review on carbon steel might be before the panel. That cannot be, for that universe is potentially extremely large."[76]

A complaining Member is not required to challenge an entire measure. Instead, it may "identify and challenge only those offending provisions of the measure it deems central in resolving the dispute."[77]

[5] Amendment of measures after the panel request

In *Chile – Price Band*, the measure at issue was amended during the course of the Panel proceedings. The Appellate Body held that the measure, as amended, is the measure that should be considered.[78] The panel request in

[72] *Id.* ¶ 10.8. [73] *Id.* ¶¶ 10.20–10.21.

[74] Panel Report, *Indonesia – Certain Measures Affecting the Automobile Industry*, WT/DS54/R, WT/DS55/R, WT/DS59/R, WT/DS64/R and Corr.1,2,3, and 4, adopted 23 July 1998, DSR 1998:VI, 2201, ¶ 14.3.

[75] Panel Report, *United States – Countervailing Duties on Certain Corrosion-Resistant Carbon Steel Flat Products from Germany*, WT/DS213/R and Corr.1, adopted 19 December 2002, as modified by the Appellate Body Report, WT/DS213/AB/R, ¶ 8.142.

[76] *Id.* ¶ 8.144.

[77] Panel Report, *European Communities – Trade Description of Sardines*, WT/DS231/R and Corr.1, adopted 23 October 2002, as modified by the Appellate Body Report, WT/DS231/AB/R, ¶ 7.34.

[78] Appellate Body Report, *Chile – Price Band System and Safeguard Measures Relating to Certain Agricultural Products*, WT/DS207/AB/R, adopted 23 October 2002, ¶ 139.

that case referred to the law "as well as the regulations and complementary provisions and/or amendments."[79] The Appellate Body explained:

> [T]he demands of due process are such that a complaining party should not have to adjust its pleadings throughout dispute settlement proceedings in order to deal with a disputed measure as a 'moving target.' If the terms of reference in a dispute are broad enough to include amendments to a measure – as they are in this case – and if it is necessary to consider an amendment in order to secure a positive solution to the dispute – as it is here – then it is appropriate to consider the measure *as amended* in coming to a decision in a dispute.[80]

[6] The "claim" or the legal basis of the complaint

The Appellate Body has stated that, "The convenient phrase, 'including but not limited to,' is simply not adequate to 'identify the specific measures at issue and provide a brief summary of the legal basis of the complaint sufficient to present the problem clearly' as required by Article 6.2 of the DSU."[81] Thus, a panel request asserting that a measure is "inconsistent with the obligations of the TRIPS Agreement, including but not necessarily limited to Articles 27, 65 and 70" is not sufficient to bring a claim relating to Article 63 within the terms of reference.[82] Similarly, the fact that a respondent first raises conformity with another provision of a covered agreement as a defense in its first written submission does not bring the question of conformity within the panel's terms of reference for purposes of finding a violation of that other provision.[83]

While it is essential that the panel request identify the treaty provisions that are the basis of the complaining Member's claims, mere listing of provisions may not be enough.[84] This must be determined case-by-case, taking "into account whether the ability of the respondent to defend itself was prejudiced, given the actual course of the panel proceedings, by the fact that the panel request simply listed the provisions claimed to have been violated."[85] In *Korea – Dairy*, the panel request listed only Article XIX of GATT 1994, which has five paragraphs in three sections, and several

[79] *Id.* ¶ 135. [80] *Id.* ¶ 144 (emphasis in original).

[81] Appellate Body Report, *India – Patents (US)*, *supra* note 34, ¶ 90.

[82] *Id.* ¶¶ 89–90. [83] *Id.* ¶ 96.

[84] Appellate Body Report, *Korea – Definitive Safeguard Measure on Imports of Certain Dairy Products*, WT/DS98/AB/R, adopted 12 January 2000, DSR 2000:I, 3, ¶ 124.

[85] *Id.* ¶ 127.

articles of the *Agreement on Safeguards* that have multiple paragraphs. The Appellate Body said that the request should have been more detailed, but found the request acceptable because the responding Member "failed to demonstrate to us that the mere listing of the articles asserted to have been violated has prejudiced its ability to defend itself in the course of the Panel proceedings."[86] This result differs from that reached when the same phrase was used in a consultation request. See, *supra* § 403 [2].

Consistent with the Appellate Body's analysis in *Korea – Dairy*, the Panel in *Mexico – Corn Syrup* upheld a panel request that "does not merely list the articles alleged to have been violated," but "also sets forth facts and circumstances describing the substance of the dispute."[87] The issue returned to the Appellate Body in *Thailand – H-Beams*:

> A defending party is entitled to know what case it has to answer, and what violations have been alleged so that it can begin preparing its defence. Likewise, those Members of the WTO who intend to participate as third parties in panel proceedings must be informed of the legal basis of the complaint. This requirement of due process is fundamental to ensuring a fair and orderly conduct of dispute settlement proceedings.[88]

Nevertheless, because of "attendant circumstances," the Panel in *US – Lamb* accepted panel requests that were very similar to the one criticized by the Appellate Body in *Korea – Dairy*.[89] It did so for a variety of reasons, including the fact that the scope of the claims raised effectively covered the contested articles in their entirety,[90] as well as discussions that were held in the Committee on Safeguards concerning the US investigation that was the subject of the dispute, the consultations that were held concerning the investigation and the measure, the DSB's consideration of the panel requests, and the timing of the US request for a ruling that the panel requests were insufficient.[91] Further, in conformity with *Korea – Dairy*, the Panel concluded that the United States had not shown that it was prejudiced in its ability to defend itself in the panel proceedings.[92]

[86] *Id.* ¶ 131.

[87] Panel Report, *Mexico – Corn Syrup*, *supra* note 41, ¶ 7.15.

[88] Appellate Body Report, *Thailand – Anti-Dumping Duties on Angles, Shapes and Sections of Iron or Non-Alloy Steel and H-Beams from Poland*, WT/DS122/AB/R, adopted 5 April 2001, ¶ 88.

[89] Panel Report, *supra* note 35, ¶¶ 5.19, 5.20.

[90] *Id.* ¶ 5.31.

[91] *Id.* ¶ 5.32. The US argument with regard to consultations is noted in § 4.03 [5] dealing with confidentiality of consultations; the effect of the late timing of the US request for a ruling is noted in § 2.06 [4].

[92] *Id.* ¶ 5.53.

In *EC – Bed Linen*, the Panel, faced with failure to list in the request for a panel a treaty article alleged to be violated, held that claims based on that article were outside its terms of reference, even if inadvertent.[93] The fact that the article was listed in the request for consultations, was discussed in consultations, and was covered in the complaining party's first written submission does not change the result.[94] In the Panel's words, "failure to state a claim in even the most minimal sense, by listing the treaty Articles alleged to be violated, cannot be cured by reference to subsequent submissions."[95] However, when there was no evidence of prejudice to the complaining party or third parties by the simple listing of an article, a request that the claim be dismissed for lack of specificity was denied.[96]

[7] Products listed in the request

In some disputes, specific products may be listed in the request for a panel. On occasion, the listing itself can lead to disputes. Under GATT, one panel observed that, "to allow the inclusion of an additional product item about which one party had not been formally advised prior to the commencement of proceedings would be to introduce an element of inequity."[97] This Report was cited by the EC in *EC – Computer Equipment* in support of its argument that a panel request relating simply to "LAN (Local Area Network) equipment" was inadequate because, with one exception, the complaining Member had failed to identify clearly the LAN products subject to the dispute.[98] The Panel distinguished the cases.

In response to a question from the Panel, the United States specified the items covered by the term "LAN equipment."[99] This did not amount to the addition of a new product in the course of the proceedings, the Panel said, but "an elucidation of the product coverage already specified in the . . . requests for the establishment of a panel in this matter."[100] The Appellate Body upheld this conclusion, noting that the panel request referred to

93 Panel Report, *European Communities – Anti-Dumping Duties on Imports of Cotton-Type Bed Linen from India*, WT/DS141/R, adopted 12 March 2001, as modified by the Appellate Body Report, WT/DS141/AB/R, ¶ 6.17.

94 *Id.* ¶¶ 6.14, 6.15. 95 *Id.* ¶ 6.15. 96 *Id.* ¶ 6.29.

97 GATT Panel Report, *EEC – Quantitative Restrictions Against Imports of Certain Products from Hong Kong*, BISD 30S/129, adopted 12 July 1983, ¶ 30.

98 Panel Report, *European Communities – Customs Classification of Certain Computer Equipment*, WT/DS62/R, WT/DS67/R, WT/DS68/R, adopted 22 June 1998, as modified by the Appellate Body Report, WT/DS62/AB/R, WT/DS67/AB/R, WT/DS68/AB/R, DSR 1998:V, 1891, ¶ 4.1.

99 *Id.* ¶ 8.8. 100 *Id.* ¶ 8.9.

"all types of LAN equipment," and that the individual types were only mentioned as examples.[101] The Appellate Body noted that it shared the concern of the complainant that, "if the EC arguments on specificity of product definition are accepted, there will inevitably be long, drawn-out procedural battles at the early stage of the panel process in every proceeding."[102]

A panel's failure to incorporate into its conclusions all of the products referred to in the terms of reference is in error.[103]

[8] Standard terms of reference

Unless the parties agree to the contrary within 20 days from the date of the establishment of a panel, panels will proceed under standard terms of reference, as set out in Article 7.1 of the DSU, which instruct them:

> To examine, in light of the relevant provisions in (name of covered agreement(s) cited by the parties to the dispute), the matter referred to the DSB by (name of party) in document . . . and to make such findings as will assist the DSB in making the recommendations or in giving the rulings provided for in that/those agreement(s).

The "document" referred to with ellipses is the complainant's request for the establishment of a panel. That document will specify the measures claimed to be inconsistent with WTO obligations and the specific WTO provisions that are said to be violated.

Article 7.2 of the DSU provides that, "Panels shall address the relevant provisions of any covered agreement or agreements cited by the parties to the dispute." Some ambiguity surrounds the reference to the relevant provisions "cited by the parties" since it is only one party, the complainant, that provides a document to the DSB requesting the establishment of a panel. Provisions of WTO agreements cited by the other party in defense are not likely to be included in the complainant's request for a panel. However, in considering the merits of a complaining Member's claim, a Panel is bound to consider the impact on that claim of any

[101] Appellate Body Report, *European Communities – Customs Classification of Certain Computer Equipment*, WT/DS62/AB/R, WT/DS67/AB/R, WT/DS68/AB/R, adopted 22 June 1998, DSR 1998:V, 1851, ¶ 72.

[102] *Id.* ¶ 71.

[103] Appellate Body Report, *Japan – Taxes on Alcoholic Beverages*, WT/DS8/AB/R, WT/DS10/AB/R, WT/DS11/AB/R, adopted 1 November 1996, DSR 1996:I, 97, § H.2(a), 117–118.

relevant provisions of any agreement raised by the defending Member. For example, a Member may assert that a measure is inconsistent with the national treatment provisions of Article III of GATT 1994. A respondent may agree, but argue that the inconsistency is excused by Article XX, which contains a series of limited exceptions to GATT obligations, including those of Article III. The complaining Member's request for the establishment of a panel alleging that a measure is inconsistent with Article III need not refer to Article XX.

In these circumstances, the respondent would not be prohibited from raising the Article XX defense, even though it is not specified in the request for establishment and, therefore, is not mentioned in the Panel's terms of reference. Article XX is an affirmative defense provided by GATT 1994 to a claim of inconsistency with Article III, and this defense is not lost even though the DSU provides no avenue for the respondent to put the defense in the complainant's request and thus into the terms of reference.

[9] Special terms of reference

If the parties agree, Article 6.3 provides that the DSB may authorize its chairman to draw special terms of reference in consultation with the parties. Use of special terms of reference is rare. They were used in *Brazil – Desiccated Coconut.*[104]

[10] Reviews and arbitrations

When a measure is found to be inconsistent with WTO obligations, the Member concerned is called upon to bring the measure into conformity.[105] If there is disagreement as to whether in fact the steps taken by the Member concerned succeed in bringing the measure into conformity, Article 21.5 of the DSU provides for referral of this disagreement to dispute settlement, if possible before the original panel. If a measure is not brought into conformity, Article 22.2 provides that the DSB may authorize the complaining Member to suspend concessions and other obligations to the Member concerned. If there is disagreement as to the level of suspension proposed by the complaining Member, that issue may be referred to arbitration under Article 22.6. The DSU is silent on the

[104] Panel Report, *Brazil – Desiccated Coconut, supra* note 29, ¶¶ 10, 288.
[105] DSU Art. 19.1.

terms of reference for Article 21.5 reviews, as well as for Article 22.2 requests for suspension and Article 22.6 arbitrations.

In *EC – Bananas III (Article 21.5 – Ecuador)*, the EC argued that the review panel's terms of reference were limited to the "matters" on which the DSB adopted its recommendations or rulings based on the original panel and Appellate Body reports.[106] The Panel disagreed, finding that its terms of reference covered all of the claims raised by Ecuador.[107] In *Canada – Aircraft (Article 21.5 – Brazil)*, the Appellate Body was more specific.[108] Proceedings under Article 21.5, the Appellate Body said, are limited to the measures taken to comply with recommendations and rulings of the DSB. "In principle," it went on to say, "a measure which has been 'taken to comply with the recommendations and rulings' of the DSB will *not* be the same measure as the measure which was the subject of the original dispute, so that, in principle, there would be two separate and distinct measures: the original measure which *gave rise* to the recommendations and rulings of the DSB, and the 'measures taken to comply' which are – or should be – adopted to *implement* those recommendations and rulings."[109] The task of an Article 21.5 panel, accordingly, is to determine whether the new measure is consistent with WTO obligations.[110]

In *EC – Bananas (Article 22.6 – 2000)*, the Arbitrators held that even though the requirements of Article 6.2 of the DSU, regarding identification of the specific measure at issue and a brief summary of the legal basis of the complaint in a panel request, were not part of Article 22, requests for arbitration under Article 22 served the same due process purpose.[111] A request for suspension of concessions under Article 22.2 and a request for referral to arbitration under Article 22.6, the Arbitrators said, give notice and permit an appropriate response. An Article 22.2 request "defines the jurisdiction of the DSB in authorizing suspension by the complaining party," while "a request for arbitration under Article 22.6 defines the terms of reference of the Arbitrators."[112]

[106] Panel Report, *European Communities – Regime for the Importation, Sale and Distribution of Bananas – Recourse to Article 21.5 of the DSU by Ecuador*, WT/DS27/RW/ECU, 12 April 1999, DSR 1999:II, 803, ¶ 6.3.

[107] *Id.* ¶ 6.12.

[108] Appellate Body Report, *Canada – Measures Affecting the Export of Civilian Aircraft – Recourse by Brazil to Article 21.5 of the DSU*, WT/DS70/AB/RW, adopted 4 August 2000, DSR 2000:IX, 4299.

[109] *Id.* ¶ 36 (emphasis in text, footnote omitted).

[110] *Id.* ¶ 40.

[111] Decision by the Arbitrators, *European Communities – Regime for the Importation, Sale and Distribution of Bananas – Recourse to Arbitration by the European Communities under Article 22.6 of the DSU*, WT/DS27/ARB/ECU, 24 March 2000, DSR 2000:V, 2243, ¶ 20.

[112] *Id.*

These topics are discussed in greater detail in §§ 7.07–7.09 and 8.05.

§ 4.05 Establishment and composition of panels

[1] Establishment

A panel will be established no later than the second meeting after the request for a panel first appears on the DSB's agenda, unless the DSB decides by consensus not to do so.[113] This is unlikely to occur because the party requesting establishment of a panel normally would not join a consensus against its establishment. Rather, if it changed its position, the requesting party more likely would simply withdraw its request. A requesting party might agree not to establish a panel at a particular meeting of the DSB if it believes further consultations are desirable. It later could place the matter on the agenda of a subsequent meeting if further consultations were not successful.

Entitlement to a panel at the DSB meeting following that at which it first appears on the agenda means, in practice, that the party complained against can "block" establishment for one DSB meeting. Of course, the party complained against could agree to the establishment of a panel at the first meeting, in which case presumably there would be consensus to do so. This has not been a frequent occurrence.

[2] Composition

Panels normally are composed of three individuals, with one serving as chair. The parties may agree, however, to a five-member panel, provided they do so within 10 days of the establishment of the panel by the DSB.[114] Panelists often are present or former members of non-party delegations to the WTO, or academics. Unless the parties agree, panelists may not be nationals of parties or third parties.[115] Panels established pursuant to the General Agreement on Trade in Services regarding specific service sectors shall have the necessary expertise relevant to the sector involved.[116] Somewhat redundantly, the Annex on Financial Services to GATS explicitly provides that, "Panels for disputes on prudential issues and other financial matters shall have the necessary expertise relevant to the specific financial service under dispute."[117]

113 DSU Art. 6. 114 DSU Art. 8.5. 115 DSU Art. 8.3.

116 *Decision on Certain Dispute Settlement Procedures for the General Agreement on Trade in Services* ¶ 4.

117 *Annex* ¶ 4.

Panelists serve in their individual capacities, not as government representatives or representatives of other organizations. Members generally are required to permit their officials to serve as panelists (a time-consuming task that can take away from their other responsibilities), and are prohibited from giving them instructions or seeking to influence them with regard to matters before the panel.[118] If a dispute involves a developing country, at least one panelist shall be from a developing country if the developing country Member so requests.[119]

[3] Nominating panelists

Although the parties themselves may agree on the composition of a panel, and notify the DSB of that fact, in practice this is extremely rare.[120] In practice, panelists are nominated by the Secretariat from Member delegations and from a roster of governmental and non-governmental individuals who are deemed qualified by virtue of their training or experience. Normally this is done by the Director of the Legal Affairs Division in collaboration with the director of the division of the Secretariat having substantive responsibility for the matter in dispute. The Secretariat routinely consults with the parties concerning the types of panelists they would or would not prefer, and attempts to reflect these views in its selection of proposed panelists.[121] In antidumping and subsidy and countervailing duty disputes, the Director of the Rules Division usually suggests the names of proposed panelists to the parties. Members are directed not to oppose nominees of the Secretariat "except for compelling reasons."[122] As a practical matter, it is up to Members to determine whether they consider their reasons for opposing a nominee "compelling," since no mechanism exists to challenge the reasons for a Member's opposition to a proposed panelist.

[118] DSU Art. 8.9. [119] DSU Art. 8.10.

[120] For one of the few examples, *see*, GATT Panel Report, *United States – Restrictions on Imports of Tuna*, 30 I.L.M. 1594 (1991) (unadopted). In this case, the GATT "Council was informed that the Panel would have the following composition." ¶ 1.2.

[121] *See* William J. Davey, *A Permanent Panel Body for WTO Dispute Settlement: Desirable or Practical?* in Kennedy & Southwick (Eds), THE POLITICAL ECONOMY OF INTERNATIONAL TRADE LAW: ESSAYS IN HONOR OF ROBERT E. HUDEC 496 (Cambridge, 2002); William J. Davey, *The Case for a Permanent Panel Body*, 6 JOURNAL OF INTERNATIONAL ECONOMIC LAW 177 (No. 1, March 2003); Thomas J. Cottier, *The WTO Permanent Panel Body, Id.* 187; Andrew W. Shoyer, *Panel Selection in WTO Dispute Settlement Systems, Id.* 203; Jacques H. J. Bourgeois, Michael Cartland, Seung Wha Chang, Luzius Wasescha, Julio Lacarte, Frieder Roessler, *Comments on a WTO Permanent Panel Body, Id.* 211.

[122] DSU Art. 8.6.

The panel selection process proceeds in an iterative fashion. Typically, before nominating panelists, the Secretariat solicits general criteria from the parties, and then provides a slate of candidates. The parties and the Secretariat then meet to discuss the slate, and, if there is no agreement, the Secretariat will propose a new slate based on the feedback received from the parties. This process may be repeated several times.

If the parties do not agree on panelists within 20 days of the establishment of the panel, however, either party may request the Director-General of the WTO, in consultation with the Chairman of the DSB and Chairman of the relevant Council or Committee, to name the panelists.[123] The Secretariat, "de facto, has the key role in selecting panelists."[124] It effectively "screens" potential panelists in selecting those that will be proposed to the parties. If the parties cannot agree on a panel from the names proposed to them, the Secretariat, while not called upon by the DSU to do so, typically recommends names to the Director-General.

A dispute over the naming of a panelist occurred in *Guatemala – Cement II*.[125] The Report of the Panel in *Guatemala – Cement I*, which found in favour of Mexico, was reversed by the Appellate Body on procedural grounds.[126] After Mexico re-introduced its claim and the parties could not agree on the composition of the panel, the Director-General was asked to nominate the panelists.[127] Guatemala protested the Director-General's nomination of a panelist who had served in the first panel, claiming that the panelist's service on the first panel detracted from the objectivity and impartiality necessary for the second panel to accomplish its task.[128] The Panel rejected Guatemala's claim on the ground that Article 8 of the DSU, relating to the nomination of panelists, did not give the Panel itself any role in the process. In its view, the only legal way for Guatemala to present its argument would be to invoke the Rules of Conduct for panelists, relating to independence and impartiality, which Guatemala did not do.[129] In the absence of such invocation, the Panel stated that

[123] DSU Art. 8.7.

[124] J. H. H. Weiler, *The Rule of Lawyers and the Ethos of Diplomats: Reflections on the Internal and External Legitimacy of WTO Dispute Settlement*, 35 JOURNAL OF WORLD TRADE 191 (No. 2, April 2001).

[125] Panel Report, *Guatemala – Definitive Anti-Dumping Measures on Grey Portland Cement from Mexico*, WT/DS156/R, adopted 17 November 2000, DSR 2000:XI, 5295

[126] Appellate Body Report, *Guatemala – Cement I*, *supra* note 69. For a more extensive discussion of this issue, see § 5.07.

[127] Panel Report, *Guatemala – Cement II*, *supra* note 125, ¶ 1.7.

[128] *Id.* ¶ 8.10. [129] *Id.* ¶ 8.11.

it lacked the authority to *ex officio* review whether its composition was consistent with the requirements of the DSU.[130]

§ 4.06 Function, authority and responsibility of panels

The formal function of panels is to assist the DSB in discharging its responsibilities under the DSU and the WTO agreements.[131] Given the near-automaticity of the WTO process for adopting reports, however, it is more realistic to say that panels, together with the Appellate Body, effectively discharge the responsibilities of the DSB. In one of the few reports in which the function of panels was discussed, the Appellate Body observed that a panel comes under a duty to address issues in at least two instances. These are, first, the duty to address issues that are put to them by the parties, and second, to address and dispose of jurisdictional issues even if they are not addressed by the parties.[132]

Panels control the dispute settlement process within the confines of the rules set out in the DSU, establishing deadlines for written submissions and otherwise establishing the schedule.[133] These time limits typically prove unrealistically short, however, and panels frequently depart from them somewhat, usually with the agreement of the parties and notice to the DSB. While normally all of the relevant information is submitted by the complainant and respondent, panels are not confined to the parties as sources of the information they need. They may take into consideration information provided by a third party.[134] They also have the right to seek information and technical advice from any source they deem appropriate.[135] However, *ex parte* communications by parties with the panel concerning matters under consideration are not permitted.[136] Panels may consult experts to obtain their opinions and, with respect to scientific and technical matters, may request an advisory report from an expert review group.[137] Procedures governing the establishment and conduct of expert review groups are set out in Appendix 4 to the DSU.

Few formal procedural rules govern the operations of panels. Consequently, panels increasingly have begun to issue fairly detailed and specific working procedures soon after they have been composed, *i.e.*, soon after

[130] *Id.* ¶ 8.12. [131] DSU Art. 11.
[132] Appellate Body Report, *Mexico – Corn Syrup (Article 21.5 – US)*, *supra* note 12, ¶ 36.
[133] DSU Arts. 12.3, 12.4, 12.5.
[134] Panel Report, *Korea – Alcoholic Beverages*, *supra* note 11, ¶ 10.58.
[135] DSU Art. 13.1. *See* § 4.11 regarding burden of proof.
[136] DSU Art. 18.1. [137] DSU Art. 13.2. *See* § 4.09 [5] regarding experts.

the panelists have been named. These procedures supplement the Working Procedures set out in Annex 3 to the DSU, and may cover topics ranging from the order of presentation at panel meetings, to the time limitations on the submission of evidence, to the form of submissions, including electronic copies. An example of panel Working Procedures is contained in the Appendix.

§ 4.07 Third parties, multiple complainants and counter-complaints

[1] Overview

Because a measure taken by any WTO Member may affect the present interests of more than one other Member, and may potentially affect the interests of all Members, the DSU provides for multiple complaints as well as for third party participation in panel proceedings. As noted above, third parties may request to participate in consultations requested by another party and, if permission is denied, may request consultations on their own and, thereby, initiate a separate panel proceeding.[138]

[2] Third parties

Any Member having a substantial interest in a dispute, and having notified the DSB of that interest, may be heard by a panel and may make written submissions to the panel.[139] The DSU does not specify a time limit within which third parties must notify the DSB of their interest in a dispute between other parties. However, since Article 8.3 provides that citizens of Members that are parties or third parties may not serve as panelists without the approval of the parties, difficulties could arise if a Member notified the DSB of its interest after one of its citizens had been named to a panel. To minimize the likelihood of this occurring, the Secretariat has adopted the informal practice of not suggesting the names of possible panelists to the parties until 10 days after the DSB has voted to establish the panel.

Third parties are entitled to receive the first written submissions of the parties "to the first meeting of the panel" in all cases.[140] In practice, this means the first written submissions and the written versions of the oral statements made by parties to the first meeting of the Panel. They may present their views at a session of the first substantive meeting of

[138] *See* § 4.03 [7]. [139] DSU Art. 10.2. [140] DSU Art. 10.3.

the panel set aside for that purpose.[141] Third parties cannot make claims before a panel, and a complainant cannot rely on them to do so on its behalf.[142] Third parties also may not appeal a panel report; however, if a party appeals, third parties may participate, as "third participants."[143]

The question of "enhanced" third party rights first arose in *Bananas III* when numerous developing country third parties requested that they be permitted to be present at all meetings between the Panel and the parties to the dispute.[144] The Panel agreed to the request,[145] but would not permit the third parties to participate in the interim review.[146] In the *EC – Hormones* cases, two separate panels, composed of the same members, were established to examine the same measures.[147] The Panels also decided to hold a joint meeting with the scientific experts with whom they consulted. Accordingly, they decided to give both Canada and the United States, each a third party in the case brought by the other, access to all of the information submitted under each proceeding, including second written submissions, written versions of oral statements, responses to questions and scientific documents.[148] The Appellate Body upheld the decision.[149]

In *US – 1916 Act (EC)*,[150] Japan, complainant in the parallel *US – 1916 Act (Japan)* case, asked for similar enhanced third party rights.[151] As in *Hormones*, the same panelists were considering the same measure in the two proceedings. The Panel denied the request, however, finding that "particular circumstances existed" in the *Hormones* cases that did not exist in the *1916 Act* cases. In referring to the *Hormones* cases, the Panel

[141] DSU Appendix 3.6.

[142] Appellate Body Report, *Chile – Price Band System*, *supra* note 78, ¶ 163.

[143] DSU Art. 17.4. *See* Chapter 6.

[144] *See* Panel Report, *EC – Bananas III (US)*, *supra* note 33, ¶ 7.4.

[145] *Id.* ¶ 7.8. [146] *Id.* ¶ 7.9.

[147] Panel Reports, *EC Measures Concerning Meat and Meat Products (Hormones) – Complaint by Canada*, WT/DS48/R/CAN, DSR 1998:II, 235, and *EC Measures Concerning Meat and Meat Products (Hormones) – Complaint by the United States*, WT/DS26/R/USA, DSR 1998:III, 699, both reports adopted 13 February 1998, as modified by the Appellate Body Report, WT/DS26/AB/R, WT/DS48/AB/R, DSR 1998:I, 135, ¶ 8.12.

[148] *Id.* ¶ 8.15.

[149] Appellate Body Report, *EC Measures Concerning Meat and Meat Products (Hormones)*, WT/DS26/AB/R, WT/DS48/AB/R, adopted 13 February 1998, DSR 1998:I, 135, ¶ 154.

[150] Panel Report, *United States – Anti-Dumping Act of 1916 – Complaint by the European Communities*, WT/DS136/R and Corr.1, adopted 26 September 2000, as upheld by the Appellate Body Report, WT/DS136/AB/R, WT/DS162/AB/R, DSR 2000:X, 4593, ¶ 6.29.

[151] Panel Report, *United States – Anti-Dumping Act of 1916 – Complaint by Japan*, WT/DS162/R and Add.1, adopted 26 September 2000, as upheld by the Appellate Body Report, WT/DS136/AB/R, WT/DS162/AB/R, DSR 2000:X, 4831.

cited "their highly technical and factually intensive nature, as well as the fact that the panels had decided to hold one single meeting with the parties and the experts."[152] That these factors were not present in the *1916 Act* cases was decisive in the Panel's view.[153] The Appellate Body affirmed, stating that, "A panel's decision whether to grant 'enhanced' participatory rights to third parties is thus a matter that falls within the discretionary authority of that panel. Such discretionary authority is, of course, not unlimited and is circumscribed, for example, by the requirements of due process."[154]

[3] Third party rights in reviews and arbitrations

The question of the rights of third parties has also arisen in reviews under DSU Article 21.5 and arbitrations under DSU Article 22.6. These topics are discussed in § 7.07 [7] and § 8.05 [9], respectively.

[4] Multiple complainants

When more than one Member requests the establishment of a panel related to the same subject matter, Article 9.1 of the DSU provides that a single panel will be established whenever feasible. The written submissions of each complainant will be made available to the other complainants, and each complainant shall have the right to be present when the other complainants present their cases to the panel.[155] The panel may issue a single report, unless one of the parties to the dispute requests separate reports, in which case separate reports shall be issued.[156] However, a request for separate reports must be timely. In *US – Offset Act (Byrd Amendment)*, the United States requested separate reports two months

[152] Panel Report, *US – 1916 Act (EC), supra* note 150, ¶ 6.33. [153] *Id.* ¶ 6.34.

[154] Appellate Body Report, *United States – Anti-Dumping Act of 1916*, WT/DS136/AB/R, WT/DS162/AB/R, adopted 26 September 2000, DSR 2000:X, 4793, ¶ 150.

[155] DSU Art. 9.2.

[156] *Id.* In the first case involving multiple complainants, a single report was issued. *United States – Standards for Reformulated and Conventional Gasoline*, WT/DS2/R, adopted 20 May 1996, as modified by the Appellate Body Report, WT/DS2/AB/R, DSR 1996:I, 29. In *European Communities – Regime for the Importation, Sale and Distribution of Bananas, supra* note 33, four separate reports were issued. The factual sections of the reports were identical, while the "findings" sections differed to take into account the fact that the complainants did not make the same arguments, but a consistent paragraph numbering system was used for all common findings. *See* ¶ 7.58.

after the panel had issued the descriptive part of its report.[157] No explanation for the delay was provided, nor did the US claim any prejudice from the issuance of a single report.[158] In denying the US request, the Panel noted that preparation of separate reports would delay its interim report, and would thereby delay the entire process, to the detriment of the other parties.[159] The Appellate Body affirmed, stating that, "We do not believe that we should lightly disturb panels' decisions on their procedure, particularly in cases such as the one at hand, in which the Panel's decision appears to have been reasonable and in accordance with due process."[160] Further, the Appellate Body added, "The Panel correctly based its decision on an assessment of the rights of all the parties, and not of one alone."[161]

In *India – Patents (EC)*, India argued that the complaint should be dismissed on the grounds that, since it was "feasible" for the EC to have brought its complaint simultaneously with an earlier complaint brought by the United States, the EC's actions did not conform to the requirements of Article 9.1 of the DSU.[162] The Panel rejected the argument.

The terms of Article 9.1 provide that, when more than one Member requests the establishment of a panel related to the same matter, "A single panel should be established to examine such complaints whenever feasible." These terms, the Panel said, "are directory or recommendatory, not mandatory."[163] They do not "affect substantive and procedural rights and obligations of individual Members under the DSU."[164]

[5] Counter-complaints

Since WTO dispute settlement is not considered to be a contentious act, counter-complaints ("counter-claims") are not provided for in DSU procedure. Consequently, if a Member responding to a complaint files its own complaint against the original complainant, with regard to a distinct matter, the DSU provides that it should not be linked to the original

157 Panel Report, *United States – Continued Dumping and Subsidy Offset Act of 2000*, WT/DS217/R, WT/DS234/R, adopted 27 January 2003, as modified by the Appellate Body Report, WT/DS217/AB/R, WT/DS234/AB/R, ¶ 7.4.

158 *Id.* 159 *Id.* ¶¶ 7.5–7.6.

160 Appellate Body Report, *United States – Continued Dumping and Subsidy Offset Act of 2000*, WT/DS217/AB/R, WT/DS234/AB/R, adopted 27 January 2003, ¶ 316.

161 *Id.*

162 Panel Report, *India – Patent Protection for Pharmaceutical and Agricultural Chemical Products – Complaint by the European Communities*, WT/DS79/R, adopted 22 September 1998, DSR 1998:VI, 2661, ¶ 7.9.

163 *Id.* ¶ 7.14. 164 *Id.*

complaint.[165] The two cases would proceed independently of each other. However, in *Brazil – Aircraft* and *Canada – Aircraft*, the panels were established and composed on the same dates and proceeded on schedules agreed to by the parties and the panels, with the final reports being issued on the same day.[166]

[6] Amicus curiae *briefs*

The issue of *amicus curiae* briefs has been contentious in the WTO.[167] In general, panels have tended to accept these submissions while stating that they did not use them in resolving the dispute.

The first instance occurred in *US – Shrimp* where two environmental organizations submitted *amicus* briefs to the Panel and served them on the parties.[168] The Panel declined to accept the documents on the ground that it had not requested them, but stated that any party could put forward all or part of these briefs as part of its own submission.[169] According to the Panel, pursuant to Article 13 of the DSU, the initiative of when and how to "seek" information rests with panels, and only parties and third parties are allowed to "submit" information.[170]

The Appellate Body found this approach too narrow, stating that the "authority to *seek* information is not properly equated with a *prohibition* on accepting information which has been submitted without having been requested by a panel. A panel has the discretionary authority either to accept and consider or to reject information and advice submitted to it, *whether requested by a panel or not*."[171] In a subsequent Article 21.5 compliance review, the Panel received two *amicus* briefs, accepted one that was attached to the submission of a party, and rejected the other.[172]

165 DSU Art. 3.10.

166 *Brazil – Aircraft, supra* note 17, and Panel Report, *Canada – Measures Affecting the Export of Civilian Aircraft*, WT/DS70/R, adopted 20 August 1999, as upheld by the Appellate Body Report, WT/DS70/AB/R, DSR 1999:IV, 1443.

167 The major disagreement has involved *amicus* briefs before the Appellate Body. *See* § 6.04 [17].

168 Panel Report, *United States – Import Prohibition of Certain Shrimp and Shrimp Products*, WT/DS58/R and Corr.1, adopted 6 November 1998, as modified by the Appellate Body Report, WT/DS58/AB/R, DSR 1998:VII, 2821, ¶ 3.129.

169 *Id.* 170 *Id.* ¶ 7.8.

171 Appellate Body Report, *United States – Import Prohibition of Certain Shrimp and Shrimp Products*, WT/DS58/AB/R, adopted 6 November 1998, DSR 1998:VII, 2755, ¶ 108 (emphasis in original).

172 Panel Report, *United States – Import Prohibition of Certain Shrimp and Shrimp Products – Recourse to Article 21.5 of the DSU by Malaysia*, WT/DS58/RW, adopted 21 November 2001, as upheld by the Appellate Body Report, WT/DS58/AB/RW, ¶ 5.16.

In *US – Lead and Bismuth II*, the Panel stated that, while it had authority to accept *amicus curiae* briefs, it declined to do so because the brief was submitted after the deadline for the parties' rebuttal submissions and after the second substantive meeting of the Panel with the parties.[173] In *EC – Asbestos*, the Panel received four *amicus* briefs from non-governmental organizations. The EC incorporated two of them by reference, and they were accepted by the Panel.[174] A fifth brief, submitted at a stage in the procedure when it could no longer be taken into account, was not accepted.[175] In *US – Softwood Lumber III*, the Panel accepted an unsolicited *amicus* brief that was submitted prior to the first substantive meeting with the parties, and on which they and the third parties had an opportunity to comment. It rejected three others, submitted after the first meeting, for "reasons relating to the timing of these submissions."[176]

§ 4.08 Role of the Secretariat

The Secretariat has the responsibility of providing legal, historical and procedural assistance to panels.[177] It also provides secretarial and technical support. Generally, panels are assisted by a representative of the Legal Affairs Division and by a representative of the Division of the Secretariat with substantive responsibility for the subject matter of the dispute. It is the role of the Legal Affairs Division to advise panelists on points of WTO law, and to assist the panel in maintaining coherent and consistent case law jurisprudence, unless the panel decides, for informed reasons, to depart from prior case law.[178] In so-called "rules" cases, involving anti-dumping, countervailing duties, and safeguards, both the legal officer and the secretary to the panel usually come from the Rules Division.

173 Panel Report, *United States – Imposition of Countervailing Duties on Certain Hot-Rolled Lead and Bismuth Carbon Steel Products Originating in the United Kingdom*, WT/DS138/R and Corr.2, adopted 7 June 2000, as upheld by the Appellate Body Report, WT/DS138/AB/R, DSR 2000:VI, 2631, ¶ 6.3.

174 Panel Report, *European Communities – Measures Affecting Asbestos and Asbestos-Containing Products*, WT/DS135/R and Add.1, adopted 5 April 2001, as modified by the Appellate Body Report, WT/DS135/AB/R, ¶¶ 6.1–6.3.

175 *Id.* ¶ 6.4.

176 Panel Report, *United States – Preliminary Determinations with Respect to Certain Softwood Lumber from Canada*, WT/DS236/R, adopted 1 November 2002, ¶ 7.2.

177 DSU Art. 27.1. *See* Robert E. Hudec, *The Role of the GATT Secretariat in the Evolution of the WTO Dispute Settlement System*, in Jagdish Bhagwati & Mathias Hirsch (Eds), The Uruguay Round and Beyond: Essays in Honour of Arthur Dunkel 101 (Springer-Verlag, 1998).

178 *See* § 3.03.

While the Secretariat frequently is asked to provide assistance and advice to Members outside the context of dispute settlement, any advice given is not controlling when disputes arise. In *Chile – Price Band System*, Chile referred to a letter from the GATT Secretariat in support of its position.[179] "The mere fact that an individual in the GATT Secretariat might have made a statement," the Panel said, "is not determinative."[180]

Yet, "[e]very WTO delegation depends on the existence of the Secretariat as an impartial guardian of shared values and institutional history. The Secretariat is central, irreplaceable, and fragile."[181] Its role in dispute settlement is both important and difficult. Indeed, Joseph Weiler has described that role as "impossible."[182] The notion that the Secretariat's role is limited to providing neutral legal, historical and procedural assistance to panels is, in Prof. Weiler's words, "comforting nonsense."[183] Because panelists are chosen *ad hoc*, while the Secretariat is relatively permanent, the Secretariat over time has developed an expertise that few panelists can match. Inevitably, this leads to the Secretariat's having a legal point of view that will be made known to panels. Not all panelists feel qualified to disagree with the Secretariat on points of law.[184] The "impossibility" of this role is based on the formal refusal of the dispute settlement system to recognize that, in a contested legal proceeding, there really can be no such thing as the kind of "objective" legal advice envisioned by the DSU. In most cases, it is safe to say, at least one of the disputants will disagree strongly with that advice and will find it anything but "objective."

The Secretariat can have a powerful influence on the outcome of a dispute, an influence that it has exercised with caution and circumspection. It is worth noting, in this regard, that a former head of the Legal Affairs Division of the Secretariat has suggested that the establishment of a permanent panel body would "increase the expertise of panelists and the quality of their work product."[185]

[179] Panel Report, *Chile – Price Band System and Safeguard Measures Relating to Certain Agricultural Products*, WT/DS207/R, adopted 23 October 2002, as modified by the Appellate Body Report, WT/DS207/AB/R, ¶ 7.94.

[180] *Id.*

[181] Amelia Porges, *Step by Step to an International Trade Court*, in Kennedy & Southwick (Eds), THE POLITICAL ECONOMY OF INTERNATIONAL TRADE LAW: ESSAYS IN HONOR OF ROBERT E. HUDEC, *supra* note 121, 528, 533.

[182] J. H. H. Weiler, *supra* note 124, § IV.5. [183] *Id.* [184] *Id.*

[185] William J. Davey, *supra* note 121, 527. One disgruntled stakeholder accused the panelists of effectively turning the decision-making process over to the Secretariat, a charge denied by a WTO spokesman who also observed that, since that stakeholder and its representatives

§ 4.09 Evidence and information

[1] General

WTO panels, like international tribunals generally, are given considerable flexibility in evaluating evidence.[186] The DSU contains no technical rules concerning the production, admissibility, or sufficiency of evidence. Article 12, dealing with panel procedures, does not mention the subject. Appendix 3 to the DSU specifies only that, before the first meeting of the panel, the parties shall file written submissions in which they present the "facts of the case" as well as their arguments. Since most WTO disputes have dealt with the "measures" of Member governments, the text of the measure at issue generally has been the factual basis for the proceeding. Accordingly, panel proceedings have tended to emphasize legal argument – the WTO consequences of the measure at issue – rather than disputes over points of fact. As disputes have become increasingly complex, however, the factual component has increased. With parties increasingly using witnesses to establish facts in a dispute, Members can expect further development by panels of necessary procedural rules.

[2] Panel's right to seek evidence and information

Article 13.1 of the DSU makes clear the right of panels to "seek information and technical advice from any individual or body it deems appropriate," while Article 13.2 authorizes panels to seek information from "any relevant source." In *Argentina – Footwear*, the Appellate Body ruled that this authority is discretionary,[187] confirming its conclusion in *Hormones* that the purpose of Article 13 is to "enable panels to seek information and advice as they deem appropriate in a particular case."[188] Similarly, in *US – Shrimp*, the Appellate Body referred to "the comprehensive nature" of a panel's authority to seek evidence and technical advice from "any

were not present during the deliberations of the Panel, they had no way of knowing how the Panel and the Secretariat interacted. *See, Kodak Charges WTO Secretariat with Unfair Intervention in Film Case*, Inside US Trade, July 3, 1998. The WTO spokesman also noted that the United States, the Member concerned, was in a better position to judge the role of the Secretariat, and had made no such claim.

186 Panel Report, *Argentina – Measures Affecting Imports of Footwear, Textiles, Apparel and Other Items*, WT/DS56/R, adopted 22 April 1998, as modified by the Appellate Body Report, WT/DS56/AB/R, DSR 1998:III, 1033, ¶ 6.39.

187 Appellate Body Report, *Argentina – Measures Affecting Imports of Footwear, Textiles, Apparel and Other Items*, WT/DS56/AB/R and Corr.1, adopted 22 April 1998, DSR 1998:III, 1003, ¶ 84.

188 Appellate Body Report, *EC Hormones, supra* note 149, ¶ 147.

individual or body" or from "any relevant source."[189] The authority of a panel to seek information "from any individual or body" includes seeking information from any WTO Member, "including *a fortiori* a Member who is a party to a dispute before a panel."[190] This authority is not conditioned on the establishment of a *prima facie* claim or defense by the other party to the dispute.[191]

Because the authority is discretionary, panels are not required to gather data.[192] Thus, despite a request based on the Appellate Body's suggestion in *India – Patents (US)*,[193] the Panel in *Canada – Aircraft* declined to engage in additional fact-finding until after it had received the first written submissions of the parties.[194] Panels also are not confined to seeking information simply from the parties or other WTO Members. Thus, in disputes involving intellectual property issues, panels have sought information from the World Intellectual Property Organization.[195]

[3] *Duty to provide evidence and information*

Paralleling the authority of panels to seek evidence and information from any source, including parties, is the obligation of parties to provide evidence and information to panels. Article 13 provides that, "A Member should respond promptly and fully to any request by a panel for such information." This duty was first referred to by the Arbitrators in *EC – Hormones*, who stated that, "The duty that rests on *all* parties to produce evidence and to collaborate in presenting evidence to the arbitrators – an issue to be distinguished from the question of who bears the burden of proof – is crucial in Article 22 arbitration proceedings."[196] A party's

[189] *Supra* note 171, ¶ 124.

[190] Appellate Body Report, *Canada – Measures Affecting the Export of Civilian Aircraft*, WT/DS70/AB/R, adopted 20 August 1999, DSR 1999:III, 1377, ¶ 185.

[191] *Id. Accord*: Panel Report, *Thailand – Anti-Dumping Duties on Angles, Shapes and Sections of Iron or Non-Alloy Steel and H-Beams from Poland*, WT/DS122/R, adopted 5 April 2001, as modified by the Appellate Body Report, WT/DS122/AB/R, ¶ 7.50. *See, infra*, § 4.11 [2] for burden of proof and *prima facie* case.

[192] Appellate Body Report, *EC Hormones, supra* note 149, ¶ 136 (referring to Article 11 and the function of panels).

[193] *Supra* note 34, ¶ 94.

[194] *Canada – Aircraft, supra* note 166, ¶ 9.50.

[195] Panel Report, *United States – Section 110(5) of the US Copyright Act*, WT/DS160/R, adopted 27 July 2000, DSR 2000:VIII, 3769, Attachment 4.1; Panel Report, *United States – Section 211 Omnibus Appropriations Act of 1998*, WT/DS176/R, adopted 1 February 2002, as modified by the Appellate Body Report, WT/DS176/AB/R, ¶ 8.13.

[196] Decision by the Arbitrators, *European Communities – Measures Concerning Meat and Meat Products (Hormones) – Original Complaint by the United States – Recourse to Arbitration by the European Communities under Article 22.6 of the DSU*, WT/DS26/ARB, 12 July 1999, DSR 1999:III, 1105, ¶ 11.

decision not to put on a defense on a particular issue, when the party denies or refuses to admit elements of the claim, does not prevent a panel from seeking information on that issue.[197]

One panel suggested that the obligation of a party to provide information in its sole possession "does not arise until the claimant has done its best to secure evidence and has actually produced some *prima facie* evidence in support of its case."[198] However, "some *prima facie* evidence" does not mean a *prima facie* case, as the Appellate Body made clear in *Canada – Aircraft*. A panel, it said:

> is vested with ample and extensive discretionary authority to determine *when* it needs information to resolve a dispute and *what* information it needs. A panel may need such information before or after a complaining or responding Member has established its complaint or defense on a *prima facie* basis. A Panel may, in fact, need the information sought in order to evaluate evidence already before it in the course of determining whether the claiming or the responding Member, as the case may be, has established a *prima facie* case or defense.[199]

The use of the word "should" in Article 13.1, moreover, is not a mere exhortation. Members are "under a duty and an obligation to 'respond fully' to requests made by panels for information under Article 13.1 of the DSU."[200]

The obligation of Members to disclose facts during the consultation process is discussed *supra* in § 4.03 [4].

[4] Adverse inferences

Panels have been reluctant – at least explicitly – to draw adverse inferences against a party that fails to provide requested information that is within its possession, although the Appellate Body has made clear their authority to do so. In *Indonesia – Autos*, Indonesia asked that the Panel draw adverse inferences based on the failure of the complainants to submit the full text of a publication. The Panel declined, noting that Indonesia had not given it any reason to believe that relevant portions of the report had been excluded. Further, because the report was "not a document to which the complainants can control access, resort to adverse inferences would not

[197] Panel Report, *Canada – Aircraft*, *supra* note 166, ¶ 9.83.

[198] Panel Report, *Argentina – Textiles and Apparel*, *supra* note 186, ¶ 6.40.

[199] Appellate Body Report, *supra* note 190, ¶ 192. *See*, *infra*, § 4.11 [2] for burden of proof and *prima facie* case.

[200] *Id.* ¶ 187.

appear appropriate."[201] In *Canada – Aircraft Credits and Guarantees*, "although one might have hoped that Canada would have been more forthcoming," the Panel did "not consider it appropriate to draw the adverse inference requested."[202] In that case, the Panel concluded that Canada was not required to provide particular details in order to respond fully to the questions as asked.[203]

The Panel in *Canada – Aircraft* declined to draw adverse inferences in several instances.[204] While the Panel's decision was upheld on appeal, the Appellate Body observed that if it had been deciding the issue in the first instance, "we might well have concluded that the facts of record did warrant" adverse inferences.[205] The Appellate Body used the occasion to elaborate on the authority of panels to draw adverse inferences when parties fail or decline to provide requested information within their possession. In noting that "the authority to draw adverse inferences from a Member's refusal to provide information" belongs to panels examining claims of prohibited export subsidies (the issue in *Canada – Aircraft*), "that authority seems to us an ordinary aspect of the task of all panels to determine the relevant facts of any dispute involving any covered agreement: a view supported by the general practice and usage of international tribunals."[206] Describing the role of adverse inferences in the WTO dispute settlement system, the Appellate Body said:

> The continued viability of that system depends, in substantial measure, on the willingness of panels to take all steps open to them to induce the parties to the dispute to comply with their duty to provide information deemed necessary for dispute settlement. In particular, a panel should be willing expressly to remind parties – during the course of dispute settlement proceedings – that a refusal to provide information requested by a panel may lead to inferences being drawn about the inculpatory character of the information withheld.[207]

In *US – Wheat Gluten*, a dispute under the *Agreement on Safeguards*, the Panel requested information that had been redacted from the public version of the report issued by the US International Trade Commission, the national investigating authority.[208] The information had been obtained by the US authorities from private parties with assurances

[201] *Supra* note 74, ¶ 14.180. [202] *Supra* note 70, ¶¶ 7.384 –7.386. [203] *Id.*
[204] *Supra* note 166, notes 577, 621 and 633, and ¶¶ 9.263 and 9.281.
[205] *Supra* note 190, ¶ 205 (footnote omitted). [206] *Id.* ¶ 202 (footnote omitted).
[207] *Id.* ¶ 204.
[208] Panel Report, *United States – Definitive Safeguard Measures on Imports of Wheat Gluten from the European Communities*, WT/DS166/R, adopted 19 January 2001, as modified by the Appellate Body Report, WT/DS166/AB/R, ¶ 8.7.

of confidentiality, pursuant to Article 3.2 of the Safeguards Agreement, and, accordingly, the US informed the Panel that it was not allowed to disclose the requested information.[209] The Panel noted "the existence of a serious systemic issue as to the relationship between, on the one hand, the confidentiality obligations under Article 3.2 [of the Safeguards Agreement] of a Member's investigating authorities with respect to confidential information obtained in the course of a domestic safeguards investigation and, on the other hand, the duties of Members when faced with a panel request for such confidential information under Article 13 [of the] DSU."[210] The Panel concluded that, while the requested information "would have facilitated our objective assessment of the facts," the record without the information was sufficient to permit it to proceed.[211]

On appeal, the EC argued that the Panel should have drawn adverse inferences from the refusal of the US to provide the requested information.[212] The Appellate Body noted its "strong agreement" with the Panel's observations on the "systemic" conflict it identified, and added, "We believe these issues need to be addressed."[213] Citing *Canada – Aircraft*, the Appellate Body said that "the refusal by a Member to provide information requested of it undermines seriously the ability of a panel to make an objective assessment of the facts and the matter, as required by Article 11 of the DSU."[214] Nevertheless, it rejected the EC's appeal.[215]

A party's refusal to provide requested information is an important fact of record, the Appellate Body said.[216] However, it is not the only fact, and a panel's disregard of other relevant facts would lead to its failure to make an "objective assessment" as required by Article 11.[217] When asking for a finding of adverse inferences, the Appellate Body said,

> an appellant must indicate clearly the manner in which a panel has improperly exercised its discretion. Taking into account the full *ensemble* of the facts, the appellant should, at least: identify the facts on the record from which the Panel should have drawn inferences; indicate the factual or legal inferences that the panel should have drawn from those facts; and, finally, explain why the failure of the panel to exercise its discretion by drawing these inferences amounts to an error of law under Article 11 of the DSU.[218]

[209] *Id.* ¶ 8.8. [210] *Id.* ¶ 8.11. [211] *Id.* ¶ 8.12.

[212] Appellate Body Report, *United States – Definitive Safeguard Measures on Imports of Wheat Gluten from the European Communities*, WT/DS166/AB/R, adopted 19 January 2001, ¶ 169.

[213] *Id.* ¶ 170. [214] *Id.* ¶ 171. [215] *Id.* ¶ 176. [216] *Id.* ¶ 174. [217] *Id.*

[218] *Id.* ¶ 175.

[5] Experts

In addition to authorizing panels to seek information from "any relevant source," Article 13.2 also authorizes them "to consult experts to obtain their opinion on certain aspects of the matter." This authority is discretionary, and panels are not required to seek expert advice.[219] Appendix 4 to the DSU sets forth rules for establishing expert review groups, and the procedures they should follow.

Article 13.2 contemplates a written report from an expert review group, and the rules of Appendix 4 reflect this. However, in the first instance of the use of experts in a WTO proceeding, the panel elected to proceed in a different fashion. In *EC – Hormones*, the Panel chose not to receive a consensus report of the experts as a group, but rather, to obtain the opinions of the experts individually.[220] This practice was affirmed by the Appellate Body.[221]

None of the parties requested the appointment of experts in *US – Shrimp*, but all of them submitted studies by experts and quoted from the same scientific documents to support opposite views. Accordingly, the Panel, on its own initiative, sought expert advice pursuant to Articles 13.1 and 13.2 of the DSU.[222] The Panel asked the parties to suggest experts and also obtained *curricula vitae* of experts from the Secretariat. Five were selected and were asked to serve in their individual capacities.[223] The parties were given time by the Panel to comment in writing on the replies of the experts to the questions of the Panel.[224]

Similarly, in *Australia – Salmon*, neither party requested that the Panel seek expert advice, but neither objected when the Panel chose to do so.[225] Four experts were chosen from names of individuals submitted by the parties and from the Office International des Épizooties.[226] The parties were given the opportunity to comment on the list of potential experts on the basis of their *curricula vitae*, and to state "any compelling objections" they might have to particular individuals.[227] In consultation with the

[219] Appellate Body Report, *Argentina – Textiles and Apparel*, *supra* note 187, ¶ 84.

[220] *Supra* note 147, ¶¶ 8.7, 8.8 and 8.9. The Panel also proceeded under Article 11 of the *Agreement on the Application of Sanitary and Phytosanitary Measures*, which also provides for the use of experts. *See* § 5.05.

[221] *Supra* note 149, ¶¶ 146–149. [222] *Supra* note 168, ¶ 5.1.

[223] *Id.* ¶¶ 5.5–5.7. [224] *Id.* ¶ 7.10.

[225] Panel Report, *Australia – Measures Affecting Importation of Salmon*, WT/DS18/R and Corr.1, adopted 6 November 1998, as modified by the Appellate Body Report, WT/DS18/AB/R, DSR 1998:VIII, 3407, ¶ 6.1.

[226] *Id.* ¶ 6.2. [227] *Id.* ¶ 6.3.

parties, the Panel prepared specific questions, which were submitted to each expert individually. The experts were requested to provide written responses to the questions they felt qualified to address. The written submissions of the parties, including the written versions of their oral presentations, were provided to each expert. The written responses of the experts were given to the parties, who in turn were given the opportunity to comment on these responses.[228] Finally, the experts met with the Panel and the parties to discuss their responses to the questions.[229] In the Article 21.5 review of *Australia – Salmon*, the Panel stated that panels are not barred from considering expert advice until after the complaining party has established a *prima facie* case.[230]

In *Japan – Agricultural Products II*, the Panel, without objection from either party, consulted with experts.[231] The Panel presented written questions to the experts and met with them, together with the parties, to discuss their written responses.[232]

In *EC – Asbestos*, the Panel decided to consult with experts after its initial meeting with the parties.[233] The consultation was with the experts individually, not as a group. However, the parties were provided with the responses of the experts to the written questions of the Panel, and met with the experts and the Panel to discuss the answers of the experts.[234] The Panel acted pursuant to Article 13.1's authorization to "seek information and technical advice from any individual or body which it deems appropriate," rather than Article 13.2's authorization to "seek an advisory report in writing from an expert review group."[235] *EC – Asbestos* was the first case under the *Agreement on Technical Barriers to Trade* and, in that regard, the Panel noted there was no conflict between Article 13 of the DSU and Article 14.2 of the TBT Agreement, which provides that a panel may establish a technical expert group. It saw this provision, as well as DSU Article 13.2, as complementary to DSU Article 13.1.[236]

The Appellate Body has stated that a panel is not duty bound to consult with particular experts; and, just as panels have discretion to determine how to seek expert advice, so also do they have discretion to determine whether to seek expert advice at all.[237]

[228] *Id.* ¶ 6.4. [229] *Id.* ¶ 6.5.

[230] Panel Report, *Australia – Measures Affecting Importation of Salmon – Recourse to Article 21.5 of the DSU by Canada*, WT/DS18/RW, adopted 20 March 2000, DSR 2000:IV, 2035, ¶ 7.118.

[231] Panel Report, *Japan – Agricultural Products II*, *supra* note 16, ¶ 6.2.

[232] *Id.* ¶ 6.3. [233] *Supra* note 174, ¶ 8.10. [234] *Id.* ¶ 5.23. [235] *Id.* ¶ 8.10.

[236] *Id.* [237] *Argentina – Textiles and Apparel, supra* note 187, ¶ 84.

Translation also has become an issue for experts. In *Japan – Film*, the Panel was faced with difficult translation issues and named a two-member panel of experts to advise it.[238]

There has been little jurisprudence on the question of the qualifications of experts. In *EC – Asbestos*, Canada argued on appeal that certain of the experts lacked expertise in particular relevant areas, but had not objected at the panel stage to the selection of these experts.[239] The Appellate Body rejected the argument, noting that the experts were instructed by the Panel to answer only those questions that fell within their areas of expertise.[240] "The Panel was entitled to assume," the Appellate Body said, "that the experts possessed the necessary expertise to answer the questions, or parts of questions, they chose to answer."[241]

In *Guatemala – Cement II*, an antidumping dispute, Mexico objected to Guatemala's inclusion of two non-governmental experts, with an alleged conflict of interest, on the verification team that would visit the investigated Mexican exporter.[242] The Panel concluded that it was reasonable for the exporter to object to the presence of these experts at the verification.[243]

In another antidumping dispute, *US – Steel Plate from India*, India presented affidavits from a former official of the United States Department of Commerce in support of its position. The United States argued that the affidavits should be rejected on the grounds that the former official was an employee of the law firm representing India in the dispute.[244] The Panel, nevertheless, accepted the affidavits as "something in the nature of 'expert opinion' in support of India's arguments."[245]

[6] Admissions and statements

If a party admits a particular fact, panels may be entitled to consider the statement as accurate and the fact as established.[246] In *India – Quantitative Restrictions*, India notified import restrictions to the Balance of

[238] Panel Report, *Japan – Film, supra* note 71, ¶¶ 1.9–1.10.

[239] Appellate Body Report, *European Communities – Measures Affecting Asbestos and Asbestos-Containing Products*, WT/DS135/AB/R, adopted 5 April 2001, ¶ 179.

[240] *Id.* [241] *Id.* ¶ 180.

[242] Panel Report, *Guatemala – Cement II, supra* note 125, ¶ 8.188.

[243] *Id.* ¶¶ 8.250–8.251.

[244] Panel Report, *United States – Anti-Dumping and Countervailing Duty Measures on Steel Plate from India*, WT/DS206/R and Corr.1, adopted 29 July 2002, ¶ 7.10.

[245] *Id.* ¶ 7.13. [246] Panel Report, *US – Shrimp, supra* note 168, ¶ 7.15.

Payments Committee.[247] The Panel found that notification was more than an admission of fact, and that it implied a recognition that the measures were "quantitative restrictions."[248] In *US – 1916 Act (Japan)*, Japan asked that statements by current and former executive branch officials regarding the status of the measure in question under GATT 1947 be treated as admissions of fact.[249] The United States disputed the factual accuracy of the statements, and for this reason, the Panel was "reluctant to consider them as 'admissions' of the United States without prior verification of the context in which they were made."[250]

In a number of disputes, parties have supported their claims by citing and quoting statements by officials of the other government. However, the Panel in *US – Section 301 Trade Act* cautioned, "A sovereign State should normally not find itself legally affected on the international plane by the casual statement of any of the numerous representatives speaking on its behalf in today's highly interactive and inter-dependent world nor by a representation in the heat of legal argument on a State's behalf."[251] In *Brazil – Aircraft (Article 21.5 – Canada II)*, the Panel did "not preclude that official statements by a Member regarding how it intends to apply a programme could be relevant to an assessment of the WTO-consistency of that programme," but did not view the statements in question as committing Brazil to applying the measure in question in any particular manner.[252]

The Panel in *Chile – Alcoholic Beverages* said that, "It goes without saying that the stated objectives by the *government* of the Member concerned may be relevant in evaluating the *design* of a measure."[253] It went on to observe that, "Statements by a government against WTO interests (*e.g.*, indicating a protective purpose or design) are most probative. Correspondingly, it is less likely that self-serving comments by a government attempting to justify its measure would be particularly probative."[254] In *US – Offset Act*

[247] Panel Report, *India – Quantitative Restrictions on Imports of Agricultural, Textile and Industrial Products*, WT/DS90/R, adopted 22 September 1999, as upheld by the Appellate Body Report, WT/DS90/AB/R, DSR 1999:V, 1799, ¶ 5.123.

[248] *Id.* ¶ 5.124. [249] *Supra* note 151, ¶¶ 6.60–6.61.

[250] *Id. Accord*: Panel Report, *US – 1916 Act (EC), supra* note 150, ¶ 6.64.

[251] Panel Report, *United States – Sections 301–310 of the Trade Act of 1974*, WT/DS152/R, adopted 27 January 2000, DSR 2000:II, 815, ¶ 7.118.

[252] Panel Report, *Brazil – Export Financing Programme for Aircraft – Second Recourse by Canada to Article 21.5 of the DSU*, WT/DS46/RW/2, adopted 23 August 2001, ¶ 5.162.

[253] Panel Report, *Chile – Taxes on Alcoholic Beverages*, WT/DS87/R, WT/DS110/R, adopted 12 January 2000, as modified by the Appellate Body Report, WT/DS87/AB/R, WT/DS110/AB/R, DSR 2000:I, 303, ¶ 7.118 (emphasis in original).

[254] *Id.* ¶ 7.119.

(Byrd Amendment), the United States argued that the stated purpose of a measure could not bring it within the scope of GATT Article VI and the Antidumping and SCM Agreements.[255] The Panel rejected the argument, noting that "acceptance of the US argument that the [measure] is not a 'specific action against dumping' would mean that the [measure] does not do what the US Congress clearly intended it to do."[256]

An issue presented in *US – Section 110(5) Copyright Act* was whether a claimed exception in national legislation met the requirements of Article 13 of the *Agreement on Trade Related Aspects of Intellectual Property Rights*.[257] The Panel said that "public policy purposes stated by lawmakers when enacting a limitation or exception may be useful from a factual perspective for making inferences about the scope of a limitation or exception or the clarity of its definition."[258]

In *Canada – Aircraft Credits and Guarantees*, Brazil pointed to statements by Canada in prior proceedings, but the Panel did not consider it necessary to resolve disagreement concerning those statements, in view of the factual record before it.[259]

[7] Deadlines for submission of evidence

Neither the DSU itself nor its Appendix 3, setting out Working Procedures for panels, establishes time limits for the submission of evidence to a panel. Normally, the Working Procedures adopted by panels for the particular case will address this matter.[260] In *Argentina – Textiles and Apparel*, Argentina objected to the submission of documentary evidence by the United States shortly before the second meeting of the Panel.[261] The Panel noted that "the rules of procedures of panels do not prohibit the practice of submitting additional evidence after the first hearing of the Panel."[262] The Panel accordingly accepted the evidence, but, expressing due process concerns, allowed Argentina an additional two weeks to comment on the documents.[263]

On appeal, the Appellate Body concluded that the Panel's acceptance of the evidence at that time did not amount to an abuse of discretion, but observed that the Panel "could well have exercised its

[255] *Supra* note 157, ¶ 7.41. [256] *Id.*
[257] Panel Report, *United States – Section 110(5) of the US Copyright Act*, WT/DS160/R, adopted 27 July 2000, DSR 2000:VIII, 3769, ¶ 6.97.
[258] *Id.* ¶¶ 6.112, 6.157. [259] *Supra* note 70, ¶ 7.195.
[260] An example of working procedures established by a panel is contained in the Appendix.
[261] *Supra* note 186, ¶ 6.54. [262] *Id.* [263] *Id.*

discretion differently."[264] Before reaching its conclusion, the Appellate Body observed that the Working Procedures in Appendix 3 contemplate two distinguishable stages in a panel proceeding, the first being the presentation of first written submissions and the first meeting of the panel with the parties, and the second being the rebuttal stage. "[T]he complaining party," the Appellate Body said, "should set out its case in chief, including a full presentation of the facts on the basis of submission of supporting evidence, during the first stage. The second stage is generally designed to permit 'rebuttals' by each party of the arguments and evidence submitted by the other parties."[265]

In *Australia – Salmon*, Australia asked that two documents offered by the complainant, Canada, be excluded on the ground that they were submitted after the deadline established by the Panel.[266] One of the documents was excluded, but the Panel allowed the other, since Australia had requested and received an additional week to respond to it. However, the Panel said that the document was not crucial to its determination, and "we shall not further consider it in our examination."[267] The Appellate Body rejected Australia's appeal, finding no evidence that the Panel, contrary to its statement, considered the document. In these circumstances, the Appellate Body "fail[ed] to see how Australia could raise due process concerns."[268] After noting that "panels are permitted to establish their own working procedures, in addition to those set out in Appendix 3," the Appellate Body cautioned that "a panel must also be careful to observe due process, which entails providing the parties adequate opportunity to respond to the evidence submitted."[269]

The Panel in *Australia – Salmon* also accepted a risk analysis conducted by a third country, New Zealand, after its deadline for new evidence. Experts advising the Panel had referred to the New Zealand risk analysis in responding to questions from the Panel, and Canada submitted a copy with its comments on the answer of the experts. In these circumstances, the Panel said it could take the New Zealand analysis into account.[270]

In *Korea – Alcoholic Beverages*, Korea submitted a market study in response to questions posed by the Panel after its first meeting with the parties.[271] When the European Communities responded by submitting its own market study at the second meeting of the Panel,[272] the Panel

[264] *Supra* note 187, ¶ 81. [265] *Id.* ¶ 79. [266] *Supra* note 225, ¶ 8.4. [267] *Id.*

[268] Appellate Body Report, *Australia – Measures Affecting Importation of Salmon*, WT/DS18/AB/R, adopted 6 November 1998, DSR 1998:VIII, 3327, ¶ 271.

[269] *Id.* ¶ 272. [270] *Supra* note 225, ¶ 8.5. [271] *Supra* note 11, ¶ 10.24. [272] *Id.*

gave Korea an extra week to respond to the EC submission, and rejected Korea's argument that this procedure violated its rights. The Panel noted that Korea did not offer its study with its first submission or at the first meeting, and that the European Communities responded at the next available opportunity.[273]

The Panel in *Canada – Aircraft* refused to order that the complaining party could not adduce new evidence after the end of the first substantive meeting of the Panel with the parties. "[A]n absolute rule excluding the submission of evidence by a complaining party after the first substantive meeting would be inappropriate," the Panel said, "since there may be circumstances in which a complaining party is required to adduce new evidence in order to address rebuttal arguments made by the respondent."[274] Shortly thereafter, the Panel in *Canada – Dairy* issued Working Procedures that provided, *inter alia*:

> Parties shall submit all factual evidence to the panel no later than during the first substantive meeting, except with respect to evidence necessary for purposes of rebuttal submissions or answers to questions. Exceptions to this procedure will be granted upon a showing of good cause. In such cases, the other party shall be accorded a period of time for comment, as appropriate.[275]

A similar provision is now included in the Working Procedures of most panels.

In *US – Offset Act (Byrd Amendment)*, Canada sought permission to submit a letter filed with US authorities that did not come into its possession until several weeks after the first Panel meeting, the deadline set in the Panel's Working Procedures for all evidence except rebuttal evidence.[276] The Panel accepted the letter, holding that Canada had shown "good cause" since the letter had not come into its possession until after the deadline, and that it was relevant to an issue the Panel had been asked to consider.[277]

[273] *Id.* ¶ 10.25.

[274] *Supra* note 166, ¶ 9.73. The Panel also noted that there may be instances in which the complaining party is required to adduce new evidence in response to questions from the Panel.

[275] Panel Report, *Canada – Measures Affecting the Importation of Milk and the Exportation of Dairy Products*, WT/DS103/R, WT/DS113/R, adopted 27 October 1999, as modified by the Appellate Body Report, WT/DS103/AB/R and Corr.1, WT/DS113/AB/R, DSR 1999:VI, 2097, ¶ 7.17.

[276] *Supra* note 157, ¶ 7.2.

[277] *Id.*

The Panel in *Chile – Price Brand System* declined to make any changes to its interim report based on the late submission of evidence at the time of the interim review, and the Appellate Body affirmed.[278]

[8] Evidence not used in reaching national decisions

In *EC – Hormones*, the issue was whether the EC had conducted a "risk assessment" prior to imposing the challenged measure. The Panel rejected "new evidence" that was not actually used by the EC.[279] "According to the terms of reference given to us as a dispute settlement panel," the Panel said, "we have no mandate to reexamine the risk assessment referred to by the European Communities in light of this 'new evidence', nor to make our own risk assessment."[280]

This issue has also arisen in trade remedy disputes. In *US – Hot-Rolled Steel*, the Panel held that it could not consider facts or evidence presented to it by a party in an attempt to demonstrate error in the national antidumping determination "unless they had been made available in conformity with the appropriate domestic procedures to the authorities of the investigating country during the investigation."[281] Japan pointed out that it is the investigating authorities themselves who establish the rules concerning the information they will accept and consider, and thus they could unjustly reject information submitted by a party. The Panel noted that "[t]his possibility raises an interesting question which is not really an issue before us."[282] It added, however, that in considering allegations under Article X of GATT, concerning the administration of trade regulations, "we should exercise our discretion to allow the presentation of evidence concerning the administration of the defending Member's anti-dumping laws, which might . . . go beyond the specific facts made available to the administering authority in accordance with appropriate domestic procedures during the course of a single anti-dumping investigation."[283]

In *US – Cotton Yarn*, however, the Panel concluded that it "should examine any evidence, without regard to whether it was available or considered at the time of investigation, for the purpose of evaluating

[278] *Supra* note 179, ¶ 6.3. [279] *Supra* note 147, ¶ 8.114n (US) and ¶ 8.117 (Canada).
[280] *Id.* ¶ 8.115 (US) and ¶ 8.118 (Canada).
[281] Panel Report, *United States – Anti-Dumping Measures on Certain Hot-Rolled Steel Products from Japan*, WT/DS184/R, adopted 23 August 2001, as modified by the Appellate Body Report, WT/DS184/AB/R, ¶ 7.6.
[282] *Id.* ¶ 7.8. [283] *Id.* ¶ 7.10

the thoroughness and sufficiency of the investigation underpinning the decision of the US authority."[284] The Panel expressed the view that it "would not be correct if panels were unable to reverse a fact-finding of a national authority even if the authority overlooked a crucial or decisive fact simply because it was not presented to the authority at the time of investigation."[285] The Appellate Body disagreed. A panel, it said, "has to put itself in the place of that Member at the time it makes its determination. Consequently, a panel must not consider evidence which did not exist *at that point in time.* A Member cannot, of course, be faulted for not having taken into account what it could not have known when making its determination. If a panel were to examine such evidence, the panel would, in effect, be conducting a *de novo* review and it would be doing so without having had the benefit of the view of interested parties."[286] Although this dispute involved the question of transitional safeguards under the *Agreement on Textiles and Clothing*, it seems likely that its reasoning would apply, *mutatis mutandis*, to antidumping and countervailing duty disputes, as well as those under the *Agreement on Safeguards.*

[9] Evidence of municipal law

"Experience suggests," writes a former member of the Appellate Body, "that the determination of the meaning of municipal law of WTO Members can be a delicate task."[287] Many, if not most, "measures" at issue in WTO disputes involve the laws and regulations of Members and, accordingly, can present WTO tribunals with a delicate task.

In the WTO, as in international law generally, municipal law is a question of fact.[288] Nevertheless, when international tribunals establish the "fact" of what "is" municipal law, almost of necessity they "interpret" that law. Thus, the Permanent Court of International Justice said:

[284] Panel Report, *United States – Transitional Safeguard Measure on Combed Cotton Yarn from Pakistan*, WT/DS192/R, adopted 5 November 2001, as modified by the Appellate Body Report, WT/DS192/AB/R, ¶ 7.33.

[285] *Id.* ¶ 7.35.

[286] Appellate Body Report, *United States – Transitional Safeguard Measure on Combed Cotton Yarn from Pakistan*, WT/DS192/AB/R, adopted 5 November 2001, ¶ 78 (emphasis in original).

[287] Claus-Dieter Ehlermann, *Six Years on the Bench of the "World Trade Court" – Some Personal Experiences as a Member of the Appellate Body of the World Trade Organization*, 36 Journal of World Trade 605 (No. 4, August 2002).

[288] Panel Report, *US – Hot-Rolled Steel*, *supra* note 281, ¶ 7.143. For discussion of the Appellate Body's jurisdiction to review panel conclusions concerning the "fact" of municipal law, *see* § 2.08 [2].

> The Court is certainly not called upon to interpret the Polish law as such; but there is nothing to prevent the Court's giving judgment on the question whether or not, in applying that law, Poland is acting in conformity with its obligations towards Germany under the Geneva Convention.[289]

This language was quoted by the Appellate Body in *India – Patents (US)* in response to the argument that the Panel had not treated India's law as a fact to be established by the United States, but as a law to be interpreted by the Panel.[290] "It is clear that an examination of the relevant aspects of Indian municipal law . . . is essential to determining whether India has complied with its obligations," the Appellate Body said.[291] It added:

> There was simply no way for the Panel to make this determination without engaging in an examination of Indian law. But, as in the case cited above before the Permanent Court of International Justice, in this case, the Panel was not interpreting Indian law "as such"; rather, the Panel was examining Indian law solely for the purpose of determining whether India had met its obligations under the *TRIPS Agreement.* To say that the Panel should have done otherwise would be to say that only India can assess whether Indian law is consistent with India's obligations under the *WTO Agreement.* This, clearly, cannot be so.[292]

The Panel in *US – Section 301 Trade Act* referred to the Appellate Body Report in *India – Patents (US)* in noting that its obligation was "to examine aspects of municipal law . . . solely for the purpose of determining whether the US meets its WTO obligations."[293] The Panel saw its task as not to interpret US law "as such," but to "establish the meaning of Sections 301–310 as factual elements and to check whether these factual elements constitute conduct by the US contrary to its WTO obligations."[294] Establishing the meaning of municipal law as a fact, the Panel

[289] *Certain German Interests in Polish Upper Silesia,* [1926], PCIJ Rep, Series A, No. 7, p. 19.

[290] *Supra* note 34, ¶¶ 64–65.

[291] *Id.* ¶ 66.

[292] *Id.* The Appellate Body cited the GATT Panel Report in *United States – Section 337 of the Tariff Act of 1930,* BISD 36S/345, adopted 7 November 1989, "where the Panel conducted a detailed examination of the relevant United States' legislation and practice, including the remedies available under Section 337 as well as the differences between patent-based Section 337 proceedings and federal district court proceedings, in order to determine whether Section 337 was inconsistent with Article III:4 of the GATT 1947." *Id.* ¶ 67. *See* also: Appellate Body Report, *United States – Anti-Dumping Measures on Certain Hot-Rolled Steel Products from* Japan, WT/DS184/AB/R, adopted 23 August 2001, ¶ 200: "Although it is not the role of panels or the Appellate Body to interpret a Member's domestic legislation as such, it is permissible, indeed essential, to conduct a detailed examination of that legislation in assessing its consistency with WTO law."

[293] *Supra* note 251, ¶¶ 7.17–7.18.

[294] *Id.* ¶ 7.18.

noted, may involve an examination of the jurisprudence of municipal courts.[295]

In *US – 1916 Act (EC)*, both parties relied on a number of not always consistent judgments of US courts interpreting the law in question.[296] After citing the ICJ judgment in the *ELSI* case, and its quotation from the PCIJ judgment in the *Brazilian Loans* case, the Panel observed that, "there is nothing in the text of the DSU, nor in the practice of the Appellate Body, that prevents us from 'weigh[ing] the jurisprudence of municipal [US] courts' if it is 'uncertain or divided.' "[297] After describing the methodology it would employ in reviewing the US case law on the 1916 Act, the Panel, reflecting the "municipal law as fact" doctrine, said:

> If, after having applied the above methodology, we could not reach certainty as to the most appropriate court interpretation, i.e. if the evidence remains in equipoise, we shall follow the interpretation that favours the party against which the claim has been made, considering that the claimant did not convincingly support its claim.[298]

The Panel in *US – Countervailing Measures*, also citing the *Brazilian Loans* judgment, quoted from the *ELSI* judgment, terming it a "well-established practice of international jurisprudence."[299] In *US – Shrimp*, the statute in question had been interpreted by a lower court, but that interpretation was appealed and could have been interpreted by the appellate court to require action inconsistent with WTO obligations. The Panel declined to anticipate this result, and noted that the appellate court's decision itself could be appealed to the Supreme Court.[300] Instead, the Panel based its determination on the situation presently before it.[301]

The judiciary is, of course, considered part of the government of Members, and Members bear responsibility for the acts of their judiciary

295 *Id.* note 635, referring to the ICJ judgment in *Elettronica Sicula S.p.A. (ELSI)* Judgment, ICJ Reports 1989, p. 47, ¶ 62, quoting from the PCIJ judgment in *Brazilian Loans*, PCIJ, Series A, Nos. 20/21, p. 124: "Where the determination of a question of municipal law is essential to the Court's decision in a case, the Court will weigh the jurisprudence of the municipal courts and if this is uncertain or divided, it will rest with the Court to select the interpretation which it considers most in conformity with the law."

296 *Supra* note 150, ¶ 6.52.

297 *Id.* ¶ 6.53. Citations to the ICJ and PCIJ judgments are provided *supra* in note 295.

298 *Id.* ¶ 6.58.

299 Panel Report, *United States – Countervailing Measures Concerning Certain Products from the European Communities*, WT/DS212/R, adopted 8 January 2003, as modified by the Appellate Body Report, WT/DS212/AB/R, ¶ 7.124.

300 *Supra* note 168, ¶ 5.109.

301 *Id.*

that may be contrary to WTO obligations.[302] Judicial decisions, however, are not the only materials available to panels in interpreting municipal law. In *US – Countervailing Measures*, the Panel found it "necessary to look to other domestic interpretive tools such as the legislative history" in establishing the meaning of the legislation, "to the extent that [these materials] form part of the effective operationalization of the legislation."[303]

Panels take seriously the explanations Members offer of their own laws.[304] Thus, in *Canada – Pharmaceutical Patents*, the Panel concluded that the complainant had not presented sufficient evidence to overcome Canada's formal declaration that an exception contained in the law at issue was not limited to pharmaceutical products and, therefore, was not *de jure* discriminatory.[305] "In reaching this conclusion, the Panel took note that its legal finding of conformity on this point was based on a finding as to the meaning of the Canadian law that was in turn based on Canada's presentations as to the meaning of that law."[306] Similarly, in *Korea – Procurement*, the Panel accepted the explanation of Korea that the references in its Government Organization Act to specific offices, such as Vice Minister, Deputy Administrator and Office Director, were, in its system, references to "subordinate linear organizations" since the areas of responsibility of the named positions correspond to the responsibilities of the subordinate organizations for which the positions are responsible.[307]

In *US – Section 301 Trade Act*, where the question was the legality of the legislation itself, the Panel stated that "in principle, internal elements legally relevant to the construction of the legislation should be determinative."[308] Accordingly, the Panel found that an official Statement of Administrative Action, made in a domestic context, before Congress on the occasion of the implementation of the Uruguay Round negotiations, was determinative of the fact that the US intended to implement the measure consistent with its international obligations, even though "we have rejected the view that the statutory language . . . itself precludes

302 Appellate Body Report, *US – Shrimp*, *supra* note 171, ¶ 173.

303 *Supra* note 299, ¶ 7.139.

304 *See* generally, Michael Lennard, *Navigating by the Stars: Interpreting the WTO Agreements*, *supra* note 4, 72–75. Also *see* § 4.09 [6].

305 Panel Report, *Canada – Patent Protection of Pharmaceutical Products*, WT/DS114/R, adopted 7 April 2000, DSR 2000:V, 2295, ¶ 7.99.

306 *Id.*

307 Panel Report, *Korea – Measures Affecting Government Procurement*, WT/DS163/R, adopted 19 June 2000, DSR 2000:VIII, 3541, ¶ 7.34.

308 *Supra* note 251, ¶ 7.114.

a determination of inconsistency."[309] Further, the Panel said, although "[a]ttributing international legal significance to unilateral statements made by a State should not be done lightly," and although a "sovereign State should normally not find itself legally affected on the international plane by the casual statement of any of the numerous representatives speaking on its behalf in today's highly interactive and inter-dependent world,"[310] the Panel concluded that statements made before it were a reflection of official policy intended to express "US understanding of its international obligations as incorporated in domestic US law."[311]

In *India – Autos*, the Panel accepted India's statement that Memoranda of Understanding between India and domestic auto manufacturers were no longer binding on the manufacturers.[312]

[10] Sufficiency and forms of evidence

WTO Panels, like other international tribunals, "are generally free to admit and evaluate evidence of every kind, and to ascribe to it the weight that they see fit."[313] There is, as a panel has observed, "a significant and substantive difference between questions concerning the admissibility of evidence, and the weight to be accorded evidence."[314] Because most "measures" involved in disputes are laws or regulations, evidentiary issues surrounding other facts are not involved in many cases. Nevertheless, these issues do arise from time to time.

In *Indonesia – Autos*, the Panel noted that evidence with regard to the planned introduction of certain models "is very general, and supporting documentation, with the exception of newspaper reports and letters prepared by GM, Ford and Chrysler for the purposes of this dispute, is non-existent."[315] The Panel went on to explain that it did "not mean to suggest that in WTO dispute settlement there are any rigid evidentiary rules regarding the admissibility of newspaper reports or the need to demonstrate factual assertions through contemporaneous source information."[316] However, the Panel noted, "the affected companies certainly had at their disposal copious evidence in support of the claims of the complainants."[317] This would have included, the Panel said, actual

309 *Id.* ¶ 7.117. 310 *Id.* ¶ 7.118. 311 *Id.* ¶ 7.121.

312 Panel Report, *India – Measures Affecting the Automotive Sector*, WT/DS146/R, WT/DS175/R and Corr.1, adopted after appeal withdrawn, 5 April 2002, ¶ 7.235.

313 Panel Report, *EC – Bed Linen*, *supra* note 93, ¶ 6.34. 314 *Id.* ¶ 6.33.

315 *Supra* note 74, ¶ 14.233. 316 *Id.* ¶ 14.234. 317 *Id.*

business plans, corporate minutes, and internal decision memoranda relating to the approval and subsequent abandonment of the plans in question. The fact that contemporaneous company documents were not submitted, and that the complainant relied instead upon news reports of its own industry's activities, led the Panel to conclude that the complainant had not demonstrated the effects of the subsidies in question "by positive evidence."[318]

It may be important to note that the panel in *Indonesia – Autos* was confronted with a situation in which the complaining party used news articles to document the alleged adverse effects upon its own industry. The situation could well be different when a party relies on press reports to document the activities of the other party or its industry, since press reports may be the only evidence available to the party.

The Panel in *Argentina – Textiles and Apparel* admitted invoices covering imports from countries other than the complainant United States because, "The issue before the Panel is whether Argentina's measures lead to the imposition of duties above its bound rate of 35 percent *ad valorem*, irrespective of source."[319] The Panel also accepted invoices relating to transactions that took place after consultations were initiated as they contributed to the Panel's understanding of "the way the Argentine tariff system functions."[320]

On appeal, Argentina challenged the Panel's conclusion that the US had adduced sufficient evidence to establish a *prima facie* case.[321] The question was whether specific duties imposed by Argentina exceeded the *ad valorem* rates bound under Article II. The US had submitted statistical evidence showing that for 118 tariff categories, the specific duties collected exceeded the bound rates. Argentina argued that this evidence did not support a finding involving all 940 relevant categories. The Panel had concluded, however, that the US had submitted sufficient evidence to establish a *prima facie* case, and that Argentina had not submitted any contrary evidence to rebut it. This result was affirmed by the Appellate Body.[322]

In *EC – Computer Equipment*, a dispute involving tariff classification, the complainant, the United States, submitted evidence that included a Binding Tariff Information issued by Ireland, letters from the UK Customs and Excise, and letters from the four leading US exporters of

[318] *Id.* ¶ 14.236. [319] *Supra* note 186, ¶ 6.60. [320] *Id.* ¶ 6.63.
[321] *Supra* note 187, ¶ 61. [322] *Id.*

the product.[323] The Panel found that the evidence was sufficient to raise a presumption that the US claim was correct.[324]

Other evidentiary rulings of panels include: acceptance of a market research report on the drinking habits of a representative sample of consumers;[325] and raw numerical data as "relevant evidence" rather than "simple assertion" within the meaning of Article 5 of the Antidumping Agreement.[326] In *US – Steel Countervailing Duties*, the Panel said that, in review proceedings, investigating authorities are required to consider factual evidence already in their possession from an original countervailing duty investigation. They "cannot remain completely passive and expect the exporters to formally submit information that is in the possession of the investigating authorities in connection with the original investigation."[327] When circumstantial evidence is used, "it must lead clearly and convincingly to the conclusion sought. Reasonable alternatives must be eliminated."[328]

While the weighing and *assessing* of evidence is outside the scope of appellate review,[329] questions of law concerning evidence are within the Appellate Body's purview. In this regard, the Appellate Body has concluded that, "evidence from other markets may be pertinent to the examination of the market at issue, particularly when demand on that market has been influenced by regulatory barriers to trade or to competition."[330]

§ 4.10 Confidential information

[1] Overview

Confidentiality is an integral part of the WTO dispute settlement process. No fewer than six articles of the DSU deal with some aspect

[323] *Supra* note 98, ¶ 8.36. [324] *Id.* ¶ 8.38.

[325] Panel Report, *Chile – Alcoholic Beverages*, *supra* note 253, ¶ 7.34.

[326] Panel Report, *Thailand – H-Beams*, *supra* note 191, ¶ 7.77.

[327] *Supra* note 75, ¶ 8.118.

[328] Panel Report, *Argentina – Measures Affecting the Exports of Bovine Hides and the Imports of Finished Leather*, WT/DS155/R and Corr.1, adopted 16 February 2001, ¶ 11.50.

[329] Appellate Body Report, *India – Quantitative Restrictions on Imports of Agricultural, Textile and Industrial Products*, WT/DS90/AB/R, adopted 22 September 1999, DSR 1999:IV, 1763, ¶ 144.

[330] Appellate Body Report, *Korea – Taxes on Alcoholic Beverages*, WT/DS75/AB/R, WT/DS84/AB/R, adopted 17 February 1999, DSR 1999:1, 3, ¶ 137.

of confidentiality, as do paragraphs of two of its appendices.[331] While any dispute settlement regime that deals with information that is inherently confidential, as does the WTO, must make provision for that fact, much of the confidentiality that applies to dispute settlement reflects the WTO's diplomatic roots in GATT, and the preference of Members who see that approach as superior to more publicly visible litigation.

Article 4.6 of the DSU provides for confidentiality of consultations, while Article 5.2 does the same for efforts at good offices, conciliation and mediation.[332] Article 13.1 provides that confidential information that is submitted to a panel shall not be revealed without authorization of the person or government that supplied it. Pursuant to Article 14.1, the panel process itself is kept confidential, while Article 17.10 provides the same for the appellate process. Article 18.2 requires panels and the Appellate Body to treat written submissions as confidential, although Members may make their own submissions public. Paragraph 3 of the Working Procedures set out in Appendix 3 to the DSU specifies that, "The deliberations of the panel and the documents submitted to it shall be kept confidential," while paragraph 5 of Appendix 4, dealing with Expert Review Groups, provides confidentiality for information submitted to those groups. All provisions providing for the confidentiality of written documents require non-confidential summaries. As the practice has developed, at the end of both the panel and appellate processes, the arguments of the parties and the reasoning of the panel are made public in the reports of the tribunals. Only information designated as confidential by the submitter is exempt from disclosure.

[2] Issues involving private counsel and advisors

The legal complexity of the WTO Agreements and the resulting complexity of dispute settlement have increased the demand for the services of lawyers, a phenomenon that began under GATT in the late 1980s and early 1990s. Most Members, particularly developing country Members, do not have the resources to support a permanent staff of legal experts. While most developed country Members do have legal specialists in Geneva or in their capitals, they increasingly support these experts with

[331] The *Agreement on Implementation of Article VI of GATT 1994* (the Antidumping Agreement), the *Agreement on Implementation of Article VII of GATT 1994* (Customs Valuation), and the *Agreement on Technical Barriers to Trade* contain special provisions regarding confidential information. *See* §§ 5.07, 5.08.

[332] Confidentiality in consultations is discussed *supra* in § 4.03 [5].

private counsel who they or interested private stakeholders retain. Indeed, Members often obtain assistance from counsel for private interests with a stake in the outcome of the proceedings.

Under GATT, private attorneys did not present cases directly to the panels; this task was performed only by government officials. Private attorneys simply advised, counseled and drafted submissions. However, the increased legalization of the WTO process soon led to efforts to have private counsel assist in the presentation of cases to panels. Initially, this was resisted by the developed countries. In *EC – Bananas III*, the Panel excluded outside counsel, in part on confidentiality grounds.[333] When the case reached the Appellate Body, the issue arose again, but with a different result: the Appellate Body held that it is for the Member concerned to determine who shall represent it, and that this may include private attorneys.[334] The issue of confidentiality, however, was not discussed by the Appellate Body.

In *Korea – Alcoholic Beverages*, the Panel granted Korea's request that it be assisted by private counsel, noting that "Korea assumes full responsibility for confidentiality of the proceedings on behalf of all members of its delegation, including non-government employees."[335] The Panel went on to note that submissions containing confidential information also may be provided to non-government advisors who are not members of a delegation. "The duty of confidentiality," it said, "extends to all governments that are parties to a dispute and to all such advisors regardless of whether they are designated as members of delegations and appear at a Panel meeting."[336]

The Appellate Body first spoke on the issue of confidentiality in the appeal of *Canada – Aircraft*, where Canada expressed the view that existing DSU provisions did not provide adequate protection, and asked that special procedures be adopted.[337] In denying Canada's request, the Appellate Body said that, "a Member's obligation to maintain the confidentiality of these proceedings extends also to the individuals whom that member selects to act as its representatives, counsel and consultants."[338]

333 *Supra* note 33, ¶ 7.11(d).

334 Appellate Body Report, *European Communities – Regime for the Importation, Sale and Distribution of Bananas*, WT/DS27/AB/R, adopted 25 September 1997, DSR 1997:II, 591, ¶ 10. The Appellate Body's action did not reverse the Panel's decision, since the issue had not been appealed; the question simply recurred when a third party sought to have private counsel present its arguments to the Appellate Body. See § 6.04 [16].

335 *Supra* note 11, ¶ 10.31.

336 *Id.* ¶ 10.32.

337 *Supra* note 190, ¶¶ 127–129.

338 *Id.* ¶ 141.

An apparent breach of confidentiality requirements occurred in *Thailand – H Beams*, where Thailand complained that an *amicus curiae* brief, submitted by an industry group, contained references to Thailand's confidential submission that indicated familiarity with that submission.[339] The same law firm was counsel to Poland, the complainant, and to the industry group that submitted the brief.[340] Poland informed the Appellate Body that it had provided no assistance to the industry group, and that it had accepted the law firm's withdrawal as legal counsel in the appeal.[341] The Appellate Body again noted that Members of the WTO involved in dispute settlement are "fully responsible under the DSU and the other covered agreements for any acts of their officials as well as their representatives, counsel or consultants."[342]

In *Brazil – Aircraft (Article 21.5 – Canada II)*, Brazil objected when a Canadian official gave a copy of the written text of Brazil's confidential statement to the Panel to persons outside the meeting room who were not members of Canada's delegation.[343] The Panel, citing the Appellate Body's language in *Canada – Aircraft* as well as its Working Procedures, which envisioned disclosure to members of a delegation "as well as any other advisors," concluded that Canada had not violated confidentiality requirements.[344] The Panel found it important that "Canada has represented that the members of the law firm who have had access to Brazil's submissions . . . are subject to a confidentiality agreement with the Government of Canada which requires them not to disclose any such information, including to . . . their client."[345]

[3] Special procedures to protect confidentiality

While the Appellate Body in *Canada – Aircraft* found that DSU rules were adequate to insure confidentiality in that appeal, several panels have exercised their discretion to make special provision for confidential information. This has been true, in particular, of "trade remedy" cases involving antidumping, subsidies, and safeguards involving so-called "business confidential information" or "BCI."

In *Indonesia – Autos*, which involved a number of issues including subsidies, the complainant United States informed the Panel that it possessed further relevant information, but "was reluctant" to provide

339 *Supra* note 88, ¶ 64. 340 *Id.* ¶ 71. 341 *Id.* 342 *Id.* ¶ 68.
343 *Supra* note 252, ¶ 3.1. 344 *Id.* ¶ 3.7. 345 *Id.* ¶ 3.13.

it to the Panel and the parties in the absence of "adequate procedures" to protect it.[346] The Panel noted that Article 18.2 of the DSU allows parties to designate information as confidential, and said that if the US believes that the protection afforded by Article 18.2 is inadequate, it could propose procedures it considers sufficient to afford protection.[347] The US did not accept this invitation, however, leading the Panel to state that, "While complainants cannot be required to submit confidential business information to WTO dispute settlement panels, neither may they invoke confidentiality as a basis for their failure to submit the positive evidence required."[348]

Canada – Aircraft was a subsidies case in which Canada, the respondent, asked the Panel to adopt special procedures for the protection of BCI, and Brazil, the complainant, agreed.[349] Although Article 18.2 provides for the protection of confidential information, the Panel said, Article 12.1 permits panels to adopt working procedures in addition to those set forth in the DSU. "Given the sensitive nature of the BCI that could be submitted to the Panel in the present case, and given the agreement between the parties on the need for additional protection of such Business Confidential Information, the Panel decided to adopt special Procedures Governing Business Confidential Information that go beyond the protection afforded by Article 18.2 of the DSU."[350]

The Panel in *Australia – Automotive Leather II*, another subsidies case, also adopted special procedures governing BCI pursuant to which only persons who filed a declaration of non-disclosure with the Chair of the Panel were granted access to BCI. Pursuant to the special procedures, the Panel was under an obligation not to disclose BCI in its interim and final reports, but could make statements of conclusion drawn from that information.[351]

A major dispute over BCI arose in the Article 22.6 arbitration in *Bananas III (Article 22.6 – 2000)*.[352] The Arbitrators asked the United States to explain the methodology it applied in calculating its proposed

[346] *Supra* note 74, ¶ 14.5. [347] *Id.* ¶ 14.7.

[348] *Id.* ¶ 14.235; *see* also, Panel Report, *Canada – Aircraft*, *supra* note 166, ¶¶ 9.56–9.69.

[349] *Supra* note 166, ¶¶ 9.54–9.55.

[350] *Id.* ¶ 9.56. Those Procedures are set forth in Annex I to the Panel Report. As noted above in Section 4.10 [2], when the case was appealed, the Appellate Body concluded that the obligations of confidentiality imposed by the DSU were adequate, and that special BCI procedures were not needed.

[351] *Supra* note 39, ¶ 4.1. [352] *Supra* note 111.

suspension of concessions.[353] Before responding, the US asked the Arbitrators to establish two categories of BCI: "regular" and "super." Regular BCI would consist of "company-specific information that was non-public and sensitive, but that could be extrapolated from other public and non-public information available to governments and the company's competitors."[354] Super BCI would include "non-public, sensitive company-specific information that could not be so extrapolated."[355]

The EC objected, arguing that working procedures on confidentiality should not be adopted case-by-case, but by the WTO as a whole. Special procedures were unnecessary, the EC said, because its officials were bound by confidentiality obligations contained in the EC Treaty. Moreover, according to the EC, the special procedures proposed would cause practical problems if the information were not available at its Brussels headquarters.[356]

After the Arbitrators decided to adopt BCI procedures – without special treatment for "super" BCI – the EC said it could not accept the procedures, and that the Arbitrators' acceptance of BCI information in these circumstances would amount to an *ex parte* contact, prohibited by Article 18.1 of the DSU.[357] The Arbitrators disagreed with the EC's conclusion that their refusal to accept the information under the procedures established by the Arbitrators would constitute an *ex parte* contact. "Acceptance of the EC argument," they said, "would mean that a party's refusal to participate in a proceeding would effectively prevent the proceeding from going forward."[358] In the end, the point was moot, since the Arbitrators did not find it necessary to use the US information.[359]

In *Canada – Dairy (Article 21.5 – New Zealand and US)*, the Panel specified that, "a party requesting the adoption of BCI procedures should clearly explain to the Panel what kind of information it may be unable to obtain and disclose but for the adoption of BCI procedures, in order to enable the Panel to assess the need for such BCI Procedures."[360]

In its first written submission in *Thailand – H-Beams*, an antidumping dispute, Thailand sought to submit confidential information only to the

[353] *Id.* ¶ 2.1. [354] *Id.* ¶ 2.3. [355] *Id.* [356] *Id.* ¶ 2.4.
[357] *Id.* ¶ 2.6. [358] *Id.* [359] *Id.* ¶ 2.7.
[360] Panel Report, *Canada – Measures Affecting the Importation of Milk and the Exportation of Dairy Products – Recourse to Article 21.5 of the DSU by New Zealand and the United States*, WT/DS103/RW, WT/DS113/RW, adopted 18 December 2001, as reversed (on other grounds) by the Appellate Body Report, WT/DS103/AB/RW, WT/DS113/AB/RW, ¶ 2.19.

Panel, stating that it did not intend to provide that information to Poland, the complainant, or to third parties.[361] Thailand cited Article 17.7 of the Antidumping Agreement which provides, *inter alia*, that "Confidential information provided to the panel shall not be disclosed without formal authorization from the person, body or authority providing such information." After consultation with the parties, the Panel established supplemental procedures concerning confidential information, and Thailand agreed to provide the information to Poland and the third parties.[362] In the end, however, the confidential information was not used by the Panel, as it declined to base its review on confidential information to which the Polish firms or their counsel did not have access at the time of the final determination in the underlying antidumping proceeding.[363]

In *EC – Bed Linen*, India submitted a dumping calculation from an investigation different from the one that was the subject of the dispute.[364] The EC objected, arguing that submission of the exhibit in the *Bed Linens* case would constitute a breach of confidentiality obligations in the other case.[365] However, the party to whom the information belonged submitted a waiver of its rights and consented to the Panel's use of the information, which was therefore accepted by the Panel.[366]

When the Panel in *US – Line Pipe*, a dispute under the Safeguards Agreement, requested information from the confidential report of the United States International Trade Commission, the US provided indexed data. The Panel determined that this was sufficient.[367] In *Argentina – Textiles and Apparel*, Argentina challenged the validity of invoices submitted as evidence because the name of the importer and all relevant data that could help identify the importer or exporter had been deleted.[368] The Panel, however, accepted the invoices in evidence, observing that, "it is often the practice in disputes, such as this one, for a party to protect commercial in-confidence information such as the names and other information of the private entities involved."[369] However, a party can go so far with redacting that the resulting document is of no use to the Panel.[370]

[361] *Supra* note 191, ¶ 5.1.

[362] *Id.* ¶ 5.2. The supplemental procedures are attached to the Report as Annex 5.

[363] *Id.* ¶ 7.247. [364] *Supra* note 93, ¶ 6.36. [365] *Id.* [366] *Id.* ¶ 6.40.

[367] Panel Report, *United States – Definitive Safeguard Measures on Imports of Circular Welded Carbon Quality Line Pipe from Korea*, WT/DS202/R, adopted 8 March 2002, as modified by the Appellate Body Report, WT/DS202/AB/R, ¶¶ 7.9–7.11.

[368] *Supra* note 186, ¶ 6.53. [369] *Id.* ¶ 6.59.

[370] *See*, Panel Report, *Canada – Aircraft, supra* note 166, ¶¶ 9.313 and 9.345.

An agreement between private parties was relevant in *US – Section 110(5) Copyright Act*, a dispute that arose under the TRIPS Agreement.[371] The US was not able to furnish a copy of the agreement because it contained a non-disclosure provision, and one of the parties, claiming that the agreement contained proprietary information, refused to permit disclosure.[372] In considering the agreement, therefore, the Panel said, "we have had to rely on other indirect information provided to us by the parties."[373]

As noted *supra* in Section 4.09 [4], in the *US – Wheat Gluten* safeguard dispute, both the Panel and the Appellate Body noted a serious systemic issue between the confidentiality requirements of Article 3.2 of the *Agreement on Safeguards* and the obligation of panels, under Article 11 of the DSU, to make an objective assessment of the facts. This issue remains unresolved.

[4] Government information

In *Australia – Salmon (Article 21.5 – Canada)*, the Panel received a request from Australia to adopt additional procedures to ensure the protection of "Government Confidential Information" that Australia had been requested to submit.[374] The information was described as reports that were open only to the Australian Government. No direct business interests were involved. "The matter [was] one mainly of government to government relationships."[375] Citing the Appellate Body's refusal to adopt special provisions in *Canada – Aircraft*, and noting Article 18.2, its own Working Procedures, and Article VII:1 of the Rules of Conduct of the DSU, the Panel concluded that only two additions needed to be made to its Working Procedures to protect the information.[376] The additions provided that the information would not be disclosed in the Panel's report and that, after circulation of the report, it would be returned.[377] In *Canada – Aircraft*, the Panel declined to accept "cabinet privilege" as a justification for withholding information.[378] In situations involving national security, the Panel said, "a Member may consider itself justified in withholding certain information from a panel. However, in such circumstances, we would expect that Member to explain clearly the basis for

[371] *Supra* note 257.
[372] *Id.* ¶ 6.203. [373] *Id.* [374] *Supra* note 230, ¶ 7.7. [375] *Id.* [376] *Id.*
[377] *Id.* [378] *Supra* note 166, ¶ 9.345.

the need to protect the information."[379] In the case before the Panel, no explanation was given.[380]

§ 4.11 Burden of proof

[1] General[381]

The burden of proof has been called "the law's response to ignorance."[382] It "compensates for the many uncertainties of litigation, allowing the judicial system to reach determinate outcomes in the absence of relevant information."[383] As dispute proceedings, first in GATT and now in the WTO, grew more complex and more juridical, the question of burden of proof became an increasingly important part of panel reports. This trend is likely to continue.

In the WTO, as in any mature legal system, the party asserting a fact, whether claimant or respondent, is responsible for providing proof of that fact.[384] The language of the Appellate Body in *US – Wool Shirts and Blouses* has been cited repeatedly in subsequent reports whenever burden of proof issues arose:

> It is a generally accepted canon of evidence in civil law, common law, and, in fact, most jurisdictions, that the burden of proof rests upon the party, whether complaining or defending, who asserts the affirmative of a particular claim or defence. If that party adduces sufficient evidence to raise a presumption that what is claimed is true, the burden then shifts to the other party, who will fail unless it adduces sufficient evidence to rebut the presumption.[385]

[379] *Id.* at footnote 633 to ¶ 9.347. [380] *Id.*

[381] *See* generally, Joost Pauwelyn, *Evidence, Proof and Persuasion in WTO Dispute Settlement*, 1 JOURNAL OF INTERNATIONAL ECONOMIC LAW 227 (1998); Rutsel Silvestre J. Martha, *Presumptions and Burden of Proof in World Trade Law*, 14 JOURNAL OF INTERNATIONAL ARBITRATION 67 (No. 1, March 1997); Mojtaba Kazazi, BURDEN OF PROOF AND RELATED ISSUES: A STUDY ON EVIDENCE BEFORE INTERNATIONAL TRIBUNALS (Kluwer, 1996).

[382] Richard H. Gaskin, BURDENS OF PROOF IN MODERN DISCOURSE 4 (Yale, 1992).

[383] *Id.*

[384] Appellate Body Report, *United States – Measure Affecting Imports of Woven Wool Shirts and Blouses from India*, WT/DS33/AB/R and Corr.1, adopted 23 May 1997, DSR 1997:I, 323, § IV, at 16.

[385] *Id.* § 14.

In a case of uncertainty, when all of the evidence and arguments remain in equipoise, the benefit of the doubt is given to the party that does not bear the burden of proof.[386]

A panel is not required to make specific findings, in each and every instance, that a party has met its burden of proof in respect of a particular claim, or that a party has rebutted a *prima facie case.*[387]

[2] Burden of proving a prima facie *case*

WTO jurisprudence raises some questions as to what – precisely – it is that parties are obliged to establish *prima facie.* It does not appear that complaining parties necessarily are obliged to establish a *prima facie* case, a case "which, in the absence of effective refutation by the defending party, requires a panel, as a matter of law, to rule in favour of the complaining party."[388] However, a complaining party that is unable to do so is running a risk of failure. Conversely, a defending party that believes the complaining party has not made *prima facie* and, consequently, decides to forego presentation of a defense also is running a risk of failure.

Lawyers trained in common law systems are particularly likely to find this confusing. Their confusion results from the fact that, contrary to what prevails in most common law proceedings, WTO panels are *not* confined to the factual record made by the parties. As detailed above, Article 13 of the DSU authorizes a panel to seek information "from any individual or body which it deems appropriate."[389] This information may supplement that provided by the parties. In this regard, WTO panels follow the practice of courts in the civil law system, as do most international tribunals.[390] For example, in *Indonesia – Autos*, the Panel considered whether the subsidies at issue were "specific" subsidies within the meaning of Articles 1 and 2 of the *SCM Agreement.* Both the complaining and responding parties agreed that they were. In most common law jurisdictions, this would be

[386] Panel Report, *US – Section 301 Trade Act, supra* note 251, ¶ 7.14; *Accord*: Panel Report, *EC – Asbestos, supra* note 239, ¶ 8.79.

[387] Appellate Body Report, *Thailand – H-Beams, supra* note 88, ¶ 134.

[388] Appellate Body Report, *EC Hormones, supra* note 149, ¶ 104.

[389] DSU Art. 13.1. *See, in particular,* §§ 4.09 [2]–4.09 [4].

[390] Even when a party fails to appear, the International Court of Justice, unlike most common law courts, cannot simply enter a default judgment against that party. Article 53 of the Statute of the ICJ provides that the Court first must satisfy itself that a claim against a non-appearing party is well founded in law. *See* Stanimir A. Alexandrov, *Non-Appearance before the International Court of Justice*, 33 COLUMBIA JOURNAL OF TRANSNATIONAL LAW 41 (1995).

the end of the matter. But it was not necessarily enough for the panel: "In light of the views of the parties, *and given that nothing in the record would compel a different conclusion*, we find that the measures in question are specific subsidies within the meaning of Articles 1 and 2 of the *SCM Agreement*."[391] Similarly, the Appellate Body, in discussing the obligation of a panel to make an "objective assessment of the facts" under Article 11 of the DSU, said, "a panel has the duty to examine and consider all the evidence before it, not just the evidence submitted by one or the other party, and to evaluate the relevance and probative force of each piece thereof."[392] A panel's duty to examine and consider all of the evidence does not mean, however, that a panel can make a case for a party that it has not made for itself. This action would be covered by the doctrine of *non ultra petita*.[393]

This practice contrasts sharply with the usual practice in common law jurisdictions where, after the complainant has presented its case, the responding party normally may move for judgment on the ground that all of the evidence presented *by the complainant* does not, in and of itself, constitute a violation of the law. There is no counterpart to such a motion in WTO practice. Thus, while a complainant whose initial submission does not adequately document a violation by a respondent obviously runs a risk, the respondent does not have a legal right to judgment at that point, since the possibility remains that additional evidence, supporting the complainant, will be or has otherwise been made available to the panel.[394]

The Panel in *Canada – Aircraft* noted that while "a critical decision for panels in every case is whether or not a *prima facie* case has been

391 *Supra* note 74, ¶ 14.155 (emphasis added). It should be noted that Article 6.8 of the *SCM Agreement* provides that, except in certain limited circumstances, "the existence of serious prejudice should be determined on the basis of the information submitted to *or obtained by* the panel." However, since panels are authorized by Article 13 of the DSU to seek information from any source, clearly their determinations in all cases can be based, at least in part, on information they *obtain*. (Emphasis added).

392 Appellate Body Report, *Korea – Dairy*, *supra* note 84, ¶ 137.

393 *See* § 2.02 [4].

394 This system is not totally unfamiliar to trade lawyers in the United States, despite their common law training. Antidumping and countervailing duty investigations before both the Department of Commerce and the United States International Trade Commission proceed in a fashion that greatly resembles the civil law procedure followed in the WTO. Proceedings before both agencies are "investigative," not adversarial, and thus, while parties have the burden of proving their claims, at the risk of having them not be accepted, the agency record is not necessarily confined to information supplied by the parties. Both agencies themselves investigate and independently develop evidence used to support their conclusions.

established, and whether or not the respondent has rebutted any such *prima facie* case, in practice these decisions are made in light of all of the evidence adduced by the parties, including both written and oral submissions. Such decisions are, therefore, necessarily made in the latter stages of the panel process."[395] The Panel went on to say that a defending party could defend itself fully "by simply assuming that Brazil had, or would, establish a *prima facie* case in respect of all its claims."[396]

When Canada declined to furnish information requested by the *Aircraft* Panel, the Panel said it "regret[ted] deeply Canada's refusal," but proceeded to find Brazil had not established its claim.[397] Brazil appealed the Panel's failure to draw adverse inferences from Canada's refusal to comply with its requests.[398] While upholding the Panel, the Appellate Body said that, "a panel should be willing expressly to remind parties – during the course of dispute settlement proceedings – that a refusal to provide information requested by the panel may lead to inferences being drawn about the inculpatory character of the information withheld."[399] However, the Appellate Body held that the Panel's declining to draw adverse inferences was not an abuse of discretion, and therefore "let the Panel's finding of *not proven* remain."[400]

Arguably, had the Panel drawn adverse inferences from Canada's failure to respond, those inferences combined with the complainant's evidence could have been enough to establish a *prima facie* case, even though Brazil's evidence, by itself, was not sufficient. This result is suggested not only by the observations of the Appellate Body in *Canada – Aircraft*, but also is the fair import of its remarks in *India – Patents (US)*, that if, after consultations, a party believes that all of the pertinent facts are not before a panel, the party should ask for additional fact finding.[401] In this regard, the Appellate Body in *Korea – Dairy* stated that no provision of the DSU "requires a panel to make an explicit ruling on whether the complainant has established a *prima facie* case of violation before a panel may proceed to examine the respondent's defence and evidence."[402] Indeed, the very power of panels to engage in independent fact-finding suggests that the information obtained is to be used by panels, when relevant, to their determinations.

395 *Supra* note 166, ¶ 9.87. 396 *Id.* ¶ 9.88. 397 *Id.* ¶¶ 9.178–9.180.

398 Adverse inferences are discussed *supra* at § 4.09 [4].

399 *Canada – Aircraft, supra* note 190, ¶ 204.

400 *Id.* ¶ 205 (emphasis in original). "Not proven" is the term used in Scottish law when neither guilt nor innocence has been established. *See* David M. Walker, THE SCOTTISH LEGAL SYSTEM 490 (1981).

401 *Supra* note 34. 402 *Supra* note 84.

Nevertheless, the Panel in *EC – Asbestos* stated that it could not utilize information furnished by experts "in order to establish the validity of a claim of one of the parties if that party has not already established a *prima facie* case."[403] Similarly, the Panel in *India – Autos* said that its "fact-finding mandate should not be utilised so as to make out a *prima facie* case where that is not achieved by the relevant party."[404] Consistent with this approach, the Panel in *Argentina – Ceramic Tiles* said, "Our role is not to make the case for either party, but we may pose questions to the parties 'in order to clarify and distill the legal arguments.' "[405] It should be noted that none of these cases was appealed.

In an earlier case that was appealed, the Appellate Body found error when a panel used information and advice from experts to establish a *prima facie* case. However, in that case, *Japan – Agricultural Products II*, the US, as complainant, had not even made claims with regard to the "sorption levels" that the experts found could support a finding of inconsistency with the *SPS Agreement*.[406]

The Panel in *Argentina – Hides and Leather* observed that in disputes involving a claim of a *de facto* restriction, "the importance of the factual analysis becomes accentuated."[407] The Panel, accordingly, asked the parties an extensive series of questions. "We felt," it said, "that there were facts of which we were not aware and which might be of importance and, therefore, we have not been fully satisfied that we have had a truly comprehensive view of some aspects of the situation. Ultimately, the burden of proof in any dispute rests with the complainant to support the claims made."[408] Further, the Panel said, "we cannot ignore the need for sufficient proof of a party's allegations simply because obtaining proof is difficult."[409]

On the narrower level of particular facts, the Panel in *US – Section 301 Trade Act* stated that the party that alleges a specific fact "has to establish a *prima facie* case that the fact exists .... [T]his *prima facie* case will stand unless sufficiently rebutted by the other party."[410]

403 *Supra* note 174, ¶ 8.81.

404 Panel Report, *India – Measures Affecting the Automotive Sector*, WT/DS146/R, WT/DS175/R and Corr.1, adopted 5 April 2002 after appeal withdrawn, ¶ 7.294.

405 Panel Report, *Argentina – Definitive Anti-Dumping Measures on Imports of Ceramic Floor Tiles from Italy*, WT/DS189/R, adopted 5 November 2001, ¶ 6.6, quoting from the Appellate Body Report in *Thailand – H-Beams, supra* note 88, ¶ 136.

406 Appellate Body Report, *Japan – Measures Affecting Agricultural Products*, WT/DS76/AB/R, adopted 19 March 1999, DSR 1999:I, 277, ¶ 130.

407 *Supra* note 328, ¶ 11.14. 408 *Id.* 409 *Id.* ¶ 11.51.

410 *Supra* note 251, ¶ 7.15.

[3] Exceptions

A party invoking an exception to justify action that would otherwise be inconsistent with its WTO obligations has the burden of proving that it has fulfilled the conditions necessary for invoking the exception.[411] Exceptions, such as Articles XI:2 and XX of GATT, "are not positive rules establishing obligations in themselves. They are in the nature of affirmative defenses. It is only reasonable that the burden of establishing such a defense should rest on the party asserting it."[412] A party invoking Article XX is not required to disprove rebuttal arguments made by the other party until the latter has established those rebuttal points with sufficient evidence.[413]

The fact that a measure is taken to comply with recommendations and rulings of the DSB does not alter the allocation of the burden of proof.[414] Thus, despite the presumption of good faith implementation of treaty obligations, a party implementing a measure to comply with rulings and recommendations of the DSB in an adopted report has the burden, in an Article 21.5 review, of establishing that a compliance measure is justified under an Article XX exception.[415]

[4] Burden of proof under specific agreements and GATT articles

Both case law and provisions of several WTO agreements establish that, under those agreements, particular burden of proof issues arise.

Agreement on Agriculture: The Agriculture Agreement provides a partial exemption to the prohibition of export subsidies imposed by Article 3 of the *Agreement on Subsidies and Countervailing Measures.* Members are permitted to provide export subsidies on agricultural products in accordance with "reduction commitments" negotiated in the Uruguay Round, but Members also undertake not to provide export subsidies otherwise than in conformity with their commitments.[416] If exports of a product

[411] Panel Report, *US – Underwear, supra* note 33, ¶ 7.16. *Accord*: Panel Report, *Canada – Pharmaceutical Patents, supra* note 305, ¶ 7.60.

[412] Appellate Body Report, *US – Wool Shirts and Blouses, supra* note 384, § IV. *Accord*: Panel Report, *US – Shrimp, supra* note 168, ¶ 7.29: "[W]hen an affirmative defence, such as Article XX, is invoked, the burden of proof should rest on the party asserting it."

[413] Panel Report, *EC – Asbestos, supra* note 174, ¶ 8.178.

[414] Panel Report, *Brazil – Export Financing Programme for Aircraft – Recourse by Canada to Article 21.5 of the DSU*, WT/DS46/RW, adopted 4 August 2000, as modified by the Appellate Body Report, WT/DS46/AB/RW, DSR 2000:IX, 4093, ¶ 66.

[415] Panel Report, *US – Shrimp (Article 21.5 – Malaysia), supra* note 172, ¶ 5.19.

[416] *Agreement on Agriculture*, Art. 8.

subject to a reduction commitment exceed the commitment level, and if the exporting Member claims that the excess quantity is not subsidized, Article 10.3 of the Agreement on Agriculture imposes on the exporting Member the burden of establishing that no subsidy has been provided for those excess quantities.

The Panel in *Canada – Dairy (Article 21.5 – New Zealand and USII)*, however, construed Article 10.3 as imposing a dual burden on the complaining party. It required not only that the complaining party establish that exports exceed reduction commitments, but also held that "an operational interpretation of Article 10.3 requires that Complainants make a *prima facie* showing that the elements of the claimed export subsides are present."[417] The Panel did not refer to an earlier report where the Panel and the parties arguably agreed that all the complaining party needs to show, in order for the burden to shift, is that exports have exceeded reduction commitments.[418]

The Appellate Body in *Canada – Dairy (Article 21.5 – New Zealand and USII)* disagreed with the Panel and reversed its holding on this point:

> The significance of Article 10.3 is that, where a Member exports an agricultural product in quantities that exceed its quantity commitment level, that Member will be treated as if it has granted WTO-*inconsistent* export subsidies, for the excess quantities, unless the Member presents adequate evidence to 'establish' the contrary. This reversal of the usual rules obliges the responding Member to bear the consequences of any doubts concerning the evidence of export subsidization.[419]

Agreement on Sanitary and Phytosanitary Measures: Articles 4.1 and 6.3 place the burden of showing "equivalence" and pest-free or disease-areas, respectively, on the exporting Member.[420] The complaining Member has the burden of showing that no relevant scientific studies or reports to

[417] Panel Report, *Canada – Measures Affecting the Importation of Milk and the Exportation of Dairy Products – Second Recourse to Article 21.5 of the DSU by New Zealand and the United States*, WT/DS103/RW2, WT/DS113/RW2, adopted 17 January 2003, as modified by the Appellate Body Report, WT/DS103/AB/RW2, WT/DS113/AB/RW2, ¶ 5.18.

[418] Panel Report, *United States – Tax Treatment for "Foreign Sales Corporations"*, WT/DS108/R, adopted 20 March 2000, as modified by the Appellate Body Report, WT/DS108/AB/R, DSR 2000:IV, 1677, ¶ 7.161.

[419] Appellate Body Report, *Canada – Measures Affecting the Importation of Milk and the Exportation of Dairy Products – Second Recourse to Article 21.5 of the DSU by New Zealand and the United States*, WT/DS103/AB/RW2, WT/DS113/AB/RW2, adopted 17 January 2003, ¶ 74.

[420] Panel Reports, *EC – Hormones (US)* and *EC – Hormones (Canada)*, *supra* note 147, footnotes 250 and 355, respectively.

support an SPS measure exist. This burden may be fulfilled by a request under Article 5.8 to the Member maintaining the measure. Failure of that Member to bring forward scientific studies or reports would be "a strong indication that there are no such studies or reports."[421]

Agreement on Subsidies and Countervailing Measures: Article 27, which provides for special and differential treatment for developing countries with regard to Article 3, the Agreement's prohibition of export subsidies, is not an affirmative defense. Therefore, a Member claiming that a developing country Member grants or maintains a prohibited export subsidy bears the burden of proving that the developing country Member is not in compliance with the requirements of Article 27.[422]

GATT 1994 Article XXIII:1(b): "[T]his is an exceptional remedy for which the complaining party bears the burden of providing a *detailed justification* to back up its allegations."[423]

GATT 1994 Article XXIV: A Member claiming justification under Article XXIV for an otherwise inconsistent measure first "must demonstrate that the measure at issue is introduced upon the formation of a customs union that fully meets the requirements of sub-paragraphs 8(a) and 5(a) of Article XXIV. And, second, that party must demonstrate that the formation of that customs union would be prevented if it were not allowed to introduce the measure at issue."[424] The Panel in *US – Line Pipe* found that the United States had made a *prima facie* showing that the North America Free Trade Agreement (NAFTA) is WTO-consistent based on submissions of the United States to the Working Party examining the compatibility of NAFTA with Article XXIV, and based on submissions of the United States to the Committee on Regional Trade Agreements, which was examining the compatibility of NAFTA with the pertinent WTO rules. The fact that the Committee had not yet issued a final decision did not rebut this *prima facie* finding.[425]

[5] "General rule-exception" analysis

A significant development in WTO jurisprudence related to burden of proof concerns the Appellate Body's apparent rejection of the so-called

[421] Appellate Body Report, *Japan – Agricultural Products II*, *supra* note 406, ¶ 137.

[422] Appellate Body Report, *Brazil – Aircraft*, *supra* note 20, ¶ 141.

[423] Panel Report, *Japan – Film*, *supra* note 71, ¶ 10.30, quoting Article 26.1 of the DSU (emphasis in original).

[424] Appellate Body Report, *Turkey – Restrictions on Imports of Textile and Clothing Products*, WT/DS34/AB/R, adopted 19 November 1999, DSR 1999:VI, 2345, ¶ 58.

[425] Panel Report, *supra* note 367, ¶ 7.144.

"general rule-exception" analysis that was used in a number of GATT panel reports.[426] Under this analysis, the party invoking an exception to a general principle of GATT – such as most-favored-nation or national treatment – effectively had a heavier burden of proof than the party invoking the provision embodying the general principle. The exception was interpreted more narrowly or more strictly than other provisions.

The Appellate Body, however, from the start has demonstrated an emphasis on text.[427] It later observed that Articles XX and XI:(2)(c)(i) of GATT are limited exceptions from other obligations, in the nature of affirmative defenses, and that the party invoking them has the burden of proving their applicability.[428] In this observation, the Appellate Body was relying on the language of the provisions themselves, and not on broader principles. In *EC Measures Concerning Meat and Meat Products (Hormones)*, it was particularly explicit. After stating that the burden of proof of showing an inconsistency with a provision is not avoided by describing that provision as an exception, the Appellate Body said:

> [M]erely characterizing a treaty provision as an "exception" does not by itself justify a "stricter" or "narrower" interpretation of that provision than would be warranted by examination of the ordinary meaning of the actual treaty words, viewed in context and in the light of the treaty's object and purpose, or, in other words, by applying the normal rules of treaty interpretation.[429]

The Appellate Body's conclusion seems to be supported by the customary rules of interpretation of public international law as set out in Articles 31 and 32 of the *Vienna Convention on the Law of Treaties.* These articles do not give grounds for preferring one portion of the text over another, construing the former broadly and the latter narrowly. The better justification for the narrow construction of some provisions of GATT lies

[426] *See, e.g., Norway – Procurement of Toll Collection Equipment for the City of Trondheim*, BISD 40S/319, adopted 13 May 1992, ¶ 4.5: "Since Article V:16(e) was an exceptions provision, its scope had to be interpreted narrowly and it would be up to Norway, as the Party invoking the provision, to demonstrate the conformity of its actions with the provision;" *United States – Measures Affecting Alcoholic and Malt Beverages*, BISD 39S/206, adopted 19 June 1992, ¶ 5.41: "The Panel also noted the practice of the CONTRACTING PARTIES of interpreting these Article XX exceptions narrowly, placing the burden on the party invoking the exception to justify its use."

[427] Appellate Body Report, *United States – Standards for Reformulated and Conventional Gasoline*, WT/DS2/AB/R, adopted 20 May 1996, DSR 1996:I, 3, III.B at 18, observing that the so-called "primarily aimed at" test developed in GATT jurisprudence to interpret the phrase "relating to" in Article XX(g) is "not itself treaty language."

[428] Appellate Body Report, *United States – Wool Shirts and Blouses, supra* note 384, at 14.

[429] Appellate Body Report, *EC – Hormones, supra* note 149, ¶ 104.

in the fact that their wording is narrow, rather than in assumed policy of favoring one article over another.

[6] Article 22.6 arbitrations

Under Article 22.6 of the DSU, if the Member concerned objects to the level of suspension of concessions or other obligations proposed by the complaining Member, the matter is referred to arbitration. As the complaining party, the Member concerned bears the burden of proof; however, arbitrators have placed on the responding Member the burden of explaining its calculation methodology. This is discussed further in § 8.05 [6].

§ 4.12 Standard of review[430]

The Dispute Settlement Understanding contains no explicit standard of review. The Appellate Body has held, however, "that the issue of failure to apply an appropriate standard of review . . . resolves itself into the issue of whether or not the Panel . . . made an 'objective assessment of the matter before it, including an objective assessment of the facts.' "[431] The quoted language is that of Article 11 of the DSU. While panels therefore must employ Article 11, they have not developed the jurisprudence of its legal content. This task has fallen to the Appellate Body as it decides claims that panels have failed to make an "objective assessment" of the matters before them, as required by Article 11.

The first appellate challenge to a panel's decision based on an alleged failure to make an objective assessment of the facts was not well received. "A claim that a panel disregarded or distorted the evidence submitted to it," the Appellate Body said, "is, in effect, a claim that the panel, to a greater or lesser degree, denied the party submitting the evidence fundamental fairness, or what in many jurisdictions is known as due process of law or natural justice."[432] The Appellate Body reiterated this approach in a number of subsequent cases. "An allegation that a panel has failed to conduct the 'objective assessment of the matter before it' required by

[430] Article 17.6 of the Antidumping Agreement contains a separate standard of review. *See* §§ 5.07 [4]–5.07 [6]. *See* generally, Maurits Lugard, *Scope of Appellate Review: Objective Assessment of the Facts and Issues of Law*, 1 Journal of International Economic Law 323 (1998).

[431] Appellate Body Report, *EC Hormones*, *supra* note 149, ¶ 119 (emphasis omitted).

[432] *Id.* ¶ 133.

Article 11 of the DSU is a very serious allegation. Such an allegation goes to the very core of the integrity of the WTO dispute settlement process itself."[433] If a panel does not "deliberately disregard," "refuse to consider," "willfully distort" or "misrepresent" the evidence, and if it does not commit an "egregious error that calls into question [its] good faith," it does not act in a manner inconsistent with Article 11.[434] Complainant's "arguments . . . do not disclose that the Panel has distorted, misrepresented or disregarded evidence, or has applied a 'double standard' of proof in this case."[435] Initially, therefore, the "standard of review" of Article 11 did not appear to provide much "review" at all.

Subsequently, the tone changed. In *US – Wheat Gluten*, the Panel's decision was reversed on the basis of Article 11, but with none of the harsh language so characteristic of the Appellate Body's earlier decisions. After stating that the question whether a panel's assessment of the facts was objective is, itself, a legal question, the Appellate Body stated what is virtually boilerplate in many national appellate reviews: "[W]e cannot base a finding of inconsistency under Article 11 simply on the conclusion that we might have reached a different factual finding from the one the Panel reached. Rather," the Appellate Body added, "we must be satisfied that the Panel has exceeded the bounds of its discretion, as the trier of facts, in its appreciation of the evidence."[436] The Appellate Body then went on to note that "we will not interfere lightly with the Panel's exercise of its discretion."[437]

The *Wheat Gluten* Panel had accepted supplemental information justifying the challenged decision, information that was not contained in the decision itself. By reaching a conclusion that upheld the challenged domestic decision in these circumstances, the Appellate Body said, "the Panel applied a standard of review which falls short of what is required by Article 11 of the DSU."[438] It then went on to give some guidance for challenging panel reports under Article 11:

> In asking us to conduct such a review, an appellant must indicate clearly the manner in which a panel has improperly exercised its discretion. Taking into account the full *ensemble* of the facts, the appellant should, at least: identify

[433] Appellate Body Report, *European Communities – Measures Affecting the Importation of Certain Poultry Products*, WT/DS69/AB/R, adopted 23 July 1998, DSR 1998:V, 2031, ¶ 133.

[434] Appellate Body Report, *Australia – Salmon, supra* note 268, ¶ 266.

[435] Appellate Body Report, *Korea – Alcoholic Beverages, supra* note 330, ¶ 164.

[436] Appellate Body Report, *US – Wheat Gluten, supra* note 212, ¶ 1.51.

[437] *Id.* [438] *Id.* ¶ 162.

> the facts on record from which the Panel should have drawn inferences; indicate the factual or legal inferences that the panel should have drawn from those facts; and, finally, explain why the failure of the panel to exercise its discretion by drawing these inferences amounts to an error of law under Article 11 of the DSU.[439]

Panels frequently are called upon to review the findings of national authorities, as was the Panel in *Wheat Gluten*, a safeguards case. This raises the question of how panels are to review those decisions. In *EC – Hormones*, the Appellate Body said, somewhat tautologically, that for panels making an objective assessment of the facts, "the applicable standard is neither *de novo* review as such, nor 'total deference,' but rather 'the objective assessment of the facts.' "[440] Subsequently, it offered further explanation:

> [U]nder Article 11 . . . panels must examine whether the competent authority has evaluated all relevant factors; they must assess whether the competent authority has examined all the pertinent facts and assessed whether an adequate explanation has been provided as to how those facts support the determination; and they must also consider whether the competent authority's explanation addresses fully the nature and complexities of the data and responds to other plausible interpretations of the data. However, panels must not conduct a *de novo* review of the evidence nor substitute their judgment for that of the competent authority.[441]

What does all of this mean in the WTO in practice? The purely legal part of the "matter" before panels is decided by them *de novo*, since the panel proceeding is the first instance in which a measure is considered in light of WTO legal standards by a WTO Body.[442] As to purely factual questions, however, there is broad and growing case law making it clear that panels are not to conduct *de novo* review.[443] That raises the question of how, precisely, panels are to make an "objective assessment" of the facts without considering them afresh. The apparent answer is something

[439] *Id.* ¶ 175. [440] Appellate Body Report, *supra* note 149, ¶ 117.

[441] Appellate Body Report, *US – Cotton Yarn*, *supra* note 286, ¶ 74.

[442] This is true even if the domestic measure is one that enacts WTO provisions *verbatim*. The national authorities are still considering a national measure, and their interpretation cannot bind a WTO panel's interpretation of a WTO provision.

[443] Appellate Body Report, *EC – Hormones*, *supra* note 149, ¶ 117; Appellate Body Report, *United States – Safeguard Measures on Imports of Fresh, Chilled or Frozen Lamb Meat from New Zealand and Australia*, WT/DS177/AB/R, WT/DS178/AB/R, adopted 16 May 2001, ¶ 106; Appellate Body Report, *US – Cotton Yarn*, *supra* note 286, ¶ 69ff.

similar to the "substantial evidence" test familiar to lawyers in the United States. If all of the witnesses say A, and the national authorities decide B, a panel most likely will find that the facts do not support the decision of the authorities. But if some witnesses say A, and others say B, panels are likely to find that the facts do provide a basis for the decision of the authorities no matter whether they decide A or B. The Appellate Body is likely to find that a panel's assessment of the facts in this manner is "objective" within the meaning of Article 11.

EC – Hormones offers one example. An issue in that case was whether the hormone ban was based on an assessment of the risks involved. After evaluating the evidence presented by the EC, the Panel concluded that none of it addressed the safety of the hormones, nor did any of that evidence indicate an identifiable risk for human health. To the contrary, all of the studies referred to by the EC came to the conclusion that the hormones were safe. The scientific experts advising the Panel confirmed these conclusions.[444] The Panel clearly viewed this situation as one in which the evidence said A and the authorities decided B. The Appellate Body held that the Panel had not "arbitrarily ignored or manifestly distorted the evidence before it,"[445] and affirmed.[446]

EC – Asbestos offers a somewhat different example. In that case, Canada challenged a French ban on the use of all varieties of asbestos.[447] The Panel sustained the ban, and, in affirming the result, the Appellate Body disposed of Canada's Article 11 challenge in short order. Characterizing Canada's argument as one that simply challenged the Panel's exercise of discretion in assessing and weighing the evidence, the Appellate Body declined to second-guess the Panel, remarking that "the Panel's appreciation of the evidence remained well within the bounds of its discretion as the trier of facts."[448]

The Appellate Body has emphasized that Article 11 obligates panels not only to make an objective assessment of the "facts," but also an objective assessment of the "matter" before it.[449] If a panel makes an assessment of a provision of a measure not before it, it does not make an objective assessment of the matter before it, and acts *ultra petita*.[450] Thus, a panel is not entitled to make a finding on an issue that is not in dispute.[451]

[444] Panel Report, *EC – Hormones (US)*, *supra* note 147, ¶ 8.124.
[445] Appellate Body Report, *EC – Hormones*, *supra* note 149, ¶ 145.
[446] *Id.* ¶ 235. [447] Panel Report, *EC – Asbestos*, *supra* note 174, ¶ 3.8.
[448] Appellate Body Report, *EC – Asbestos*, *supra* note 239, ¶ 177.
[449] Appellate Body Report, *Chile – Price Band System*, *supra* note 78, ¶ 172.
[450] *Id.* ¶ 173. [451] *Id.* ¶ 174.

§ 4.13 Written submissions to panels

[1] General

Soon after its members are named, usually within one week, the panel will hold an organizational meeting at which it will consult with the parties and establish Working Procedures.[452] These will include a timetable for written submissions and a schedule for meetings of the parties with the Panel.[453] Normally, the complaining party will present its first submission two-to-three weeks prior to the responding party, unless the panel decides, after consultation with the parties, that they should make their initial submissions simultaneously.[454] This normally would occur three-to-six weeks after the panel is established.

[2] First written submission

The first submissions of all parties should set forth their view of the facts of the case and their arguments flowing from those facts.[455] Working Procedures typically provide that, except for rebuttal evidence, all factual information should be submitted no later than the first meeting of the Panel with the parties. Presentation of extensive factual material for the first time after the first meeting can lead to confusion and thereby dilute its effectiveness. Late presentation of extensive factual material is also likely to lead the Panel to offer more time to the other party to respond.

In *Korea – Alcoholic Beverages*, Korea submitted a marketing study done by an independent firm as part of its responses to questions presented by the Panel to the parties after its first meeting with the parties.[456] The EC responded, at the second meeting, with its own survey. The Panel gave Korea an extra week to respond to the EC's new evidence, which Korea considered insufficient. The Panel rejected Korea's complaint, noting that "[h]ad Korea chosen to submit its survey at the first substantive meeting and the European Communities failed to respond at the next opportunity (in such a case, it would have been in the rebuttal submission), there obviously would have been more merit to the claim because then the European Communities, it could have been argued, delayed submitting their evidence."[457]

[452] DSU Art. 12.3. *See* the Appendix for an example of panel working procedures.

[453] DSU Art. 12.5. [454] DSU Art. 12.4; App. 3, Art. 12(a)(2).

[455] DSU Appendix 3.4. [456] *Supra* note 11, ¶ 10.24. [457] *Id.* ¶ 10.25.

The complainant's first written submission normally would include such things as the texts or other information concerning the "measure" complained of, together with any relevant translations, as well as an exposition of its legal theory as to why the measure is inconsistent with specific WTO provisions. As the *Korea – Alcoholic Beverages* case indicates, the complaining party's first written submission also should include any surveys, studies or other evidentiary material intended to support the claim. The responding party's later-filed first submission inherently will be somewhat in the nature of a rebuttal, but it also should set out any affirmative defenses that may be claimed, keeping in mind that a party asserting an affirmative defense has the burden of establishing it.[458] It should also set out the responding party's factual view of the measure at issue.

It is not always necessary for a complaining party to include a discussion of all of its claims in its first written submission to the panel, although such an omission might not be advisable as a tactical matter. In *EC – Bananas III*, Mexico, Guatemala, and Honduras, in their first written submissions to the Panel, omitted any reference to some claims that had been made in their request for the establishment of the panel, which had been made jointly with other parties.[459] The Panel declined to consider these claims on the ground that to do so would be unfair to the respondent, as it would have little or no time to respond.

The Appellate Body, however, disagreed, apparently concluding that what the Panel considered to be a claim was actually an argument in support of a claim: "There is no requirement in the DSU or in GATT practice for arguments on all claims relating to the matter referred to the DSB to be set out in the complaining party's first written submission to the panel."[460] The Appellate Body added that, "Any omissions in the arguments contained in the first written submissions were rectified in joint presentations with other Complaining Parties made at the first meeting of the parties with the panel, as well as in their joint written rebuttal submission and in their joint representations made at the second meeting of the panel."[461]

In *Korea – Dairy*, the Appellate Body elaborated on the distinction between claims and arguments:

[458] *See* § 4.13. [459] *Supra* note 33, ¶ 7.57.

[460] Appellate Body Report, *EC – Bananas III*, *supra* note 33, ¶ 145. Article 4 of Appendix 3 to the DSU provides that prior to the first meeting of the panel, the parties shall transmit written submissions "in which they present the facts of the case and their arguments."

[461] *Id.* ¶ 146.

> [A] party to a dispute settlement proceeding may not introduce a new claim during or after the rebuttal stage. Indeed, any claim that is not asserted in the request for the establishment of a panel may not be submitted at any time after submission and acceptance of that request. By "*claim*" we mean a claim that the respondent party has violated, or nullified or impaired the benefits arising from, an identified provision of a particular agreement. Such a *claim of violation* must, as we have already noted, be distinguished from the *arguments* adduced by a complaining party to demonstrate that the responding party's measure does indeed infringe upon the identified treaty provision. Arguments supporting a claim are set out and progressively clarified in the first written submissions, the rebuttal submissions and the first and second panel meetings with the parties. Both "claims" and "arguments" are distinct from the "evidence" which the complainant or respondent presents to support its assertions of fact and arguments.[462]

At the first substantive meeting of the parties in *EC – Pipe Fittings (Brazil)*, the EC requested that the Panel refuse to consider certain claims of Brazil on the grounds that they were "vaguely defined" in Brazil's first written submission.[463] The Panel declined, finding that all of the allegedly "vague" claims described in Brazil's first submission were within its terms of reference.[464] It is the nature of the process, the Panel said, "that the claims made by a party may be progressively clarified and refined throughout the proceeding."[465]

[3] Second written submission

The parties submit their second written submissions to the Panel simultaneously.[466] These are the formal rebuttal submissions, which would include rebuttal not only to the first submission of the other party, but also rebuttal to oral statements made at the first meeting. Panels generally prefer that rebuttal evidence be submitted with the second written submission. If rebuttal evidence is not submitted until the second meeting of the panel, additional time may be given for the other party to respond.[467]

Parties typically have further opportunities to present written submissions to panels in the form of written answers to questions presented by a panel. Usually questions are given to both parties after each meeting,

[462] *Supra* note 84, ¶ 139.

[463] Panel Report, *European Communities – Anti-Dumping Duties on Malleable Cast Iron Tube or Pipe Fittings from Brazil*, WT/DS219/R, report dated 7 March 2003, ¶ 7.10 (1).

[464] *Id.* ¶ 7.10(5). [465] *Id.* ¶ 7.10(6). [466] DSU Art. 12.6.

[467] Panel Report, *Argentina – Textiles and Apparel*, *supra* note 186, ¶ 6.55.

and parties are normally permitted to respond to questions presented to the other party as well. Depending on time, panels may permit parties to comment on the answers submitted by the other party.

[4] Executive summaries of submissions

In *Argentina – Preserved Peaches Safeguard*, the working procedures adopted by the Panel required the parties to provide executive summaries of their arguments for the descriptive part of the Panel's report.[468] Argentina objected, arguing that this requirement imposed an additional procedural burden since it limited the time available to the parties for preparation of their submissions.[469] The Panel rejected Argentina's argument, noting that other panels now commonly require summaries, and holding that the working procedures were adopted after consultation with the parties.[470]

§ 4.14 Meetings of panels with the parties

[1] General

The few formal rules that govern the proceedings of panels, apart from the Working Procedures issued by a panel, may be stated briefly. Panels meet in closed sessions, and the parties, including interested third parties, attend only by invitation of the panel.[471] A panel's deliberations, as well as the documents submitted to it are confidential, although, as previously noted, parties may make their own submissions public, and non-confidential summaries that may be made public are required of confidential submissions.[472] Parties are required to provide to the panel written versions of their oral statements.[473] All submissions are made available to all parties.[474]

[2] First meeting of the Panel with the parties

At the first meeting, the complaining party presents its case first, followed by the party against whom the complaint was brought.[475] The panel may, at any time, put questions to the parties. Panels vary greatly in their

[468] Panel Report, *Argentina – Definitive Safeguard Measure on Imports of Preserved Peaches*, WT/DS238/R, adopted 15 April 2003, ¶ 4.2. Regarding the descriptive part of panel reports, *see* § 4.18 [2].

[469] *Id.* ¶ 4.3. [470] *Id.* ¶ 4.4. [471] DSU Appendix 3.3. [472] *Id.*

[473] DSU Appendix 3.9. [474] DSU Appendix 3.10. [475] DSU Appendix 3.5.

degree of activity during meetings with the parties. Some will interrupt presentations to ask questions as they arise; others will ask questions after a presentation is concluded; still others do so only after both sides have finished their presentations; and a few present no oral questions at all, but rely entirely on written questions. The members of the Secretariat assisting a panel normally do not ask questions directly of the parties, but may privately make suggestions to a panel as to the content of written questions. Third parties usually meet with the panel, and with the parties to the proceeding, at a separate session of the first substantive meeting.[476]

The first meeting of the Panel is a critical time for the parties. Following the meeting, the panelists normally meet with the Secretariat and sketch out the outlines of its decision. Since many panelists are not resident in Geneva, this meeting provides one of the few times they will be together in one room to discuss the merits of the case. Although rebuttal submissions, written responses to questions, and the second meeting are very important, it is fair to say that, after the first meeting, it will be more difficult to change the minds of the panelists, and convince them to alter the course they decided upon after the first meeting.

[3] Second meeting of the Panel with the parties

The second meeting of the panel considers the rebuttal arguments of the parties, and any other issues the panel may wish to review. Third parties normally do not participate in or attend the second panel meeting, nor receive the second written submissions of the parties. However, in one dispute, the third parties requested that they be allowed to be present at all meetings between the Panel and the parties to the dispute.[477] The Panel agreed to permit the third parties to observe the second substantive meeting of the Panel with the parties, but declined to offer further participation.[478]

Just as the second written submissions are important, so is the second meeting of the panel. By this time, the panel will have had the opportunity of hearing the parties during the first meeting, possibly receiving their responses to questions posed, and simply to reflect on the issues. The second meeting normally will be the panel's last opportunity to request information from the parties and to hear their responses to issues that may be troubling the panel. It also normally will be the last opportunity

[476] DSU Appendix 3.6.

[477] Panel Report, *EC – Bananas III*, *supra* note 33, ¶¶ 7.4 to 7.9.

[478] *Id.*

of the parties, apart from written responses to questions, to make their case to the panel.

Submission of new evidence at the second meeting of a panel may lead to a third written submission for both parties. In *Australia – Salmon*, a situation arose that was somewhat similar to that in *Korea – Alcoholic Beverages*. Australia claimed that Canada's oral statement, at the second meeting with the Panel, introduced fundamental changes in the nature of its legal claims which were of such significance that Australia should be allowed to submit a formal written submission to rebut them.[479] The Panel granted Australia's request and provided a like opportunity to Canada, specifying that "both third submissions had to be limited to the 'fundamental changes' introduced by Canada as they were identified in an oral statement made by Australia at the second substantive meeting."[480] Although Australia argued that the additional time it was given was insufficient, the Appellate Body affirmed the Panel's decision.[481]

§ 4.15 Computation of time

Prompt resolution of disputes was an important goal of the negotiators of the Uruguay Round and, consequently, the DSU imposes a number of time limits on the various stages of the process. However, the DSU does not provide flexibility for many of these limits, particularly if they expire on weekends or holidays. Accordingly, the DSB subsequently agreed on the following practice:

> When, under the DSU (and its special or additional rules and procedures), a time-period within which a communication must be made or action taken by a Member to exercise or preserve its rights expires on a non-working day of the WTO Secretariat, any such communication or action will be deemed to have been made or taken on the WTO non-working day if lodged on the first working day of the WTO Secretariat following the day on which such time-period would normally expire.[482]

The fact that this practice would extend some time-periods by a day or more would not serve to extend subsequent time-periods;[483] consequently, these subsequent time-periods could in fact be shortened.

479 *Supra* note 225, ¶ 7.8. 480 *Id.* 481 *Supra* note 268, ¶ 278.

482 *Expiration of Time-Periods in the DSU – Proposal by the Chairman*, WT/DSB/W/10 and WT/DSB/W/10/Add.1, 20 July 1995. The proposal was agreed to by the DSB at its meeting of 27 September 1995, WT/DSB/M/7, 27 October 1995, agenda item 10.

483 *Id.*

The DSU calls for panels normally to issue their final reports to the parties within six months from the date of the composition of the panel.[484] "In no case should the period from the establishment of the panel to the circulation of the report to the Members exceed nine months."[485] Despite this relatively clear injunction, panels have exceeded the nine-month deadline.[486] In truth, given the complexity of many disputes, it is not realistically possible for many panels to meet the nine-month deadline set out in the DSU. Panels have interpreted the word "should" to be hortatory, not mandatory; the Dispute Settlement Body and the parties thus far have agreed. In fact, panels and the parties often negotiate a specific time-table for a dispute that might differ from the DSU time-lines, but which reaches an expeditious result while protecting the due process interests of the parties. As one panel observed, "most of the time-limits in the DSU are either minimum time-limits without ceilings or maximum time-limits that are, nonetheless, indicative only."[487]

§ 4.16 "Violation," "non-violation" and "other situation" complaints

[1] General

Most WTO disputes involve claims under Article XXIII:1(a) of GATT 1994, that a Member has failed to carry out its obligations under a covered agreement, *i.e.*, that a Member is in violation of its commitments. However, Article XXIII:1 also provides two other bases for complaints:

(b) the application by another contracting party of any measure, whether or not it conflicts with the provisions of this Agreement; or
(c) the existence of any other situation.

Thus, a complaint may allege that benefits accruing to a Member under a covered agreement are being nullified or impaired by: (1) a violation on

[484] DSU Art. 12.8. [485] DSU Art. 12.9.

[486] For example, the Panel in *Bananas* was composed on 7 June 1996, but its final report was not circulated until 22 May 1997, more than 11 months later. Panel Report, *EC – Bananas III (US)*, *supra* note 33. Similarly, the Panel in *Hormones* was constituted on 2 July 1996, but its report was not circulated until 18 August 1997, more than 13 months later. Panel Report, *EC – Hormones (US)*, *supra* note 147.

[487] Panel Report, *United States – Import Measures on Certain Products from the European Communities*, WT/DS165/R and Add.1, adopted 10 January 2001, as modified by the Appellate Body Report, WT/DS165/AB/R, ¶ 6.135.

the part of another Member; (2) action by another Member that does not violate a covered agreement; and (3) any other situation.

[2] Violation complaints

Most disputes involve violation complaints. The DSU elaborates and applies Article XXIII:1(a) to the WTO covered agreements. Article 3.8 of the DSU provides that infringement of obligations under any covered agreement "is considered *prima facie* to constitute a case of nullification or impairment." This presumption places on the Member against whom a complaint has been brought the burden of rebuttal – a burden that has not yet been met.

Guatemala attempted to meet the burden in *Guatemala – Cement II.* Guatemala argued that its failure to notify Mexico of the receipt of an antidumping petition prior to initiating its investigation, as required by Article 5.5 of the Antidumping Agreement, did not result in nullification or impairment of Mexico's rights because Guatemala did not take any actual steps to begin the investigation until Mexico had been notified, and that it granted the Mexican exporter an additional two months to respond to the questionnaire.[488] The Panel rejected the argument, finding that, "There is no way to ascertain what Mexico might have done if it had received a timely notification," and that the extra time granted to the Mexican exporter had no bearing on the failure to notify Mexico on time.[489]

[3] Non-violation complaints

The somewhat unusual notion that one Member can nullify or impair its commitments to another Member without violating an agreement is grounded in the fact that the benefits governments expect to obtain from trade agreements may be negated by unrelated and permissible actions of another government that could not reasonably have been anticipated at the time of the negotiation.[490] Article 26 of the DSU provides

[488] *Supra* note 125, ¶ 8.107. [489] *Id.* ¶ 8.109.

[490] GATT panels found "non-violation" nullification and impairment in four of 14 instances in which it was alleged: *Australia – Subsidy on Ammonium Sulphate,* BISD II/188, adopted 3 April 1950; *Germany – Imports of Sardines,* BISD IS/53, adopted 31 October 1952; *Germany – Import Duties on Starch and Potato Flour,* BISD 3S/77, noted 16 February 1955; *European Communities – Payments and Subsidies Paid to Processors and Producers of Oilseeds and Related Animal Feed Proteins,* BISD 37S/86, adopted 25 January 1990.

special procedures for dealing with these complaints, as well as the "other situation" complaints.

When a Member brings a "non-violation" complaint of the type described in Article XXIII:1(b), it must comply with all of the requirements that apply to other complaints. In addition, the complaining Member must present a detailed justification in support of its position.[491] However, Article 26 does not state where or when the complaining party must do this: in its request for consultations, in its request for the establishment of a panel, or in its submissions to the panel. Presumably, a detailed justification would not be necessary in the request for consultations, so long as the request gives "the reasons for the request including identification of the measures at issue and an indication of the legal basis for the complaint."[492] Prudence would dictate, however, that the complaining Member should present as detailed a justification as possible in its request for consultations, as well as in its panel request, at least until a panel or the Appellate Body makes clear that it is not necessary to do so. A simple reference to Article XXIII as the legal basis for a request for the establishment of a panel will not suffice to include a claim for an Article XXIII:1(b) violation within a panel's terms of reference. Explicit reference to Article XXIII:1(b) is necessary.[493]

If the panel agrees with the complaining Member, there is, nevertheless, no obligation on the responding Member to withdraw the measure.[494] However, in such cases, the panel or the Appellate Body shall recommend that the responding Member concerned make a mutually satisfactory adjustment.[495]

[4] "Other situation" complaints

A party alleging nullification and impairment of benefits based on "any other situation" also shall present a detailed justification in support of its argument.[496] As with allegations of non-violation nullification and impairment, prudence would dictate that this justification be included both in the request for consultations and in the request for the establishment of a panel.

[491] DSU Art. 26.1(a). [492] DSU Art. 4.5.
[493] Panel Report, *Australia – Salmon*, *supra* note 225, ¶ 8.28.
[494] DSU Art. 26.1(b). [495] *Id. See* Chapter 8 with regard to implementation.
[496] DSU Art. 26.2(a).

In cases encompassing findings concerning both "other situation" claims and violation or non-violation claims, the panel shall prepare and circulate separate reports for the other disputes and the "other situation" dispute.[497]

The DSU applies to "other situation" disputes only to the point when the report has been circulated to the Members.[498] Consideration for adoption, and surveillance and implementation of recommendations and rulings of "other situation" reports, are governed by the Decision of 12 April 1989, the so-called "Montreal Rules."[499] The most significant consequence of this is that the Montreal Rules contain GATT's requirement of a positive consensus to adopt a report and to act upon an adopted report.[500] This is the only remaining relic of the former system's consensus practice in dispute settlement, and is likely to mean few "other situation" disputes, since the losing party can always prevent consensus.

Article XXIII:3 of the General Agreement on Trade in Services ("GATS") contains special provisions concerning non-violation complaints involving services. These are discussed in § 5.11 [3].

§ 4.17 Representation by private attorneys

The legal complexity of the WTO Agreements – 558 pages of text in the English version – increased the demand for the services of lawyers, a phenomenon that had begun under GATT in the late 1980s and early 1990s. Many Members, particularly developing country Members, did not have the resources to support a permanent staff of legal experts, and found themselves in need of legal help, particularly in disputes involving developed countries that were well-staffed with legal expertise. Traditionally, however, private attorneys did not present cases directly to the panels; this task was performed by government officials. Private attorneys advised, counseled, drafted submissions, and remained available during panel meetings to answer questions.

In *Bananas III*, some third parties included private attorneys in their delegations. Upon objection from the complaining party, the Panel excluded the private attorneys from attendance in the Panel meetings.[501]

When the case reached the Appellate Body, the issue arose again, but

[497] DSU Art. 26.2(b). [498] DSU Art. 26.2.

[499] *Id.* The "Montreal Rules" are published at BISD 36S/61. *See* also, §§ 7.09 and 8.09.

[500] Montreal Rules ¶ G.3. [501] *Supra* note 33, ¶¶ 7.10–7.12.

with a different result: the Appellate Body held that it is for the Member concerned to determine who shall represent it, and that this may include private attorneys.[502] The Appellate Body's action, however, did not reverse the Panel's decision since the issue had not been appealed; the question simply recurred when the third parties sought to have private attorneys present their arguments to the Appellate Body.[503]

While the *Bananas III* appeal did not formally reverse the Panel on the point, its rationale left little room for excluding private lawyers. Thus, when the issue next arose, the Panel in *Indonesia – Autos* permitted private lawyers to present the case for a Member government, observing:

> [W]e find no provision in the WTO Agreement or the DSU, including the standard rules of procedure included therein, which prevents a WTO Member from determining the composition of its delegation to WTO panel meetings.[504]

§ 4.18 Panel reports

[1] General

Prior to the issuance of the final report, panels are required by Article 15 of the DSU to offer the parties the opportunity to review the descriptive portion of the report and an interim report. These are intended to insure factual accuracy, as well as to offer an additional opportunity to settle the dispute. They are not intended to give the parties opportunity for further argument on the merits.

[2] Descriptive portions of the report

GATT panels developed the practice of giving the parties an opportunity to comment on the descriptive portions of their reports – the summary of the arguments of the parties – prior to the issuance of the final report. The purpose was to ensure the accuracy of the panel's summary or paraphrase of each party's position. Most WTO panels, and all of the earlier ones, followed this practice. However, as submissions became lengthier, some

502 *See* § 6.04 [16].

503 The third parties could not appeal issues of their own, but were confined to addressing the issues appealed by the parties themselves. *See* § 6.03.

504 Panel Report, *Indonesia – Autos, supra* note 74, ¶ 14.1.

panels sought to ease the burden on the Secretariat (which prepares the summaries) simply by including the entire texts of the actual submissions of the parties, thus obviating the need for summarizing and the need for review of descriptive parts of the report.

However, this practice in turn created an increased burden on the Language Services and Documentation Division, which is required to translate the entire report and its appendices from the original language into the other two official WTO languages before the report may be sent to the parties. To ease this burden, some panels have required the parties themselves to prepare executive summaries of their arguments for inclusion in the final report.[505] Thus, panels now follow different procedures with regard to the inclusion of the arguments of the parties, and thus different procedures with regard to review of the descriptive parts of the report. The methodology of a panel usually is established when it issues its Working Procedures.

[3] Interim reports

After consideration of the comments of the parties on the descriptive portion of the report, the panel then issues an interim report that includes not only its descriptive portion, but also its findings and recommendations.[506] This usually occurs two-to-four weeks after the submission of comments on the descriptive portion.[507]

Again within a time set by the panel, usually one week, parties may submit a written request for a review of precise aspects of the interim report, including a further meeting with the panel to review the issues identified in the written request.[508] The review, including the possible meeting with the parties, normally will occur within two weeks.[509] In most instances, parties do not request a meeting with the panel, but simply submit written comments on the report. If no review is requested through the submission of comments or a meeting, or both, the interim report is considered to be the final report.[510] The DSU requires that the findings of the final panel report include a discussion of the arguments made at the interim review stage.[511] However, it does not limit the panel to modifying

505 *See* § 4.13 [4]. 506 DSU Art. 15.1. 507 DSU Art. 15.2; App. 3.12(g).
508 DSU Art. 15.2; App. 3.12(h). 509 DSU App. 3.12(j). 510 DSU Art. 15.2.
511 DSU Art. 15.3.

only those paragraphs of the interim report commented upon by the parties.[512]

The main purpose of requiring identification of the precise issues to be reviewed is to provide the other party with adequate notice of the issues so that it may prepare a rebuttal.[513] Therefore, merely enumerating the numbers of the paragraphs of the findings section of the interim report for which review is requested, and not stating the precise aspects of those paragraphs for which review is requested, normally would not meet the requirements of Article 15.2 of the DSU.[514] However, where the written request for review of the findings section related only to such factual aspects as the correct reflection of the requestor's arguments and the names and references of scientific experts, the responding party normally would not be prejudiced.[515] Sometimes, parties have simply avoided the issue by putting all of their comments in their request for an interim review, treating their request as their interim review filing.

"The interim review stage is not a time to introduce new evidence," and panels are justified in not taking into account evidence submitted at this stage.[516]

[4] Final reports

The Working Procedures set out in Appendix 3 to the DSU call for issuance of the final report approximately two weeks after completion of the interim review. Article 12.7 of the DSU calls for the panel to set out, in its report, "the basic rationale behind any findings and recommendations that it makes." In *Mexico – Corn Syrup (Article 21.5 – US)*, the Appellate Body provided its gloss on Article 12.7:

> [T]he duty of panels under Article 12.7 of the DSU to provide a "basic rationale" reflects and conforms with the principles of fundamental fairness and due process that underlie and inform the provisions of the DSU. In particular, in cases where a Member has been found to have acted inconsistently with its obligations under the covered agreements, that Member is entitled to know the reasons for such finding as a matter of due process. In addition, the requirement to set out a "basic rationale" in the panel report assists such Member to understand the nature of its obligations and to make informed decisions about: (i) what must be done in order to implement

512 Panel Report, *EC – Hormones, supra* note 147, ¶ 7.6.

513 *Id.* ¶ 7.4. 514 *Id.* 515 *Id.*

516 Appellate Body Report, *European Communities – Trade Description of Sardines*, WTDS231/AB/R, adopted 23 October 2002, ¶ 301.

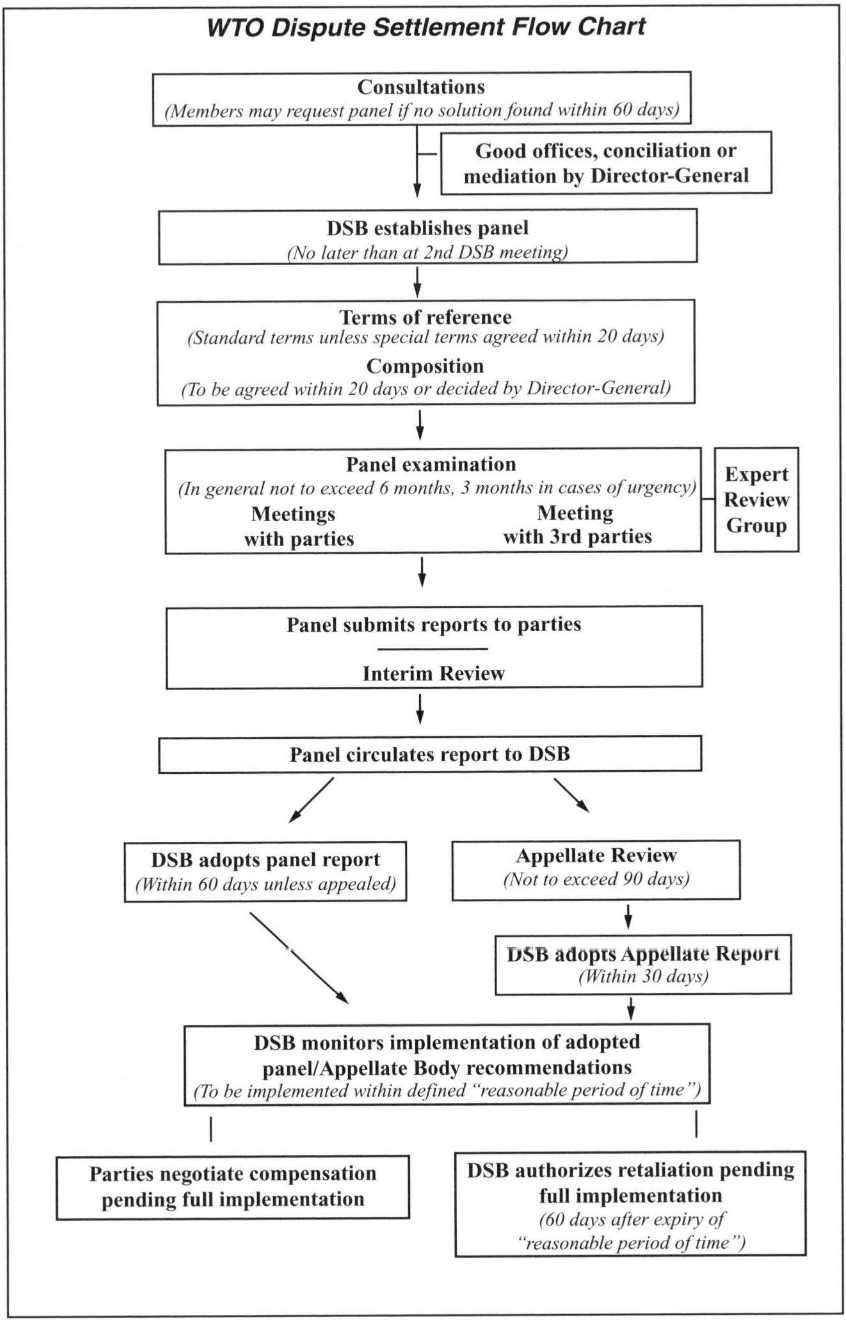
WTO Dispute Settlement Flow Chart
Consultations
(Members may request panel if no solution found within 60 days)
Good offices, conciliation or mediation by Director-General
DSB establishes panel
(No later than at 2nd DSB meeting)
Terms of reference
(Standard terms unless special terms agreed within 20 days)
Composition
(To be agreed within 20 days or decided by Director-General)
Panel examination
(In general not to exceed 6 months, 3 months in cases of urgency)
Meetings with parties
Meeting with 3rd parties
Expert Review Group
Panel submits reports to parties
Interim Review
Panel circulates report to DSB
DSB adopts panel report
(Within 60 days unless appealed)
Appellate Review
(Not to exceed 90 days)
DSB adopts Appellate Report
(Within 30 days)
DSB monitors implementation of adopted panel/Appellate Body recommendations
(To be implemented within defined "reasonable period of time")
Parties negotiate compensation pending full implementation
DSB authorizes retaliation pending full implementation
(60 days after expiry of "reasonable period of time")

> the eventual rulings and recommendations made by the DSB; and (ii) whether and what to appeal. Article 12.7 also furthers the objectives, expressed in Article 3.2 of the DSU, of promoting security and predictability in the multilateral trading system and of clarifying the existing provisions of the covered agreements, because the requirement to provide "basic" reasons contributes to other WTO Members' understanding of the nature and scope of the rights and obligations in the covered agreements.[517]

The Appellate Body went on to explain, however, that Article 12.7 does not require panels to expound at length on the reasons for their findings and recommendations. In some cases, those reasons may be set out in other documents, such as previous panel or Appellate Body reports. In these cases, simple quotation or even incorporation by reference could suffice.[518]

[517] *Supra* note 12, ¶ 107.
[518] *Id.* ¶ 109.

5

Special Rules and Procedures

§ 5.01 Overview

Appendix 2 to the Dispute Settlement Understanding lists a number of special or additional rules and procedures contained in specific covered agreements that apply when the provisions of those agreements are in issue. To the extent that there is a difference between the provisions of the DSU and any of these special rules, the special rules prevail.[1] If there is no difference between the provisions of the DSU and the special or additional rules and procedures of a covered agreement, then both apply.[2] Since it is only when there is a conflict between the DSU and the special or additional rules and procedures that the latter prevail, it is the task of the interpreter to determine whether in fact there is a difference or inconsistency.[3]

A number of agreements have consultation and dispute settlement provisions, but these are not meant to replace the rules and procedures of the DSU as a coherent system of dispute settlement.[4] The DSU also contains several provisions applicable to disputes involving developing countries. These too prevail over the standard rules of the DSU when applicable. Finally, the DSU contains special rules that apply to "non-violation" and "other situation" complaints of the type described in Article XXIII (1)(b) and (c) of GATT, as well as arbitration.

§ 5.02 GATT and WTO rules for developing countries

Developing countries have long been a concern of the GATT and now of the WTO.[5] Article XVIII of GATT 1947 deals with Governmental

[1] DSU Art. 1.2.

[2] Appellate Body Report, *Guatemala – Anti-Dumping Investigation Regarding Portland Cement from Mexico*, WT/DS60/AB/R, adopted 25 November 1998, DSR 1998:XI, 3767, ¶ 65.

[3] *Id.* [4] *Id.* ¶ 67.

[5] *See* generally, Robert E. Hudec, GATT AND THE DEVELOPING COUNTRIES (Trade Policy Research Centre, 1988).

Assistance to Economic Development, a topic of primary interest to developing countries. The entirety of Part IV of GATT, dealing with Trade and Development, was added in the 1960s at the behest of the developing countries. In 1966, GATT adopted an Understanding regarding the application of dispute settlement procedures to developing countries.[6] Article 3.12 of the DSU makes certain provisions of the 1966 Understanding applicable to developing countries as optional alternatives to the corresponding DSU provisions. In addition, several articles of the DSU contain provisions that apply specifically to developing countries. Finally, Article 27 of the *Agreement on Subsidies and Countervailing Measures* and Article 15 of the *Agreement on Implementation of Article VI of GATT 1994* ("Antidumping Agreement") provide for special and differential treatment for developing countries.[7]

§ 5.03 The 1966 Understanding and developing countries

The 1966 Understanding provides alternative provisions to four DSU articles to developing countries which bring complaints under any WTO agreement against a developed country Member. These are: Article 4 (Consultations); Article 5 (Good Offices, Conciliation and Mediation); Article 6 (Establishment of Panels); and Article 12 (Panel Procedures).[8]

[1] Consultations

Despite the fact that the DSU offers the 1966 Understanding as an alternative to the consultation provisions of Article 4 of the DSU, there do not appear to be any important differences between the Understanding and Article 4. The Understanding simply refers to steps to be taken "[i]f consultations between a less-developed contracting party and a developed contracting party in regard to any matter falling under paragraph 1 of Article XXIII do not lead to a satisfactory settlement."[9] The Understanding has no provisions governing the course and conduct of consultations, apart from paragraph 4's reference to a "two months" time frame which would closely coincide with the 60 days provided for in Article 4. Accordingly, it does not seem likely that developing countries will often invoke the Understanding in lieu of Article 4.

[6] *Procedures Under Article XXIII*, BISD 14S/18.
[7] *See*, §§ 5.07 [8] and 5.09 [9].
[8] DSU Art. 3.12.
[9] Understanding ¶ 1.

[2] Good offices, conciliation or mediation

The provisions for good offices, conciliation or mediation ("good offices") contained in the Understanding are more elaborate than those contained in the DSU and, in an appropriate case, could offer an attractive alternative to a developing country complainant.

Perhaps the most important difference is that, under the DSU, good offices are undertaken only if both parties agree.[10] The Understanding, in contrast, permits a developing country complainant, if consultations are unsuccessful, to refer the matter to the Director-General, who may use his good offices with a view to facilitating a solution.[11] This provision permits the Director-General to become involved in the matter even over the opposition of the developed country respondent.

The Understanding also requires the parties, at the request of the Director-General, to furnish all relevant information.[12] This requirement could be a useful vehicle for developing country complainants that, during consultations, experience difficulty in obtaining relevant information concerning developed country programs.

[3] Establishment of panels

The 1966 Understanding provides that, after two months of consultations, the Director General shall – at the request of either of the parties – bring the matter to the attention of the DSB, to whom he shall submit a report.[13] A panel shall be appointed "forthwith,"[14] rather than at the meeting of the DSB following the meeting at which the request first appears on the agenda, as is normally the case.[15]

[4] Panel procedures

A panel established pursuant to the Understanding is to submit its findings and recommendations within 60 days from the date on which the matter was referred to it.[16] This short deadline contrasts sharply with the six to nine months normally provided to panels.[17] The DSU therefore relaxes

[10] DSU Art. 5.1. [11] Understanding ¶ 1. [12] Understanding ¶ 2.

[13] Understanding ¶ 4. The text of this paragraph actually refers to the CONTRACTING PARTIES or the GATT Council. Their dispute settlement responsibilities are now handled by the DSB.

[14] Understanding ¶ 5. [15] DSU Art. 6.1.

[16] Understanding ¶ 7. [17] DSU Art. 12.9.

the requirement of the Understanding by permitting a panel to extend the 60-day limit if it considers the time insufficient.[18]

§ 5.04 Developing country-related provisions of the DSU

[1] Consultations

Members are required by Article 4.10 of the DSU to "give special attention to the particular problems and interests of developing country Members" in the consultation process. Article 12.10 gives this general requirement some degree of specificity when a measure of a developing country is the subject of the consultations. The parties may agree to extend the time for consultations and, if they cannot agree to do so, the Chairman of the Dispute Settlement Body, after consulting with the parties, may extend the consultation period.

[2] Panel process

The difficulties developing countries may have in dealing with the complex WTO process are recognized by a further requirement of Article 12.10. When examining a complaint against a developing country Member, the panel shall accord sufficient time for the developing country to prepare and present its argumentation in defense of its measure. However, any extra time provided may not extend the normal time limits for the panel to issue the report, or for its recommendations and rulings to be implemented. When a developing country is involved as either complainant or respondent, panels are required to state in their reports explicitly how they have taken into account, when raised by a developing country, any relevant provisions on differential and more-favourable treatment for developing countries in the particular agreement at issue.[19]

In any dispute in which a developing country is involved, the panel shall include at least one panelist from a developing country, if the developing country Member involved in the dispute so requests.[20] Finally, the Secretariat provides legal advice and assistance to developing country Members upon request.[21]

[18] DSU Art. 3.12.
[19] DSU Art. 12.11.
[20] DSU Art. 8.10.
[21] DSU Art. 27.2.

§ 5.05 Agreement on the Application of Sanitary and Phytosanitary Measures

The *Agreement on the Application of Sanitary and Phytosanitary Measures* ("SPS Agreement") applies to measures designed to protect human, plant, and animal life or health from pests and disease.[22] Such measures are, for the most part, highly technical. Article 11.2 of the SPS Agreement, therefore, specifies that panels should seek the advice of experts in disputes involving scientific or technical issues which, as a practical matter, will be most of them.[23] A panel may establish an advisory technical experts group or consult with relevant international organizations, either on its own initiative or upon the request of a party.[24]

To facilitate the invitation of scientific experts to the WTO, an agreement between the WTO and the Office International des Épizooties provides that the organizations may agree "on administrative arrangements for designating scientific and technical experts with a view to the application of the provisions of the SPS Agreement, notably as provided for in Article 11, paragraph 2, in respect of dispute settlement."[25]

§ 5.06 Agreement on Technical Barriers to Trade

[1] General

The *Agreement on Technical Barriers to Trade* ("TBT Agreement") applies to standards and technical regulations applicable to all products, including agricultural and industrial products, other than those covered by the *Agreement on the Application of Sanitary and Phytosanitary Measures.*[26] Article 14 specifies that consultations and the settlement of disputes shall be governed by the Dispute Settlement Understanding.[27] In addition, it authorizes a panel, at the request of a party or on its own initiative, to establish a technical experts group to assist in questions of a technical nature, requiring detailed consideration by experts.[28]

[22] *See* definition in SPS Agreement, Annex A.

[23] SPS Agreement Art. 11.2.

[24] *Id. See* § 4.09 [5].

[25] *Agreement between the World Trade Organization and the Office International des Épizooties*, WT/L/272, 8 July 1998, ¶ 10. (The Organization International des Épizooties, headquartered in Paris, comprises 164 member countries. Its mission is to: inform governments of the occurrence and course of animal diseases; coordinate studies devoted to the surveillance and control of animal diseases; and harmonize regulations for trade in animals and animal products among its members.)

[26] TBT Agreement Arts. 1.3 and 1.5.

[27] TBT Agreement Art. 14.1.

[28] TBT Agreement Art. 14.2.

[2] Measures covered by the TBT Agreement

A technical regulation is a "[d]ocument which lays down product characteristics or their related processes and production methods, including the applicable administrative provisions, with which compliance is mandatory."[29] In *EC – Asbestos*, its first examination of the TBT Agreement, the Appellate Body discussed this definition extensively, including a thorough exploration of dictionary definitions of the operative terms.[30]

A standard is a "[d]ocument approved by a recognized body, that provides, for common and repeated use, rules, guidelines or characteristics for products or related processes and production methods, with which compliance is not mandatory."[31]

[3] Experts

Annex 2 to the TBT Agreement sets out simple procedures for technical expert groups: their terms of reference are set by the panels to whom they report; participation is restricted to persons of recognized experience and standing in the field; citizens of parties to the dispute shall not serve without the joint agreement of the parties, other than in exceptional circumstances when the need for specialized expertise cannot be satisfied otherwise; officials of governments of parties to the dispute may not serve; and governments or organizations shall not give instructions to experts, who serve in their individual capacities.[32]

Technical expert groups, in turn, may consult and seek information and technical advice from any source they deem appropriate.[33] Parties shall have access to all relevant information provided to an expert group, other than confidential information, which shall not be released without formal authorization from the government, organization or person providing the information.[34] If confidential information is not released, a non-confidential summary will be provided by the government, organization or person supplying the information.[35] A draft report of the expert group shall be submitted for comment to the Members. Comments shall be taken into account in the final report which is circulated both to the Members and to the panel.[36]

[29] TBT Annex 1.1.

[30] Appellate Body Report, *European Communities – Measures Affecting Asbestos and Asbestos-Containing Products*, WT/DS135/AB/R, adopted 5 April 2001, ¶¶ 67–77.

[31] TBT Annex 1.2. [32] TBT Annex 2.1–2.3. [33] TBT Annex 2.4.

[34] TBT Annex 2.5. [35] *Id.* [36] TBT Annex 2.6.

There is no comparable provision in the SPS Agreement, raising the issue as to whether a panel established under the TBT Agreement could use experts in their individual capacity, rather than as a group, as was done by the Panel in *EC – Hormones* under the SPS Agreement.[37] This issue was avoided by the Panel in *EC – Asbestos*, which decided to consult experts on an individual basis, pursuant to Articles 13.1 and 13.2, first sentence, of the DSU.[38] The Panel in *EC – Asbestos* also noted that Article 14.2 of the TBT Agreement provides that panels "may" establish a technical expert group. "Nevertheless," the Panel said, "it does not exclusively prescribe the establishment of a technical expert group, and this possibility, in our opinion, is not incompatible with the general authorization given under Article 13 of the DSU to consult with individual experts. The two provisions can be read as complementing each other."[39]

The TBT Agreement's provisions regarding experts may be invoked when a Member considers that another Member has not achieved satisfactory results under that agreement's provisions dealing with local government bodies and non-governmental bodies, as well as central government bodies, provided its trade interests are significantly affected. In these circumstances, the results of the dispute settlement process shall be the equivalent to those as if the body in question were a Member.[40] Several provisions of the TBT Agreement require that Members take reasonable measures available to them in achieving compliance with the Agreement by local governmental bodies and non-governmental organizations.[41]

§ 5.07 Agreement on Implementation of Article VI of GATT 1994 (Antidumping Agreement)

[1] General

Article 17 of the *Agreement on Implementation of Article VI of GATT 1994* ("Antidumping Agreement") covers consultations and dispute settlement

[37] Panel Reports, *EC Measures Concerning Meat and Meat Products (Hormones) – Complaint by Canada*, WT/DS48/R/CAN, DSR 1998:II, 235, and *EC Measures Concerning Meat and Meat Products (Hormones) – Complaint by the United States*, WT/DS26/R/USA, DSR 1998:III, 699, both reports adopted 13 February 1998, as modified by the Appellate Body Report, WT/DS26/AB/R, WT/DS48/AB/R, DSR 1998:I, 135, ¶ 8.12. *See*, §§ 4.09 [5] and 5.05.

[38] Panel Report, *European Communities – Measures Affecting Asbestos and Asbestos-Containing Products*, WT/DS135/R and Add.1, adopted 5 April 2001, as modified by the Appellate Body Report, WT/DS135/AB/R, ¶ 5.6.

[39] *Id.* ¶ 5.18. *See* § 4.09 [5].

[40] TBT Agreement Art. 14.4.

[41] TBT Agreement Arts. 3, 4, 7, 8 and 9.

concerning antidumping matters.[42] Paragraphs 4 through 7 of Article 17 are listed as special or additional rules and procedures in Appendix 2 of the DSU, and therefore take precedence over any conflicting provisions of the DSU. Article 17 does not, however, replace the DSU as a coherent or complete system of dispute settlement for antidumping.[43] Interpretation of Article 17 has been the subject of several significant panel and Appellate Body reports.

In *US – DRAMS*, a challenge to an administrative review of an antidumping measure, the Panel held that the scope of WTO review of antidumping measures applies only to those parts of a pre-WTO measure that are included in the scope of a review that took place after the Antidumping Agreement became effective.[44]

[2] Establishment of a panel

Article 17.4 of the Antidumping Agreement, like Article 6.2 of the DSU, concerns requests for the establishment of a panel when consultations do not resolve the dispute. They are complementary and are to be read together.[45] Article 17.4 does not set out any additional requirements with respect to the specificity with which claims must be set forth in a request for establishment challenging an antidumping determination. Accordingly, a request that satisfies Article 6.2 of the DSU also satisfies the requirements of Article 17.4.[46]

Article 17.5, however, requires that the request indicate how a benefit accruing to the complaining Member is nullified or impaired, or that the achieving of the objectives of the Agreement is being impeded. While this does not require the complaining Member to use the words "nullify" or "impair," it must be clear from the request that such an allegation is

[42] For a general discussion of the Antidumping Agreement, *see*, David Palmeter, *A Commentary on the WTO Anti-Dumping Code*, 30 JOURNAL OF WORLD TRADE 43 (No. 4, August 1996).

[43] Panel Report, *United States – Anti-dumping Act of 1916 – Complaint by the European Communities*, WT/DS136/R and Corr.1, adopted 26 September 2000, as upheld by the Appellate Body Report, WT/DS136/AB/R, WT/DS162/AB/R, DSR 2000:X, 4593, ¶ 67.

[44] Panel Report, *United States – Anti-Dumping Duty on Dynamic Random Access Memory Semiconductors (DRAMS) of One Megabit or Above from Korea*, WT/DS99/R, adopted 19 March 1999, DSR 1999:II, 521, ¶ 6.14.

[45] Panel Report, *Mexico – Anti-Dumping Investigation of High Fructose Corn Syrup (HFCS) from the United States*, WT/DS132/R and Corr.1, adopted 24 February 2000, DSR 2000:III, 1345, ¶ 7.11.

[46] *Id.* ¶ 7.14.

being made; moreover, the request must explicitly indicate how benefits are being nullified or impaired.[47]

[3] The "matter" before an antidumping panel

The term "matter" in Article 17.4 of the Antidumping Agreement has the same meaning as "matter" in Article 6.2 of the DSU.[48] However, in *Guatemala – Cement I*, the Appellate Body held that Article 17.4 limits the "measures" that may be the subject of an antidumping matter referred to a panel to three: definitive antidumping duties, provisional measures, and price undertakings.[49] Nevertheless, in *US – 1916 Act*, the Appellate Body concluded that Article 17.4 does not preclude review of antidumping legislation as such for aspects of that legislation other than definitive antidumping duties, provisional measures, and price undertakings.[50]

[4] Article 17.6 – standard of review[51]

Perhaps the most significant part of Article 17 is paragraph 6, which provides a standard of review for panels considering antidumping measures. No other agreement, including the DSU, contains an explicit standard of review provision.[52] Article 17.6 was included, reportedly at the insistence of the United States, as a last minute "deal breaker."[53] It provides a detailed standard of deference to the decisions of national authorities imposing antidumping duties.

Article 17.6(i) requires panels to determine whether the establishment of the facts by the national authorities was proper, and whether their evaluation of those facts was unbiased and objective. If so, panels should not overturn the factual evaluation of the national authorities, even though

47 *Id.* ¶ 7.26.

48 Appellate Body Report, *Guatemala Cement – I, supra* note 2, ¶ 72.

49 *Id.* ¶ 79.

50 Appellate Body Report, *United States – Anti-Dumping Act of 1916*, WT/DS136/AB/R, WT/DS162/AB/R, adopted 26 September 2000, DSR 2000:X, 4793, ¶ 72.

51 *See* generally, § 4.12.

52 During the Uruguay Round, negotiators reached a *Decision on Review of Article 17.6 of the Agreement on Implementation of Article VI of the General Agreement on Tariffs and Trade 1994*, in which they agreed to review the antidumping standard of review within three years "with a view to considering the question of whether it is capable of general application." The three-year deadline was not met.

53 Ernst-Ulrich Petersmann, *The Dispute Settlement System of the World Trade Organization and the Evolution of the GATT Dispute Settlement System Since 1948*, 31 Common Mkt. L. Rev. 1157, 1204, 1224 (1994); *see* also, John Croome, Reshaping the World Trading System 374 (WTO, 1995).

the panel might have reached a different conclusion on the same facts. Article 17.6(i) can be seen as applying to panels reviewing factual findings of national authorities a standard of review that echoes the DSU Article 11 standard applied by the Appellate Body to factual findings by panels. The Appellate Body has distinguished the obligation of a panel under Article 17.6(i) and the obligation of national authorities under Article 3.1 of the Antidumping Agreement, which requires the authorities to base a determination of injury on "positive evidence."[54]

Article 17.6(ii) directs panels first to interpret the relevant provisions of the Agreement in accordance with the customary rules of interpretation of public international law; this requirement is consistent with DSU Article 3.2. Second, Article 17.6(ii) provides that, "Where the panel finds that a relevant provision of the Agreement admits of more than one permissible interpretation, the panel shall find the authorities' measure to be in conformity with the Agreement if it rests upon one of those permissible interpretations."

The requirements of subparagraphs (i) and (ii) are cumulative.[55]

[5] Article 17.6(i) – review of factual determinations

The question whether the "establishment of the facts was proper" is different from the question whether their evaluation was "unbiased and objective." The question of establishment of the facts does not, for example, involve the question whether all the relevant facts were considered. That question goes to evaluation.[56]

The "facts" upon which a determination is made, for purposes of review under Article 17.6(i), include both the confidential and non-confidential record of the national investigation.[57] However, panels are not required to scrutinize the entire record on their own. It is the responsibility of

[54] Appellate Body Report, *Thailand – Anti-Dumping Duties on Angles, Shapes and Sections of Iron or Non-Alloy Steel and H-Beams from Poland*, WT/DS122/AB/R, adopted 5 April 2001, ¶ 137.

[55] Appellate Body Report, *Mexico – Anti-Dumping Investigation of High Fructose Corn Syrup (HFCS) from the United States – Recourse to Article 21.5 of the DSU by the United States*, WT/DS132/AB/RW, adopted 21 November 2001, ¶ 130.

[56] Panel Report, *United States – Anti-Dumping Measures on Certain Hot-Rolled Steel Products from Japan*, WT/DS184/R, adopted 23 August 2001, as modified by the Appellate Body Report, WT/DS184/AB/R, ¶ 7.26.

[57] Panel Report, *Thailand – Anti-Dumping Duties on Angles, Shapes and Sections of Iron or Non-Alloy Steel and H-Beams from Poland*, WT/DS122/R, adopted 5 April 2001, as modified by the Appellate Body Report, WT/DS122/AB/R, ¶ 7.52.

the national authorities to make a record of their own establishment and evaluation of the facts for the panel to review.[58] The Appellate Body made clear, in *Mexico – Corn Syrup (Article 21.5 – US)*, that panels are not authorized "to engage in a new and independent fact-finding exercise."[59] In the words of one Panel:

> [W]e are precluded from basing our findings on our own *de novo* review of the record evidence, and our own conclusions about each factor and the existence of injury and causation overall. We are, rather, to consider whether the conclusions reached in the investigation *could* have been reached by an objective and unbiased investigating authority on the basis of its analysis of the evidence of record at the time of the determination.[60]

In *Guatemala – Cement I*, in considering whether the evidence available to the authorities was sufficient to justify the initiation of the investigation, the Panel quoted extensively, with approval, from the GATT Panel report in *United States – Measures Affecting Imports of Softwood Lumber from Canada*.[61] The Panel stated that its task was not to evaluate anew the evidence and information available to the authorities, but to examine "whether an unbiased and objective investigating authority evaluating that evidence could properly have determined that sufficient evidence of dumping, injury, and causal link existed to justify initiating the investigation."[62] The Panel in *US – Hot-Rolled Steel* followed this understanding, holding that evidence not submitted to an investigating authority cannot be submitted for the first time before a panel.[63]

The responsibility imposed on national authorities by Article 17.6(i) has been considered by several panels. The Panel in *US – Hot-Rolled Steel* stated that the authorities must collect "relevant and reliable information," including evidence which "might detract from the decision actually reached by the investigating authorities."[64] In *Mexico – Corn Syrup*, the Panel found that the national authorities must examine all of the factors relevant to an injury finding listed in Article 3.4 of the Antidumping Agreement.[65]

[58] Panel Report, *Mexico – Corn Syrup*, *supra* note 45, ¶ 7.192. [59] *Supra* note 55, ¶ 84.
[60] Panel Report, *Egypt – Definitive Anti-Dumping Measures on Steel Rebar from Turkey*, WT/211/R, adopted 1 October 2002, ¶ 7.126.
[61] BISD 40S/358, adopted 17 October 1993.
[62] Panel Report, *Guatemala – Anti-Dumping Investigation Regarding Portland Cement from Mexico*, WT/DS60/R, adopted 25 November 1998, as modified by the Appellate Body Report, WT/DS60/AB/R, DSR 1998:IX, 3797, ¶ 7.57.
[63] *Supra* note 56, ¶¶ 7.6–7.7. [64] *Id.* ¶ 7.26. [65] *Supra* note 45, ¶ 7.128.

[6] *Article 17.6(ii) – review of legal determinations*

Article 17.6(ii) provides a standard of review to be applied to questions of law. It first instructs panels to interpret the relevant provisions of the Antidumping Agreement in accordance with the customary rules of interpretation of public international law. It next instructs panels, when they find that a provision of the Agreement admits of more than one permissible interpretation, to uphold the decision of the authorities if they reach one of those permissible interpretations.

The customary rules of interpretation of public international law for purposes of Article 17, as with DSU Article 3.2, are those set out in Articles 31 and 32 of the *Vienna Convention on the Law of Treaties.*[66] Prof. Steven P. Croley and Prof. John H. Jackson have noted that Articles 31 and 32 of the Vienna Convention are intended to resolve textual ambiguities. Thus, they observe, "Once a panel has invoked Articles 31 and 32 of the Vienna Convention, it presumably will have already settled on a nonambiguous, nonabsurd interpretation."[67] In other words, a panel following the text of Article 17.6(ii) and applying the customary rules of interpretation of public international law would reach a single, correct interpretation of the treaty provision in question. It would not find that "a relevant provision of the Agreement admits of more than one permissible interpretation," and therefore would not have occasion to "find the authorities' measure to be in conformity with the Agreement if it rests upon one of those permissible interpretations."

In *US – Hot-Rolled Steel*, the Appellate Body suggested rather strongly that this is the likely result. "The second sentence of Article 17.6(ii)," it said, "*presupposes* that application of the rules of treaty interpretation in Articles 31 and 32 of the Vienna Convention could give rise to, at least, two interpretations of some provisions of the Antidumping Agreement."[68] It went on to state that "a permissible interpretation is one which is found to be appropriate *after* application of the pertinent rules of the Vienna Convention."[69] It then went on to say that "which provisions" of the Antidumping Agreement "admit of more than one 'permissible

[66] Appellate Body Report, *United States – Anti-Dumping Measures on Certain Hot-Rolled Steel Products from Japan*, WT/DS184/AB/R, adopted 23 August 2001, ¶ 57.

[67] Steven P. Croley & John H. Jackson, *WTO Dispute Procedures, Standard of Review, and Deference to National Governments*, 90 AMERICAN JOURNAL OF INTERNATIONAL LAW 193, 201 (April 1996).

[68] Appellate Body Report, *supra* note 66, ¶ 59 (emphasis in original).

[69] *Id.* ¶ 60 (emphasis in original).

interpretation' can only be addressed in the context of particular disputes."[70]

In *EC – Bed Linen*, the Panel explicitly stated that it would determine whether the EC's interpretation was one that was permissible under the customary rules of interpretation.[71] In no instance, however, did the Panel reach more than one interpretation. On appeal, the Appellate Body affirmed, noting that "the Panel was not faced with a choice among multiple 'permissible' interpretations which would have required it, under Article 17.6(ii), to give deference to the interpretation relied upon by the European Communities. Rather, the Panel was faced with a situation in which the interpretation relied upon by the European Communities was . . . 'impermissible.' "[72]

[7] Confidential information

Many of the relevant facts in antidumping investigations are confidential. In this regard, Article 17.7, in conformity with the DSU, specifies that confidential information disclosed to the panel shall not be disclosed without formal authorization of the submitter, but that if confidential information is withheld, a non-confidential summary will be released.[73]

An additional provision in Article 17 deals, indirectly, with the issue of confidentiality. Article 17.5(ii) provides that panels shall examine matters based upon "the facts made available in conformity with appropriate domestic procedures to the authorities of the importing Member." In *Thailand – H-Beams*, the Appellate Body held that Article 17.5, as well as Article 17.6(i), "require a panel to examine the facts made available to the investigating authority of the importing Member. These provisions do not prevent a panel from examining facts that were not disclosed to, or discernable by, the interested parties at the time of the final determination."[74]

In *US – Line Pipe*, a dispute involving the *Agreement on Safeguards*, the Panel requested information from the confidential report to the President

[70] *Id.* ¶ 61.

[71] Panel Report, *European Communities – Anti-Dumping Duties on Imports of Cotton-Type Bed Linen from India*, WT/DS141/R, adopted 12 March 2001, as modified by the Appellate Body Report, WT/DS141/AB/R, ¶ 6.46.

[72] Appellate Body Report, *European Communities – Anti-Dumping Duties on Imports of Cotton-Type Bed Linen from India*, WT/DS141/AB/R, adopted 12 March 2001, ¶ 65.

[73] *See* § 4.14.

[74] Appellate Body Report, *supra* note 54, ¶ 118.

from the United States International Trade Commission. The US did not provide the information, but did supply indexed data, which the Panel found was sufficient to permit it to make an "objective assessment of the matter."[75]

[8] Developing countries

WTO Members are called upon by Article 15 of the Antidumping Agreement to recognize the special situation of developing countries when considering the application of antidumping measures, and to explore "constructive remedies" provided for by the Agreement before applying antidumping duties, "where they would affect the special interests of developing country Members." However, this provision "imposes no specific or general obligation on Members to undertake any particular action."[76] Further, the fact that a company is operating in a developing country "does not mean that it somehow shares the 'special situation' of the developing country Member."[77]

[9] Overlap with countervailing duties

There is considerable substantive overlap between antidumping and countervailing duty proceedings, particularly with regard to questions of injury. To further consistency in these areas, the Ministers at the Uruguay Round issued a Declaration "recognizing the need for the consistent resolution of disputes arising from anti-dumping and countervailing duty measures."[78] This is likely to mean, in practice, that parties, panels, and the Appellate Body will treat prior reports dealing with injury under the Antidumping Agreement as the equivalent of a report under the Agreement on Subsidies and Countervailing Measures and vice versa.[79]

[75] Panel Report, *United States – Definitive Safeguard Measures on Imports of Circular Welded Carbon Quality Line Pipe from Korea*, WT/DS202/R, adopted 8 March 2002, as modified by the Appellate Body Report, WT/DS202/AB/R, ¶¶ 7.9–7.11.

[76] Panel Report, *United States – Anti-Dumping and Countervailing Measures on Steel Plate from India*, WT/DS206/R and Corr.1, adopted 29 July 2002, ¶ 7.110.

[77] *Id.* ¶ 7.111.

[78] *Declaration on Dispute Settlement Pursuant to the Agreement on Implementation of Article VI of the General Agreement on Tariffs and Trade 1994 or Part V of the Agreement on Subsidies and Countervailing Measures.*

[79] *See* § 3.03.

§ 5.08 Agreement on Implementation of Article VII of GATT 1994 (Customs Valuation Agreement)

A Technical Committee on Customs Valuation, established by Article 18.2 of the *Agreement on Implementation of Article VII of GATT 1994* (the "Customs Valuation Agreement") serves, *inter alia*, as an institutionalized expert group available to assist panels and parties to valuation disputes.

An important difference between the Technical Committee on Customs Valuation and other expert groups is that the Technical Committee is directed to provide, upon request, advice and assistance to Members engaged in consultations.[80] This responsibility is in addition to the normal expert group responsibility, which the Technical Committee also has, of carrying out an examination of any question requiring technical consideration upon the request of a panel.[81]

The terms of reference for the Technical Committee are set by the panel, and the panel, in turn, is required to take the Committee's report into consideration in its own deliberations.[82] If the Committee is unable to reach consensus on the matter referred to it, the panel will afford the parties an opportunity to present their views on the matter.[83]

Article 19 to the Customs Valuation Agreement makes clear that the DSU is generally applicable to disputes arising under the Agreement.[84] It also provides that confidential information provided to the panel shall not be disclosed without formal authorization of the submitter, but that when such information is not disclosed, a non-confidential summary shall be provided.[85]

§ 5.09 Agreement on Subsidies and Countervailing Measures

The entire subject of subsidies and countervailing measures – usually termed "countervailing duties" – is contentious, and the *Agreement on Subsidies and Countervailing Measures* ("SCM Agreement"), in its complexity, reflects this policy contentiousness. The SCM Agreement initially deals with two types of subsidies: (1) prohibited and (2) actionable, as well as with domestic measures taken to offset, or "countervail," prohibited and actionable subsidies.[86] It also establishes a Permanent Group of Experts with the responsibility, *inter alia*, of assisting panels in disputes concerning prohibited subsidies.[87]

[80] Customs Valuation Agreement Art. 19.3. [81] *Id.* Art. 19.4. [82] *Id.*
[83] *Id.* [84] *Id.* Art. 19.1. [85] *Id.* Art. 19.5. *See* also, § 4.10 [1].
[86] A former third category, "non-actionable" subsidies, is no longer in effect. *See* § 5.09 [7].
[87] SCM Agreement Art. 24.3. As noted above at § 5.07 [9], there is considerable substantive overlap between countervailing duty and antidumping proceedings, particularly with

[1] Prohibited subsidy procedures

Subsidies that are contingent upon export performance or upon the use of domestic rather than imported goods are prohibited by the SCM Agreement.[88] Reflecting the concern of the Members of the WTO with such subsidies, the SCM Agreement provides expedited procedures for dealing with disputes concerning them.

Whenever a Member has reason to believe that a prohibited subsidy is being granted or maintained by another Member, it may request consultations with that other Member. The Member requested to consult must do so "as quickly as possible."[89] If no mutually agreed solution is reached within 30 days of the request for consultations, the matter may be referred to the Dispute Settlement Body for the immediate establishment of a panel.[90] This contrasts sharply with regular DSU proceedings which provide 60 days for consultations before a request for the establishment of a panel can be made, and for the establishment of a panel at the second meeting after a request first was placed on the agenda of the DSB.[91] Apart from the time limits specified in the SCM Agreement, other time periods specified in the DSU for the conduct of dispute settlement panels are reduced by half for prohibited subsidy disputes.[92]

No provision is made for interim reports of panels concerned with prohibited subsidy disputes. Instead, panels are directed simply to submit their final reports to the parties to the dispute and to circulate the final report to the Members within 90 days of the date of the composition of the panel and the establishment of its terms of reference.[93] In practice, no panel has been able to issue its report within 90 days of its composition.[94] Two panels have required more than 300 days.[95]

regard to questions of injury, and, to further consistency in these areas, the Ministers at the Uruguay Round issued a Declaration "recognizing the need for the consistent resolution of disputes arising from anti-dumping and countervailing duty measures."

[88] SCM Agreement Art. 3.1. [89] *Id.* Art. 4.3. [90] *Id.* Art. 4.4.

[91] DSU Arts. 4.7 and 6.1. [92] SCM Agreement Art. 4.12. [93] *Id.* Art. 4.6.

[94] For the first eight plus years of the WTO, the shortest time was 180 days from composition to report. *See* Panel Report, *Brazil – Export Financing Programme for Aircraft*, WT/DS46/R, adopted 20 August 1999, as modified by the Appellate Body Report, WT/DS46/AB/R, DSR 1999:III, 1221, and Panel Report, *Canada – Measures Affecting the Export of Civilian Aircraft*, WT/DS70/R, adopted 20 August 1999, as upheld by the Appellate Body Report, WT/DS70/AB/R, DSR 1999:IV, 1443.

[95] *See* Panel Report, *United States – Tax Treatment for "Foreign Sales Corporations,"* WT/DS108/R, adopted 20 March 2000, as modified by the Appellate Body Report, WT/DS108/AB/R, DSR 2000:IV, 1677, and Panel Report, *Canada – Certain Measures Affecting the Automotive Industry,* WT/DS139/R, WT/DS142/R, adopted 19 June 2000, as modified by the Appellate Body Report, WT/DS139/AB/R, WT/DS142/AB/R, DSR 2000:VII, 3043.

If the measure in question is found to be a prohibited subsidy, the panel shall recommend that it be withdrawn without delay; in this regard, the panel will specify the time within which the measure must be withdrawn "without delay."[96] Expedited provisions also govern the appeal of prohibited subsidy panel reports, and the adoption and implementation of those reports.[97]

[2] Requests for consultations – SCM Article 4.2

Article 4.2 of the SCM Agreement specifies that a request for consultations in a prohibited subsidy dispute "shall include a statement of available evidence with regard to the existence and nature of the subsidy in question."[98] In *US – FSC*, the United States argued to the Panel that the request for consultations, which simply referred to the legislation at issue, did not contain the required statement of evidence.[99] The Panel held that identification of the measure was sufficient.[100] It went on to say that even if the request did not contain a statement of available evidence, "the sole prerequisite to requesting establishment of a panel is that consultations have been held or requested to be held and that the relevant specified time-period has elapsed."[101] It went on to say that no provision of either the DSU or SCM Article 4 required the dismissal of a claim for failure to include a statement of available evidence in the consultation request.[102]

The Appellate Body affirmed the result, but with very different reasoning.[103] As an initial matter, the Appellate Body said that SCM Article 4.2 and DSU Article 4.4 should be read and applied together.[104] The requirements of SCM Article 4.2 are distinct from and are not satisfied by compliance with DSU Article 4.4.[105] Thus, Article 4.2 requires evidence of the nature of the subsidy, not simply evidence of the existence of the measure. "We would have preferred that the Panel gave less relaxed treatment to this important distinction," the Appellate Body said.[106] While the Appellate Body strongly implied that an SCM Article 4.2 request for consultations that does not contain a statement of available evidence could be fatally defective, on the facts of the *US – FSC* case it effectively

[96] *Id.* Art. 4.8. [97] *See* § 8.07.

[98] A comparable provision with regard to actionable subsidies is contained in SCM Article 7.2. *See* § 5.09 [4]

[99] *Supra* note 95, ¶ 7.1. [100] *Id.* ¶ 7.5. [101] *Id.* ¶ 7.7. [102] *Id.*

[103] Appellate Body Report, *United States – Tax Treatment for "Foreign Sales Corporations,"* WT/DS108/AB/R, adopted 20 March 2000, DSR 2000:III, 1619.

[104] *Id.* ¶ 159. [105] *Id.* ¶ 161. [106] *Id.*

found – without using the words – that the United States had waived any right to objection it might have had, or was estopped from asserting that the request was defective.

The parties had engaged in three separate sets of consultations over a period of nearly five months, the Appellate Body noted, and during this time the United States did not object to the consultation request.[107] The United States, it said, "acted as if it had accepted the establishment of the Panel in this dispute, as well as the consultations preceding such establishment."[108] It went on to cite DSU Article 3.10, which commits Members to engage in dispute settlement proceedings "in good faith," and stated that the principle of good faith "requires that responding Members seasonably and promptly bring claimed procedural deficiencies to the attention of the complaining Member, and to the DSB or the Panel, so that corrections, if needed, can be made to resolve disputes."[109]

The Panel in *US – FSC* noted that, as a practical matter, all evidence presented by a complainant to the Panel was available to the complainant at the time of the request.[110] The Panel in *Australia – Automotive Leather II* stated that, "Article 4.2 does not require a complaining Member to disclose arguments in the request for consultations."[111] "The statement of available evidence," it said, "thus informs the beginning of the dispute settlement process – it does not limit the scope of evidence and argument for the entire proceeding that may ensue to only what is in the request for consultations."[112]

[3] Procedures before the Permanent Group of Experts

Panels established to consider prohibited subsidies may request the assistance of the Permanent Group of Experts ("PGE") with regard to the issue of whether the measure in question is or is not a prohibited subsidy.[113] The PGE's conclusions on that question "shall be accepted by the panel without modification."[114]

The SCM Agreement also provides that the PGE "shall provide an opportunity for the Member applying or maintaining the measure to demonstrate that the measure in question is not a prohibited subsidy."[115]

[107] *Id.* ¶ 162. [108] *Id.* ¶ 165. [109] *Id.* ¶ 166.
[110] Panel Report, *supra* note 95, ¶ 7.6.
[111] Panel Report, *Australia – Subsidies Provided to Producers and Exporters of Automotive Leather*, WT/DS126/R, adopted 16 June 1999, DSR 1999:III, 951, ¶ 9.26.
[112] *Id.* ¶ 9.29. [113] SCM Agreement Art. 4.5. [114] *Id.* [115] *Id.*

It is not clear from this language whether the accused Member has the burden of establishing that the measure is not prohibited, or that the accuser has the burden of establishing that it is.[116] In 1996, the PGE issued Draft Rules of Procedure, but has never issued Final Rules.

Part III of the Draft Rules deal with Assistance to Panels.[117] These rules reflect the accelerated pace of prohibited subsidy proceedings. Parties, and any interested third parties, may make written submissions within seven days of the request for the establishment of a panel to the PGE for assistance.[118] The submission should address the issue of whether the measure identified by the panel is a prohibited subsidy, and should contain any relevant information concerning the measure, including legislation, regulations, or other documentation relating to the establishment and operation of the measure.[119] Parties to the dispute, but not third parties, may submit written rebuttal within fourteen days of the request for assistance.[120]

At the request of a party, or on its own initiative, the PGE may hold one hearing which, normally, will take place 21 days after the request for assistance.[121] Parties' requests for a hearing should be included in their initial written submissions.[122] Third parties, as well as parties, may be present at the hearing, but only for the duration of their oral presentations.[123]

In exceptional circumstances, where strict adherence to these time periods would result in "manifest unfairness," the PGE may, at the request of a party, modify the time period for filing documents or scheduling a hearing.[124] Documents filed by a party or a third party must be served, by the most expeditious means possible, on each of the other parties to the dispute and to third parties.[125] This service requirement is unusual in WTO practice; the PGE Rules do not specify how a service list is to be compiled so that parties may comply with this requirement.

The PGE may be consulted by any Member, and may give confidential advisory opinions, which may not be invoked in any dispute settlement proceeding involving actionable subsidies.[126]

Through the first nine years of the WTO's existence, no Member has requested the assistance of the PGE.

[116] *See* § 4.13 concerning burden of proof.

[117] *Draft Rules of Procedure for the Permanent Group of Experts*, G/SCM/W/365/Rev.1, 26 June 1996 (hereafter PGE Rules).

[118] PGE Rule 9(1). [119] PGE Rule 9(2). [120] PGE Rule 9(3).

[121] PGE Rule 10(1). [122] PGE Rule 10(2). [123] PGE Rule 10(3) and (4).

[124] PGE Rule 13(2). [125] PGE Rule 15(2) and (3). [126] SCM Agreement Art. 24.4.

[4] *Actionable subsidy procedures*

Actionable subsidies are those which, though not prohibited, cause "adverse effects to the interests of other Members."[127] Adverse effects are those that cause injury to the domestic industry of another Member, nullify or impair benefits accruing to another Member, or cause serious prejudice to the interests of another Member.[128] Only a Member that believes that it has itself suffered serious prejudice as a result of subsidization may invoke the actionable subsidy provisions of Article 7 of the SCM Agreement.[129]

As is the case with prohibited subsidies, a request for consultations regarding an actionable subsidy must include a statement of available evidence with regard to the existence and nature of the subsidy.[130] In addition, the request must contain a statement of available evidence with regard to the adverse effects, *i.e.*, the injury, nullification and impairment, or serious prejudice.[131] In the event that serious prejudice is alleged, the available evidence may be limited to specific factors: the level of the subsidization; whether the subsidy covers operating losses sustained by an industry or, in some instances, a single enterprise; or whether it constitutes forgiveness of debt.[132] Annex V to the SCM Agreement sets out procedures for developing information concerning serious prejudice.[133]

Also, as is the case with prohibited subsidies, a Member receiving a consultation request shall enter into consultations "as quickly as possible."[134] If consultations do not result in an agreed solution within 60 days, establishment of a panel may be requested, and the panel will be established absent consensus to the contrary.[135] The composition of the panel and its terms of reference shall be established within 15 days from the date when it is established.[136] The final report of the panel shall be circulated to all Members within 120 days.[137] Expedited provisions also govern the appeal of actionable subsidy panel reports, and the adoption and implementation of those reports.[138]

[127] SCM Agreement Art. 5. [128] *Id.*

[129] Panel Report, *Indonesia – Certain Measures Affecting the Automobile Industry*, WT/DS54/R, WTDS55/R, WT/DS59/R, WT/DS64/R and Corr.1, 2, 3, and 4, adopted 23 July 1998, DSR 1998:IV, 2201, ¶ 14.203.

[130] SCM Agreement Art. 7.2. *See* § 5.09 [2]. [131] SCM Agreement Art. 7.2.

[132] SCM Agreement Art. 7, n. 19. The factors are set out in detail in Art. 6.1.

[133] *See*, § 5.09 [5]. [134] SCM Agreement Art. 7.3. [135] SCM Agreement Art. 7.4.

[136] *Id.* [137] SCM Agreement Art. 7.5. [138] *See* §§ 5.09 [4] and 8.07.

[5] Annex V procedures for developing information concerning serious prejudice

To establish that a program is inconsistent with the actionable subsidy provisions of the SCM Agreement, the complaining Member must demonstrate adverse effects – injury to its domestic industry, nullification or impairment, or serious prejudice. Information regarding injury to a domestic industry, as well as that relating to nullification and impairment to the complaining Member, is information uniquely available to that Member. However, information regarding serious prejudice may be uniquely in the possession of the Member complained against or of third parties.[139] Annex V to the SCM Agreement contains procedures for developing information concerning serious prejudice.

Members are required to cooperate in the development of evidence to be provided to a panel examining an allegation of an actionable subsidy.[140] In this regard, the parties to the dispute, as well as any interested third parties, are required to notify the DSB, as soon as a panel has been requested, of the organization within its territory responsible for administering the information requirement and the procedures to be followed in requesting information.[141] The DSB, upon request, shall initiate the procedure necessary to obtain relevant information from the government of the subsidizing Member.[142] This process may include the presentation of questions to both the complaining Member and the subsidizing Member.[143]

When third-country effects are at issue, a party to the dispute may collect third-country information through the use of questions to the government of the third-country Member.[144] The information to be supplied by third-country Members is that which already is available or readily can be made available; third-country Members are not required to make a market or price analysis specially for the purpose of responding to questions.[145] However, if a party undertakes a detailed market analysis at its own expense, the authorities of the third country should cooperate by making available all non-confidential information which is normally maintained by the government.[146]

[139] Serious prejudice is defined in Art. 6 of the SCM Agreement and includes, *inter alia*, the *ad valorem* level of the subsidy, whether it is used to cover operating losses or debt forgiveness, or whether the effect is to displace or impede imports of a Member in third country markets, or to undercut prices.

[140] SCM Agreement Annex V.1. [141] *Id.* [142] SCM Agreement Annex V.2.

[143] *Id.* [144] SCM Agreement Annex V.3. [145] *Id.* [146] *Id.*

Annex V specifies that a representative shall be appointed by the DSB to serve the function of facilitating the timely completion of the information-gathering process.[147] One of the responsibilities of the representative is to advise the panel of the reasonableness of any requests for information and the efforts made by parties to comply with these requests in a cooperative and timely manner.[148]

If the subsidizing Member, or third-country Members, fail to cooperate in the information-gathering process, the complaining Member shall present its case based on the evidence available to it.[149] The panel shall make its determination based on the best information available.[150] In making that determination, "the panel should draw adverse inferences from instances of non-cooperation by any party involved in the information-gathering process."[151] The panel retains its basic power to seek additional information on its own initiative.[152]

Paragraph 5 of Annex V provides that the information-gathering process by the facilitator "shall be completed within 60 days of the date on which the matter was referred to the DSB under paragraph 4 of Article 7." Paragraph 4 of Article 7 allows a complaining party "to refer the matter to the DSB for the establishment of a panel" when consultations have not resulted in an agreed solution. This language would seem to suggest that the 60-day period for the information-gathering process should begin with the request for the establishment of a panel, *i.e.*, even before the DSB has agreed to establish a panel. However, in *Indonesia – Autos*, the first dispute in which the Annex V process was requested, the DSB and the parties proceeded in a different manner.[153] Three complainants each requested the Annex V process and for each, the 60-day period began on the dates of their respective requests for the establishment of a panel.[154] The parties then agreed that the complainants' first submissions would be due four weeks after the completion of the last Annex V procedures.[155]

However, when Brazil requested Annex V procedures in its request for the establishment of a panel in *United States – Upland Cotton*, the process did not go as smoothly.[156] No facilitator was named, and the formal Annex V process was not initiated by the DSB when it established

[147] SCM Agreement Annex V.4.
[148] SCM Agreement Annex V.8.
[149] SCM Agreement Annex V.6.
[150] *Id.*
[151] SCM Agreement Annex V.7.
[152] SCM Agreement Annex V.9.
[153] Panel Report, *supra* note 129, ¶ 1.17.
[154] *Id.* ¶ 1.18.
[155] *Id.* ¶ 1.19.
[156] *United States – Subsidies on Upland Cotton – Request for the Establishment of a Panel by Brazil*, WT/DS267/7, 7 February 2003.

a panel.[157] Objections raised by the United States, including objections to the names of potential facilitators proposed by the Chairman of the DSB, led to an absence of consensus. The Chairman appears to have been of the view that a facilitator could not be named over the objection of the defending party. He stated that it had been his intention to appoint the facilitator at the meeting establishing the Panel, but because consultations on the identity of that person had not been completed, he was not in a position to do so.[158] This interpretation by the Chairman, if followed in subsequent cases, would have the practical effect of making the process subject to a positive consensus rule by giving the defending party the opportunity to block the process.[159]

[6] Multiple subsidy procedures

A Member may wish to argue that a subsidy is both prohibited and actionable, or that it is otherwise inconsistent with Article XVI of GATT. However, the time-tables prescribed for these procedures differ greatly. Allegations of prohibited subsidies and actionable subsidies are subject to different time-tables under the terms of Articles 4 and 7 of the SCM Agreement, while Article XVI proceedings would be subject to the even different times provided for in the DSU.

This issue arose when Canada requested the establishment of a panel to determine whether export financing for civil aircraft provided by Brazil was a prohibited subsidy as well as a violation of Articles XVI and XXIII of GATT.[160] Canada withdrew the request after the procedural problem was raised by Brazil in the DSB, and subsequently refiled the request with the Articles XVI and XXIII counts dropped.[161] Several

[157] Dispute Settlement Body, 18 March 2003, *Minutes of Meeting*, WT/DSB/M/145, 7 May 2003, ¶ 35.

[158] *Id.* ¶ 37. *See* also, *U.S. Raises Latest Obstacle to Brazil WTO Cotton Subsidies Challenge*, INSIDE US TRADE, April 18, 2003.

[159] The United States also argued that before a facilitator began work, it would be necessary for the Panel to determine whether, in view of the so-called "peace clause" of Article 13 of the Agriculture Agreement, the Panel could even proceed to consider the case. That provision precludes actionable subsidy proceedings against measures that conform to a Member's domestic support commitments, for a period of nine years. Dispute Settlement Body, 31 March 2003, *Minutes of Meeting*,WT/DSB/M/146.

[160] *Brazil – Export Financing Programme for Aircraft, Request for Establishment of a Panel by Canada*, WT/DS46/2, 17 September 1996.

[161] *Brazil – Export Financing Programme for Aircraft, Request for the Establishment of a Panel by Canada*, WT/DS46/4, 4 October 1996. This request also was withdrawn prior to the meeting at which it was to be considered. World Trade Organization, *WTO Focus*, No. 21, at 2 (August 1997).

months later, Brazil in turn sought consultations with Canada concerning the latter's programs affecting exports of civil aircraft. In this instance, Brazil filed two separate requests for consultations, the first alleging that the programs were prohibited subsidies, the second that they were actionable.[162]

As noted in § 5.09 [1], the "fast track" deadlines of the prohibited subsidy procedure have not been followed by panels; instead, panels and the parties have agreed to working procedures that extend the deadlines. Presumably, such a practice would permit a single panel to consider multiple subsidy complaints utilizing the longest times applicable to any claim.

[7] Non-actionable subsidies

For the first five years of the WTO, subsidies that provided assistance for certain research activities or to disadvantaged regions, as well as those that promoted adaptation of existing facilities to new environmental requirements, were not actionable provided they met the criteria of the SCM Agreement.[163] By operation of Article 31 of the SCM Agreement, this exemption was limited to five years unless renewed; it was not renewed.

[8] Countervailing measures

Countervailing measures, in the form of duties, may be taken to offset subsidies that injure a domestic industry. Disputes concerning the imposition of countervailing measures are governed generally by the Dispute Settlement Understanding.

Footnote 35 to Article X of the SCM Agreement specifies that countervailing measures may be imposed to offset both prohibited and actionable subsidies. However, they may not be imposed if counter-measures under dispute settlement procedures have been imposed. Countervailing measures could not be imposed against non-actionable subsides. However, as noted *supra* in § 5.09 [7], this category no longer exists.

[162] *Canada – Measures Affecting the Export of Civilian Aircraft*, WT/DS/70 and WT/DS/71, 10 March 1997.

[163] SCM Agreement Arts. 8.1 and 8.2.

[9] Developing countries

Article 27 of the SCM Agreement provides for special and differential treatment of developing countries. With regard to dispute settlement, it provides that the prohibited subsidy provisions shall not apply for a period of eight years from the date of entry into force of the WTO Agreement, *i.e.*, 31 December 2003, provided certain substantive standards are met.[164] During this period, the actionable subsidy provisions of Article 7, with their requirement of a showing of adverse effects, apply to what otherwise would be prohibited subsidies.[165]

In its report on *Brazil – Aircraft*, the Appellate Body held that it is not the obligation of a defending developing country to show that it meets the standards of Article 27. To the contrary, the Appellate Body said, the complaining party had the burden of showing that a defending developing country did not comply with of Art. 27.4.[166]

[10] Remedies

Articles 4 and 7 specify actions Members must take when a measure has been found to be prohibited or actionable, and provide for the imposition of countermeasures in the event that the Member concerned fails to implement a report properly. These are discussed in Chapters 7 and 8, *infra*.

§ 5.10 Agreement on Textiles and Clothing (ATC)

[1] Overview

International trade in textiles and clothing ("textiles") traditionally has been and, at least temporarily, effectively remains subject to a strict regulatory regime, the *Arrangement Regarding International Trade in Textiles*, commonly known as the "MFA." The MFA is not, however, an integral part of the WTO Agreement, nor was it made "in connexion with the conclusion of" the WTO Agreement.[167]

[164] The substantive standards are set out in paragraphs 2 through 5 of Article 27.

[165] SCM Agreement Art. 27.7.

[166] Appellate Body Report, *Brazil – Export Financing Programme for Aircraft*, WT/DS46/AB/R, adopted 20 August 1999, DSR 1999:III, 1161, ¶ 141.

[167] Panel Report, *United States – Transitional Safeguard Measure on Combed Cotton Yarn from Pakistan*, WTDS192/R, adopted 5 November 2001, as modified by the Appellate Body Report, WT/DS192/AB/R, ¶ 7.73.

The *Agreement on Textiles and Clothing* ("ATC") brings textile trade into the GATT/WTO system by phasing out the import quotas established by the MFA over a period of 10 years.[168] During this transition period, restrictions continue to apply, subject to the rules of the ATC. This system of restrictions is supervised by the Textiles Monitoring Body ("TMB").[169] Its responsibilities include resolving disagreements over such matters as changes in import restrictions, and, if necessary, making findings and recommendations to the parties. In addition, pursuant to the ATC, the TMB has established its own rules of procedure.[170] Ultimately, if a matter remains unresolved despite TMB recommendations, it may be referred to the Dispute Settlement Body for consideration by a panel pursuant to the Dispute Settlement Understanding.[171] Prior consultations pursuant to the DSU are not required.[172]

As described more fully below, the role and function of DSU panels differ substantially from those of the TMB. Unlike panels, for example, the TMB is not limited to any specific terms of reference.[173] The function of the TMB is to supervise the implementation of the ATC generally; panels have no such general responsibility.[174] The TMB's membership is composed of constituencies; DSU panelists, by contrast, are not selected on the basis of constituencies.[175] During the review process, the TMB – unlike a panel – is not limited to the initial information submitted by the importing Member, as parties may submit additional and other information in support of their positions, which relate to subsequent events.[176]

[2] ATC procedures

The ATC provides that WTO Members should not make changes in practices, rules, procedures and categorization of textile products, or take specified action with regard to import levels, which upset the balance of negotiated rights and obligations under the ATC, adversely affect or

[168] ATC Art. 8. [169] ATC Art. 8.1. [170] ATC Art. 8.2. *See* § 5.10 [3].
[171] ATC Art. 8.10. [172] *Id.*
[173] Panel Report, *United States – Measure Affecting Imports of Woven Wool Shirts and Blouses from India*, WT/DS33/R, adopted 23 May 1997, as upheld by the Appellate Body Report, WT/DS33/AB/R, DSR 1997:I, 343, ¶ 7.19.
[174] *Id.* [175] *Id.*
[176] *Id.* ¶ 7.20. The Appellate Body, however, termed this statement *dicta*. Appellate Body Report, *United States – Measure Affecting Imports of Woven Wool Shirts and Blouses from India*, WT/DS33/AB/R and Corr.1, adopted 23 May 1997, § V, at 19, DSR 1997:I, 323, 338.

impede market access of a Member, or disrupt trade.[177] When changes in an import regime are made, the Member taking action should inform and, if possible, consult with affected Members prior to taking action.[178] If this is not possible, the Member taking action should consult within 60 days, if possible, with a view to reaching a mutually satisfactory solution regarding appropriate and equitable adjustments.[179] If a mutually satisfactory solution is not reached, any Member involved may refer the matter to the TMB for recommendations.[180]

Referral to the TMB is also available for a variety of other issues that may arise under the ATC. With regard to possible circumvention by transshipment, re-routing, false declarations of origin or of official documents, and inadequate measures in response, consultations should be held promptly, within 30 days if possible.[181] Any measures taken to counter these activities must be notified to the TMB. If a mutually agreed upon solution is not reached, any Member concerned may refer the matter to the TMB for review and recommendations.[182] Should any Member believe that no action, or inadequate action, is being taken in response to false declarations concerning fibre content, quantities, description or classification, frustrating the objectives of the ATC, it should consult promptly with the Member concerned. If a solution is not reached, any Member involved may refer the matter to the TMB for recommendations.[183]

In certain circumstances, Members may impose import restraints pursuant to a "transitional safeguard mechanism."[184] The Panel in *US – Underwear* concluded that, consistent with prior GATT practice, this provision should be interpreted narrowly.[185] This point was not reviewed on appeal; however, subsequent decisions of the Appellate Body cast serious doubt on this "narrow interpretation" conclusion.[186]

Transitional safeguard restraints are applied on a Member-by-Member basis, not on a most-favored-nation basis.[187] The Member proposing to take safeguard action must consult with the Members that would be affected by the measure.[188] The request for consultations must be accompanied by specific and relevant information with regard to the impact of the imports on the domestic industry concerned and the source of

177 ATC Arts. 4.2, 4.3. 178 ATC Art. 4.4. 179 *Id.* 180 *Id.* 181 ATC Art. 5.2.
182 ATC Art. 5.4. 183 ATC Art. 5.6. 184 ATC Art. 6.
185 Panel Report, *United States – Restrictions on Imports of Cotton and Man-made Fibre Underwear*, WT/DS24/R adopted 25 February 1997, as modified by the Appellate Body Report, WT/DS24/AB/R, DSR 1997:I, 31, ¶ 7.21.
186 *See* § 4.11 [5]. 187 ATC Art. 6.4. 188 ATC Art. 6.7.

the imports.[189] The Member should also state the level of the proposed restraint, and communicate the request for consultations, together with the relevant data, to the Chairman of the TMB.[190] Consultations should be held "without delay," and normally would be completed within 60 days of the date on which the request was received.[191]

If the Members concerned agree on a restraint measure, the details must be communicated to the TMB within 60 days from the date of the conclusion of the agreement.[192] The TMB shall determine whether the agreement is consistent with the safeguard requirements of the ATC, and shall make such recommendations as it deems appropriate to the Members.[193] If the Members concerned do not agree on a restraint measure within 60 days from the date on which the request for consultations was requested, the Member which proposed to take safeguard action may apply the restraint, in accordance with the requirements of the ATC, within 30 days following the 60-day period for consultations.[194] At the same time, the Member applying the restraint must refer the matter to the TMB.[195] Either Member may refer the matter to the TMB prior to the expiration of the 60-day period for consultations.[196] The TMB shall make its recommendations to the Members concerned within 30 days.[197]

In "highly unusual and critical circumstances, where delay would cause damage which would be difficult to repair," safeguard restraints may be imposed provisionally.[198] In such a case, the request for consultations and the notification to the TMB shall be made by the Member taking action no more than five working days after the action is taken.[199] The TMB shall be notified at the conclusion of the consultations if they do not produce agreement; in no case shall it be notified later than 60 days from the date of implementation of the action.[200] The TMB shall examine the matter and make its recommendations to the Members concerned within 30 days.[201] If consultations are successful, the Members shall notify the TMB upon their conclusion, but in any case, no later than 90 days from the date of the implementation of the action.[202] The TMB may make such recommendations as it deems appropriate to the Members concerned.[203]

Members shall endeavor to accept in full the recommendations of the TMB.[204] If a Member is unable to do so, it shall inform the TMB

[189] *Id.* [190] *Id.* [191] *Id.* [192] ATC Art. 6.9. [193] *Id.* [194] ATC Art. 6.10.
[195] *Id.* [196] *Id.* [197] *Id.* [198] ATC Art. 6.11. [199] *Id.* [200] *Id.*
[201] *Id.* [202] *Id.* [203] *Id.* [204] ATC Art. 8.9.

as to why it is unable to do so not later than one month after receipt of the recommendations.[205] The TMB may then issue any further recommendations it deems appropriate and, if the matter remains unresolved, either Member may bring it before the Dispute Settlement Body, invoking Article XXIII:2 of GATT 1994, and the relevant provisions of the Dispute Settlement Understanding.[206]

[3] Textiles Monitoring Body Working Procedures

The TMB consists of a chairman and 10 members.[207] The ATC provides that its membership is to be balanced and broadly representative of the Members, and shall be rotated at "appropriate intervals."[208] The members of the TMB are appointed by WTO Members designated by the WTO Council for Trade in Goods; they serve in their personal capacities.[209]

The TMB's Working Procedures with regard to dispute settlement are brief. Representatives of parties to a dispute shall be invited to present their views fully to the TMB and to answer questions put by TMB Members.[210] If a member of the TMB is a representative of a party to a dispute, that member should not present the party's case.[211] Parties to a dispute may designate a representative who may be present during the discussion phase of the TMB's consideration of the dispute. If a national of a party to a dispute is a member of the TMB, the designated representative may not be present during the drafting of recommendations, findings or observations. However, the representative of a party to a dispute of which no member of the TMB is a national may be present, but may not take part during the drafting of the recommendations, findings or observations.[212] Parties to the dispute are required to notify the Chairman of the TMB, in writing, prior to the TMB's examination of the dispute of the composition of their delegations.[213]

Unless otherwise decided by the TMB, support material, working documents or information prepared by the Secretariat shall be confidential to the TMB and shall have no official standing.[214] Information supplied to the TMB by WTO Members shall remain confidential to the

[205] ATC Art. 8.10. [206] *Id.* [207] ATC Art. 8.1. [208] *Id.* [209] *Id.*

[210] *Working Procedures for the Textiles Monitoring Body, Annex to Textiles Monitoring Body, Report of the First Meeting*, G/TMB/R/1, ¶ 6.1.

[211] *Id.* [212] *Id.* ¶ 6.2. [213] *Id.* ¶ 6.3. [214] *Id.* ¶ 4.3.

TMB, if supplied on a confidential basis.[215] The TMB Working Procedures do not require a non-confidential summary.[216]

[4] TMB jurisdiction and panel jurisdiction

In *Turkey – Textiles*, the Panel held that the ATC, providing jurisdiction to the TMB, and the DSU, providing jurisdiction for panels to interpret covered agreements, apply together.[217] Therefore, panels are entitled to interpret the ATC to the extent necessary to determine whether a Member has valid WTO claims based on provisions of the ATC.[218] In *US – Cotton Yarn*, the Appellate Body held that panels, in transitional safeguard proceedings under the ATC, do not have jurisdiction to examine evidence that did not exist when the national authorities were conducting their investigation.[219]

§ 5.11 General Agreement on Trade in Services (GATS)

[1] General

The consultation and dispute settlement provisions of the Dispute Settlement Understanding apply to consultations concerning disputes under the *General Agreement on Trade in Services* ("GATS").[220] Additionally, at the request of a Member, the Council for Trade in Services or the Dispute Settlement Body may consult with any Member or Members with regard to any matter for which regular consultations have not produced a satisfactory solution.[221]

[215] *Id.* ¶ 4.4. At its first meeting, the TMB decided to continue discussion on the adoption of the following sentence: "In cases where the TMB has based its recommendations, findings or observations, *inter alia*, on confidential information provided to it by a party to a dispute, the TMB should ensure that the other party directly concerned [can] have access to such information." TMB, *Report of the First Meeting*, G/TMB/R/1, 26 July 1995, ¶ 5 at 2.

[216] *See* § 4.10.

[217] Panel Report, *Turkey – Restrictions on Imports of Textile and Clothing Products*, WT/DS34/R, adopted 19 November 1999, as modified by the Appellate Body Report, WT/DS34/AB/R, DSR 1999:VI, 2363, ¶ 9.82.

[218] *Id.*

[219] Appellate Body Report, *United States – Transitional Safeguard Measure on Combed Cotton Yarn from Pakistan*, WT/DS192/AB/R, adopted 5 November 2001, ¶ 78.

[220] GATS Art. XXII:1 and Art. XXIII:1.

[221] GATS Art. XXII:2.

[2] Double taxation treaties

A Member may not request consultations (or dispute settlement) under the national treatment provisions of Article XVII of GATS with regard to measures that fall within the scope of international agreements between them concerning the avoidance of double taxation.[222] In the case of disagreement between the Members as to whether a measure falls within the scope of such an agreement, and if the agreement in question was entered into after the date of entry into force of the WTO Agreement, either Member may bring the matter before the Council on Trade in Services, which shall refer the question to binding arbitration.[223] If the agreement existed on the date on which the WTO Agreement entered into force, the question may be brought before the Council only with the consent of both parties to the agreement.[224]

[3] Non-violation nullification and impairment[225]

If a Member considers that any benefit it could reasonably have expected to accrue to it under a specific commitment of another Member under Part III of GATS is being nullified or impaired as a result of the application of a measure which does not conflict with GATS, it may have recourse to the DSU.[226] If nullification and impairment is found, the Member affected would be entitled to a mutually satisfactory adjustment on the basis of Article XXI:2 ("Modification of Schedules"). If an agreement cannot be reached on the basis of Article XXI:2, the compensation and suspension of concessions provisions of Article 22 of the DSU apply.[227]

[4] Modification of schedules

A Member may modify or withdraw any service commitment made in its Schedule of specific commitments at any time after three years have elapsed from the date on which the commitment entered into force, in accordance with the provisions of Article XXI of GATS. However, compensatory adjustments in its Schedule must be made at the request of an affected Member.[228]

At the request of an affected Member, the Member proposing to modify or withdraw a commitment, shall enter into negotiations with regard to

[222] GATS Art. XXII:3. [223] *Id.* [224] *Id.*, n. 1. [225] *See* § 4.23.
[226] GATS Art. XXIII:3. [227] *Id. See* Chapter 8. [228] GATS Art. XXI:2.

compensatory adjustments, and "shall endeavor to maintain a general level of mutually advantageous commitments not less favourable to trade than that provided for in Schedules of specific commitments prior to such negotiations."[229] If agreement is not reached before the end of the period provided for negotiations, the affected Member may refer the matter to arbitration. Any affected Member that wishes to enforce a right that it may have to compensation must participate in the arbitration.[230] The proposed modification or withdrawal may not occur until compensatory adjustments have been made in conformity with the findings of the arbitration.[231]

[5] Air transport services

GATS does not apply to air traffic rights, however granted, or to services directly related to the exercise of traffic rights, other than measures affecting aircraft repair and maintenance services, the selling and marketing of air transport services, and computer reservation systems.[232] The DSU may be invoked with regard to air transport services only where obligations or specific commitments have been assumed by a Member, and only where any dispute settlement procedures in bilateral or other multilateral agreements or arrangements have been exhausted.[233]

[6] Panelists

Among the Ministerial Decisions and Declarations adopted with the WTO Agreement was the *Decision on Certain Dispute Settlement Procedures for the General Agreement on Trade in Services.* This five-paragraph Decision deals with panelists for GATS disputes, providing for a roster of qualified individuals who have experience in issues related to the GATS. It specifically provides that, "Panels for disputes regarding sectoral matters shall have the necessary expertise relevant to the specific services sectors which the dispute concerns."[234] This requirement that "panels" have the expertise appears to mean that at least one of the panelists, but not necessarily all, should possess the required expertise.

[229] *Id.* [230] GATS Art. XXI:3(a). [231] GATS Art. XXI:4(a).
[232] *Annex on Air Transport Services,* ¶¶ 2–3. [233] *Id.* ¶ 4.
[234] *Decision on Certain Dispute Settlement Procedures for the General Agreement on Trade in Services,* ¶ 4.

§ 5.12 Agreement on Trade-Related Aspects of Intellectual Property Rights (TRIPS)

The non-violation nullification and impairment provisions and the "other situation" provisions of GATT Article XXIII:(b) and (c) did not apply to disputes under the *Agreement on Trade-Related Aspects of Intellectual Property Rights* ("TRIPS") for a period of five years from the date of entry into force of the WTO Agreement.[235] During this five-year period, the Council for TRIPS was directed to examine the scope and modalities for non-violation and "other situation" complaints.[236] That "examination" has not resulted in any agreement on the subject.[237]

§ 5.13 Agreement on Government Procurement

[1] Background

The *Agreement on Government Procurement* ("GPA") is a plurilateral agreement applicable only to the minority of WTO Members that have signed it. The GPA is not listed in Appendix 2 of the DSU with the agreements whose special dispute settlement provisions take precedence over the DSU in case of conflict, although it contains special dispute settlement provisions. It is, however, listed in Appendix 1 as one of the agreements covered by the DSU, but with the proviso that the applicability of the DSU shall be subject to a decision of the parties to the GPA setting out the terms for the applicability of the DSU and the GPA's special terms.

On 8 July 1996, the Committee on Government Procurement officially notified the Dispute Settlement Body that the special or additional rules and procedures contained in the GPA, Article XXII:2–7, would be applicable to disputes involving the GPA.[238] Article XXII:1 specifies that the DSU is applicable to disputes under the GPA, subject to the remaining paragraphs of the Article.

235 *Agreement on Trade-Related Aspects of Intellectual Property Rights* ("TRIPS") Art. 64.2.

236 TRIPS Art. 64.3.

237 *See, e.g., Annual Report (2002) of the Council for TRIPS*, IP/C/27, 6 December 2002, ¶¶ 30–31.

238 Committee on Government Procurement, *Special or Additional Rules and Procedures on Dispute Settlement in the Agreement on Government Procurement* (1994), GPA/5, 19 July 1996.

[2] Proposals and DSU notification

A party to the GPA that believes that benefits accruing to it under the Agreement are being nullified or impaired by the actions of another party, whether or not those actions violate the GPA, may begin dispute settlement by making written representations or proposals to the other party.[239] The written representations or proposals should be notified to the DSB at the same time.[240]

The GPA does not specify that consultations should be requested. Presumably, however, inasmuch as the DSU applies, the panel process would begin with a request for consultations in accordance with Article 4 of the DSU. The consultation request presumably would include, or accompany, the written representations and proposals required by Article XXII:2. Pursuant to Article 4.4, this consultation request should simultaneously be notified to the Committee on Government Procurement.

[3] DSB authority

Although Article XXII gives overall dispute settlement authority to the DSB, only WTO Members party to the GPA may participate in decisions or actions taken by the DSB with respect to GPA disputes.[241] In the event of disputes involving the GPA and another covered agreement, however, all DSB Members shall participate in the non-GPA aspects of the DSB's activities.[242]

[4] Terms of reference

Unless the parties to the dispute within 20 days of the establishment of a panel agree otherwise, the following standard terms of reference shall apply to GPA disputes:

> To examine, in the light of the relevant provisions of this Agreement and of (name of any other covered Agreement cited by the parties to the dispute), the matter referred to the DSB by (name of party) in document . . . and to make such findings as will assist the DSB in making the recommendations or in giving the rulings provided for in this Agreement.[243]

[239] GPA Art. XXII:2. For non-violation nullification and impairment, *see* § 4.23.
[240] *Id.* [241] GPA Art. XXII:3. [242] GPA Art. XXII:4. [243] *Id.*

[5] Time limits

Article XXII imposes tighter time limits on GPA dispute settlement than apply generally under the DSU. This could create difficulties of the kind experienced under the Agreement on Subsidies and Countervailing Measures when other agreements, with different time-tables, are included in the dispute.[244]

Panels shall "attempt" to provide their final reports to the parties not later than four months, or, in case of delay, seven months from the date on which the composition and terms of reference of the panel were agreed.[245] This contrasts with the six and nine months specified in the DSU.[246] Further, "every effort shall be made" to reduce by two months the DSU's nine to 12 month limit between the date of the establishment of the panel until the report is considered for adoption, and the DSU's 15 to 18 month period from the date of the establishment of the panel until the date of determination of the reasonable period of time for compliance with an adopted report.[247]

In the first case under the GPA, the Panel submitted the Interim Report to the Parties slightly more than six months after it was composed.[248] The Final Report was circulated eight months after the Panel was composed.[249]

In the case of a disagreement as to the existence or consistency with a covered agreement of measures taken to comply with the recommendations and rulings of an adopted report, the time for the panel to resolve the dispute is set at 60 days, rather than the 90 days provided for by the DSU.[250]

[6] No cross-retaliation

Notwithstanding DSU Article 22.2, concessions granted under the GPA shall not be suspended as a result of a dispute involving another covered agreement, nor shall concessions granted under any other covered agreement be suspended as a result of a dispute involving the GPA.[251]

[244] *See* § 5.09[5]. [245] GPA Art. XXII:6. [246] DSU Art. 12.8, 9.

[247] GPA Art. XXII:6, referring to DSU Arts. 20.1 and 21.4.

[248] Panel Report, *Korea – Measures Affecting Government Procurement*, WT/DS163/R, adopted 19 June 2000, DSR 2000:VIII, 3541, ¶¶ 1.5–1.6.

[249] *Id.* [250] *Id.*, referring to DSU Art. 21.5.

[251] GPA Art. XXII:7. *See* § 8.05.

§ 5.14 Agreement on Trade in Civil Aircraft

The *Agreement on Trade in Civil Aircraft* ("TCA"), like the Agreement on Government Procurement, is a plurilateral agreement, listed in Appendix 1 to the DSU as a covered agreement, but not in Appendix 2 as one whose dispute settlement terms automatically prevail over the DSU. Unlike the GPA, however, the Committee on Trade in Civil Aircraft has never notified the DSB of the adoption of a decision setting out the terms for the application of the DSU to the TCA. This creates considerable legal uncertainty, as the Committee on Trade in Civil Aircraft itself has recognized.[252]

The uncertainty is compounded by the fact that the specific dispute settlement procedures of the TCA incorporate the somewhat dated rules of the GATT's 1979 Understanding Regarding Notification, Consultation, Dispute Settlement and Surveillance.[253]

§ 5.15 Arbitration[254]

[1] Generally

Parties that wish may by-pass WTO dispute settlement altogether and arbitrate their differences.[255] Apart from instances in which the DSU permits a single Member to seek arbitration of a particular issue, mutual agreement to arbitrate is required.[256] Agreement to arbitrate must be notified to all WTO Members "sufficiently in advance of the actual commencement of the arbitration process."[257]

However, other Members may become party to an arbitration proceeding only upon agreement of the parties that have agreed to arbitration.[258] Thus, unlike regular dispute settlement before panels established by the DSB, third parties have no rights as such in arbitration. However, they may seek dispute settlement on their own if they are affected by the measure in question.

[252] Committee on Trade in Civil Aircraft, *Report (1997) of the Committee on Trade in Civil Aircraft*, WT/L/247 (26 November 1997): "At the meeting of 16 June 1997 (TCA/M/5), the Chairman recalled that significant legal uncertainty surrounded the relationship between the Agreement and other WTO Agreements as a result of the continuing failure to adapt the Agreement to the WTO Structure."

[253] TCA Art. 8.8. The Understanding is set out at BISD 26S/210.

[254] For arbitration of issues surrounding implementation of panel reports, *see* Chapter 8.

[255] DSU Art. 25.1.

[256] DSU Art. 25.2. These instances are noted in the subsequent subsections.

[257] DSU Art. 25.2. [258] DSU Art. 25.3.

The parties to arbitration are required (1) to notify awards to the DSB and to any relevant Council or Committee of the WTO and (2) abide by the arbitration award.[259] Arbitration awards must be consistent with the WTO agreements, and should not nullify or impair benefits under those agreements, or impede the attainment of any objective of those agreements.[260]

The first WTO dispute to be submitted to Article 25 arbitration was *US – Section 110(5) Copyright Act*, where the European Communities and the United States asked for arbitration to determine the level of nullification or impairment of benefits to the EC as a result of the operation of Section 110(5) of the US Copyright Act.[261] The measure had previously been found to be inconsistent with the WTO obligations of the United States.[262]

The parties requested that the original panelists serve as arbitrators, but two of them were unable to do so. Accordingly, the Director-General appointed two replacements, and the remaining original panelist served as chair.[263] The Arbitrators and the parties held an organizational meeting on the day the replacements were named, after which the Arbitrators developed Working Procedures and a timetable on the basis of an agreement submitted by the parties in their request for arbitration.[264]

The organizational meeting was held on 13 August 2001.[265] The EC submitted a methodology paper on 14 August. The parties made concurrent written submissions on 21 August and concurrent rebuttals 28 August. They met with the Arbitrators 5 September, filed replies to questions of the Arbitrators on 11 September, and commented on the other's replies on 14 September.[266] The award was issued to the parties on 12 October, and was notified to the DSB and the TRIPS Council on 9 November.[267] Thus, the entire process, from the 23 July notification of the parties of their agreement to arbitrate to the 9 November notification of the DSB and the TRIPS Council, took less than four months.

The Arbitrators found, *inter alia*, that, like any international tribunal, they were competent to consider questions of their jurisdiction on their own initiative.[268]

[259] *Id.* [260] DSU Art. 3.5.

[261] Award of the Arbitrators, *United States – Section 110(5) of the US Copyright Act – Recourse to Arbitration under Article 25 of the DSU*, WT/DS160/ARB25/1, 9 November 2001.

[262] Panel Report, *United States – Section 110(5) of the US Copyright Act*, WT/DS160/R, adopted 27 July 2000, DSR 2000:VIII, 3769.

[263] Award of the Arbitrators, *supra* note 261, ¶¶ 1.3–1.4. [264] *Id.* ¶ 1.5. [265] *Id.*

[266] *Id.* ¶ 1.7. [267] *Id.* ¶ 1.8. [268] *See* § 2.06 [2].

[2] Non-actionable subsidies

An individual Member may request arbitration of a determination by the Committee on Subsidies and Countervailing Measures as to whether a program qualifies as a non-actionable subsidy, or the failure of the Committee to make such a determination.[269] An individual Member also may request arbitration of alleged violation, in individual cases, of the conditions for non-actionability set out in a notified program.[270]

The arbitrator is required to present its conclusions within 120 days from the date of referral. In all other aspects, the DSU applies to non-actionable subsidy arbitrations.[271]

The SCM Agreement also provides for arbitration of whether counter-measures taken in response to actionable and prohibited subsidies are appropriate.[272]

The arbitration rules adopted by the Committee on Subsidies and Countervailing Measures for Article 8.5 issues require that requests for arbitration be addressed to the chair of the Committee and that they include the basis for the request, the specific questions to be addressed by the arbitration body, and a brief summary of the information on which the request is based.

Rule 8 of the Committee's procedures provides that the only parties to an arbitration proceeding shall be the Member which has notified the subsidy in question, the Member which requested the arbitration, and any other Member that has become a party. Third parties may participate, but they are not considered "parties" to the proceeding. Members wishing to become parties may do so by notifying the Committee chair, within 15 days of the date of circulation of the initial request, and including in the notification the information required for a request for arbitration. Members wishing simply to become third parties may do so by notifying the Committee chair, in writing, within 20 days of the circulation of the request for arbitration. Third parties may intervene only with respect to specific questions raised by the parties.

[3] Services

In specified circumstances, Members may modify or withdraw commitments in their Schedule of Commitments made pursuant to the General

[269] SCM Agreement Art. 8.5. [270] *Id.* [271] *Id.*
[272] SCM Agreement Arts. 4.11 and 7.10. *See* § 8.07 [2].

Agreement on Trade in Services. However, such a step requires compensatory adjustments.[273] If an agreement is not reached concerning compensatory adjustments, an affected Member may refer the matter to arbitration.[274] Any affected Member wishing to enforce a right to compensation must participate in the arbitration.[275]

[273] GATS Art. XXI. [274] GATS Art. XXI:3(a). [275] *Id.*

6

The Appellate Process

§ 6.01 Overview

The WTO Appellate Body consists of seven Members, three of whom serve on any particular case.[1] Its jurisdiction is limited to issues of law covered in a panel report and to legal interpretations developed by a panel.[2] The Appellate Body may uphold, modify or reverse the legal findings and conclusions of a panel.[3] However, if it modifies or reverses the findings, it may not remand the matter to the panel for further proceedings.[4] The Appellate Body's proceedings are confidential.[5] As is the case with panels, *ex parte* communications with the Appellate Body concerning matters under its consideration are not permitted.[6]

§ 6.02 The task of the Appellate Body

In its Report in *US – Certain EC Products*, the Appellate Body reflected on its task:

> [W]e observe that it is certainly not the task of either panels or the Appellate Body to amend the DSU or to adopt interpretations within the meaning of Art. IX:2 of the *WTO Agreement.* Only WTO Members have the authority to amend the DSU or to adopt such interpretations. Pursuant to Article 3.2 of the DSU, the task of panels and the Appellate Body in the dispute settlement system of the WTO is 'to preserve the rights and obligations of Members under the covered agreements, and to *clarify the existing provisions* of those agreements in accordance with customary rules of interpretation of public international law'. (emphasis added) Determining what the rules and procedures of the DSU ought to be is not our responsibility nor the

[1] DSU Art. 17.1. [2] DSU Art. 17.6. [3] DSU Art. 17.13.
[4] *See* § 6.06. [5] DSU Art. 17.10. [6] DSU Art. 18.1.

responsibility of panels; it is clearly the responsibility solely of the Members of the WTO.[7]

In *EC – Hormones*, the Appellate Body observed that:

> Under Article 17.6 of the DSU, appellate review is limited to appeals on questions of law covered in a panel report and legal interpretations developed by the panel.
>
> . . . Determinations of the credibility and weight properly to be ascribed to (that is, the appreciation of) a given piece of evidence is part and parcel of the fact finding process and is, in principle, left to the discretion of the panel as the trier of facts.[8]

In *Korea – Alcoholic Beverages*, the Appellate Body rejected a claim relating to the weight the Panel had given to evidence, and refused to "second-guess the Panel in appreciating either the evidentiary value of such studies or the consequences, if any, of alleged defects in those studies."[9]

The "fact/law" distinction normally is not of great significance in international law because international tribunals typically are tribunals of first instance that decide both factual and legal questions. The WTO Appellate Body is the unique exception in public international law – the only appellate tribunal, and the only tribunal whose jurisdiction is confined to questions of law. However, what is "fact" and what is "law" is not always clear and, as one scholar has observed, "some of the most interesting and important current international issues involve, not questions solely of fact or solely of law, but rather 'mixed questions of fact and law' – for example, whether particular actions are 'reasonable,' 'discriminatory,' 'necessary,' or 'proportionate.' "[10]

[7] Appellate Body Report, *United States – Import Measures on Certain Products from the European Communities*, WT/DS165/AB/R, adopted 10 January 2001, ¶ 92 (emphasis in original).

[8] Appellate Body Report, *EC Measures Concerning Meat and Meat Products (Hormones)*, WT/DS26/AB/R, WT/DS48/AB/R, adopted on 13 February 1998, DSR 1998:I, 135, ¶ 132.

[9] Appellate Body Report, *Korea – Taxes on Alcoholic Beverages*, WT/DS75/AB/R, WT/DS 84/AB/R, adopted 17 February 1999, ¶ 160. Presumably, however, the Appellate Body could review a panel's evaluation of evidence under Article 11 of the DSU. *See* § 4.12.

[10] Richard B. Bilder, *The Fact/Law Distinction in International Adjudication*, in Richard B. Lillich (Ed) FACT-FINDING BEFORE INTERNATIONAL TRIBUNALS 95, 98 (Transnational, 1991).

§ 6.03 Right of appeal

Only parties to the dispute, not third parties, may appeal a panel report.[11] In the event of an appeal by a party, however, the Appellate Body's *Working Procedures* allow for third party participation in the appellate process. See § 6.04 [11].

§ 6.04 Appellate Body Rules

[1] Overview

The DSU requires the Appellate Body to prepare working procedures, in consultation with the Chairman of the DSB and the Director-General.[12] These were first issued in early 1996, shortly after the Members of the Appellate Body were appointed, and have been amended incrementally. These *Working Procedures for Appellate Review* constitute the rules by which the appellate process is conducted.[13] Part I of the Rules deals with internal organizational matters, while Part II deals with the process.

Most of the terms used by the Appellate Body are self-explanatory. A few terms, however, are specialized: the Appellate Body uses the term "participant" for those who participate in an appeal. Appellants and appellees are simply "participants," while third parties before the Panel are "third participants" in the appeal. The terms "party to the dispute" and "third party" refer to those who participated in the panel process. A list of definitions is set out at the beginning of the *Working Procedures.*

[2] Prohibited subsidy cases

Part II of the *Agreement on Subsidies and Countervailing Measures* provides a special, "fast-track" procedure for dealing with disputes concerning alleged prohibited subsidies.[14] This Agreement reduces the time provided for appeals of prohibited subsidy cases from the normal 60 to 90 days to 30 to 60 days.[15] Pursuant to Rule 31 of its *Working Procedures,* the Appellate Body, accordingly, has established a separate, shorter, time-table

[11] DSU Art. 17.4. [12] DSU Art. 17.9

[13] WT/AB/WP/7, 1 May 2003. For earlier versions, see WT/AB/WP/4, 24 January 2002; WT/AB/WP/3, 28 February 1997; and WT/AB/WP/1, 15 February 1996.

[14] *Agreement on Subsidies and Countervailing Measures* Art. 4. *See* § 5.09 [1].

[15] *Id.* Art. 4.9.

for appeals of prohibited subsidy cases. These basically cut the already truncated appellate time limits in half.

[3] Divisions of the Appellate Body

The DSU specifies that three of the seven Members of the Appellate Body shall hear a case.[16] In its *Working Procedures*, the Appellate Body has used the term "Division" for this group of three members.[17] The Members constituting a Division are selected on the basis of a non-disclosed rotation intended to insure random selection, unpredictability and opportunity for all Members to serve regardless of their national origin.[18] The Members of a Division select a Presiding Member, whose responsibilities include coordinating the overall conduct of the proceeding, chairing oral hearings and meetings, and coordinating the drafting of the appellate report.[19]

A Member assigned to a Division, whose term expires while the Division is sitting, may, with the authorization of the Appellate Body and upon notification to the DSB, complete that appeal.[20] When the terms of office of two Members of the Division expired during the appeal in *US – Lead and Bismuth II*, they were deemed to be Members of the Appellate Body until the circulation of the report in that case.[21]

[4] Decision making and collegiality

Decisions relating to an appeal are taken only by Members of the Division hearing the appeal.[22] If a Division cannot reach consensus, the decision will be made by majority vote.[23] The DSU specifies that opinions of the Appellate Body shall be anonymous.[24] It does not discuss the possibility of a dissenting opinion. In *EC – Asbestos*, one Member of the Division hearing the appeal made a "concurring statement."[25] That Member remained anonymous.

To further collegiality, all Members of the Appellate Body receive all documents filed in all appeals, including those Members not serving on

[16] DSU Art. 17.1. [17] Appellate Body Rule (hereafter "AB Rule") 6(1).

[18] AB Rule 6(2). [19] AB Rule 7. [20] AB Rule 15.

[21] *United States – Imposition of Countervailing Duties on Certain Hot-Rolled Lead and Bismuth Carbon Steel Products Originating in the United Kingdom – Communication from the Appellate Body*, WT/DS138/7, 4 April 2000.

[22] AB Rule 3(1). [23] AB Rule 3(2). [24] DSU Art. 17.11.

[25] Appellate Body Report, *European Communities – Measures Affecting Asbestos and Asbestos-Containing Products*, WT/DS135/AB/R, adopted 5 April 2001, ¶ 149.

the Division deciding the case. All Members also exchange views on each appeal before the Division finalizes the appellate report for circulation to WTO Members.[26] The Division, however, retains "full authority and freedom" to decide the appeal.[27]

Because Divisions have the authority to decide cases before them, even in the face of disagreement from other Members of the Appellate Body, the collegial approach is critical. It is also likely to make Divisions less ready to reverse prior decisions of their colleagues, even if they believe those decisions were wrongly decided. Each report is in the name of the Appellate Body itself, and not a particular Division. Indeed, because opinions – even potential dissenting opinions – are anonymous, if Members of a Division did not greatly respect the prior decisions of their colleagues, the result could be a "see-saw" of interpretations, as the three Members of one Division reverse the holdings of a prior case, only to be reversed themselves by three other Members in a subsequent case. However far-fetched such a scenario might seem, it clearly would be disastrous for the Appellate Body and the WTO itself should it occur. This is likely to mean long-term stability of Appellate Body jurisprudence, even jurisprudence Members of the Appellate Body themselves privately question.[28]

[5] Documents

No document is considered filed with the Appellate Body unless it is received by the Appellate Body Secretariat within the time period set out for filing in the appellate rules.[29] Unless specifically provided for in the rules to the contrary, every document filed must be served on all other parties, including third parties, to the dispute before the panel, and participants, including third participants, in the appeal.[30] Documents must be served by the most expeditious means available, including delivery to the service address of the participants, transmission by facsimile, expedited courier or expedited mail service.[31] Each filed document shall include proof of service.[32] In practice, documents tend to be hand delivered or sent electronically.

The Division may authorize participants, including third parties, to correct clerical errors in their submissions, provided the corrections are

[26] AB Rule 4(2) and (3). [27] AB Rule 4(4).
[28] For discussion of Appellate Body decisions as sources of law, *see* § 3.03 [5].
[29] AB Rule 18(1). [30] AB Rule 18(2). [31] AB Rule 18(4). [32] AB Rule 18(3).

made within three days of the filing. A copy of the revised version must be filed with the Appellate Body Secretariat and served upon the other participants.[33]

[6] Notice of appeal

An appeal is commenced by notification in writing to the DSB in accordance with Article 16.4 of the DSU, and with simultaneous filing of a Notice of Appeal with the Appellate Body Secretariat.[34] The Notice of Appeal should contain:

(a) the title of the panel report under appeal;
(b) the name of the party filing the Notice of Appeal;
(c) the service address, telephone and facsimile numbers of the party to the dispute; and
(d) a brief statement of the nature of the appeal, including the allegations of errors in the issues of law covered in the panel report and in the legal interpretations developed by the panel.[35]

Appellees are not required to notify the Secretariat, the appellant, or other parties of their intent to participate prior to filing a written Appellee's Submission pursuant to Rule 22.[36]

The Notice of Appeal is not expected to contain the reasons why the appellant regards the findings and interpretations of the Panel erroneous.[37] It is not designed to be a summary or outline of the arguments to be made by the appellant.[38] However, failure to note a particular finding of a panel in the claims of error set out in the Notice of Appeal will result in exclusion of the finding from the scope of the appeal.[39]

The Appellate Body has noted "the important balance that must be maintained between the right of Members to exercise the right of appeal meaningfully and effectively, and the right of appellees to receive notice through the Notice of Appeal of the findings under appeal, so that they

[33] AB Rule 18(5). [34] AB Rule 20(1). [35] AB Rule 20(2). [36] *See* § 6.03 [9].
[37] Appellate Body Report, *United States – Import Prohibition of Certain Shrimp and Shrimp Products*, WT/DS58/AB/R, adopted 6 November 1998, DSR 1998:VII, 2755, ¶ 95.
[38] *Id.*
[39] Appellate Body Report, *European Communities – Regime for the Importation, Sale and Distribution of Bananas*, WT/DS27/AB/R, adopted 25 September 1997, DSR 1997:II, 591, ¶ 152.

may exercise their right of defence effectively."[40] For these reasons, a Notice of Appeal that simply refers to the paragraph numbers found in the "Conclusions and Recommendations" section of a panel report, or that quotes them in full, will not meet the requirements of Article 20(2)(d) of the Appellate Body's *Working Procedures.*[41]

In *US – Offset Act (Byrd Amendment)*, the Appellate Body elaborated on the point:

> Generic statements . . . cannot serve to give the appellees adequate notice that they will be required to defend against a claim that the Panel exceeded its terms of reference. This is particularly so for procedural errors; it can be especially difficult to discern a claim of procedural error by a panel from general references to panel findings or from extracts of a panel report, because allegations of procedural error by a panel may not necessarily be raised until the appellate stage.[42]

A claim of error under Article 11 of the DSU, asserting that a panel failed to make an objective assessment of the facts, is only possible in the context of an appeal. There would, of course, be no reference to Article 11 in a request for establishment of a panel, nor would panels themselves normally refer to Article 11. Accordingly, an Article 11 claim must be referred to in the Notice of Appeal "in a way that will enable appellees to discern it and know the case they have to meet."[43]

[7] Working schedule

Immediately after the commencement of an appeal, the Division will prepare a working schedule for the appeal. It will contain the dates for the filing of documents and a timetable for the Division's work and, if possible, the date for an oral hearing. The Appellate Body Secretariat shall serve the working schedule on the appellant, the parties to the dispute, and any third parties.[44] This is likely to include finalization of the service list, since it is only the appellant, in its Notice of Appeal, that is required

[40] Appellate Body Report, *United States – Countervailing Measures Concerning Certain Products from the European Communities*, WT/DS212/AB/R, adopted 8 January 2003, ¶ 62.

[41] *Id.* ¶ 70.

[42] Appellate Body Report, *United States – Continued Dumping and Subsidy Offset Act of 2000*, WT/DS217/AB/R, WT/DS234/AB/R, adopted 27 January 2003, ¶ 200.

[43] Appellate Body Report, *US – Countervailing Measures on Certain EC Products*, *supra* note 40, ¶ 74.

[44] AB Rule 26.

to furnish a service address, but all participants are required to serve all documents on all other participants.

Because the DSU calls for a decision by the Appellate Body within 60 days as a "general rule," and in no case more than 90 days from the initiation of the appeal, the working schedule will reflect these tight time constraints.[45] Time limits and their impact, which give the Appellate Body little room to maneuver, are noted *passim* in the sections below which discuss the appellate process, and are treated in greater detail in § 6.05.

[8] Appellant's submission

The Appellant's written submission must be filed within 10 days of the Notice of Appeal, and served on the other parties to the dispute and third parties. The submission must be dated and signed by the appellant, and contain:

(a) the legal arguments in support of the appellant's position, including a precise statement of the grounds for appeal, including the specific allegations of errors in the issues of law covered in the panel report, and in the legal interpretations developed by the panel;
(b) a precise statement of the provisions of the covered agreements and other legal sources relied on; and
(c) the nature of the decision or ruling sought.[46]

Apart from a written version of its statement at the oral hearing and possible written responses to inquiries from Members of the Appellate Body, the appellant's submission is the only written opportunity the appellant has to make its case on appeal. Since the document must be filed and served within 10 days of the Notice of Appeal, and since that Notice might have to be filed in as little as 20 days after the circulation of the panel report,[47] appellants frequently begin their preparation for appeal as early as the circulation to the parties of the full interim report containing the panel's proposed findings and recommendations.[48]

It should be noted that parties that have prevailed before a panel may, nevertheless, appeal that result. This has not been a common occurrence, since prevailing parties normally do not desire to question the result, but it does occur. In *Canada – Dairy (Article 21.5 – New Zealand and US II)*, for example, Canada appealed from the Panel's interpretation of Article 10.3 of the *Agreement on Agriculture*, which deals with the burden of proof

[45] DSU Article 17.5. [46] AB Rule 21. [47] *See* § 6.04 [1]. [48] *See* § 4.18 [3].

in cases involving alleged export subsidies on agricultural products.[49] Although the Panel's interpretation was in its favour, Canada successfully argued that the Panel's interpretation was "plainly erroneous."[50]

In addition, prevailing parties often file cross appeals as "other appeals" under Rule 23 of the *Working Procedures*.[51] In *US – FSC (Article 21.5 – EC)*, the European Communities made four conditional appeals, requesting the Appellate Body to consider claims in respect of which the Panel exercised judicial economy. The EC stated that it did not challenge the Panel's exercise of judicial economy, but that it wished to have the claims adjudicated in the event that the Appellate Body should reverse those of the Panel's findings that led to the exercise of judicial economy.[52] Since the Appellate Body upheld the Panel's findings, it concluded that "none of the conditions on which the European Communities' appeal is predicated arise, and there is no need for us to examine any of the conditional appeals."[53]

[9] Appellee's submission

Any party to the dispute before a panel wishing to respond to allegations raised in an appellant's submission may file a written submission with the Secretariat, serving a copy on the appellant, other parties to the dispute and third parties.[54] The submission must be made no later than 25 days after the filing of the Notice of Appeal, which means that, normally, a potential appellee will have access to the appellant's arguments for only 15 days before its submission is due, since normally the appellant's submission would be filed 10 days after the Notice of Appeal.[55]

The appellee's submission, which must be dated and signed, should set out:

(a) a precise statement of the grounds for opposing the specific allegations of errors in the issues of law covered in the panel report and in the legal interpretations developed by the panel that have been raised in

[49] Appellate Body Report, *Canada – Measures Affecting the Importation of Milk and the Exportation of Dairy Products – Second Recourse to Article 21.5 of the DSU by New Zealand and the United States*, WT/DS103/AB/RW2, WT/DS113/AB/RW2, adopted 17 January 2003, ¶ 15.

[50] *Id.*, also ¶ 159.

[51] *See* § 6.04 [10].

[52] Appellate Body Report, *United States – Tax Treatment for "Foreign Sales Corporations" – Recourse to Article 21.5 of the DSU by the European Communities*, WT/DS108/AB/RW, adopted 29 January 2002, ¶ 253.

[53] *Id.* ¶ 255.

[54] AB Rule 22(1).

[55] *Id. See* also, § 6.03 [8].

the appellant's submission, and in the legal arguments raised by the appellant in support of its points;

(b) an acceptance of, or opposition to, each ground set out in the appellant's submission;

(c) a precise statement of the provisions of the covered agreements and other legal sources relied on; and

(d) the nature of the decision or ruling sought.[56]

[10] Multiple or "cross" appeals

Within 15 days after the date of the filing of the Notice of Appeal, a party to the dispute before the panel, other than the original appellant, may join in that appeal or may itself appeal on the basis of other alleged errors in the issues of law covered in the panel report and legal interpretations developed by the panel.[57] This would be accomplished by filing and serving a written submission in conformity with the requirements set out in Article 21(2) for appellants' submissions.[58] These are, typically, "cross appeals" by the prevailing party seeking to protect the result, particularly in light of the fact that the Appellate Body lacks remand authority.[59]

The original appellant, any appellee, and any other party to the dispute that wishes to respond to a later appeal may do so by filing a written submission within 25 days after the date of the filing of the Notice of Appeal. Such submission should conform to the requirements set out in Article 22(2) for appellees' submissions.[60]

[11] Third participants

In May 2003, the Appellate Body amended Rule 24 of its *Working Procedures* to broaden the right of third parties before the panel to participate in an appeal.[61]

From the start, the *Working Procedures* provided that any third party before the panel may file a written submission stating its intention to participate as a third participant in the appeal, and stating the grounds and legal arguments in support of its position. This submission must be made within 25 days of the date of filing of the Notice of Appeal.[62] A third

[56] AB Rule 22(2). [57] AB Rule 23(1). [58] AB Rule 23(2).

[59] *See* § 6.06 and Appellate Body Report, *Canada – Dairy (Article 21.5 – New Zealand and US II)*, *supra* note 49.

[60] AB Rule 23(3). [61] WT/AB/WP/7, 1 May 2003. [62] AB Rule 24.

participant who has filed a written submission may appear and make oral argument or presentations at the Appellate Body's hearing.[63]

Under these *Working Procedures*, but prior to the 1 May 2003 amendments, in *Argentina – Footwear (EC)*, Paraguay, which had been a third party before the Panel, did not file a written submission with the Appellate Body. It argued, however, that it had the right to attend and "participate passively" in the oral hearing of the Appellate Body in the dispute. Since no participant or third participant objected to its passive participation, Paraguay was allowed to attend.[64] Similarly, in *Chile – Price Band System*, Japan and Nicaragua, who were third parties in the Panel proceedings, were allowed to attend the oral hearing of the Appellate Body, as passive observers, without filing a written submission.[65]

The May 2003 revision of Rule 24 establishes three ways in which third parties may participate at the oral hearing of the Appellate Body. First, as before, third parties that file written submissions within 25 days of the filing of the Notice of Appeal will continue to have the right to appear and make an oral statement.[66] Second, third parties that, within the same 25-day period, notify the Appellate Body of their intention to appear will have the right to make an oral statement even if they do not file a written submission.[67] Third, third parties that notify the Appellate Body of their intention to appear after the expiration of the 25-day period may attend the hearing, but their entitlement to make an oral statement will be subject to the discretion of the Appellate Body Division hearing the appeal.[68] That discretion will be exercised in light of due process considerations.

[12] Record on appeal

The parties have no responsibility for preparing or filing the record on appeal. This is the direct responsibility of the Director-General and the indirect responsibility of the Secretariat.[69] The record includes, but is not limited to:

(a) written submissions, rebuttal submissions, and supporting evidence attached to the submissions by the parties and third parties to the panel dispute;

[63] AB Rule 27(3).

[64] Appellate Body Report, *Argentina – Safeguard Measures on Imports of Footwear*, WT/DS121/AB/R, adopted 12 January 2000, DSR 2000:I, 515, ¶ 7.

[65] Appellate Body Report, *Chile – Price Band System and Safeguard Measures Relating to Certain Agricultural Products*, WT/DS207/AB/R, adopted 23 October 2002, ¶ 6.

[66] AB Rule 24(1). [67] AB Rule 24(2). [68] AB Rule 24(4). [69] AB Rule 25(1).

(b) written arguments submitted at the panel meetings with the parties to the dispute and third parties, the records of those meetings, and any written answers to questions posed at the meetings;
(c) correspondence relating to the dispute between the panel or the WTO Secretariat and the parties to the dispute or third parties; and
(d) any other documentation submitted to the panel.

[13] Oral hearing

The Appellate Body's Rules require an oral hearing in each appeal. This normally will be held 30 days after the Notice of Appeal.[70] The Secretariat will notify all interested parties and participants of the date as soon as possible.[71] The Presiding Member of the Appellate Body, who chairs the hearing, may set time-limits for oral arguments and presentations.[72] Third participants may also appear and participate at the hearing in accordance with Rule 24.[73] Of course, statements made at the oral hearing are part of the record and are relied upon by the Appellate Body.[74]

[14] Written responses to questions

At any time during the appellate process, and particularly during the hearing, Members of the Division may address questions to participants and third participants and specify the time periods in which responses should be made. They may also request memoranda, usually on a legal question, and again set the time for response.[75] Any questions, responses, or memoranda shall be made available to other participants and third participants, who shall be given an opportunity to reply.[76]

[15] Failure to appear and withdrawal of appeal

Where a participant fails to file a submission within the required time, or fails to appear at the hearing, the Division shall, after hearing the views of the participants, issue such order as it deems appropriate. This could include dismissal of the appeal.[77]

[70] AB Rule 27(1). [71] AB Rule 27(2). [72] AB Rule 27(4).
[73] AB Rule 27(3). *See* also, § 604 [11].
[74] *See, e.g.*, Appellate Body Report, *US – FSC (Article 21.5 – EC)*, *supra* note 52, ¶ 117.
[75] AB Rule 28(1). [76] AB Rule 28(2). [77] AB Rule 29.

An appellant may withdraw its appeal at any time by notifying the Appellate Body.[78] In *India – Autos*, on the day before the oral hearing, India notified the Appellate Body of its withdrawal of the appeal pursuant to Rule 30(1) of the *Working Procedures*.[79]

In *EC – Sardines*, the EC withdrew its initial Notice of Appeal three days after it was filed, subject to its right to file a new Notice of Appeal, which it did on the same day.[80] Peru challenged the right of the EC to withdraw conditionally and to file a second Notice of Appeal.[81] The Appellate Body allowed the second notice, stating that nothing in Rule 30(1) prohibits an appellant from exercising its right to withdraw an appeal subject to a condition, unless the Member attaching the condition is not engaging in the dispute settlement procedures in a good faith effort to resolve the dispute.[82] In this instance, the Appellate Body said there was no denial of due process, and both the withdrawal and the refiling took place within the time available for an initial appeal. The Appellate Body cautioned that "there may be situations where the withdrawal of an appeal on condition of refiling a new notice, and the filing thereafter of a new notice, could be abusive and disruptive."[83] It went on to note that "in such cases, we would have the right to reject the condition, and also to reject any filing of a new notice of appeal."[84]

In *US – FSC*, the original Notice of Appeal was withdrawn for scheduling reasons, pursuant to an agreement between the parties, and a second notice was later filed.[85] Similarly, again for scheduling reasons, the original notice in *US – Line Pipe* was withdrawn and a second notice was filed.[86]

Where a mutually agreed solution to a dispute which is the subject of an appeal has been notified to the DSB pursuant to Article 3.6 of the DSU, it shall be notified as well to the Appellate Body.[87]

[78] AB Rule 30(1).

[79] Appellate Body Report, *India – Measures Affecting the Automotive Sector*, WT/DS146/AB/R, WT/DS175/AB/R, adopted 5 April 2002, ¶ 15.

[80] Appellate Body Report, *European Communities – Trade Description of Sardines*, WT/DS231/AB/R, adopted 23 October 2002, ¶¶ 11–13.

[81] *Id.* ¶ 15. [82] *Id.* ¶ 141. [83] *Id.* ¶ 146. [84] *Id.*

[85] Appellate Body Report, *United States – Tax Treatment for "Foreign Sales Corporations,"* WT/DS108/AB/R, adopted 20 March 2000, DSR 2000:III, 1619, ¶ 4.

[86] Appellate Body Report, *United States – Definitive Safeguard Measures on Imports of Circular Welded Carbon Quality Line Pipe from Korea*, WT/DS202/AB/R, adopted 8 March 2002, ¶ 13.

[87] AB Rule 30(2).

[16] Representation by private attorneys

The Appellate Body has held that it is for a WTO Member to decide who should represent it as members of its delegation in an oral hearing of the Appellate Body, and that this may include private lawyers.[88]

[17] Amicus curiae *briefs*

The Appellate Body has held that, "we have the legal authority under the DSU to accept and consider *amicus curiae* briefs in an appeal in which we find it pertinent and useful to do so."[89] This includes the authority to accept *amicus curiae* briefs from WTO Members that are not parties to the dispute.[90]

In *EC – Asbestos*, the Division hearing the appeal decided, "in the interests of fairness and orderly procedure" to adopt an additional procedure to deal with the many *amicus* briefs anticipated.[91] The additional procedure required anyone other than a party or third party to the dispute wishing to file a written brief to apply for leave to file. This procedure provoked strong opposition among developing country Members of the WTO. At the request of Egypt, on behalf of the Informal Group of Developing Countries, a special meeting of the DSB was convened at which many voiced their objections.[92] The Appellate Body received 11 timely applications under the Additional Procedure, but denied leave to file in each instance.[93]

In *EC – Sardines*, an *amicus* brief was submitted by Morocco, a WTO Member that did not exercise its right to appear as a third party before the

[88] Appellate Body Report, *European Communities – Regime for the Importation, Sale and Distribution of Bananas*, WT/DS27/AB/R, adopted 25 September 1997, DSR 1997:II, 591, ¶¶ 10–12.

[89] Appellate Body Report, *United States – Imposition of Countervailing Duties on Certain Hot-Rolled Lead and Bismuth Carbon Steel Products Originating in the United Kingdom*, WT/DS138/AB/R, adopted 7 June 2000, ¶ 42.

[90] Appellate Body Report, *EC – Sardines*, *supra* note 80, ¶ 163.

[91] *European Communities – Measures Affecting Asbestos and Asbestos-Containing Products – Communication from the Appellate Body*, WT/DS135/9, 8 November 2000.

[92] General Council, *Minutes of Meeting Held in the Centre William Rappard on 22 November 2000*, WT/GC/M/60, 23 January 2001.

[93] Appellate Body Report, *EC – Asbestos, supra* note 25, ¶ 56. *See*, Geert A. Zonnekeyn, *The Appellate Body's Communication on* Amicus Curiae *Briefs in the* Asbestos *Case*, 35 Journal of World Trade 553 (No. 3, June 2001); Robert Howse & Reinhard Quick, *Trade, Environment and the Role of NGOs*, 4 Journal of World Intellectual Property 277, 281 (March 2001).

Panel.[94] The Appellate Body reiterated its holding that it had the authority to accept *amicus curiae* briefs,[95] and held further that the explicit right of WTO Members to participate as third parties does not deprive them of the right to submit *amicus* briefs in proceedings in which they do not appear as third parties.[96] Acceptance of any such brief remains a matter of discretion.[97]

§ 6.05 Time elements

Because the DSU imposes tight time constraints on the appellate process, the Appellate Body's Rules, in turn, impose tight time constraints on the participants. These constraints can have tactical importance.

[1] Limits imposed by the DSU

Article 16.4 of the DSU provides that a panel report shall be adopted, absent consensus to the contrary, at a meeting of the Dispute Settlement Body occurring within 60 days after its circulation to the Members – unless a party to the dispute formally notifies the DSB of its intention to appeal. However, the report shall not be considered for adoption until 20 days after it has been circulated.[98] If a meeting of the DSB is not scheduled between the 20th and 60th days after circulation, a special meeting shall be held to consider the report.[99]

The practical impact of these provisions, taken together, is that a party wishing to appeal a panel report must so notify the DSB and file a Notice of Appeal prior to any meeting scheduled between the 20th and 60th days after circulation of the report, or prior to any special meeting convened to consider the report.

The Appellate Body, as noted previously, normally must issue its decision within 60 days from the date a party formally notifies its decision to appeal. When the Appellate Body considers that it cannot provide its report within 60 days, it is to inform the DSB of this fact, in writing. According to the DSU, "In no case shall the proceedings exceed 90 days."[100] However, on occasion, the Appellate Body, like some panels, simply has found it impossible to complete the task even within the time prescribed by the DSU. In *EC – Hormones*, the Appellate Body informed the DSB,

[94] *Supra* note 80, ¶ 153. [95] *Id.* ¶ 157. [96] *Id.* ¶ 163. [97] *Id.* ¶ 167.
[98] DSU Art. 16.1. [99] DSU Art. 16.4, n. 7. [100] DSU Art. 17.5.

"after consultation with the parties to the dispute," that it would not be able to circulate its report by the 90th day, and specified a date on which it intended to circulate its report.[101] Following the death of a Member of the Division after the oral hearing in *US – Lead and Bismuth II*, the Appellate Body selected a replacement, and held a second oral hearing before the reconstituted Division.[102] Due to these extraordinary circumstances, the participants and third participants agreed to a two-week extension of the 90-day time limit.[103] The "exceptional work load of the Appellate Body" and the agreement of the parties were cited as the reasons for an extension of approximately six weeks in *EC – Asbestos.*[104] The report in *US – Countervailing Measures on Certain EC Products* was issued in English within 90 days, but it was issued without translations into French and Spanish, the other official languages of the WTO, because of a "work-to-the-rule" action by the Secretariat.[105]

[2] Limits imposed by the Appellate Body

The short time limits allowed the Appellate Body by the DSU result, in turn, in the imposition of short time limits on the participants in an appeal. However, the *Working Procedures* provide that the time limits set out in any of the rules for filing documents or for an oral hearing may, in exceptional circumstances, "where strict adherence to a time period set out in these Rules would result in a manifest unfairness, a party to the dispute, a participant, a third party or a third party participant may request" that the Appellate Body modify the time limits set out in its working schedule.[106] Obviously, the Appellate Body's flexibility in granting extensions of time is limited.

In actual practice, parties frequently consult informally with the Appellate Body Secretariat prior to filing a Notice of Appeal. This process allows them and the Appellate Body some flexibility in scheduling, while still adhering to the applicable time limits. For example, the parties may

[101] *See, EC Measures Concerning Meat and Meat Products (Hormones) – Complaint by the United States – Communication from the Appellate Body*, WT/DS26/11 and *Complaint by Canada – Communication from the Appellate Body*, WT/DS48/9, 10 December 1997.

[102] *Supra* note 89, ¶ 8. [103] *Id.* [104] *Supra* note 25, ¶ 8.

[105] *United States – Countervailing Measures Concerning Certain Products from the European Communities – Communication from the Appellate Body*, WT/DS212/10, 12 December 2002.

[106] AB Rule 16(2).

agree on the date on which a Notice of Appeal will be filed and on the dates on which their respective submissions might be due. The remainder of the process could follow normally from these dates, or could itself be modified in cooperation with the Appellate Body.

The Appellate Body has adopted the DSB's *Decision on Expiration of Time-Periods in the DSU* for the appeal process.[107] In computing any time period stipulated in the DSU, or in the special or additional provisions of the covered agreements, or its own rules, the day from which the time period begins to run shall be excluded, and the last day of the time-period shall be included, subject to the *Decision on Expiration of Time-Periods in the DSU*.[108]

[3] Timing – tactical considerations

The *Working Procedures*, which designate the date of the Notice of Appeal as Day zero, require the appellant's submission on Day 10. Practical consequences flow both from the decision to date everything from Day zero, instead of allowing a fixed number of days from the previous event, and from the decision to allow the appealing party 10 days from Day zero to file its submission.

The decision to measure each action from Day zero can crucially shorten the time allowed for some actions. For example, if a Notice of Appeal is filed on a Wednesday, Day 10 falls on Saturday; the appellant's submission then becomes due on the following Monday, Day 12.[109] Appellant thus gains two days, while appellee gains one, since, with Day zero on Wednesday, Day 25 is Sunday and appellee's submission would be due on Monday, Day 26. More important for the cross-appeal process, an appellee's cross-appeal remains due on Day 15, a Thursday. Thus, an appellee's time to consider and prepare a cross-appeal after reviewing appellant's submission is cut from five days to three – from Monday to Thursday. Even the full 15 days for filing a cross-appeal submission is extremely short, particularly when five of those days overlap with the 15 days scheduled by the *Working Procedures* for the response on the merits of appellees to the appellant's submission.

[107] AB Rule 17(2) referring to WT/DSB/M/7. *See* § 4.15.

[108] AB Rule 17(1).

[109] *See*, Dispute Settlement Body, *Expiration of Time-Periods in the DSU, Proposal by the Chairman*, WT/DSB/W/10 (20 July 1995). If Monday is a holiday, timing could become even more skewed. *See* § 4.15.

In practice, this often means that prevailing parties operate on the assumption that the Report will be appealed, and begin their review and preparation for cross-appeals when the Report is issued, rather than begin only if the losing party appeals.

§ 6.06 Lack of remand authority

[1] The problem

With the establishment of an appellate body, the legal system of the World Trade Organization acquired an important characteristic of all mature legal systems: the separation of the judicial power from the other organs of governance (or, in this case, of the organization). Panels were not – and are not – formally independent of the organization.

The significance of an appellate tribunal to consider appeals only of questions of law should not be underestimated. It appears to have no international counterpart. Even the International Court of Justice is a court of original jurisdiction which decides both questions of fact and of law, and from which there is no appeal. Yet, this important institution lacks one of the most important powers of an appellate body: the power to remand cases to the lower tribunal – the panel – whose decision has been appealed.[110]

The issue arises because panels have often decided disputes on narrow grounds, adopting the practice known as "judicial economy." In one of its early decisions, *US – Wool Shirts and Blouses*, the Appellate Body endorsed the practice, holding that, "A panel need only address those claims which must be addressed in order to resolve the matter in issue in the dispute."[111]

There are good reasons why judicial tribunals, including panels and the Appellate Body, should practice judicial economy: it not only economizes on judicial resources, it also avoids deciding issues that do not have to be decided in order to reach a conclusion on the dispute before the panel, thereby reducing the intrusiveness of the process. Judicial economy is a less expansive approach which seems particularly appropriate to bodies reviewing the programs and actions of sovereign governments. Despite

110 *See* David Palmeter, *The WTO Appellate Body Needs Remand Authority*, 32 JOURNAL OF WORLD TRADE No. 1 (February 1998).

111 Appellate Body Report, *United States – Measure Affecting Imports of Woven Wool Shirts and Blouses from India*, WT/DS33/AB/R and Corr.1, adopted 23 May 1997, DSR 1997:I, 323, § VI, at 22.

the Appellate Body's endorsement of the utilization of the practice by panels, however, experience has shown that in the absence of remand authority, the practice of judicial economy can cause difficulties. Indeed, after endorsing the practice, the Appellate Body soon took a different tack:

> The principle of judicial economy has to be applied keeping in mind the aim of the dispute settlement system. This aim is to resolve the matter at issue and "to secure a positive solution to a dispute." To provide only a partial resolution of the matter at issue would be false judicial economy. A panel has to address those claims on which a finding is necessary in order to enable the DSB to make sufficiently precise recommendations and rulings so as to allow for prompt compliance by a Member with those recommendations and rulings "in order to ensure effective resolution of disputes to the benefit of all Members."[112]

Problems with judicial economy can arise in two ways – when panels do not decide an issue of law and when panels have not found the relevant facts.

[2] Legal issues undecided by a panel

The first case to be appealed, *US – Gasoline*, presented the Appellate Body with the consequence of its reversal of the basis of the Panel's legal conclusion.[113] The question was whether the measure at issue was consistent with the national treatment provisions of GATT Article III. The United States argued first, that the measure was consistent and second, even if it was inconsistent, it was permitted by Article XX(g) which permits measures "relating to" an exhaustible natural resource, if they are "made effective in conjunction with restrictions on domestic production or consumption," and if, in the words of the chapeau of Article XX, they are not applied in such a manner as to constitute "arbitrary or unjustifiable discrimination" or a "disguised restriction on international trade."

The Panel found that the measure was inconsistent with Article III and that it was not a measure "relating to" an exhaustible natural resource. It did not find it necessary, therefore, to consider whether the measure was

[112] Appellate Body Report, *Australia – Measures Affecting Importation of Salmon*, WT/DS18/AB/R, adopted 6 November 1998, DSR 1998:VIII, 3327, ¶ 223.

[113] Appellate Body Report, *United States – Standards for Reformulated and Conventional Gasoline*, WT/DS2/AB/R, adopted 20 May 1996, DSR 1996:I, 3.

"made effective in conjunction with restrictions on domestic production or consumption" or whether it constituted "arbitrary or unjustifiable discrimination" or a "disguised restriction on international trade." The US appealed on the "relating to" finding, and the Appellate Body reversed.

When the Appellate Body reversed the Panel on "relating to," its choices were limited. It could not remand the case to the Panel for consideration of the remaining Article XX(g) issues. It either could tell the appellees to start the process over, or it could decide the necessary undecided Article XX(g) issues itself, *de novo*. It chose to do the latter, and upheld the Panel's conclusion that the US measure was not justified by other requirements of Article XX(g). The Appellate Body could hardly have done otherwise. To have sent the complainants back to the starting line a year after they had begun the process, simply because the Panel – reasonably practicing judicial economy – did not decide all of elements of Article XX(g), would have been an unacceptable result to most WTO Members, particularly in the first matter to proceed through the new dispute settlement process.

In *Canada – Periodicals*, the issue arose again.[114] There Canada successfully appealed the Panel's conclusions regarding the first sentence of Article III:1 of GATT. In light of its decision as to the first sentence, the Panel had concluded that it did not need to consider Article III's second sentence, and this aspect of its decision was not appealed. Canada argued that the Appellate Body lacked jurisdiction even to consider the unappealed second sentence. The Appellate Body disagreed:

> As the legal obligations in the first and second sentences are two closely-linked steps in determining the consistency of an internal tax measure with the national treatment obligations of Article III:2, the Appellate Body would be remiss in not completing the analysis of Article III:2. In the case at hand, the Panel made legal findings and conclusions concerning the first sentence of Article III:2, and because we reverse one of those findings, we need to develop our analysis based on the Panel Report in order to issue legal conclusions with respect to Article III:2, second sentence, of the GATT 1994.[115]

While the Appellate Body's confirmation of the results in *US – Gasoline* and *Canada – Periodicals* no doubt was the correct approach in those

[114] Appellate Body Report, *Canada – Certain Measures Concerning Periodicals*, WT/DS31/AB/R, adopted 30 July 1997, DSR 1997:I, 449.

[115] *Id.* § VI.A, at 25, DSR 1997:I, 449, 469.

cases, these decisions themselves lack the benefit of the "second look" that normal appellate review provides. The practice amounts to the making of *de novo* legal findings without benefit of the analysis of the Panel or of the argument of the parties as to the merits of that analysis. These findings are effectively unreviewed and unreviewable.[116] There is evidence that the Appellate Body is aware of this difficulty, and that it will avoid completing the analysis of legal issues undecided by panels in some instances.

An early instance of this kind of difficulty occurred in *EC – Poultry*, where two of the issues raised before the Panel by Brazil, the complainant, were not the subject of legal findings or conclusions by the Panel.[117] Brazil had included both issues in its Notice of Appeal and in its appellant's submission. The Appellate Body, however, did not decide these issues. Instead, it referred to Article 17.6 of the DSU, which limits appeals "to issues of law covered in the panel report and legal interpretations developed by the panel," and to Article 17.13 of the DSU, which specifies that the Appellate Body may only, "uphold, modify or reverse the legal findings and conclusions of the panel." Since the Panel did not deal with these issues, the Appellate Body reasoned, there was "no finding nor any 'legal interpretation developed by the panel' that may be the subject of an appeal of which the Appellate Body may take cognizance."[118]

In *EC – Asbestos*, the Appellate Body referred to its decision in *Canada – Periodicals*, stating that, "embarking there on an analysis of a provision that the Panel had not considered, we emphasized that 'the first and second sentences of Article III:2 are *closely related*' and that those two sentences are 'part of a *logical continuum*' (emphasis added)."[119] At issue in *EC – Asbestos* were four claims under the *Agreement on Technical Barriers to Trade* that the Panel, which decided the case under GATT 1994, had not considered. The Appellate Body noted that the provisions at issue not only had not been considered by the Panel in the *Asbestos* case, they also had never been interpreted by any panel or by the Appellate Body. Moreover, their predecessor terms in the Tokyo Round *Agreement*

[116] This is because Appellate Body reports are adopted by the Dispute Settlement Body and unconditionally accepted by the parties unless there is consensus not to adopt. DSU Art. 17.14. *See* § 1.04.

[117] Appellate Body Report, *European Communities – Measures Affecting the Importation of Certain Poultry Products*, WT/DS69/AB/R, adopted 23 July 1998, DSR 1998:V, 2031, ¶ 107.

[118] *Id.*

[119] Appellate Body Report, *EC – Asbestos, supra* note 25, ¶ 79 (emphasis in original).

on Technical Barriers to Trade had never been interpreted by a GATT panel.

"In light of their novel character," the Appellate Body said, "we consider that Canada's claims under the TBT Agreement have not been explored before us in depth. As the Panel did not address these claims, there are no 'issues of law' or 'legal interpretations' regarding them to be analyzed by the parties, and reviewed by us under Article 17.6 of the DSU."[120]

EC – Asbestos, however, was a very different case from either *US – Gasoline* or *Canada – Periodicals* in that the measures already had been found to be inconsistent with GATT 1994; the undecided TBT issues would not have changed the result, but were merely cumulative. In *Gasoline* and *Periodicals*, on the other hand, the Appellate Body's failure to complete the analysis would have left the cases completely undecided.

Panels very early became aware of the lack of remand problem, and some of them explicitly decided issues with that problem in mind. Thus, the Panel in *India – Patents (US)* said, "[W]e believe it necessary to make our findings clear on the issue of transparency in order to avoid a legal vacuum in the event that, upon appeal, the Appellate Body were to reverse our findings on Article 70.8."[121] The Panel in *US – Lamb* made explicit reference to the Appellate Body's endorsement of judicial economy in *US – Wool Shirts and Blouses* and its subsequent caution in *Australia – Salmon*[122] and decided, "in the spirit of the Appellate Body's statements in *Australia – Salmon*," to "continue with an analysis of other claims in the alternative."[123]

In *US – Wheat Gluten*, the Panel's exercise of judicial economy itself was appealed.[124] The Appellate Body affirmed the Panel, however, stating that a finding on the non-decided issue "would not, in our view, have added anything to the ability of the DSB to make sufficiently precise

[120] *Id.* ¶ 82.

[121] Panel Report, *India–Patent Protection for Pharmaceutical and Agricultural Chemical Products – Complaint by the United States*, WT/DS50/R, adopted 16 January 1998, as modified by the Appellate Body Report, WT/DS50/AB/R, DSR 1998:I, 41, ¶ 7.44.

[122] *Supra* notes 111 and 112, respectively.

[123] Panel Report, *United States – Safeguard Measures on Imports of Fresh, Chilled or Frozen Lamb Meat from New Zealand and Australia*, WT/DS177/R, WT/DS178/R, adopted 16 May 2001, as modified by the Appellate Body Report, WT/DS177/AB/R, WT/DS178/AB/R, ¶ 7.119.

[124] Appellate Body Report, *United States – Definitive Safeguard Measures on Imports of Wheat Gluten from the European Communities*, WT/DS166/AB/R, adopted 19 January 2001, ¶¶ 29–30.

recommendations and rulings in this dispute."[125] This reasoning is somewhat puzzling, in that the non-decided issue was not necessary only because the Appellate Body had affirmed the overall result reached by the Panel – that the measure was inconsistent with US obligations – both by upholding some findings and by completing the analysis on others.[126] However, had the Appellate Body reversed the Panel on those findings, it might well have been necessary to consider the non-decided issue. Judicial economy is certainly available to the Appellate Body; but its lack of remand authority, as it noted in *Australia – Salmon*, can make its use by panels risky.

[3] Factual issues undecided by a panel

When the Appellate Body "completes the analysis" of a panel, it does so on the basis of the factual record developed during the panel process. If a panel does not make the required factual findings for any reason, including judicial economy, the Appellate Body cannot complete the analysis, and since it cannot remand the matter, the complainant is left without a ruling.

In *Canada – Dairy (Article 21.5 – New Zealand and US)*, for example, the Appellate Body held that the Panel had applied the wrong benchmark for determining whether a "payment" had occurred within the meaning of Article 9.1(c) of the *Agreement on Agriculture*.[127] However, the Panel did not make the factual findings necessary for the Appellate Body to complete the analysis using what it had found to be the correct benchmark. "We are simply not in a position to make a ruling on this issue," the Appellate Body said.[128] This led the complainants, New Zealand and the United States, to begin the process anew by requesting a second Article 21.5 panel.[129]

In *Korea – Dairy*, the absence of the required factual findings, or undisputed facts in the Panel record, led the Appellate Body to observe that, "we are not in a position, within the scope of our mandate set forth in Article 17

[125] *Id.* ¶ 183. [126] *Id.* ¶ 187.

[127] Appellate Body Report, *Canada – Measures Affecting the Importation of Milk and the Exportation of Dairy Products – Recourse to Article 21.5 of the DSU by New Zealand and the United States*, WT/DS103/AB/RW, WTDS113/AB/RW, adopted 18 December 2001, ¶ 82.

[128] *Id.* ¶ 103.

[129] Panel Report, *Canada – Measures Affecting the Importation of Milk and the Exportation of Dairy Products – Second Recourse to Article 21.5 of the DSU by New Zealand and the United States*, WT/DS103/RW2, WT/DS113/RW2, adopted 17 January 2003, as modified by the Appellate Body Report, WT/DS103/AB/RW2, WT/DS113/AB/RW2, ¶ 1.10.

of the DSU, to complete the analysis and make a determination."[130] Similarly, in *Canada – Autos*, the Appellate Body found that it lacked the factual foundation to complete the analysis, and, "Therefore, we make no finding and reserve our judgment."[131] In neither of these cases was a further proceeding undertaken by the complainants.

[130] Appellate Body Report, *Korea – Definitive Safeguard Measure on Imports of Certain Dairy Products*, WT/DS98/AB/R, adopted 12 January 2000, DSR 2000:I, 3, ¶ 92.

[131] Appellate Body Report, *Canada – Certain Measures Affecting the Automotive Industry*, WT/DS139/AB/R, WT/DS142/AB/R, adopted 19 June 2000, DSR 2000:VI, 2995, ¶ 134.

7

Adoption and Implementation of Reports

§ 7.01 Overview

If the Dispute Settlement Understanding arguably is the most significant achievement of the Uruguay Round, its provisions concerning adoption and implementation of reports arguably are the most significant parts of the DSU. Under GATT, a consensus in favor of a report was required for its adoption. In practice, this meant that a dissatisfied party could block consensus and prevent adoption of a report. The DSU reverses this requirement. WTO reports are adopted unless there is a consensus not to adopt them.[1] This "negative consensus" requirement has made WTO dispute settlement into what is, in all probability, the most effective area of adjudicative dispute settlement in the entire area of public international law.

§ 7.02 Consideration and adoption of reports

The DSB has a minimum of 20 days from the date of circulation of a final report to consider its adoption.[2] Members having objections to a report must give their reasons in writing at least 10 days prior to the DSB meeting at which the report will be considered.[3] Of course, parties to a dispute have the right to participate fully in the DSB's consideration of a report.[4]

Reports will be adopted within 60 days after the circulation of the panel report to the Members, unless a party formally notifies the DSB of its intention to appeal, or unless the DSB decides by consensus not to adopt the report. This latter, of course, is the "negative consensus" that makes WTO dispute settlement so different from that of GATT. If a DSB meeting is not scheduled for the period between the 20th day after circulation of a report and the 60th day, a special meeting of the DSB shall be held to consider adoption.[5] An Appellate Body report shall be adopted

[1] DSU Art. 16.4. [2] DSU Art. 16.1. [3] DSU Art. 16.2.
[4] DSU Art. 16.3. [5] DSU footnote 7.

by the DSB and unconditionally accepted by the parties to the dispute within 30 days of its circulation, unless the DSB decides by consensus not to adopt it.[6] If a DSB meeting is not scheduled during this period, a special meeting shall be held to consider an Appellate Body report.[7]

The DSB utilizes the rules of procedure of the WTO General Council for its consideration of panel reports.[8] These rules specify that meetings are to be convened by written notice at least 10 days prior to the date of the meeting, and that the notice be accompanied by a proposed agenda.[9] Members may place items on the agenda up to, but not including the day on which the notice is to be issued. It is normal practice for a Member seeking to have adoption of a report placed on the agenda to notify the Secretariat within the time limits specified by the rules of the General Council.

The DSU *Working Practices Concerning Dispute Settlement Procedures* specify that the "date of circulation" of a report is the date printed on the document to be circulated, "with the assurance of the Secretariat that the date printed on the document is the date on which this document is effectively put in the pigeon holes of delegations in all three working languages."[10]

§ 7.03 Notification of implementation intentions

When a panel or the Appellate Body concludes that a measure is inconsistent with the requirements of a covered agreement, it recommends that the "Member concerned" bring its measure into conformity with that agreement.[11] When the report is adopted, its recommendations and rulings become those of the DSB itself. At a DSB meeting held within 30 days of the adoption of a report, the Member concerned must inform the DSB of its intentions concerning the DSB's recommendations and rulings.[12] If a DSB meeting is not scheduled within the 30 days following the adoption of a report, a special meeting will be called for the purpose of hearing from the Member concerned regarding its intentions.[13]

[6] DSU Art. 17.14. [7] DSU footnote 8.

[8] *Rules of Procedure for Meetings of the Dispute Settlement Body*, WT/DSB/9. The General Council rules are *Rules of Procedure for Sessions of the Ministerial Conference and for Meetings of the General Council*, WT/L/161.

[9] General Council Rules 2 and 3. [10] WT/DSB/6.

[11] DSU Art. 19.1. However, in cases involving prohibited or actionable subsidies, different terminology is used. *See*, § 8.07. In situations involving "non-violation" complaints, the Member is not required to withdraw the measure. DSU Art. 26.1(a).

[12] DSU Art. 21.3. [13] DSU footnote 11.

§ 7.04 "Reasonable period of time"

[1] Legal framework

If it is not practicable to comply immediately with the DSB's recommendations and rulings, the Member concerned shall have a "reasonable period of time" to do so. The reasonable period of time shall be:

a) a period proposed by the Member concerned, provided it is approved by the DSB; in the absence of DSB approval,
b) a time mutually agreed by the parties to the dispute within 45 days of the adoption of the report; in the absence of such an agreement,
c) a period determined through binding arbitration within 90 days of adoption of the report.[14]

The prevailing Member has clear control over the first two alternatives, but there is some ambiguity regarding the interplay of the second and third. This is discussed *infra* at § 7.04 [6].

As to the first alternative, if the period proposed by the Member concerned is acceptable to the Member that prevailed in the dispute, then it may be approved by the DSB; however, if it is not acceptable to the prevailing Member, that Member could prevent the consensus needed to approve it.[15] Similarly, as to the second alternative, the prevailing Member, by definition, must consent to an agreement of the parties reached within 45 days.

[2] The Arbitrator

If the parties are unable to agree on an arbitrator within 10 days after referring the matter to arbitration, the Director-General will appoint the Arbitrator within an additional 10 days.[16] Typically, the parties are not able to agree and the Arbitrator is named by the Director-General. Although footnote 13 to Article. 21.3(c) provides that "the expression 'Arbitrator' shall be interpreted as referring either to an individual or a group," in most instances a single Arbitrator has been named, usually a member of the Appellate Body. In *EC – Hormones*, the Director-General appointed two Arbitrators, a Member of the Appellate Body and the former chair of the Dispute Settlement Body and the General Council. However, the

[14] DSU Art. 21.3. With regard to Arbitration generally, *see* § 5.15.

[15] The positive consensus requirement is set out in the *Marrakesh Agreement Establishing the World Trade Organization* Article IX:1.

[16] DSU Art. 21.3, footnote 12.

latter appointee was unable to accept the nomination, so the proceeding went forward with a single Arbitrator.[17]

[3] Jurisdiction of the Arbitrator

In *EC – Hormones*, the Arbitrator observed that the parties disagreed "as to what constitutes 'implementation of the recommendations and rulings of the DSB' under Article 21.3 of the DSB."[18] However, noting that the Arbitrator's task is to determine the reasonable period of time, the Arbitrator said that, "It is not within my mandate under Article 21.3(c) of the DSU to suggest ways or means to the European Communities to implement" the adopted reports.[19] Members have discretion in choosing the means of implementation, the Arbitrator added.[20]

In *Australia – Salmon*, the Arbitrator cited the *EC – Hormones* award, saying, "I am mindful of the limits of my mandate in this arbitration. I am particularly aware that suggesting ways and means of implementation is not part of my mandate and that my task is confined to the determination of the 'reasonable period of time.' Choosing the means of implementation is, and should be, the prerogative of the implementing Member."[21] The Arbitrator in *Korea – Alcoholic Beverages* cited with agreement both the *EC – Hormones* and the *Australia – Salmon* awards, stating that, "Choosing the means of implementation is, and should be, the prerogative of the implementing Member, as long as the means chosen are consistent with the recommendations and rulings of the DSB and the provisions of the covered agreements."[22]

This raises the question: Who determines whether "the means chosen are consistent with the recommendations and rulings of the DSB and the provisions of the covered agreements"? In the next award, the Arbitrator in *Canada – Pharmaceutical Patents*, while expressing agreement with the award in *Korea – Alcoholic Beverages*, stated that whether the means chosen by a Member are "consistent with that Member's obligations under the WTO covered agreements is not a question that falls within

[17] Award of the Arbitrator, *EC Measures Concerning Meat and Meat Products (Hormones) – Arbitration under Article 21.3(c) of the DSU*, WT/DS26/15, WT/DS48/13, 29 May 1998, DSR 1998:V, 1833.

[18] *Id.* ¶ 32. [19] *Id.* ¶ 38. [20] *Id.*

[21] Award of the Arbitrator, *Australia – Measures Affecting Importation of Salmon – Arbitration under Article 21.3(c) of the DSU*, WT/DS18/9, 23 February 1999, DSR 1999:I, 267, ¶ 35.

[22] Award of the Arbitrator, *Korea – Taxes on Alcoholic Beverages – Arbitration under Article 21.3(c) of the DSU*, WT/DS75/16, WT/DS84/14, 4 June 1999, DSR 1999:II, 937, ¶ 45.

the jurisdiction of an arbitrator under Article 21.3(c)."[23] The Arbitrator went on to say that his responsibility does not "include in any respect a determination of the *consistency* of the proposed implementing measure with the recommendations and rulings of the DSB. The proper concern of an arbitrator under Article 21.3(c) is with *when*, not *what*."[24]

In *Chile – Alcoholic Beverages*, the Arbitrator stated that, "the Member concerned has the sovereign prerogative and responsibility of determining for itself the most appropriate, and probably effective, method of implementing the recommendations and rulings of the DSB by securing the passage of the amendatory law. The choice and the timing of the detailed operating steps in enacting a new law are properly left to the Member concerned."[25] The view was repeated by the Arbitrator in *Chile – Price Band System*, who said, "I am not asked to determine or even suggest the manner in which a Member should implement its international obligations."[26] In a similar vein, the Arbitrator in *US – Hot-Rolled Steel* stated, "I do not believe that an arbitrator acting under Article 21.3(c) of the DSU is vested with jurisdiction to make any determination of the proper scope and content of implementing legislation."[27]

Although the Arbitrator should "avoid deciding what a Member must do for proper implementation," the more information the Arbitrator has about the details of the implementing measure, the more likely the period selected will fairly balance the needs of the implementing Member with those of the complaining Member.[28]

In *US – Offset Act (Byrd Amendment)*, the Panel had suggested that the United States bring the measure into conformity simply by repealing it.[29] However, in the arbitration of the reasonable period of time, the Arbitrator held that although a panel suggestion "could serve as a useful contribution

[23] Award of the Arbitrator, *Canada – Patent Protection of Pharmaceutical Products – Arbitration under Article 21.3(c) of the DSU*, WT/DS114/13, 18 August 2000, ¶ 40.

[24] *Id.* ¶ 41 (emphasis in original).

[25] Award of the Arbitrator, *Chile – Taxes on Alcoholic Beverages – Arbitration under Article 21.3(c) of the DSU*, WT/DS87/15, WT/DS110/14, 23 May 2000, DSR 2000: V, 2589, ¶ 42.

[26] Award of the Arbitrator, *Chile – Price Band System and Safeguard Measures Relating to Certain Agricultural Products – Arbitration under Article 21.3(c) of the DSU*, WT/DS207/13, 17 March 2003, ¶ 32.

[27] Award of the Arbitrator, *United States – Anti-Dumping Measures on Certain Hot-Rolled Steel Products from Japan – Arbitration under Article 21.3(c) of the DSU*, WT/DS184/13, 19 February 2002, ¶ 30.

[28] *Chile – Price Band System*, *supra* note 26, ¶ 13.

[29] Panel Report, *United States – Continued Dumping and Subsidy Offset Act of 2000*, WT/DS217/R, WT/DS234/R, adopted 27 January 2003, as modified by the Appellate Body Report, WT/DS217/AB/R, WT/DS234/AB/R, ¶ 8.6.

to the decision-making process in the implementing Member," it did not affect the prerogative of the implementing Member to choose the means of implementation, and therefore did not determine the reasonable period of time.[30]

[4] *Agreements establishing the reasonable period of time*

On a number of occasions, the parties have been able, pursuant to Article 21.3(b) of the DSU, to agree on the reasonable period of time without the necessity of arbitration. In *Canada – Dairy*, the parties reached agreement on a four-stage implementation process, with consultations scheduled for each stage.[31] The parties in *India – Quantitative Restrictions* also agreed on staged implementation, with some steps to take place a full year after others.[32] In *Korea – Dairy*, a dispute under the *Agreement on Safeguards*, the Panel Report was adopted on 12 January 2000, and the parties agreed that the reasonable period of time for implementation would expire less than five months later, on 20 May 2000.[33] In another safeguards case, *US – Wheat Gluten*, the parties agreed on four months and 14 days.[34] In *Mexico – Corn Syrup*, which involved antidumping, agreement was reached on a period of six months and 29 days for implementation.[35]

In *US – Line Pipe*, while arbitration under Article 21.3(c) was underway, and after written submissions had been made to the Arbitrator, the parties requested a delay in the issuance of the award to allow time for additional bilateral negotiations. The parties eventually reached agreement, and the Arbitrator, accordingly, found it unnecessary to issue the award.[36]

[30] Award of the Arbitrator, *United States – Continued Dumping and Subsidy Offset Act of 2000*, WT/DS217/14, WT/DS234/22, 13 June 2003, ¶ 52.

[31] Agreement under Article 21.3(b) of the DSU, *Canada – Measures Affecting the Importation of Milk and the Exportation of Dairy Products*, WT/DS103/10 and Corr.1, WT/DS113/10 and Corr.1, 7 January 2000.

[32] Agreement under Article 21.3(b) of the DSU, *India – Quantitative Restrictions on Imports of Agricultural, Textile and Industrial Products*, WT/DS90/15, 17 January 2000.

[33] Agreement under Article 21.3(b) of the DSU, *Korea – Definitive Safeguard Measure on Imports of Certain Dairy Products*, WT/DS98/11, 24 March 2000.

[34] Agreement under Article 21.3(b) of the DSU, *United States – Definitive Safeguard Measure on Imports of Wheat Gluten from the European Communities*, WT/DS166/12, 12 April 2001.

[35] Agreement under Article 21.3(b) of the DSU, *Mexico – Anti-Dumping Investigation of High Fructose Corn Syrup* (HFCS) *from the United States*, WT/DS132/5, 26 April 2000.

[36] Award of the Arbitrator, *United States – Definitive Safeguard Measures on Imports of Circular Welded Carbon Quality Line Pipe from Korea – Arbitration under Article 21.3(c) of the DSU*, WT/DS202/17, 26 July 2002.

[5] Time within which to request arbitration

Article 21.3(c) specifies that the Arbitrator is to determine the reasonable period of time within 90 days after adoption of the report. However, the article also allows 45 days for the parties to attempt to reach agreement on the issue before resorting to arbitration. If this 45 days is fully consumed in unsuccessful negotiations, this leaves only 45 days for the arbitration, including the naming of an arbitrator.

In the first Article 21.3(c) arbitration, *Japan – Alcoholic Beverages*, the report was adopted on 1 November 1996, while arbitration was not requested until 24 December, some 54 days after adoption. The parties agreed to extend the 90-day period for arbitration itself for two weeks.[37] Similar extensions have been granted in many other Article 21.3 arbitrations.[38] Indeed, there have been instances when the full 90 days expired before the parties even requested arbitration.[39]

Reasonable period of time arbitrations under Article 21.3 are an excellent example of the flexibility of WTO Members to set their own rules by mutual agreement.

[6] Time allowed for implementation

Arbitral decisions establishing the reasonable period of time have not always been outstanding examples of clarity. The DSU does not mandate a specific period as the reasonable period of time. It simply offers as "a guideline for the Arbitrator" that the reasonable period normally should not exceed 15 months from the date of adoption of the report.[40]

[37] Award of the Arbitrator, *Japan – Taxes on Alcoholic Beverages – Arbitration under Article 21.3(c) of the DSU*, WT/DS8/15, WT/DS10/15, WT/DS11/13, 14 February 1997, DSR 1997:I, 3, at 1.

[38] *See, e.g.*, Awards of the Arbitrators in *Australia – Salmon, supra* note 21, ¶ 3 (extended by 19 days); *Korea – Alcoholic Beverages, supra* note 22, ¶ 4 (extended by 20 days); *Chile – Taxes on Alcoholic Beverages – Arbitration under Article 21.3(c) of the DSU*, WT/DS87/15, WT/DS110/14, 23 May 2000, DSR 2000:V, 2589, ¶ 3 (extended by 51 days); *Canada – Certain Measures Affecting the Automotive Industry – Arbitration under Article 21.3(c) of the DSU*, WT/DS139/12, WT/DS142/12, 4 October 2000, DSR 2000:X, 5079, ¶ 3 (extended by 18 days); *US – Line Pipe, supra* note 36, ¶ 3 (extended by 36 days).

[39] *See, e.g.* Award of the Arbitrator, *United States – Section 110(5) of the US Copyright Act – Arbitration under Article 21.3(c) of the DSU*, WT/DS160/12, 15 January 2001 (report adopted 27 July 2000; parties request arbitration 22 November 2000); *US – Hot-Rolled Steel, supra* note 27, (report adopted 23 August 2001; parties request arbitration 6 December 2001).

[40] DSU Art. 21.3(c). *See* generally, Pierre Monnier, *The Time to Comply with an Adverse WTO Ruling*, 35 JOURNAL OF WORLD TRADE 825 (No. 5, October 2001).

In *Japan – Taxes on Alcoholic Beverages*, the complaining party argued for a period of less than 15 months; Japan argued for a longer period. The Arbitrator found that neither party had made a case for departing from the 15-month guideline, which, he concluded, was the reasonable period of time.[41] In *EC – Bananas III*, the Arbitrator used a similar rationale, with a slight adjustment.[42] The Arbitrator said that the complaining parties "have not persuaded me that there are 'particular circumstances' in this case to justify a shorter period of time than stipulated by the guideline in Article 21.3(c) of the DSU."[43] The "complexity of the implementation process," the Arbitrator said, "would suggest adherence to the guideline, with a slight modification, so that the 'reasonable period' of time for implementation would expire by 1 January 1999."[44] This extended the period from 15 months to 15 months and one week.[45]

The Arbitrator in *EC – Hormones* also awarded 15 months but, in doing so, elaborated on standards that should be used to establish the reasonable period of time. "[T]he 15-month guideline," the Arbitrator said, "is an outer limit or maximum in the usual case. For example, where the implementation can be effected by administrative means, the reasonable period of time should be considerably shorter than 15 months."[46] Article 21.3(c), the Arbitrator added, requires that the reasonable period of time "should be the shortest period possible within the legal system of the Member to implement the recommendations and rulings of the DSB."[47] However, "the party seeking to prove that there are 'particular circumstances' justifying a shorter or longer time has the burden of proof under Article 21.3(c)."[48]

The Arbitrators in the first three Article 21.3(c) arbitrations effectively treated 15 months as the default reasonable period of time unless a party could establish that a longer or shorter period was appropriate. But this did not last. The next 10 arbitrations resulted in periods of less than 15 months, running from six months in *Canada – Pharmaceutical Patents*[49] to 14 months and nine days in *Chile – Alcoholic Beverages*.[50] It was not until the 14th arbitration, *US – Hot-Rolled Steel*, that a 15-month reasonable period was again awarded by the Arbitrator.[51] The average reasonable

41 *Supra*, note 37, ¶ 27.

42 Award of the Arbitrator, *European Communities – Regime for the Importation, Sale and Distribution of Bananas – Arbitration under Article 21.3(c) of the DSU*, WT/DS27/15, 7 January 1998, DSR 1998:I, 3.

43 *Id.* ¶ 19. 44 *Id.* 45 *Id.* ¶ 20. 46 *Supra* note 17, ¶ 25.

47 *Id.* ¶ 26. 48 *Id.* ¶ 27. 49 *Supra* note 23, ¶ 64.

50 *Supra* note 25, ¶ 46. 51 *Supra* note 27, ¶ 40.

period of time awarded in the first 14 arbitrations was approximately 11.7 months.

In *Canada – Pharmaceutical Patents*, the Arbitrator broke sharply with the rationale of the Arbitrators' earlier awards. The default position was not 15 months, but "immediately." "Implicit in the wording of Article 21.3 seems to me to be the assumption that, ordinarily, Members will comply with recommendations and rulings of the DSB 'immediately,' " the Arbitrator said.[52] "The 'reasonable period of time' to which Article 21.3 refers is, thus, a period of time in what is implicitly not the ordinary circumstance, but a circumstance in which 'it is impracticable to comply *immediately* . . . .' "[53] Since immediate compliance is the "preferred option under Article 21.3," the Arbitrator continued, it is "for the implementing Member to bear the burden of proof in showing – '[i]f it is impracticable to comply immediately' – that the duration of any proposed period of implementation, including its supposed component steps, constitutes a 'reasonable period of time.' And the longer the proposed period of implementation, the greater the burden will be."[54]

However, the Arbitrator in *US – Offset Act (Byrd Amendment)* formulated the standard in different terms, and in so doing seemed to give greater status to the 15-month guideline. "Where the implementing Member fails to establish that the period of time requested by it is indeed the shortest period possible within its legal system, the arbitrator must determine the 'shortest period possible' for implementation, which will be shorter than proposed by the implementing Member, on the basis of the evidence presented by all parties in their submissions, and taking into account the 15-month guideline provided by Article 21.3(c)."[55]

§ 7.05 Factors affecting time allowed for implementation

[1] Overview

While Article 21.3(c) provides, as a "guideline" for the Arbitrator, that the reasonable period of time should not exceed 15 months from the date of adoption of the report, the article concludes, as discussed *supra* in § 7.04, "that time may be shorter or longer, depending upon the particular circumstances." The "particular circumstances" that are most often raised in Article 21.3(c) arbitrations concern: complexity; whether there is need for legislation, or whether the measure can be brought into conformity by

[52] *Supra* note 23, ¶ 45. [53] *Id.* (emphasis in original).
[54] *Id.* ¶ 47. [55] *Supra* note 30, ¶ 51.

simpler administrative action; the extent of any domestic opposition; and how and whether, pursuant to Article 21.2, particular attention should be paid to matters affecting the interests of developing country Members. Typically, these factors are interrelated.

[2] Complexity

The complexity of the proposed implementation is a factor that has been considered by several arbitrators. In *Canada – Pharmaceutical Patents*, the Arbitrator expressed the view that, if the proposed implementation required extensive new regulations affecting many sectors of activity, then more time would be required for drafting and consulting with the parties than would be the case if the proposed implementation called only for the repeal of "a sentence or two."[56] Relevant to the evaluation of complexity is the question of the need to take legally required – as opposed to discretionary – steps in the process.[57] In *Indonesia – Autos*, the Arbitrator accepted Indonesia's request to account for legally binding, domestic, rule-making requirements.[58] Complexity also was mentioned by the Arbitrator in *EC – Bananas III* as a relevant factor.[59]

In *US – 1916 Act*, the Arbitrator declined to consider relevant to the determination of a reasonable period of time such factors as the volume of legislation brought before the US Congress or the small percentage of bills that become law, or that most legislation is passed at the end of the session.[60] "What is relevant to my determination in this case," the Arbitrator said, "are the treaty obligations explicitly undertaken by Members pursuant to the covered agreements."[61] Accordingly, "Since this is a case where the United States has to enact a piece of legislation to bring it into compliance with its international treaty obligations under the covered agreements, the United States Congress may reasonably be expected to use all the flexibility available within its normal legislative procedures to enact the required legislation as speedily as possible."[62]

[56] *Supra* note 23, ¶ 50. [57] *Id.* ¶ 51.

[58] Award of the Arbitrator, *Indonesia – Certain Measures Affecting the Automobile Industry – Arbitration under Article 21.3(c) of the DSU*, WT/DS54/15, WT/DS55/14, WT/DS59/13, WT/DS64/12, 7 December 1998, DSR 1998:IX, 4029, ¶ 22.

[59] *Supra* note 42, ¶ 19.

[60] Award of the Arbitrator, *United States – Anti-Dumping Act of 1916 – Arbitration under Article 21.3(c) of the DSU*, WT/DS136/11, WT/DS162/14, 28 February 2001, ¶ 38.

[61] *Id.* [62] *Id.* ¶ 39.

[3] Need for legislative action

Often central to the question of whether complexity is a factor is the question of whether legislative or administrative action is required. Implementation through administrative means normally will justify a shorter period than implementation through legislative means. In *EC– Hormones*, the Arbitrator said that, "when implementation can be effected by administrative means, the reasonable period of time should be considerably shorter than 15 months."[63]

While the reasonable period of time should be the shortest possible within the legal system of the Member concerned, the Arbitrator in *Korea – Alcoholic Beverages* found that this does not require that a Member "utilize an *extraordinary* legislative procedure, rather than the *normal* legislative procedure, in every case."[64] Accordingly, the Arbitrator found it "reasonable to allow Korea to follow its *normal* legislative procedure for the consideration and adoption of a tax bill with budgetary implications, that is, to submit the proposed amendments to the next regular session of the National Assembly."[65] In *Canada – Autos*, the complaining party argued that the fact that Canada, in another case, had been able to take action to withdraw a prohibited subsidy within 90 days in accordance with Article 4.7 of the *Agreement on Subsidies and Countervailing Measures*, was relevant to how much time it would need to implement the recommendation and ruling of the DSB.[66] The Arbitrator disagreed:

> Canada's ability to take "extraordinary action" to withdraw the export subsidy "without delay," in accordance with the provisions of Article 4.7 of the *SCM Agreement* and pursuant to the recommendation of the DSB, is not relevant for determining the "reasonable period of time" under Article 21.3(c) of the DSU for implementation of the recommendations of the DSB relating to Article I:1 and Article III:4 of the GATT 1994 and Article XVII of GATS.[67]

However, the Arbitrator stated that factors within a Member's legal system unrelated to an assessment of the shortest period of time possible are not relevant to a determination of the "reasonable period of time" under Article 21.3(c). Accordingly, the Arbitrator did not allow additional time so that the DSB's recommendation could be implemented on the same timetable as a planned reform of Canada's customs regime, even though it might be more convenient for Canada to do so.[68]

[63] *Supra* note 17, ¶ 25.
[64] *Supra* note 22, ¶ 42 (emphasis in original).
[65] *Id.* (emphasis in original).
[66] *Supra* note 38, ¶ 26.
[67] *Id.* ¶ 53.
[68] *Id.* ¶ 55.

[4] Domestic opposition

Neither the "contentiousness" of a measure nor the "controversy" surrounding it is relevant to a determination of the reasonable period of time for implementation.[69] In *Canada – Patent Term*, the United States argued that, in Canada's parliamentary system, "the Government of Canada can essentially pass any legislation it wishes in whatever time it likes."[70] The Arbitrator, however, was "very reluctant to take these factors into account in determining the 'reasonable period of time.' These factors vary from country to country, and from constitution to constitution," the Arbitrator said. "Even within a given country, they will change over time. In addition, their evaluation will often be difficult and highly speculative."[71] This argument notwithstanding, the Arbitrator in *Canada – Patent Term* also observed that, "Ultimately, the 'reasonable period of time' appears to be a function of the priority which Canada attributes to the amendment of its *Patent Act* in order to bring it into conformity with its obligations."[72]

While the "simple contentiousness" of a proposed implementation measure normally would not be a consideration for determination of the reasonable period of time, the Arbitrator in *Chile – Price Band System* stated that "the longstanding nature" of the measure and its "fundamental integration into the central agricultural policies of Chile," among other factors, including its "unique role and impact on Chilean society is a relevant factor in my determination."[73]

Something close to a "good faith" effort to implement recommendations and rulings promptly was suggested by the Arbitrator in *US – Section 110(5) Copyright Act*:

> [A]n implementing Member must use the time after adoption of a panel and/or Appellate Body report to begin to implement the recommendations and rulings of the DSB. Arbitrators will scrutinize very carefully the actions an implementing Member takes in respect of implementation during the period after adoption of a panel and/or Appellate Body report and prior to any arbitration proceeding. If it is perceived by an arbitrator that an implementing Member has not adequately begun implementation after adoption so as to effect "prompt compliance," it is to be expected that the arbitrator will take this into account in determining the "reasonable period of time."[74]

[69] *US – Section 110(5) Copyright Act*, *supra* note 39, ¶ 42.

[70] Award of the Arbitrator, *Canada – Term of Patent Protection – Arbitration under Article 21.3(c) of the DSU*, WT/DS170/10, 28 February 2001, ¶ 59.

[71] *Id.* ¶ 60. [72] *Id.* ¶ 64. [73] *Supra* note 26, ¶¶ 47–48. [74] *Supra* note 39, ¶ 46.

[5] Economic harm

The fact that exporters may suffer particular economic harm during the period of implementation is not in itself relevant to the determination of the reasonable period of time.[75] The need to remove any economic harm that might result from inconsistent measures is reflected in Article 21.1's principle of prompt compliance, and is the reason for the requirement that the time for implementation be the shortest possible.[76]

[6] Developing countries

Article 21.2 provides that, "Particular attention should be paid to matters affecting the interests of developing country Members with respect to measures which have been subject to dispute settlement." This requirement has been noted in arbitrations and, in one of them, resulted in a longer period of time.

In *Indonesia – Autos*, after quoting Article 21.2, the Arbitrator observed that, "Indonesia is not only a developing country; it is a developing country that is currently in a dire economic and financial situation."[77] Accordingly, the Arbitrator awarded "an additional period of six months over and above the six-month period required for the completion of Indonesia's domestic rule-making process."[78] In both *Chile – Alcoholic Beverages*[79] and *Argentina – Hides and Leather*,[80] the developing country Member concerned raised Article 21.2. However, the Arbitrator noted that neither country had "been very specific about how its interests as a developing country Member actually bear upon the duration of the 'reasonable period of time'" required to take appropriate action.[81] In these circumstances, the Arbitrator concluded, "Article 21.2, whatever else it may signify, usefully enjoins, *inter alia*, an arbitrator functioning under Article 21.3(c) to be generally mindful of the great difficulties that a developing country Member may, in a particular case, face as it proceeds to implement the recommendations and rulings of the DSB."[82]

[75] *US – Offset Act (Byrd Amendment), supra* note 30, ¶ 79. [76] *Id.* ¶ 80.

[77] *Supra* note 58, ¶ 24. [78] *Id.* [79] *Supra* note 25.

[80] Award of the Arbitrator, *Argentina – Measures Affecting the Export of Bovine Hides and Import of Finished Leather – Arbitration under Article 21.3(c) of the DSU*, WT/DS155/10, 31 August 2001.

[81] *Chile – Alcoholic Beverages, supra* note 25, ¶ 44; *Argentina – Hides and Leather, supra* note 80, ¶ 51.

[82] *Chile* and *Argentina, Id.* ¶ 45 and ¶ 51, respectively.

Chile – Price Band System, in which Argentina was the complaining party, was the first arbitration involving developing countries as both complainant and respondent.[83] Chile was unable to point to any additional, specific obstacles it faced, as a developing country.[84] At the same time, the Arbitrator said, "the acuteness of Argentina's burden as a developing country complainant that has been successful in establishing the WTO-inconsistency of a challenged measure, is amplified by Argentina's daunting financial woes at present."[85] In the unusual circumstances of the case, therefore, the Arbitrator was "not swayed" towards either a longer or shorter period by virtue of the fact that each of the parties was a developing country.[86]

§ 7.06 Surveillance by the DSB

Implementation of all adopted recommendations and rulings is kept under surveillance by the DSB until the process is completed, and the issue of implementation may be raised in the DSB by any Member at any time.[87] Unless it is (by consensus) agreed to the contrary, six months after establishment of the reasonable period of time for implementation, the issue of implementation is placed on the agenda of the DSB and remains on the agenda until the issue is resolved.[88]

At least 10 days prior to each meeting of the DSB, the Member subject to the recommendations and rulings is required to provide the DSB with a written status report of its progress in the implementation of the DSB's recommendations and rulings.[89] When a Member does not implement within a reasonable period of time, surveillance by the DSB continues even if compensation has been provided or the DSB has authorized "sanctions" or "retaliation" in the form of suspension of concessions.[90] Compensation and retaliation are considered to be temporary measures, and are not preferred to full implementation.[91] This process usually creates an incentive for Members to implement adopted rulings and recommendations.

§ 7.07 Disputes regarding implementation

[1] Overview

The initial decision as to the "modalities of implementation of a panel, or Appellate Body, report," and, thereby, the decision as to how to

[83] *Supra* note 26, ¶ 55. [84] *Id.* ¶ 56. [85] *Id.* [86] *Id.*
[87] DSU Art. 21.6. [88] *Id.* [89] *Id.* [90] *See* § 8.05.
[91] DSU Art. 22.1. Compensation and retaliation are discussed in Chapter 8.

comply with the rulings and recommendations of the DSB, belongs to the Member taking those steps.[92] However, the remedy selected by the Member concerned may not, in the view of the prevailing complainant, in fact bring the measure into conformity. When disagreement occurs as to the existence or consistency with a covered agreement of measures taken to comply, that further disagreement itself shall be decided through recourse to dispute settlement.[93]

Article 21.5 of the DSU provides that, whenever possible, this shall be done through referral to the original panel, which should circulate its report within 90 days of referral. When the panel considers that it cannot provide its report within 90 days, it will inform the DSB in writing of the reasons for the delay, together with an estimate of the time within which it will submit its report. No maximum time is provided in the DSU.[94] In proceedings under the *Agreement on Government Procurement*, the 90-day period is reduced to 60 days.[95]

The short time available to complete an Article 21.5 review led the Panel in *EC – Bananas III (Article 21.5 – Ecuador)*, the first compliance panel, not to include an interim review in its timetable.[96] Subsequent panels generally, but not always, have followed this practice.[97]

The question of compliance with the recommendations and rulings of the DSB is linked to the question of remedies, in particular because of an apparent flaw in the drafting of the timing requirements of the relevant provisions of the DSU, Articles 21.5 and 22.6. This is discussed, *infra*, in Chapter 8.

[92] Panel Report, *Guatemala – Anti-Dumping Investigation Regarding Portland Cement from Mexico*, WT/DS60/R, adopted 25 November 1998, as modified by the Appellate Body Report, WT/DS60/AB/R, DSR 1998:IX, 3797, ¶ 8.3.

[93] DSU Art. 21.5. [94] *Id.*

[95] *Agreement on Government Procurement*, Art. XXII:6. *See* § 5.13 [5].

[96] Panel Report, *European Communities – Regime for the Importation, Sale and Distribution of Bananas – Recourse to Article 21.5 of the DSU by Ecuador*, WT/DS27/RW/ECU, 12 April 1999, DSR 1999:II, 803, ¶ 6.2.

[97] For panels that have issued interim reports, *see, e.g.*, Panel Report, *Brazil – Export Financing Programme for Aircraft – Recourse by Canada to Article 21.5 of the DSU*, WT/DS46/RW, adopted 4 August 2000, as modified by the Appellate Body Report, WTDS46/AB/RW, DSR 2000:IX, 4093; Panel Report, *Canada – Measures Affecting the Export of Civilian Aircraft – Recourse by Brazil to Article 21.5 of the DSU*, WT/DS70/RW, adopted 4 August 2000, as modified by the Appellate Body Report, WT/DS70/AB/RW, DSR 2000:IX, 4315; Panel Report, *Brazil – Export Financing Programme for Aircraft – Second Recourse by Canada to Article 21.5 of the DSU*, WT/DS46/RW/2, adopted 23 August 2001; Panel Report, *United States – Tax Treatment for "Foreign Sales Corporations" – Recourse to Article 21.5 of the DSU by the European Communities*, WT/DS108/RW, adopted 29 January 2002, as modified by the Appellate Body Report, WT/DS108/AB/RW.

[2] Scope of Article 21.5 "compliance" review

The question of the scope of review by a "compliance panel" instituted pursuant to Article 21.5 of the DSU arose at the start in *EC – Bananas III (Article 21.5 – Ecuador)*, and has been an issue in several subsequent reviews. In *Bananas III*, the EC argued that the Panel's terms of reference were limited, by Article 21.5, to the "matters" on which the DSB had adopted its recommendations or rulings based on the original Panel and Appellate Body reports.[98] The Panel rejected the argument. First, the Panel noted, pursuant to its terms of reference, it was required to consider the matter referred to the DSB by Ecuador, "and that matter consists of the measures and claims specified by Ecuador [in its request for establishment of the Panel]."[99] Second, the Panel observed, Article 21.5 directs compliance panels to consider "the existence or consistency with a covered agreement of measures taken to comply with the recommendations and rulings" of the DSB.[100] Accordingly, the Panel held, its terms of reference covered all of the claims raised by Ecuador.[101]

Similarly, in *Australia – Salmon (Article 21.5 – Canada)*, the compliance Panel rejected the argument that its jurisdiction was limited by the fact that the original Panel did not deal with a claim. To the contrary, the Panel held, the scope of its review was governed by Article 21.5 and the specific terms of reference of the compliance panel, which include the relevant provisions of covered agreements referred to in the request for establishment of the Panel.[102]

The Appellate Body took the occasion of its review of the compliance Panel's report in *Canada – Aircraft* to confirm this analysis. Its statement merits full quotation:

> Proceedings under Article 21.5 do not concern just *any* measure of a Member of the WTO; rather, Article 21.5 proceedings are limited to those "measures *taken to comply* with the recommendations and rulings" of the DSB. In our view, the phrase "measures taken to comply" refers to measures which have been, or which should be, adopted by a Member to bring about compliance with the recommendations and rulings of the DSB. In principle, a measure which has been "taken to comply with the recommendations and rulings" of the DSB will *not* be the same measure as the measure which was the subject of the original dispute, so that, in principle, there would be

[98] *Supra* note 96, ¶ 6.3. [99] *Id.* ¶ 6.7. [100] *Id.* ¶ 6.8. [101] *Id.* ¶ 6.12.

[102] Panel Report, *Australia – Measures Affecting Importation of Salmon – Recourse to Article 21.5 of the DSU by Canada*, WT/DS18/RW, adopted 20 March 2000, DSR 2000:IV, 2035, ¶ 7.10 (9) and (14).

> two separate and distinct measures: the original measure which *gave rise* to the recommendations and rulings of the DSB, and the "measures taken to comply" which are – or should be – adopted to *implement* these recommendations and rulings.[103]

The Appellate Body went on to elaborate that:

> [I]n carrying out its review under Article 21.5 of the DSU, a panel is not confined to examining the "measures taken to comply" from the perspective of the claims, arguments and factual circumstances that related to the measure that was the subject of the original proceedings. Although these may have some relevance in proceedings under Article 21.5 of the DSU, Article 21.5 proceedings involve, in principle, not the original measure, but rather a new and different measure which was not before the original panel. In addition, the relevant facts bearing upon the "measure taken to comply" may be different from the relevant facts relating to the measure at issue in the original proceedings. It is natural, therefore, that the claims, arguments and factual circumstances which are pertinent to the "measure taken to comply" will not, necessarily, be the same as those which were pertinent in the original dispute. Indeed, the utility of the review envisaged under Article 21.5 of the DSU would be seriously undermined if a panel were restricted to examining the new measure from the perspective of the claims, arguments and factual circumstances that related to the original measure, because an Article 21.5 panel would then be unable to examine fully the "consistency with a covered agreement of the measures taken to comply," as required by Article 21.5 of the DSU.[104]

The Appellate Body has also stated that when the issue concerns the consistency of a new measure, taken to comply with DSB recommendations and rulings, the task of an Article 21.5 panel "is to consider the new measure in its totality."[105] However, it "is not part of a panel's task to go beyond the particular claims that have been made with respect to the consistency of a new measure with a covered agreement when a matter is referred to it by the DSB for an Article 21.5 proceeding."[106]

In *Australia – Salmon (Article 21.5 – Canada)*, Australia also argued that a measure was not properly before the compliance Panel, even though it was included in the terms of reference by way of the request for the establishment of the Panel, because it was not a "measure taken to comply"

[103] *Supra* note 97, ¶ 36 (emphasis in original, footnote omitted).

[104] *Id.* ¶ 41.

[105] Appellate Body Report, *United States – Import Prohibition of Certain Shrimp and Shrimp Products – Recourse to Article 21.5 of the DSU by Malaysia*, WT/DS58/AB/RW, adopted 21 November 2001, ¶ 87.

[106] *Id.* ¶ 88.

with recommendations and rulings of the DSB.[107] Australia had made the same argument shortly before in *Australia – Automotive Leather II (Article 21.5 – US)*.[108] Both panels rejected the argument.

The Panel in *Salmon* reasoned that "an Article 21.5 panel cannot leave it to the full discretion of the implementing Member to decide whether or not a measure is one 'taken to comply.' "[109] The Panel in *Leather* agreed, noting that, "In general, it is the complaining Member in WTO dispute settlement which establishes the scope of the measures before a panel."[110] To hold to the contrary, the Panel reasoned, "would allow Australia to establish the scope of our terms of reference by choosing what measure or measures it will notify, or not notify, to the DSB in connection with its implementation of the DSB's ruling."[111] In the specific case, the Panel noted that the measure in question, a loan, "is inextricably linked to the steps taken by Australia in response to the DSB's ruling in this dispute, in view of both its timing and its nature."[112]

The same conclusion was reached by the Panel in *EC – Bed Linen (Article 21.5 – India)*. After quoting from both the *Australia – Salmon* and the *Australia – Automotive Leather II* compliance panels, the *Bed Linens* Panel said that:

> [I]t is clear that it is the Panel, and not the EC, which decides whether the measures cited by India in the request for establishment are to be considered 'measures taken to comply' and therefore fall within the purview of this dispute. That said, however, it is also not India's right to determine which measures taken by the EC are measures taken to comply. Rather, this is an issue which must be considered by an Article 21.5 panel.[113]

While the early Article 21.5 cases, following *Canada – Aircraft*, tended to include, as measures taken to comply, measures that were not before the original panel, subsequent Article 21.5 proceedings cases have distinguished between that case and those cases that involved findings that had not been pursued by the complainant and were subsequently adopted by the DSB when it adopted the original Panel or Appellate Body report. These were held not to be subject to review by a compliance panel.

107 *Supra* note 102, ¶ 7.10 (20).

108 Panel Report, *Australia – Subsidies Provided to Producers and Exporters of Automotive Leather – Recourse to Article 21.5 of the DSU by the United States*, WT/DS126/RW and Corr.1, adopted 11 February 2000, DSR 2000:III, 1189, ¶ 6.1.

109 *Supra* note 102, ¶ 7.10 (22). 110 *Supra* note 108, ¶ 6.4. 111 *Id.* 112 *Id.* ¶ 6.5.

113 Panel Report, *European Communities – Anti-Dumping Duties on Imports of Cotton-Type Bed Linen from India – Recourse to Article 21.5 of the DSU by India*, WT/DS141/RW, adopted 24 April 2003, as modified by the Appellate Body Report, WT/DS141/AB/RW, ¶ 6.15.

Thus, in *US – Shrimp (Article 21.5 – Malaysia)*, the Panel noted that in the original appeal, the Appellate Body had found that a provision of US law, "Section 609," was "provisionally justified" under Article XX(g), and that, "as long as the implementing measure before us is identical to the measure examined by the Appellate Body in relation to paragraph (g), we should not reach a different conclusion from the Appellate Body."[114] Thus, the Panel did not re-examine Section 609 in the compliance review. This approach was affirmed by the Appellate Body, which referred to the text of Article 17.4 of the DSU providing that Appellate Body reports "shall be" adopted by the DSB, and that adopted Appellate Body reports shall be unconditionally accepted by the parties to the dispute.[115]

The Panel in *EC – Bed Linen (Article 21.5 – India)* referred with approval to *US – Shrimp (Article 21.5 – Malaysia)* in declining to rule on a claim as not properly before it. In the original investigation, India claimed, *inter alia*, that the EC failed properly to consider "other factors" besides imports that might have caused injury within the meaning of the Antidumping Agreement. The original Panel found that India had not presented a *prima facie* case on the issue, and India had not appealed that finding.[116]

The compliance Panel rejected India's argument that the claim could be re-visited in the Article 21.5 proceeding as a "measure taken to comply" with the recommendations and rulings of the DSB. This situation was very different from the situation presented in *Canada – Aircraft (Article 21.5 – Brazil)*, the Panel said. In that case, Canada had implemented by adopting a new and different measure. Claims involving that new measure could not have been raised by Brazil in the original proceeding.[117] In contrast, *Bed Linens* involved claims that: (1) were raised and rejected before the original panel; (2) were not pursued on appeal; and (3) were the subject of findings in the Report adopted by the DSB.[118] "Thus," the Panel concluded, "the portions of the original Report of the Panel that are not appealed, together with the Appellate Body report resolving the issues appealed, must, in our view, be considered as the final resolution of the dispute, and must be treated as such by the parties, and by us, in this proceeding."[119]

[114] Panel Report, *United States – Import Prohibition of Certain Shrimp and Shrimp Products – Recourse to Article 21.5 of the DSU by Malaysia*, WT/DS58/RW, adopted 21 November 2001, as upheld by the Appellate Body Report, WT/DS58/AB/RW, ¶ 5.39.

[115] Appellate Body Report, *US – Shrimp (Article 21.5 – Malaysia)*, *supra* note 105, ¶ 97.

[116] *Supra* note 113, ¶ 6.41. [117] *Id.* ¶ 6.48. [118] *Id.*

[119] *Id.* ¶ 6.51. *See*, *Res judicata* and Estoppel at §§ 2.06 [3] and [4].

In a far-reaching opinion, the Appellate Body agreed. Its analysis began with the observation that, "If a *claim* challenges a *measure* which is not a 'measure taken to comply,' that *claim* cannot properly be raised in Article 21.5 proceedings."[120] In agreeing with the Panel that *Bed Linens* differed importantly from *Canada – Aircraft*, the Appellate Body said that in *Bed Linens*, "India did not raise a *new* claim before the Article 21.5 Panel; rather, India reasserted in the Article 21.5 proceedings the *same* claim that it had raised before the *original* panel in respect of a component of the implementation measure which was the same as the original measure. This *same* claim was dismissed by the original panel, and India did not appeal that finding."[121]

Because the original Panel's finding was not appealed, the Appellate Body said, Article 17.4, which deals with the adoption of Appellate Body reports, is not dispositive of the case. Nevertheless, "in our view, an *unappealed* finding included in a panel report that is *adopted* by the DSB must be treated as a *final resolution* to a dispute between the parties in respect of the *particular* claim and the *specific* component of a measure that is the subject of that claim."[122]

[3] Standing of respondent to initiate Article 21.5 proceedings

In *EC – Bananas III (Article 21.5 – EC)*, the EC itself, the respondent in the case, took the unusual step of requesting review of the measure it had enacted to implement the recommendations and rulings of the DSB.[123] The EC did so in the context of a procedurally complex case that presented, for the first time, the question of how compliance review under Article 21.5 should interact with potential remedies under Article 22 for failure to bring a measure into conformity. The Article 21.5-Article 22 issue is discussed in Chapter 8.

For its part, the EC requested establishment of a compliance panel "to find that the implementing measures of the European Communities must be presumed to conform to WTO rules unless their conformity had been duly challenged under the appropriate WTO procedures."[124] "From

[120] Appellate Body Report, *European Communities – Anti-Dumping Duties on Imports of Cotton-Type Bed Linen from India – Recourse to Article 21.5 of the DSU by India*, WT/DS141/AB/RW, adopted 24 April 2003, ¶ 78.

[121] *Id.* ¶ 80. [122] *Id.* ¶ 93.

[123] Panel Report , *European Communities – Regime for the Importation, Sale and Distribution of Bananas – Recourse to Article 21.5 of the DSU by the European Communities*, WT/DS27/RW/EEC and Corr.1, 12 April 1999, DSR 1999:II, 783.

[124] *Id.* ¶ 1.4.

the beginning of the reasonable period of time," the EC argued, "the original complainants had not ceased to affirm in the press and in the DSB their conviction that the measures first envisaged, then proposed, then adopted by the Council, then finally adopted by the Commission, did not comply with the recommendations and rulings of the DSB in this case."[125]

The Panel noted its agreement with the EC that there is normally no presumption of inconsistency attached to a Member's measures; however, the Panel added, the failure, at a given point in time, of one Member to challenge a measure cannot create a presumption that the Member failing to challenge accepts the measure as consistent with WTO obligations.[126] Further, the Panel noted, it did not have authority to compel the original complainants to participate as parties in an Article 21.5 proceeding.[127]

In the end, the Panel treated the EC's request in the context of an Article 21.5 request that had been filed by Ecuador, noting that, "Since we have found in the proceeding initiated by Ecuador that the EC's implementing measures are *not* consistent with its WTO obligations, it is clear that they cannot be presumed to be consistent in this proceeding."[128] As a formal matter, the Panel explicitly did not consider whether the respondent is authorized to initiate an Article 21.5 proceeding. It noted practical problems that had been mentioned by third parties, such as the requirement that a party asserting a fact have the burden of proving it. The absence of a complainant in a respondent-initiated proceeding would raise serious questions as to a panel's ability to accomplish its task.[129] Nevertheless, it said, "we would not rule out the possibility of using Article 21.5 in such a manner, particularly when the purpose of such initiation was clearly the examination of the WTO-consistency of implementing measures."[130] The Panel concluded, however, simply by not making the findings requested by the EC.[131]

[125] *Id.* ¶ 2.1. [126] *Id.* ¶ 4.13.
[127] *Id.* ¶ 4.12. [128] *Id.* ¶ 4.15. [129] *Id.* ¶ 4.18.
[130] *Id.* Prof. Hudec has pointed out that, "The language of Article 21.5 would seem to permit such actions, for the text does not identify the initiating party. The traditions of GATT dispute settlement would certainly favor such a result, recalling that pro-adjudication governments led by the United States fought for two decades to establish the firm right of a party to have its rights adjudicated." Robert E. Hudec, *Broadening the Scope of Remedies in WTO Dispute Settlement*, in Friedl Weiss (Ed) Improving WTO Dispute Settlement Procedures: Issues & Lessons from the Practice of Other International Courts & Tribunals 369, 398 (Cameron May, 2000).
[131] *Id.* ¶ 5.1.

[4] "Existence" of an implementing measure

Article 21.5 deals with both the "existence" and the "consistency" of measures to comply. In *Australia – Salmon*, the Panel said that a measure exists when the new "regime sets out all the requirements and criteria under which the product concerned *can* enter the market of the implementing Member."[132] A "framework" regulation, setting out basic – but not all – new requirements is not sufficient for a new regime to "exist."[133]

In the specific case, the effective date of the measures taken to comply occurred after the expiration of the "reasonable period of time." Accordingly, the Panel held, "no measures taken to comply existed or will exist in the sense of Article 21.5."[134]

[5] Requirement of consultations

Article 21.5 reviews generally have proceeded without consultations. In *Mexico – Corn Syrup (Article 21.5 – US)*, the EC, as a third party, challenged this practice.[135] The EC argued that Article 21.5 provides that compliance panels will proceed under "these dispute settlement procedures," and that "these procedures" included the consultation requirements of the DSU.[136] Parties cannot dispense with the consultation requirements of Article 4, the EC claimed. It also noted that Article 6.2 of the DSU requires a Member requesting the establishment of a panel to state in its request whether consultations were held.

The Appellate Body explicitly did not decide whether the general obligations in the DSU regarding consultations were applicable to Article 21.5 compliance reviews.[137] It did conclude that "the lack of prior consultations is not a defect that, by its very nature, deprives a panel of its authority to deal with and dispose of a matter."[138] It also concluded that the requirement in Article 6.2 to state "whether consultations were held" was not a requirement to hold consultations. To the contrary, Article 6.2 "envisages the possibility that a panel may be validly established without being preceded by consultations."[139] Accordingly:

[132] *Supra* note 102, ¶ 7.28. [133] *Id.* [134] *Id.* ¶ 7.30.

[135] Appellate Body Report, *Mexico – Antidumping Investigation of High Fructose Corn Syrup (HFCS) from the United States – Recourse to Article 21.5 of the DSU by the United States*, WT/DS132/AB/RW, adopted 21 November 2001.

[136] The EC argument is set out in *Id.* at ¶¶ 30–33.

[137] *Id.* ¶ 65. [138] *Id.* ¶ 64. [139] *Id.* ¶ 62.

> [W]here the responding party does not object, explicitly and in a timely manner, to the failure of the complaining party to request or engage in consultations, the responding party may be deemed to have consented to the lack of consultations and, thereby, to have relinquished whatever right to consult it may have had.[140]

In reaching its conclusion, the Appellate Body no doubt was aware that a consultation requirement for compliance reviews under Article 21.5 would exacerbate the procedural conflict of that article with Article 22 of the DSU. See Chapter 8.

[6] Burden of proof

In Article 21.5 reviews, as in other panel proceedings, the party asserting a fact has the burden of proving it, and the party asserting an affirmative defence has the burden of establishing it. In *Brazil – Aircraft (Article 21.5 – Canada)*, Brazil argued that changes made in the program at issue qualified it for an exemption to the SCM Agreement's general prohibition of export subsidies. It argued further that, since the new measure was designed to comply with WTO requirements, it enjoyed a presumption of compliance, and that it was up to the challenging party to establish the contrary.[141]

The Appellate Body disagreed. The fact that a measure was taken to comply with recommendations and rulings of the DSB, the Appellate Body held, does not alter the allocation of the burden of proof. A party asserting eligibility for an affirmative defence has the burden of establishing that eligibility in an Article 21.5 review, as well as in a regular panel proceeding.[142]

[7] Third party rights

Before several compliance panels, the EC raised the issue of the rights of third parties to receive all of the submissions of the parties to the panel. The issue centers on the text of Article 10.3 of the DSU which provides that, "Third parties shall receive the submissions of the parties to the dispute to the first meeting of the panel." In a normal panel proceeding, this

[140] *Id.* ¶ 63.

[141] Appellate Body Report, *Brazil – Export Financing Programme for Aircraft – Recourse by Canada to Article 21.5 of the DSU*, WT/DS46/AB/RW, adopted 4 August 2000, DSR 2000:VIII, 4067, ¶ 66.

[142] *Id.*

means that third parties do not receive the second, rebuttal submissions of the parties that typically are submitted to the second meeting of the panel. But, because of the shorter time allowed by the DSU for compliance proceedings, Article 21.5 panels typically hold a single meeting with the parties that is preceded by the filing by each party of an initial and a rebuttal submission.

In *Australia – Automotive Leather II (Article 21.5 – US)*, the Panel's working procedures allowed for one meeting with the parties, and also provided for third parties to receive only the first submissions of the parties, not the rebuttal submissions.[143] The Panel disallowed the EC's objection, reasoning that, had it decided to hold two sessions with the parties, third parties would have been entitled to only the first submissions. The Panel saw its practice in the compliance proceeding as conforming to that usual practice.[144] At approximately the same time, the Panel in *Australia – Salmon (Article 21.5 – Canada)*[145] reached the same result, as did the Panel in *US – FSC (Article 21.5 – EC)*.[146] While Article 10.3 does not expressly address the extent of third party access to submissions of the parties, the *US – FSC (Article 21.5 – EC)* Panel said that article "must be understood as limiting third party rights in these proceedings to access to the first written submissions only."[147]

However, in *Canada – Dairy (Article 21.5 – New Zealand and US)*, the Panel reached the opposite result.[148] Although the Panel's working procedures initially allowed third parties to receive only the first submissions, the Panel accepted the EC's request and amended its procedures.[149] The Panel observed that the text of Article 10.3 clearly requires that third parties receive "*the* submissions of the parties to the dispute to the first meeting of the panel."[150] Not only does the text require that third parties receive "the submissions" of the parties to the first meeting, the Panel said, the object and purpose of the article call for such action as well. "In the Panel's view, the object and purpose of Article 10.3 of the DSU is to allow third parties to participate in an informed and, hence, meaningful, manner in a session of the meeting with the parties specifically set aside for that purpose. Third parties can only do so if they have received all the

[143] *Supra* note 108, ¶ 3.7. [144] *Id.* ¶ 3.9. [145] *Supra* note 102, ¶ 7.5.

[146] *Supra* note 97. [147] *Id.* ¶ 6.3.

[148] Panel Report, *Canada – Measures Affecting the Importation of Milk and the Exportation of Dairy Products – Recourse to Article 21.5 of the DSU by New Zealand and the United States*, WT/DS103/RW, WT/DS113/RW, adopted 18 December 2001, as reversed (on other grounds) by the Appellate Body Report, WT/DS103/AB/RW, WT/DS113/AB/RW.

[149] *Id.* ¶ 2.32. [150] *Id.* ¶ 2.33 (emphasis supplied by Panel).

information exchanged between the parties before that session."[151] The Panel's conclusion on this point was not included in the appeal.

[8] Suggestions as to implementation

Although Article 19.1 of the DSU authorizes panels, including Article 21.5 compliance panels, to suggest ways in which the Member concerned could bring the measure into compliance, most panels have been reluctant to do so, preferring to leave the mode of implementation to the Member. However, in *EC – Bananas III (Article 21.5 – Ecuador)*, the Panel observed that after one implementation attempt has proven to be at least partly unsuccessful, suggestions by an Article 21.5 panel may be appropriate.[152] Suggestions as to implementation by panels, other than compliance panels and by the Appellate Body, are discussed in § 8.08.

§ 7.08 Prohibited and actionable subsidies

The provisions of the *Agreement on Subsidies and Countervailing Measures* dealing with the adoption and implementation of reports concerning prohibited and actionable subsidies reflect the accelerated procedures that agreement provides generally.

If a measure is found by a panel to be a prohibited subsidy, Article 4.7 of the *SCM Agreement* provides that the Panel shall recommend that it be withdrawn "without delay." Article 4.7 also provides, however, that the Panel "shall specify in its recommendation the time period within which the measure must be withdrawn."

The Panels in *Brazil – Aircraft* and *Canada – Aircraft*, the first to confront the issue, said they were required by this language to take into account the nature of the procedures and the difficulties likely to be faced in implementing the recommendation when specifying what period would represent withdrawal "without delay."[153] Both Panels allowed the Members concerned 90 days to withdraw the subsidy.[154] The Panel in *Australia – Automotive Leather II* adopted the same 90-day period for

[151] *Id.* ¶ 2.34. [152] *Supra* note 96, ¶ 6.154.

[153] Panel Report, *Brazil – Export Financing Programme for Aircraft*, WT/DS46/R, adopted 20 August 1999, as modified by the Appellate Body Report, WT/DS46/AB/R, DSR 1999:III, 1221, ¶ 8.5; Panel Report, *Canada – Measures Affecting the Export of Civilian Aircraft*, WT/DS70/R, adopted 20 August 1999, as upheld by the Appellate Body Report, WT/DS70/AB/R, DSR 1999:IV, 1443, ¶ 10.4.

[154] *Id.*

withdrawal of the subsidy "without delay."[155] However, in *US – FSC*, the Panel, citing the need for legislative action, required withdrawal by 1 October 2000 in a report scheduled for circulation to the Members in September 1999, more than a year earlier.[156] The Panel in *Canada – Aircraft Credits and Guarantees* returned to the 90-day standard of the earlier reports.[157]

Article 7.9 of the SCM Agreement requires that Members take "appropriate steps" to "remove the adverse effects" of an actionable subsidy, or withdraw the subsidy, "within six months from the date when the DSB adopts the panel report or the Appellate Body report."

A report dealing with either prohibited or actionable subsidies shall be adopted by the DSB within 30 days of its issuance, unless it is appealed or unless the DSB decides by consensus not to adopt it.[158] If a report dealing with either prohibited or actionable subsidies is appealed, the appellate report shall be adopted by the DSB and unconditionally accepted by the parties unless the DSB decides by consensus not to adopt it within 20 days of its issuance to the Members.[159]

If a meeting of the DSB is not scheduled during the 30-day period for consideration of a panel report dealing with prohibited or actionable subsidies, or the 20-day period for dealing with an appellate report on either prohibited or actionable subsidies, a special meeting shall be held for the purpose of adopting the report.[160]

The Panel in *Australia – Automotive Leather II (Article 21.5 – US)* was the first to consider the meaning of the term "withdraw the subsidy" in Article 4.7 of the SCM Agreement. The question considered by the Panel was whether "withdraw the subsidy" meant "repay the subsidy." Australia, the United States and the EC as third party all argued that an interpretation of Article 4.7 to allow a retroactive remedy would be inconsistent with Article 19 of the DSU.[161] The Panel disagreed, arguing, "An interpretation of Article 4.7 of the SCM Agreement which would allow exclusively 'prospective' action would make the recommendation to 'withdraw the subsidy' under Article 4.7 indistinguishable

[155] Panel Report, *Australia – Subsidies Provided to Producers and Exporters of Automotive Leather*, WT/DS126/R, adopted 16 June 1999, DSR 1999:III, 951.

[156] Panel Report, *United States – Tax Treatment for "Foreign Sales Corporations"*, WT/DS108/R, adopted 20 March 2000, as modified by the Appellate Body Report, WT/DS108/AB/R, DSR 2000:IV, 1677, ¶ 8.8.

[157] Panel Report, *Canada – Export Credits and Loan Guarantees for Regional Aircraft*, WT/DS222/R and Corr.1, adopted 19 February 2002, ¶ 8.4.

[158] SCM Agreement Arts. 4.8, 7.6.

[159] SCM Agreement Arts. 4.9, 7.7.

[160] SCM Agreement notes 3, 8, and 9.

[161] *Supra* note 108, ¶ 6.29.

from the recommendation to 'bring the measure into conformity' under Article 19.1 of the DSU thus rendering Article 4.7 redundant."[162] The Panel went on to state:

> A subsidy may take the form of a one-time financial contribution conferring a benefit, or it may take the form of a programme or practice pursuant to which financial contributions conferring a benefit are provided on a recurrent basis. For 'withdraw the subsidy' to be a meaningful remedy, that is, for it to effectuate the prohibition on the grant or maintenance of certain types of subsidies, it must be effective regardless of the form in which a prohibited subsidy is found to exist.[163]

In *Brazil – Aircraft (Article 21.5 – Canada)*, Canada argued that the "continued" issuance of bonds in respect of commitments previously made was inconsistent with Brazil's obligation to "withdraw the subsidy."[164] "Thus," the Panel said, "we need not for the purposes of this dispute develop a comprehensive understanding of the scope of the obligation to 'withdraw' a prohibited subsidy."[165] In a footnote referring to the *Australia – Automotive Leather II* report, the *Brazil – Aircraft* Panel said that it would address only the issue before it, and added that, "Our silence on issues that that are not before us should not be taken as expressing any view, express or implied, as to whether or not a recommendation to 'withdraw' a prohibited subsidy may encompass repayment of that subsidy."[166]

In *US – FSC (Article 21.5 – EC)*, the Panel, in an approach that closely resembled that of the Panel in *Brazil – Aircraft*, practiced "judicial economy" and did not rule on the issue.[167]

Canada – Dairy (Article 21.5 – New Zealand and US) involved claims under the *Agreement on Agriculture*, as well as the SCM Agreement, and raised the issue of the relationship of the implementation provisions of the two treaties. While the SCM Agreement calls for Members to "withdraw" prohibited subsidies, the Agriculture Agreement permits some export subsidies on agricultural products. In the actual case, the Panel did not make a finding with regard to the SCM Agreement claim, so the issue became moot. In *dicta*, however, it said that, even if it had made a finding with regard to the SCM Agreement, in light of the provisions of the Agriculture Agreement, it could not have recommended that Canada be

[162] *Id.* ¶ 6.31. [163] *Id.* ¶ 6.36 (footnote omitted). [164] *Supra* note 97, ¶ 6.8.
[165] *Id.* [166] *Id.* footnote 17. [167] *Supra* note 97, ¶ 8.171.

requested to withdraw "measures constituting an export subsidy, exclusively in respect of agricultural products."[168]

§ 7.09 "Other situation" complaints

The DSU provides that when the provisions of Article XXIII:1(c), involving so-called "other situations," are applicable to a covered agreement, the DSU itself applies only up to and including the point in the proceedings where the panel report has been circulated to the Members. Adoption of the report, as well as surveillance and implementation of rulings, is governed by the Montreal Rules.[169] These rules retain GATT's requirement of a positive consensus for the adoption of a report. Consequently, few disputes are likely to be brought under this provision.[170]

[168] Panel Report, *Canada – Measures Affecting the Importation of Milk and the Exportation of Dairy Products – Recourse to Article 21.5 of the DSU by New Zealand and the United States*, WT/DS103/RW, WT/DS113/RW, adopted 18 December 2001, as reversed (on other grounds) by the Appellate Body Report, WT/DS103/AB/RW, WT/DS113/AB/RW, ¶ 6.99.

[169] DSU Art. 26.2. *Decision of 12 April 1989*, BISD 36S/61. *See* § 4.23.

[170] Montreal Rules ¶ G.3.

8

Remedies

§ 8.01 General

Public international law has long recognized the duty of governments to repair or remedy damage they have caused. The Permanent Court of International Justice stated the principle in the *Factory at Chorzów* case: "Reparation must, as far as possible, wipe out all the consequences of the illegal act and re-establish the situation which would, in all probability, have existed if that act had not been committed."[1] In its first decision, the *Corfu Channel* case, the International Court of Justice awarded damages to the United Kingdom as compensation for injury incurred.[2] The Draft Articles of the International Law Commission on State Responsibility provide that, "The responsible State is under an obligation to make full reparation for the injury caused by the internationally wrongful act."[3] GATT practice with regard to remedy was, for the most part, very different. WTO practice, thus far, is different as well, but it appears to be an evolving practice, the final shape of which is yet to appear.

§ 8.02 GATT practice

Practice under the GATT with regard to remedies was inconsistent. Panels usually recommended that the offender bring its measure into conformity with the relevant provision of the General Agreement or the relevant

[1] P.C.I.J. (ser. A) No. 17 at 47-48.

[2] ICJ Reports at 4. The government of the respondent, Albania, refused to pay the damages. It was not until the change in regime and the resumption of diplomatic relations between Albania and the United Kingdom, in 1992, that the damages were paid in full. *See*, Shabtai Rosenne, The World Court 44 (5th ed., Martinus Nijhoff, 1995).

[3] Report of the International Law Commission 132, Art. 31 (United Nations, 2000). *See* generally, Malcolm Evans (Ed) Remedies in International Law: The Institutional Dilemma (Hart, 1998); Christine Gray, Judicial Remedies in International Law (Oxford, 1990).

Tokyo Round Code. This remedy usually was prospective only, providing no relief for past damages suffered.

In a number of instances, however, in cases involving antidumping duties, GATT panels did recommend relief for past damages in the form of reimbursement of duties paid pursuant to a non-conforming antidumping measure. The Panel in *Electrical Transformers from Finland*, for example, stated:

> The Panel proposes to the Council that it addresses to New Zealand a recommendation to revoke the anti-dumping determination and to reimburse the antidumping duty paid.[4]

However, the United States consistently opposed reimbursement and refused to adopt the report in *Stainless Steel Hollow Products from Sweden* for this reason.[5] There, the Panel recommended that the United States "revoke the anti-dumping duties imposed" and "reimburse the anti-dumping duties paid."[6] In *Cement from Mexico*, also unadopted, the Panel was even more specific:

> The Panel recommends that the Committee request the United States to revoke the anti-dumping duty order on grey portland cement and cement clinker from Mexico and to reimburse any anti-dumping duties paid or deposited under this order.[7]

The EC appears to have agreed with the United States on this issue. As complaining party before a countervailing duty panel conducted under the Tokyo Round Subsidies Code, the EC originally asked for reimbursement, but then, mid-proceeding, changed its position.[8]

[4] GATT Panel Report, *New Zealand – Imports of Electrical Transformers from Finland*, BISD 32S/55, adopted 18 July 1985, ¶ 4:11. This and the other reports recommending reimbursement are discussed by Ernst-Ulrich Petersmann in *GATT Dispute Settlement Proceedings in the Field of Antidumping Law*, 28 COMMON MARKET LAW REVIEW 69 (1991).

[5] GATT Panel Report, *United States – Imposition of Anti-Dumping Duties on Imports of Seamless Stainless Steel Hollow Products from Sweden*, ADP/47, circulated 20 August 1990, unadopted. The U.S. took the position that correction of the error prospectively would suffice. *See*, Robert E. Hudec, ENFORCING INTERNATIONAL TRADE LAW: THE EVOLUTION OF THE MODERN GATT LEGAL SYSTEM 253-4 (Butterworth, 1993).

[6] *Id.* ¶ 5.24.

[7] GATT Panel Report, *United States – Anti-Dumping Duties on Gray Portland Cement and Cement Clinker from Mexico*, ADP/82, circulated 9 July 1992, unadopted, ¶ 6.2.

[8] GATT Panel Report, *Brazil – Imposition of Provisional and Definitive Countervailing Duties on Milk Powder and Certain Types of Milk from the European Economic Community*, BISD 41S/467, adopted 28 April 1994, ¶ 200: "The EEC initially requested that the Panel also recommend that Brazil reimburse any provisional and definitive countervailing duties

A particularly difficult issue with regard to remedy arose in the *Trondheim Case*, which involved the Tokyo Round *Agreement on Government Procurement*.[9] There, the Panel found that, in awarding the contract for an electronic and mainly unmanned toll collection system for the city of Trondheim, the Government of Norway had not complied with its obligations under the Agreement. However, by the time the Panel ruled, performance of the contract had been completed. Faced with a *fait accompli*, the Panel observed that the only way "that Norway could bring the Trondheim procurement into line with its obligations under the Agreement would be by annulling the contract and recommencing the procurement process. The Panel did not consider it appropriate to make such a recommendation."[10]

The United States, the complaining party, explicitly stated that it was not asking the Panel to recommend negotiation of compensation for past losses.[11] The Panel recommended that the Government Procurement Committee request Norway to take the measures necessary to ensure that future procurements were conducted in accordance with its substantive findings.[12]

Something similar to the *fait accompli* problem that faced the GATT Panel in the *Trondheim Case* has confronted WTO panels dealing with some subsidies. These are discussed *infra* in § 8.07.

If a GATT contracting party failed to bring its measure into conformity, the remedy was "compensation" from the offending party to the victim, in the form of reduced barriers on other products, or "retaliation" by the victim in the form of increased barriers against imports from the offending party. (The more formal term for "retaliation" is "suspension of concessions or other obligations.") Perhaps the closest municipal law analogue to this system is that of partial recission of a contract, where equivalent non-performance by one party excuses performance by another, without vitiating the entire contract.

levied on these imports. Subsequently, the EEC indicated that it was no longer seeking such a recommendation, on the ground that it should generally be left to a signatory found to have acted inconsistently with its obligations under the Agreement to determine the means by which to bring its measure into conformity with its obligations."

9 GATT Panel Report, *Norway – Procurement of Toll Collection Equipment for the City of Trondheim*, BISD 40S/319, adopted 13 May 1992.

10 *Id.* ¶ 4.17. 11 *Id.* ¶ 4.20.

12 *Id.* ¶ 5.2. For a detailed analysis of the remedies issue in this case, *see* Petros C. Mavroidis, *Government Procurement Agreement: The Trondheim Case*, 49 AUSSENWIRTSCHAFT 77 (1993).

§ 8.03 Overview of the WTO remedy regime

As was the case with GATT, "compensation" and "suspension of concessions or other obligations" are the remedies made available by the DSU when a Member fails to bring a non-conforming measure into compliance with Dispute Settlement Body recommendations and rulings within a reasonable period of time. Compensation typically would take the form of a reduction in tariffs or other bound trade barriers, on a most favoured nation basis, implemented by the Member concerned in lieu of compliance. Compensation must be on a most favoured nation basis because the Member granting it would otherwise be according an advantage to the Member receiving the compensation *vis-à-vis* other Members.[13]

Suspension of concessions or other obligations typically would take the form of imposition of tariffs or other trade barriers, on a non-most favoured nation basis, against the non-complying Member by the successful complainant. Suspension of concessions or other obligations "to the Member concerned" discriminates against the non-complying Member only, and not against other Members, who are entitled to the continued benefit of the WTO Agreements.

Article 22.1 of the DSU specifies that both compensation and suspension are considered to be temporary measures, and that neither is preferred to full implementation. The system provides for negotiation of compensation and arbitration of the level of suspension of concessions or other obligations.

§ 8.04 Negotiation on compensation

If the Member concerned fails to comply with the recommendations and rulings of an adopted report within the reasonable period of time allowed,[14] the Member shall, if requested – and no later than the expiration of the reasonable period of time – enter into negotiations, with a view to agreeing on compensation, with any party having invoked the dispute settlement procedures.[15]

Because it is trade-liberalizing rather than trade-restricting, compensation is to be preferred – from an economic perspective – to suspension

[13] DSU Art. 22.1 provides that compensation "shall be consistent with the covered agreements." This would include the most-favoured-nation requirement of Art. I of GATT 1994.

[14] *See* § 7.04. [15] DSU Art. 22.2.

of concessions or other obligations. However, compensation usually has serious drawbacks for both complainants and defendants and is, for that reason, comparatively rare. From the complainant's point of view, compensation by way of lower barriers in other areas does nothing to eliminate non-compliance in the area that was the subject to the dispute. Particularly from the perspective of the concerned industry in the territory of the complaining Member, compensation does nothing. By the same token, Members whose measures are found not to be in compliance have difficulty "volunteering" a sector of the economy for increased foreign competition for the explicit reason of protecting another sector that benefits from that violation.

§ 8.05 Suspension of concessions or other obligations

[1] Request for authorization to suspend concessions

If an agreement on compensation is not reached within 20 days of the expiration of the reasonable period of time, Article 22.2 of the DSU provides that the complainant ("any party having invoked the dispute settlement procedures") may request authorization from the DSB to suspend the application of concessions or other obligations under covered agreements to the Member concerned.

In *EC – Hormones (Article 22.6 – EC)*, the Arbitrators set out the minimum requirements of a request for authorization under Article 22.2:

> (1) the request must set out a specific level of suspension, *i.e.*, a level equivalent to the nullification and impairment caused by the WTO-inconsistent measure, pursuant to Article 22.4; and (2) the request must specify the agreement and sector(s) under which concessions or other obligations would be suspended, pursuant to Article 22.3.[16]

Although, as discussed in § 8.05[6] below, dealing with burden of proof, arbitrators typically ask Members seeking authorization to submit their calculation methodologies, neither these nor any other submissions

[16] Decision by the Arbitrators, *European Communities – Measures Concerning Meat and Meat Products (Hormones) – Original Complaint by the United States – Recourse to Arbitration by the European Communities under Article 22.6 of the DSU*, WT/DS26/ARB, 12 July 1999, DSR 1999:III, 1105, ¶ 16; Decision by the Arbitrators, *European Communities – Measures Concerning Meat and Meat Products (Hormones) – Original Complaint by Canada – Recourse to Arbitration by the European Communities under Article 22.6 of the DSU*, WT/DS48/ARB, 12 July 1999, DSR 1999:III, 1135, ¶ 16. Because in all respects relevant to this chapter the two *Hormones* reports are the same, for simplicity's sake, subsequent citation in this chapter will be only to the US report, DS26, the earlier of the two.

not made to the DSB form a part of the Arbitrators' terms of reference. "Belated supplementary requests and arguments concerning additional amounts of alleged nullification or impairment," the Arbitrators stated in *EC – Bananas III (Ecuador) (Article 22.6 – EC)*, are "not compatible with the minimum specificity requirements for such a request because they were not included in Ecuador's request for suspension under Article 22.2 of the DSB."[17]

In *EC – Bananas III (US) (Article 22.6 – EC)*, which was the first request for suspension of concessions under Article 22.2,[18] the United States attached to its request to the DSB a list of products that, according to the United States, corresponded to the estimate of nullification or impairment.[19] In *EC – Hormones*, the US and Canada included in their requests for authorization lists of products that covered a significantly higher amount of trade than the amount of the suspension actually proposed.[20] They stated that no determination had yet been made as to which products on the lists would be subject to suspension.[21]

The EC objected, requesting that the US and Canada be required to submit lists of proposed suspensions equivalent to the level of nullification and impairment, after that level was determined by the Arbitrators.[22] The Arbitrators declined, noting that the DSU did not impose such a requirement.[23] However, the Arbitrators limited any potential suspension to the products on the lists, seeing them as "linked" to the DSB authorization. "In the event that tariff concessions are to be suspended," the Arbitrators said, "only products that appear on the product list attached to the request for suspension can be subject to suspension."[24]

Although nothing in the DSU explicitly requires that Members seeking authorization from the DSB to suspend concessions or other obligations include a list of potential target products with their request, the Arbitrators in *EC – Bananas III* effectively read such a requirement into the DSU and, it appears, subsequent requests have included lists.[25] According to the

[17] Decision by the Arbitrators, *European Communities – Regime for the Importation, Sale and Distribution of Bananas – Recourse to Arbitration by the European Communities under Article 22.6 of the DSU*, WT/DS27/ARB/ECU, 24 March 2000, DSR 2000:V, 2243, ¶ 24.

[18] Decision by the Arbitrators, *European Communities – Regime for the Importation, Sale and Distribution of Bananas – Recourse to Arbitration by the European Communities under Article 22.6 of the DSU*, WT/DS27/ARB, 9 April 1999, DSR 1999:II, 725.

[19] This is not apparent from the Decision in *Bananas III*, but is discussed by the Arbitrators in *EC – Hormones (US) (Article 22.6 – EC)*, *supra* note 16, at footnote 13.

[20] *Id.* ¶ 13. [21] *Id.* [22] *Id.* ¶ 14. [23] *Id.* ¶ 15. [24] *Id.* ¶ 16.

[25] *Brazil – Export Financing Programme for Aircraft*, WT/DS/46/16, 11 May 2000; *United States – Tax Treatment for "Foreign Sales Corporations,"* WT/DS108/13, 17 November 2000; *Canada – Export Credits and Loan Guarantees for Regional Aircraft*, WT/DS222/7, 24 May 2002.

Arbitrators in *EC – Hormones*, the US, as the party seeking to suspend concessions, "has to – and did – identify the products that may be subject to suspension in a way that allowed us to attribute annual trade value to each of these products when subject to the additional tariff proposed, namely a 100 percent tariff (assuming this tariff is prohibitive)."[26] The Arbitrators went on to state that, "Once this is done, however, the US is free to pick products from that list – not outside the list – equaling a total trade value that does not exceed the amount of trade impairment we find."[27]

In *EC – Bananas III (Ecuador) (Article 22.6 – EC)*, Ecuador included in its Article 22.2 request the statement that it "reserves the right to suspend tariff concessions or other obligations granted in the framework of the GATT 1994 in the event that these may be applied in a practicable and effective manner."[28] The Arbitrators did not consider this "reserves the right" statement compatible with the minimum due process requirements of Article 22.2 and, accordingly, construed its terms of reference as covering only those requests that were to specific sectors under the WTO agreements.[29]

To the extent that a list is "linked" to DSB authorization, there would appear to be strong grounds for the Arbitrators' holding that the action must be confined to the list. However, since the DSU does not itself specify that a list is required – as the Arbitrators observed – their holding that the party seeking to suspend concessions "has to" provide a list identifying the products that may be subject to suspension seems not to have as strong a legal basis supporting it.

The issue may be largely academic, however, since Members use lists for a very practical reason: the itemization of potential target products serves to notify elements of the private sector in the territory of the Member concerned that they may be required to "pay" for the non-complying measure that benefits some other element of the economy. Notification, presumably, could lead to internal pressure on the Member concerned to bring the measure into conformity and avoid suspension altogether. The practice of submitting a list that itemizes a target total higher than the amount of suspension claimed has raised the question of whether a Member may change products subject to retaliation from time to time based on a single authorization from the DSB. This is sometimes called "carousel" suspension or retaliation.

[26] *EC – Hormones, supra* note 16, ¶ 21. [27] *Id.*
[28] *Supra* note 17, ¶ 27. [29] *Id.* ¶ 29.

[2] "Carousel" suspension

In *EC – Hormones*, the EC objected to statements made by US officials that the US would be "free to resort to a 'carousel' type of suspension where the concessions and other obligations subject to suspension would change every now and then, in particular in terms of product coverage."[30] This would be done by periodically substituting a product on the list for another on which concessions previously had been suspended. The purpose of such an "on-and-off" practice would be to cause disruption and uncertainty through periodic changes in the products subject to suspension. This, it is widely believed, would make non-compliance more difficult for the Member concerned.

The US stated to the Arbitrators in *EC – Hormones*, however, that it had "no current intent" to suspend concessions on a carousel basis, and the Arbitrators, accordingly, concluded that it did not need to consider the issue.[31] Nevertheless, less than a year later, the United States Congress attached a carousel provision to a bill liberalizing trade with Africa and the Caribbean.[32] The US administration has yet to implement the provision, and it has not been subject to challenge in the WTO. The European Communities, however, has stated that it would challenge the provision should it be implemented.[33]

[3] Jurisdiction of the arbitrators

Article 22.7, which sets forth the scope of the jurisdiction or mandate of arbitrators, begins by limiting that jurisdiction: "The arbitrator shall not examine the nature of the concessions or other obligations to be suspended." Accordingly, all qualitative aspects of the proposed suspension, those that touch upon the "nature" of the concessions to be withdrawn, are outside the jurisdiction of an arbitrator.[34] Thus:

> in case a proposal for suspension were to target, for example, only biscuits with a 100 per cent tariff *ad valorem*, it would not be for the Arbitrators to decide that, for example, cheese and not biscuits should be targeted; that a 150 per cent tariff should be imposed instead of a 100 per cent tariff; or that tariff increases should be levied on a product weight basis, not *ad valorem*.[35]

[30] *Supra* note 16, ¶ 22. [31] *Id.*

[32] Trade and Development Act of 2000, § 407.

[33] European Commission, REPORT ON UNITED STATES BARRIERS TO TRADE AND INVESTMENT 13 (November 2002).

[34] *EC – Bananas III (US) (Article 22.6 – EC)*, *supra* note 18, ¶ 19. [35] *Id.*

Affirmatively, Article 22.7 specifies that an arbitrator "shall determine whether the level of such concession is equivalent to the level of nullification or impairment." In addition, an arbitrator's mandate includes the authority to determine whether the principles and procedures that apply to suspension have been followed.[36] Where arbitrators find that the proposed level of suspension is not equivalent to the nullification or impairment, the Arbitrators in *EC – Bananas III (Ecuador) (Article 22.6 – EC)* held, they are required to estimate the amount that it did consider to be equivalent.[37]

Suspension of concessions or other obligations under the *Agreement on Trade-Related Aspects of Intellectual Property Rights* (TRIPS Agreement) can have implications for a Member's compliance with the international intellectual property rights treaties that are incorporated into the TRIPS Agreement. However, Arbitrators, acting pursuant to Article 22.6 of the DSU, do not have jurisdiction to determine whether suspension of WTO obligations involves a violation of the intellectual property rights treaties. That is a question for the parties to those treaties.[38]

The Arbitrators in *EC – Bananas III (US) (Article 22.6 – EC)*, on their own motion, raised and resolved a potential problem relating to their jurisdiction based on some infelicitous drafting in Article 22 dealing with the principles and procedures to be applied when a Member considers which concessions to suspend. Article 22.3 lists three principles: (a) the Member should seek to suspend in the same sector; (b) if that is not effective or practicable, the Member should consider other sectors in the same agreement; and (c) only if that is not effective or practicable, may the Member consider any other covered agreement. Article 22.6 refers to "the principles and procedures set forth in paragraph 3," but then refers only to a request to suspend under (b) and (c), not under (a). Article 22.7, in contrast, authorizes the Arbitrators to consider claims that the "principles and procedures set forth in paragraph 3 have not been followed," a jurisdictional grant that includes (a) as well as (b) and (c).

The Arbitrators held that the authority granted by Article 22.6 to review claims that the principles and procedures in subparagraphs (b) and (c) have not been followed "must imply the Arbitrators' competence to examine whether a request made under subparagraph (a) should have been made – in full or in part – under subparagraphs (b) or (c)."[39]

[36] These are discussed *infra* in § 8.05 [8].
[37] *Supra* note 17, ¶ 12.
[38] *Id.* ¶ 152.
[39] *Id.* ¶ 3.7.

[4] Consequences of arbitration

A request for arbitration of the amount of the suspension of concessions or other obligations effectively replaces the complaining party's original request to the DSB for authority to suspend. Article 22.7 provides that the DSB shall be informed "promptly" of the results of the arbitration, but beyond this the DSB does not act unless requested. Article 22.7 goes on to provide that the DSB "shall, upon request, grant authorization to suspend concessions or other obligations where the request is consistent with the decision of the Arbitrators." Accordingly, before the complaining party can suspend, it must make a new request to the DSB consistent with the arbitration award.[40]

[5] Time limits

Article 22.6 specifies, rather explicitly, that arbitration "shall be completed within 60 days after the date of expiry of the reasonable period of time." This can be a difficult, if not impossible time limit, particularly since any delay by the complaining party in requesting authorization to suspend, after the expiry of the reasonable period of time, would consume some of the 60 days.

The issue arose in the first Article 22.6 arbitration, *EC – Bananas III (US) (Article 22.6 – EC)*. There, the Arbitrators noted the 60-day limit, but went on to state that, "given that our own decisions cannot be appealed, we consider it imperative to achieve the greatest degree of clarity possible with a view to avoiding future disagreements between the parties. Reaching this objective required the parties to have more time to submit to us the information necessary for us to complete our tasks."[41] In that case, the reasonable period of time expired on 1 January 1999; the award of the Arbitrators was made on 9 April 1999.

A large part of the difficulty in the *EC – Bananas III (US) (Article 22.6 – EC)* arbitration stemmed from the problem of "sequencing" the proceeding with a compliance review by the Panel under Article 21.5. This issue is discussed in § 8.06. In subsequent Article 22.6 arbitrations, time limits have been agreed upon by the parties in conjunction with Article 21.5 reviews.

[40] *See, e.g., EC – Hormones, supra* note 16, footnote 13 of the Report: "Once the Arbitrators had lowered the level of trade impairment to US $191.4 million, the US submitted a new request to the DSB meeting."

[41] *Supra* note 18, ¶ 2.12.

[6] Burden of proof

As a formal matter, the burden of proof in Article 22.6 arbitrations is no different from the burden of proof in any other WTO proceeding. Members are presumed to act in conformity with their WTO obligations, and a Member claiming the contrary has the burden of proof. Thus, in *EC – Hormones (US) (Article 22.6 – EC)*, the Arbitrators said that a Member seeking authorization to suspend concessions or other obligations is presumed to be acting in accordance with its obligations in doing so, and that it is up to the challenging Member to prove otherwise.[42] Subsequent arbitrators routinely recite this statement, and just as routinely note that there is a "duty that rests on *all* parties to produce evidence and to collaborate in presenting evidence to the Arbitrators," and that, while this duty is not the same as the burden of proof, it "is crucial in Article 22 arbitration proceedings."[43]

In reality, however, the duty to collaborate in presenting evidence is much more intertwined with the burden of proof than the statements in the arbitration reports might suggest. In fact, both the Member seeking authorization and the Member disputing the level of authorization requested are, effectively, required to justify their positions, and fail to do so at their peril. This is a consequence of the legal awkwardness inherent in Article 22.6 arbitrations in which the challenged action is not a "measure" in the WTO traditional sense of that term. It is not a law or regulation or the application of a law or regulation. Instead, it is a calculation of the amount of nullification or impairment that a Member claims it has suffered. A consideration of whether that calculation is correct must begin with the presumably correct calculation itself. This is where the "duty to collaborate in presenting evidence" imposes what is, in all but name, a burden of proof on the Member being challenged.

In the first Article 22.6 arbitration, *EC – Bananas III (US) (Article 22.6 – EC)*, the Arbitrators – even before they met with the parties to establish working procedures – "invited" the United States to submit a communication "explaining the methodology it applied in calculating its proposed level of suspension."[44] The Arbitrators said that they "considered the request to the United States to be of an informative nature only, aimed at saving time."[45] As to whether this communication really was looked upon as "informative" only, it is worth observing that, subsequently, the Arbitrators said, "As to burden of proof, if the United States has not convinced us that there is a positive level of nullification or

[42] *EC – Hormones (US) (Article 22.6 – EC)*, *supra* note 16, ¶ 9. [43] *Id.* ¶ 11.
[44] *Supra* note 18, ¶ 2.1. [45] *Id.* footnote 2.

impairment, then we will set the level of suspension of concessions at zero."[46] An "invitation" from an arbitrator to a Member for a submission explaining its methodology is an invitation that few Members are likely to decline.

In *Canada – Aircraft Credits and Guarantees (Article 22.6 – Canada)*, the Arbitrators distinguished between the methodology paper and the proof supporting it. After noting the duty of parties to provide relevant information, the Arbitrators said, "This is why, even though Canada bears the original burden of proof, we also requested Brazil to submit a 'methodology paper' describing how it arrived at the level of proposed countermeasures it proposes. Later, we asked it to come forward with evidence supporting various factual assertions made in its 'methodology paper.' "[47] Structurally, therefore, the process could be viewed as involving first a methodology paper consisting only of calculations, followed by "evidence" supporting the factual assertions on which the calculations were based, once those calculations had been challenged. Yet, if the methodology paper is to have any use in the process both for arbitrators and for the challenging Member, presumably it would have to consist of more than just calculations.

As discussed below in § 8.05[8], Article 22.3 generally requires Members seeking authorization to suspend concessions or other obligations to seek to do so first with respect to the same sectors found to be in violation. When a Member seeks to suspend concessions or other obligations other than in the same sectors found to be in violation, Article 22.3(e) specifies that "it shall state the reasons therefor in its request." The Arbitrators in *EC – Bananas III (Ecuador) (Article 22.6 – EC)* held that the party seeking authorization "had to come forward and submit information giving reasons and plausible explanations for its initial consideration of the principles and procedures set forth in Article 22.3 that caused it to request authorization under another sector and agreement than those where violations were found."[48] Once this is done, however, it is for the other Member to establish that suspension within the sector where the violation was found is "both practicable as well as effective" for the Member seeking authorization.[49]

All of this formulaic language appears to be directed at the very reasonable goal of providing the Arbitrators, in a timely fashion, with

46 *Id.* ¶ 4.13.

47 Decision by the Arbitrators, *Canada – Export Credits and Loan Guarantees for Regional Aircraft – Recourse to Arbitration by Canada under Article 22.6 of the DSU and Article 4.11 of the SCM Agreement*, WT/DS222/ARB, 17 February 2003, ¶ 2.8 (footnote omitted).

48 *Supra* note 17, ¶ 60. 49 *Id.* ¶ 75.

the information needed to make a decision. Once that is done, as noted by the Arbitrators in *EC – Hormones (US) (Article 22.6 – EC)*, there is a very important difference between the task of Arbitrators and the task of a dispute settlement or compliance panel. The difference is that, if Arbitrators decide that the proposed suspension is not WTO-consistent because it exceeds the level of nullification or impairment, "we should not end our examination the way panels do, namely by requesting the DSB to recommend that the measure be brought into conformity with WTO obligations."[50] Arbitrators must do more. They must estimate the level of suspension that they consider to be equivalent to the impairment suffered.[51] "If this were not done," the Arbitrators in *Hormones* said, "the Member requesting suspension would need to make new estimates and arguably submit a new proposal. This proposal could again meet objections and might be referred back to arbitration. To avoid this potentially endless loop," Arbitrators need to arrive at their own figure in the event they find the proposed amount not justified.[52]

[7] *Information submitted by private parties*

WTO disputes, as government-to-government proceedings, do not formally involve private parties. Nevertheless, private parties usually have a strong interest in these proceedings and, in many ways, can sometimes be considered the real parties in interest. It is often their information that is the basis of the record of the dispute.

In *Brazil – Aircraft (Article 22.6 – Brazil)*, some of the information on which the challenged calculations were based was provided by the private sector. The Arbitrators assumed that the private sector was independent of the government, and for that reason chose not to treat statements from that sector "as we would have if they had originated from a subject of international law."[53] The Arbitrators requested that Brazil support the private sector information "with materials usually regarded as evidence, such as articles or statements reproduced in the specialized press, company annual reports or any other certified information originating in [the private sector] or other reliable sources."[54] In contrast, as to information supplied by the Brazilian government, the Arbitrators "assumed good faith and accepted the information and the supporting evidence provided by Brazil

[50] *Supra* note 16, ¶ 12. [51] *Id.* [52] *Id.* footnote 9.

[53] Decision by the Arbitrators, *Brazil – Export Financing Programme for Aircraft – Recourse to Arbitration by Brazil under Article 22.6 of the DSU and Article 4.11 of the SCM Agreement*, WT/DS46/ARB, 28 August 2000, ¶ 2.11.

[54] *Id.*

to the extent Canada also accepted it or did not provide sufficient evidence to put in doubt the accuracy of Brazil's statements and/or evidence."[55]

[8] Applicable principles

The WTO, covering trade in services, aspects of intellectual property, as well as trade in goods, is a far broader agreement than was GATT. This breadth is reflected in the principles the DSU establishes for the suspension of concessions.

The first principle is that the complaining party initially should seek to suspend concessions or other obligations with respect to the same sector or sectors as that in which the adopted report has found nullification and impairment.[56] Next, if the complaining party considers that it is not practicable or effective to do this, it may seek to suspend in other sectors under the same agreement.[57] Finally, if the complaining party considers that it is not practicable or effective to suspend with respect to other sectors under the same agreement, and that the circumstances are serious enough, it may seek to suspend under another covered agreement.[58] The term "sector" is defined

(i) with respect to goods, to include all goods;

(ii) with respect to services, those identified in the current version of the "Services Sectoral Classification List." Eleven services sectors were so identified in the Uruguay Round: business, communication, construction and related engineering, distribution, educational, environmental, financial, health and related social services, tourism and travel-related services; recreational, cultural and sporting; and transport;[59]

(iii) with respect to trade-related intellectual property rights, each of the categories covered in the first seven sections of Part II of the TRIPS Agreement: copyright and related rights, trademarks, geographical indications, industrial designs, patents, lay-out designs (topographies) of integrated circuits, and protection of undisclosed information; the enforcement obligations of Part III of the TRIPS Agreement, and the obligations of Part IV, dealing with the acquisition and maintenance of intellectual property rights and related inter partes procedures.[60]

[55] *Id.* ¶ 2.10. [56] DSU Art. 22.3(a). [57] DSU Art. 22.3(b).
[58] DSU Art. 22.3(c). [59] *Services Sectoral Classification List*, MTN.GNS/W/120.
[60] DSU Art. 22.3(f).

If a party decides to request authorization other than in the same sector in which the adopted report has found a violation or other nullification and impairment, *i.e.*, if a party decides to "cross-retaliate," it must state its reasons in its request. At the time that the request is forwarded to the DSB, it must also be forwarded to the Councils or sectoral bodies concerned.[61]

The request by the United States for authorization to suspend concessions in *EC – Bananas III (US) (Article 22.6 – EC)* covered only goods obligations under GATT 1994, although the underlying violation covered both goods and services under GATS.[62] The EC objected, arguing that when findings of nullification or impairment are found in more than one sector, suspension must be commensurate with the harm experienced in each sector.[63] The Arbitrators disagreed, holding "that the United States has the right to request suspension of concessions in either of these two sectors, or in both, up to the overall level of nullification or impairment suffered, if the inconsistencies with the EC's obligations under the GATT and the GATS found in the original dispute have not been removed fully in the EC's revision of its regime."[64]

The second *Bananas III* arbitration, involving Ecuador, was the first in which "cross-retaliation" occurred. An important factor in the arbitration was that it presented "considerable economic differences between a developing WTO Member and the world's largest trader."[65] Where "a great imbalance in terms of trade volume and economic power exists between the complaining party seeking suspension and the other party which has failed to bring WTO-inconsistent measures into compliance," the Arbitrators said, "a consideration by the complaining party in which sector or under which agreement suspension may be expected to be least harmful to itself would seem sufficient for us to find a consideration by the complaining party of the effectiveness criterion" of Article 22.3.[66]

Ecuador argued that most of its imports of goods from the EC were "primary goods" or "investment goods," rather than "consumer goods."[67] Accordingly, Ecuador argued that it was not practicable or effective for it to suspend concessions in the goods sector. Instead, Ecuador requested authorization to suspend concessions under the GATS, where a violation also occurred, and under the TRIPS Agreement where no violation had

61 DSU Art. 22.3(e). 62 *Supra* note 18, ¶ 1.1. 63 *Id.* ¶ 3.8. 64 *Id.* ¶ 3.10.

65 *EC – Bananas III (Ecuador) (Article 22.6 – EC)*, *supra* note 17, ¶ 126.

66 *Id.* ¶ 73. The Arbitrators also noted the economic truism that "Of course, suspension of concessions or other obligations is always likely to be harmful to a certain, limited extent also for the complaining party requesting authorization by the DSB." *Id.* footnote 29.

67 *Id.* ¶ 88.

been found.[68] The Arbitrators determined that the EC had failed to show that it was both practicable and effective for Ecuador to suspend concessions with regard to goods in the "primary" and "investment" goods areas.[69] However, the Arbitrators went on to find that it was both practicable and effective for Ecuador to suspend with respect to "consumer goods."[70] As to services, the Arbitrators also found that because Ecuador's concessions were limited, it was correspondingly limited in its ability to suspend services concessions, and accepted Ecuador's proposal.[71]

Where the arbitration broke new ground was in allowing suspension of intellectual property rights concessions based on a violation in the goods sector. The Arbitrators found that Ecuador, in requesting authorization to suspend intellectual property concessions, had properly taken into account the requirements of Article 22.3. They then went on, however, to observe potential problems in suspending concessions in the three intellectual property areas selected by Ecuador: copyright and related rights of performers, producers of phonograms, and broadcasting organizations; geographical indications; and industrial designs.[72] For example, although Ecuador would be entitled to produce phonograms without the rights holder's permission, that rights holder continued to enjoy protection in the markets of other WTO Members who, in turn, had a continuing WTO obligation to honor those rights.[73] Thus, the Arbitrators observed, "Distortions in third-country markets could be avoided if Ecuador would suspend the intellectual property rights in question only for the purposes of supply destined for the domestic market."[74]

Finally, it should be noted that the plurilateral *Agreement on Government Procurement* is an exception to the cross-retaliation provision. Concessions or other obligations under the GPA may not be suspended as a result of obligations under other agreements, and disputes involving the GPA may not lead to the suspension of concessions or other obligations under other agreements.[75]

[9] Third party rights

Article 22 does not address the issue of third party participation in arbitration proceedings. Based on the absence of a third party provision, and on the fact that the Arbitrators did not believe its rights would be

[68] *Id.* ¶¶ 2, 66. [69] *Id.* ¶ 96. [70] *Id.* ¶ 101.
[71] *Id.* ¶ 103. [72] *Id.* ¶¶ 159–165. [73] *Id.* ¶ 155.
[74] *Id.* ¶ 156. Implementation suggestions by WTO tribunals are addressed *infra* in § 8.08.
[75] GPA Art. XXII:7.

affected, Ecuador was denied third party status in *EC – Bananas III (US) (Article 22.6 – EC)*.[76]

In *EC – Hormones (Canada) and (US) (Article 22.6 – EC)*, however, the Arbitrators allowed both Canada and the United States to participate as third parties in the arbitration concerning the other's request for authorization to suspend concessions applicable to the EC.[77] Each Arbitrator noted that DSU provisions regarding panel proceedings, "referred to by analogy" in their working procedures, gave the Arbitrators discretion to establish working procedures on matters not regulated by the DSU. Since the DSU does not address third party participation, the Arbitrators reasoned, they may do so.[78]

Both Arbitrators found that Canadian and US rights might be affected in the other proceeding, and that the EC had "not shown how third-party participation would prejudice its rights."[79]

The Arbitrators in *Brazil – Aircraft (Article 22.6 – Brazil)* denied third party participation rights to Australia, which had participated as a third party in the Article 21.5 panel proceeding.[80] Australia's situation in *Brazil – Aircraft* was very different from the positions of Canada and the US in *EC – Hormones*, the Arbitrators said, and even different from Ecuador's in *Bananas III*.[81] Australia had never initiated dispute settlement proceedings against Brazil with regard to the measure at issue, the Arbitrators noted, and did not claim that any of its WTO rights would be affected by the decision.[82]

§ 8.06 The "sequencing" problem

[1] Overview

The procedural conundrum that has become known as the "sequencing" problem begins with the expiration of the reasonable period of time within which the Member concerned must bring its non-conforming measure into compliance with WTO requirements. It involves the relationship between compliance reviews under Article 21.5 and requests for authorization to suspend concessions or other obligations under Article 22. The

[76] *Supra* note 18, ¶ 2.8. [77] *Supra* note 16, ¶ 7. [78] *Id.*
[79] *Id.* [80] *Supra* note 53, ¶¶ 2.4–2.5. [81] *Id.* 2.6.
[82] *Id.* At footnote 11, the Arbitrators said that its decision "may have been different if Australia had demonstrated that the countermeasures which Canada plans to adopt may affect Australia's rights or benefits under the WTO Agreement."

problem is that each provision was drafted with no apparent reference to the other.

Article 21.5 provides, "Where there is disagreement as to the existence or consistency with a covered agreement of measures taken to comply," that disagreement "shall be decided through recourse to these dispute settlement procedures." This is the source of the authority for compliance panels to review the steps taken to implement DSB recommendations and rulings. Article 21.5 provides further that the original panel should, wherever possible, be selected to make the determination, and that a compliance panel "shall circulate its report within 90 days after the date of referral of the matter to it." In a typical case, this would be 90 days after the expiration of the reasonable period of time inasmuch as agreement, in theory at least, is always possible prior to that expiration. In practice, Members will frequently wish to use most, if not all, of the time to postpone confronting a difficult situation.

Article 22.2 refers to situations in which "the Member concerned fails to bring the measure found to be inconsistent with a covered agreement into compliance" within the reasonable period of time. However, Article 22.2 makes no reference as to how or by whom that failure is to be determined. In some instances, of course, the Member concerned itself may state that it does not intend to comply. Where, however, the Member concerned asserts that it has complied, and the complaining Member disagrees, Article 22.2, arguably, could be said to imply that the question has previously been resolved by a compliance panel established under Article 21.5. Article 22.2 then goes on to state that, if the measure has not been brought into compliance – however that is determined – "no later than the expiry of the reasonable period of time," the Member concerned shall enter into compensation negotiations. If negotiations do not result in an agreement on compensation within 20 days, according to Article 22.2, the complaining Member then may request authorization to suspend.

At this point, Article 22.6 becomes relevant. As an initial matter, Article 22.6 provides that when "the situation described in paragraph 2 occurs," *i.e.*, when the Member concerned has failed to bring the measure into conformity (however that is determined), the complaining Member may request authorization to suspend concessions "within 30 days of the expiry of the reasonable period of time." Recall that paragraph 2 calls for 20 of these 30 days to be given to compensation negotiations; arguably, therefore, the complaining Member has a window of only 10 days, from day 20 to day 30 after the expiry of the reasonable period of time within which to ask for authorization.

The sequencing problem arises next – with arbitration, pursuant to Article 22.6, of the amount of authorization to suspend requested by the complaining Member. Article 22.6 (also providing that the arbitration shall be carried out by the original panel members if possible) calls upon the Arbitrators to issue their award "within 60 days of the expiry of the reasonable period of time." But if an Article 21.5 compliance panel does not render its report until 90 days after the expiry of the reasonable period of time, then it would be impossible for Arbitrators to issue their award within 60 days of that same date, if the complaining Member was required to wait for the compliance report before requesting authorization. In fact, if Article 21.5's reference to a compliance dispute's being resolved according to "these dispute settlement procedures" includes the consultation requirements of the DSU, the normal 60-day consultation period would consume all of the ostensible time for the Article 22.6 Arbitrators to reach their decision. But if the complaining Member does not wait, on what basis can it claim that the Member concerned has not brought its measure into compliance? All of this came to a head in *Bananas III.*[83]

[2] Bananas III

The reasonable period of time in *EC – Bananas III* expired on 1 January 1999.[84] Even before that date, the parties had consulted as to the adequacy of the measures proposed by the EC to bring its regime into compliance.[85] Consultations did not resolve the issue, however, and two requests for the establishment of Article 21.5 compliance panels were made, both before the expiration of the reasonable period of time: on 14 December 1998, the EC requested a panel to examine its own measure;[86] and on

[83] *See* generally, Petros C. Mavroidis, *Proposal for Reform of Article 22 of the DSU: Reconsidering the Sequencing Issue and Suspension of Concessions*, in E. U. Petersmann (Ed), PREPARING FOR THE DOHA DEVELOPMENT ROUND 81 (European University Institute, Florence, 2002); Cherise M. Valles and Brendan P. McGivern, *The Right to Retaliate under the WTO Agreement: The "Sequencing" Problem*, 34 JOURNAL OF WORLD TRADE 63 (Vol. 2, 2000).

[84] Award of the Arbitrators, *European Communities – Regime for the Importation, Sale and Distribution of Bananas – Arbitration under Article 21.3(c) of the DSU*, WT/DS27/15, 7 January 1998, DSR 1998:I, 3, ¶ 20.

[85] Panel Report, *European Communities – Regime for the Importation, Sale and Distribution of Bananas – Recourse to Article 21.5 of the DSU by Ecuador*, WT/DS27/RW/ECU, 12 April 1999, DSR 1999:II, 803, ¶ 1.1.

[86] Panel Report, *European Communities – Regime for the Importation, Sale and Distribution of Bananas – Recourse to Article 21.5 of the DSU by the European Communities*, WT/DS27RW/EEC and Corr.1, 12 April 1999, DSR 1999:II, 783. This request is discussed *supra* in § 7.07 [3].

18 December 1998, Ecuador requested a compliance panel.[87] Both panels were established by the DSB on 12 January 1999.[88]

Two days later, on 14 January 1999, the United States, which had not requested a compliance review, requested authorization under Article 22.2 to suspend concessions or other obligations.[89] On 25 January, the EC requested arbitration under Article 22.6, and on 29 January, the DSB submitted the US request to arbitration.[90]

All three proceedings – Ecuador's Article 21.5 review, the EC's Article 21.5 review, and the Article 22.6 arbitration of the US request – were submitted to the members of the original Panel in their new capacities as compliance panelists and Arbitrators. The chair of the DSB, very much aware of the situation, stated:

> There remains the problem of how the Panel and the Arbitrators would coordinate their work, but as they will be the same individuals, the reality is that they will find a logical way forward, in consultation with the parties.[91]

In finding "a logical way forward," the three individuals, in their capacity as panelists in the compliance review requested by Ecuador, found that the steps taken by the EC to come into compliance were not sufficient.[92] In their capacity as panelists in the compliance review requested by the EC, they stated, "Since we have found in the proceeding initiated by Ecuador that the EC's implementing measures are *not* consistent with its WTO obligations, it is clear that they cannot be presumed to be consistent in this proceeding."[93]

In their capacity as Arbitrators in the Article 22.6 proceeding requested by the EC, they effectively reached the same substantive conclusion on the consistency of the revised EC regime as they did in the compliance reviews, and only then addressed the level of suspension. But the arbitration report was issued three days prior to the compliance panel reports and in it, the Arbitrators found a way out of the difficulty that had not been widely anticipated.

First, they noted that paragraphs 4 and 7 of Article 22 both require that the level of suspension be "equivalent" to the level of nullification or impairment.[94] Consequently, they reasoned, they could not fulfil

[87] *EC – Bananas III (Article 21.5 – Ecuador), supra* note 85.

[88] *Id.* ¶ 1.3; *EC – Bananas III (Article 21.5 – EC), supra* note 86, ¶ 1.4.

[89] *EC – Bananas III (US) (Article 22.6 – EC), supra* note 18, ¶ 1.1. [90] *Id.*

[91] *EC – Bananas III (Article 21.5 – EC), supra* note 86, ¶ 4.16; *EC – Bananas III (US) (Article 22.6 – EC), supra* note 18, ¶ 4.9.

[92] *EC – Bananas III (Article 21.5 – Ecuador), supra* note 85, ¶ 7.1.

[93] *EC – Bananas III (Article 21.5 – EC), supra* note 86, ¶ 4.15.

[94] *EC – Bananas III (US) (Article 22.6 – EC), supra* note 18, ¶ 4.1.

their "task to assess the *equivalence* between the two levels before we have reached a view on whether the revised regime is, in light of our and the Appellate Body's findings in the original dispute, fully WTO-consistent."[95] Accordingly, the Arbitrators, without reference to their compliance review conclusions, analyzed the EC's revised regime, found it inconsistent, and proceeded to establish the level of suspension equivalent to the nullification or impairment that was caused by the inconsistency. "In the special circumstances of this case," the Arbitrators said, "and in the absence of agreement of WTO Members over the proper interpretation of Article 21 and Article 22, it is necessary to find a logical way forward that ensures a multilateral decision, subject to DSB scrutiny, of the level of suspension of concessions. In our view, we have accomplished this task."[96]

While this solution solved the immediate problem in *Bananas III*, its viability as a future solution was seriously called into question by a subsequent opinion of the Appellate Body in *US – Certain EC Products*,[97] a dispute that grew out of *Bananas III.* Prior to the issuance of the Arbitrators' Report in *EC – Bananas III (US) (Article 22.6 – EC)*, the United States withheld "liquidation" on imports on the original list of products for which it sought authority to suspend concessions under Article 22.2 in *Bananas III.*[98] This action made those products contingently liable for suspension of concessions – and, therefore, for 100 percent duties – from that date forward if the Article 22.6 Arbitrator approved the level of suspension requested by the United States.[99] In the course of its analysis, the Panel in *Certain EC Products* discussed, with approval, the action of the Arbitrator in *EC – Bananas III (US) (Article 22.6 – EC)*, stating, *inter alia*, that "it is legally impossible to assess the level of suspension based on the level of nullification before assessing whether the implementing measure nullifies or impairs WTO rights."[100] Accordingly, "[s]ince the Article 22.6 arbitration process was given the authority to determine 'a level of suspension equivalent to the level of nullification,' it has the authority to

[95] *Id.* ¶ 4.8. [96] *Id.* 4.15.

[97] Appellate Body Report, *United States – Import Measures on Certain Products from the European Communities*, WT/DS165/AB/R, adopted 10 January 2001.

[98] Panel Report, *United States – Import Measures on Certain Products from the European Communities*, WT/DS165/R and Add.1, adopted 10 January 2001, as modified by the Appellate Body Report, WT/DS165/AB/R, ¶ 2.21. "Liquidation" is the term used to describe the completion of the customs entry process for imports, including the assessment of duties.

[99] *Id.* ¶ 6.2. [100] *Id.* ¶ 6.122.

assess both variables of the equation, including whether the implementing measure nullifies any benefit and the level of such nullified benefits."[101]

The Appellate Body disagreed on procedural grounds.[102] As to the substance, the Appellate Body went on to state that it was "cognizant of the important systemic issue of the relationship between Articles 21.5 and 22.6 of the DSU."[103] Nevertheless, it said, "it is certainly not the task of either panels or the Appellate Body to amend the DSU or to adopt interpretations within the meaning of Article IX:2 of the *WTO Agreement*. . . . Determining what the rules and procedures of the DSU ought to be is not our responsibility nor the responsibility of panels; it is clearly the responsibility solely of the Members of the WTO."[104] It found that the Panel erred in stating that Article 22.6 Arbitrators can determine the WTO-consistency of a measure taken by a Member to comply with DSB recommendations and rulings, and concluded that "the Panel's statements on this issue have no legal effect."[105]

The Appellate Body was able to opine on the statement of the Panel in *US – Certain EC Products* because the statement was exactly that – the statement of a panel. But in the *Bananas III* Article 22.6 arbitration, the individuals who concluded that they had the authority to determine the WTO-consistency of the EC measures were not panelists, they were arbitrators. The decisions of arbitrators, it should be noted, are not subject to appeal. Consequently, despite the statement of the Appellate Body in *US – Certain EC Products*, should another Arbitrator under Article 22.6 decide to determine the WTO-consistency of a measure for itself, that decision could be questioned only by the DSB. The DSB would be required to accept the action of the Arbitrator unless there was a consensus not to do so.

The reports in *US – Certain EC Products* were issued, in any event, well after the DSB authorized suspension of concessions in *Bananas III*, and did not affect the action taken in that dispute from the date of authorization forward. There remained, however, one issue in *Bananas III*: the final disposition of Ecuador's claim that the EC's revised banana regime was not WTO-consistent. As noted, the compliance panel circulated its Article 21.5 report in Ecuador's case on 12 April 1999. Ecuador did not request authority to suspend concessions until 8 November 1999, some seven months later, and more than 10 months after the expiration of the reasonable period of time.[106] On 19 November, the EC requested

[101] *Id.* [102] *Supra* note 97, ¶ 89. [103] *Id.* ¶ 90. [104] *Id.* ¶ 92.
[105] *Id.* ¶ 128 (b). [106] *EC – Bananas III (Ecuador) (Article 22.6 – EC)*, *supra* note 17, ¶ 1.

arbitration under Article 22.6 and, on the same day, the DSB submitted the matter to arbitration.[107] It was, of course, impossible at that point for the Arbitrators to complete their work, in the words of Article 22.6, "within 60 days after the date of expiry of the reasonable period of time." On 20 March 2000, some 415 days after the expiry of the reasonable period of time, the Arbitrators circulated their report authorizing Ecuador to suspend concessions or other obligations.[108] While the EC challenged Ecuador's calculations on the merits, there is no suggestion in the report that the EC raised the issue of time, nor did the Arbitrators do so.

[3] Ad hoc *solutions*

The experience of *Bananas III* led parties in subsequent disputes to reach *ad hoc* agreements on the sequencing of Article 21.5 compliance reviews and Article 22.6 arbitrations. The first agreement was reached between Australia and Canada in *Australia – Salmon.* An Article 21.5 panel was established at the request of Canada, the complainant, and its contemporaneous request for authorization to suspend concessions or other obligations under Article 22.2 was referred to arbitration under Article 22.6 at the request of Australia.[109] Australia and Canada then agreed to hold the Article 22.6 arbitration "in abeyance" until after circulation of the Article 21.5 compliance report. They agreed further that if the Article 21.5 Panel found that Australia's revised measure was inconsistent with its WTO obligations, then both Australia and Canada would request the immediate resumption of the Article 22.6 arbitration, regardless of whether either party appealed the Article 21.5 report.[110]

With modifications, the Australia–Canada agreement has served as a template for agreements in subsequent cases. A few months later, Australia and the United States entered into a comparable agreement whereby the US would ask for the establishment of an Article 21.5 panel; the parties would agree to cooperate to permit circulation of the report of that panel within 90 days; and that they would accept the report without appeal. In the event that the review panel found Australia's measure inconsistent, the parties agreed, Australia would not object to a US request for authorization to suspend concessions under Article 22.2, but Australia would

[107] *Id.* ¶¶ 7, 9. [108] *Id.*

[109] Panel Report, *Australia – Measures Affecting Importation of Salmon – Recourse to Article 21.5 of the DSU by Canada*, WT/DS18/RW, adopted 20 March 2000, DSR 2000:IV, 2035, ¶ 1.3.

[110] *Id.*

be free to request arbitration under Article 22.6. They further agreed on the deadline for the Article 22.6 report and DSB action on that report.[111]

When these two agreements were made, no Article 21.5 report had been appealed, and it was not known whether the Appellate Body would accept an appeal of an Article 21.5 report. That question was resolved in *Brazil – Aircraft (Article 21.5 – Canada)*, where an appeal was accepted without discussion of the issue.[112]

The appeal in *Brazil – Aircraft* added some complexity to the subsequent Article 22.6 arbitration, however, because the bilateral agreement between Brazil and Canada did not explicitly provide for appeal. It provided that if the compliance Panel found that Brazil had not complied, the DSB could authorize Canada to suspend concessions subject to Brazil's right to request arbitration under Article 22.6. Arbitration should be completed within 30 days of referral of the matter.[113]

At the DSB meeting held on 22 May 2000 to consider Canada's request for authorization to suspend concessions, the DSB, at Brazil's request, submitted the matter to arbitration.[114] Pursuant to the agreement, the arbitration report would have been due within 30 days, or by June 21. However, at the same meeting, Brazil notified the DSB of its intention to appeal.[115] The Appellate Body Report was not circulated until 21 July 2000, some 60 days after referral of Canada's Article 22.2 request to arbitration, and 30 days beyond the date specified for the arbitration report in the agreement.

The Arbitrators noted that the time periods contained in the agreement "were difficult to reconcile with the situation created by Brazil's appeal."[116] Because the report of the Appellate Body could affect the rights of the parties, due process required that they be given time to address that report. Accordingly, "the Arbitrators adopted a timetable which, in their opinion, respected the spirit of Articles 21 and 22 of the DSU and the purpose of arbitration under Article 22.6 of the DSU . . . while not unduly delaying

111 *Australia – Subsidies Provided to Producers and Exporters of Automotive Leather – Recourse to Article 21.5 of the DSU by the United States*, WT/DS126/8, 4 October 1999.

112 Appellate Body Report, *Brazil – Export Financing Programme for Aircraft – Recourse by Canada to Article 21.5 of the DSU*, WT/DS46/AB/RW, adopted 4 August 2000, DSR 2000:VIII, 4067.

113 *Brazil – Export Financing Programme for Aircraft*, WT/DS46/13, 26 November 1999.

114 *Supra* note 53, ¶¶ 1.1, 1.2.

115 Appellate Body Report, *Brazil – Export Financing Programme for Aircraft – Recourse by Canada to Article 21.5 of the DSU*, WT/DS46/AB/RW, adopted 4 August 2000, DSR 2000:VIII, 4067.

116 *Brazil – Aircraft (Article 22.6 – Brazil), supra* note 53, ¶ 2.1.

the issuance of the award."[117] This timetable provided for two dates: one if the Appellate Body declined jurisdiction of the Article 21.5 appeal or if it completely upheld the conclusions of the compliance panel; the other if either party considered that the conclusion of the Appellate Body would require additional submissions.[118] At the conclusion of the appeal, the parties did file comments with the Arbitrators, who issued the report to the parties on August 21, approximately 60 days after it would have been due under the timetable originally agreed to by the parties, and circulated it on August 28.[119]

In *US – FSC*, the agreement of the parties covered the possibility of an appeal.[120] This practice was followed subsequently in *Canada – Dairy*.[121]

The first case in which the parties reached a sequencing agreement, *Australia – Salmon*, was an SPS Agreement dispute. *Canada – Dairy* concerned the *Agreement on Agriculture*. The other cases, *Australia – Automotive Leather II*, *Brazil – Aircraft*, and *US – FSC*, were all prohibited subsidies disputes that were also subject to the special or additional dispute settlement rules of Article 4 of the SCM Agreement. Footnote 6 to SCM Article 4 provides, "Any time periods mentioned in this Article may be extended by mutual agreement." The same text appears at footnote 20 to SCM Article 7, dealing with actionable subsidies. While no comparable language appears in the DSU, the SPS Agreement, or the Agriculture Agreement, the long tradition, dating from GATT, of party control over proceedings suggests that WTO Members that are parties to a dispute may extend DSU timetables by mutual agreement. *Australia – Salmon* and *Canada – Dairy* might be said to confirm it. Subsidy cases are discussed further in § 8.07.

[4] Proposals for change

A number of proposals have been made to remedy the sequencing problem that was revealed in *Bananas III*. In September 2000, Japan, on behalf

[117] *Id.* (footnote omitted). [118] *Id.* ¶ 2.2. [119] *Id.* ¶ 2.3.

[120] *United States – Tax Treatment for "Foreign Sales Corporations" – Understanding between the European Communities and the United States Regarding Procedures under Articles 21 and 22 of the DSU and Article 4 of the SCM Agreement*, WT/DS108/12, 5 October 2000.

[121] *Canada – Measures Affecting the Importation of Milk and the Exportation of Dairy Products – Understanding between Canada and the United States Regarding Procedures under Articles 21 and 22 of the DSU*, WT/DS103/14, 5 January 2001; *Canada – Measures Affecting the Importation of Milk and the Exportation of Dairy Products – Understanding between Canada and New Zealand Regarding Procedures under Articles 21 and 22 of the DSU*, WT/DS113/14, 5 January 2001.

of itself and 10 other Members, addressed the sequencing problem in a proposal to amend a number of aspects of the DSU.[122] This proposal provided, *inter alia*, that a complaining party could request authorization to suspend concessions under Article 22.2 after a compliance panel found that the Member concerned failed to bring its measures into conformity.[123] This request could be submitted to arbitration under Article 22.6. The arbitration award would be circulated within 45 days of referral of the matter to arbitration.[124] The same Members submitted a similar proposal to the Fourth Ministerial Conference at Doha.[125]

The EC submitted a proposal that would, *inter alia*, provide for consultations following a compliance panel or Appellate Body report that the Member concerned had acted inconsistently with a covered agreement.[126] It, too, would allow 45 days for Article 22.6 arbitration, also from the date of referral of the matter to arbitration.[127] The EC explained its reasoning by referring to the *ad hoc* solutions reached post-*Bananas III*, and stating, "it would appear that Members now broadly agree that completing the procedure established under Article 21.5 DSU is a pre-requisite for invoking the provisions of Article 22 DSU, in case of disagreement among the parties about implementation."[128]

After consultations with the EC, Japan amended its proposal to allow for early determination of the level of nullification or impairment, and to exempt "*en route*" products from the application of the suspension of concessions.[129] A proposal from Mexico would have required that Article 22.6 arbitration should be completed 60 days after referral.[130]

[122] *Proposal to Amend Certain Provisions of the Understanding on Rules and Procedures Governing the Settlement of Disputes (DSU) Pursuant to Article X of the Marrakesh Agreement Establishing the World Trade Organization – Submission by Canada, Colombia, Costa Rica, Ecuador, Japan, Korea, New Zealand, Norway, Peru, Switzerland and Venezuela for Examination and Further Consideration by the General Council*, WT/GC/W/410, 29 September 2000. Chile, Add.1, Bolivia, Add.2, and Uruguay, Add.3, subsequently requested to be added to the list of sponsors.

[123] *Id.* ¶ 5. [124] *Id.* ¶ 6.

[125] *Amendment of Certain Provisions of the Understanding on Rules and Procedures Governing the Settlement of Disputes – Submission by Bolivia, Canada, Chile, Colombia, Costa Rica, Ecuador, Japan, Korea, New Zealand, Norway, Peru, Switzerland, Uruguay and Venezuela*, WT/MIN(01)/W/6, 1 November 2001.

[126] *Contribution of the European Communities and Its Member States to the Improvement of the WTO Dispute Settlement Understanding*, TN/DS/W/1, 13 March 2002, ¶ 25.

[127] *Id.* ¶ 26. [128] *Id.* § II.A.

[129] *Amendment of the Understanding on Rules and Procedures Governing the Settlement of Disputes – Proposal by Japan*, TN/DS/W/32, 23 January 2003.

[130] *Amendment to the Understanding on Rules and Procedures Governing the Settlement of Disputes – Communication from Mexico*, TN/DS/W/40, 27 January 2003.

While the situation presented by *Bananas III* was truly difficult, Members have found a way around the problem, as the subsequent *ad hoc* solutions demonstrate. This, perhaps, explains the failure of both the General Council and the Ministerial Conference to address the sequencing problem in isolation from other proposals to amend the DSU. In the words of the EC, in light of the *ad hoc* solutions, "The problem is therefore clearly less acute than in the past."[131]

[5] The safeguards "sequencing" problem

A problem similar to the DSU Article 21.5/Article 22.6 problem appears in Article 8 of the *Agreement on Safeguards*, a provision that sets forth what is perhaps the most important change in GATT/WTO safeguards requirements made by the Uruguay Round. Prior to adoption of the Safeguards Agreement, safeguards were governed only by GATT Article XIX, which provides, *inter alia*, that if the party limiting imports does not offer compensation in a form acceptable to other interested parties, the latter may suspend equivalent concessions.[132] Paragraphs 1 and 2 of Article 8 continue this requirement, but paragraph 3 provides that the right of suspension "shall not be exercised for the first three years that a safeguard measure is in effect, provided that the measure has been taken as a result of an absolute increase in imports and that such a measure conforms to the provisions of this Agreement." This three-year "holiday" from the need to compensate for safeguards was viewed by many as necessary to make safeguards more readily available, thereby discouraging the use of non-transparent "gray area" measures.

The difficulty arises, as it does with the DSU Article 21.5/Article 22.6 problem, when there is disagreement as to whether, in fact, there is an absolute increase in imports or whether the measure otherwise conforms to the provisions of the Agreement. May the affected Members decide these issues for themselves, or must they seek a panel determination confirming their views?

Permitting an exporting Member to decide for itself that the Member imposing safeguards has not complied with the Agreement, or that imports are not increasing absolutely, would permit uncontrolled, unilateral limitations on trade. But Article 8.2 authorizes the suspension of concessions by affected Members "not later than 90 days after the measure is applied." If resort must be had to a panel, to say nothing of a possible appeal, the process would take far more than 90 days, arguably denying

[131] *Supra* note 126, § II.A.

[132] GATT Art. XIX:3.

the exporting Members the legal right to take action even after a panel or the Appellate Body confirms their views. Moreover, even if this problem is resolved, the Member concerned will have enjoyed the benefit of an illegal safeguard for the rather lengthy period of the panel and appellate processes.[133]

As they did with the DSU Article 21.5/Article 22.6 sequencing problem, Members devised *ad hoc* solutions to the Safeguards Agreement sequencing problem. In some instances, they extended the 90-day period set forth in Article 8.2 to a specified date.[134] They have also extended the specified date.[135] Parties have also agreed to extend the 90-day period for as long as the safeguard measure remains in force.[136] Typical of these *ad hoc* agreements is the language set forth in an agreement between Australia and the United States concerning a US safeguard measure on steel products:

> The United States and Australia are pleased to notify the Council for Trade in Goods that they have agreed that their reciprocal rights and obligations in respect of the above-referenced action under the Agreement on Safeguards and the General Agreement on Tariffs and Trade 1994 will be maintained, and for this purpose they have agreed that as between them the 90-day period set forth in Article 8.2 of the Agreement on Safeguards and Article XIX:3(a) of the General Agreement on Tariffs and Trade 1994 shall be considered to expire on 20 March 2005.[137]

[133] GATT Art. XIX:3 also provides that other parties are entitled to suspend concessions "not later than ninety days after such action is taken," but this did not present a sequencing problem because, under GATT, there was no "holiday" from the obligation to compensate or face retaliation. The suspension of concessions was justified by the uncompensated safeguard measure itself, even if it otherwise conformed to Article XIX.

[134] *Immediate Notification under Article 12.5 of the Agreement on Safeguards to the Council for Trade in Goods Concerning United States Action in Respect of Fresh, Chilled or Frozen Lamb Meat – Joint Communication from Australia and the United States*, G/L/339, G/SG/N/AUS/1, G/SG/N/12/USA/1, 27 October 1999.

[135] *Immediate Notification under Article 12.5 of the Agreement on Safeguards to the Council for Trade in Goods Concerning Brazil's Action in Respect of Toys – Joint Communication from Brazil and the European Communities*, G/SG/N/12/BRA/1, G/SG/N/12/EEC/2 and Corr.1, 1 March 2000; G/SG/N/12/BRA/1/Add.1 and Corr.1, and G/SG/N/12/EEC/2/Add.1 and Corr.1, 9 June 2000.

[136] *Immediate Notification under Article 12.5 of the Agreement on Safeguards to the Council for Trade in Goods Concerning Argentina's Action in Respect of Imports of Footwear – Joint Communication from Argentina and the European Communities*, G/L/366, G/SG/N/12/ARG/1, G/SG/N/12/EEC/3, 19 April 2000.

[137] *Immediate Notification under Article 12.5 of the Agreement on Safeguards to the Council for Trade in Goods Concerning United States Action in Respect of Certain Steel Products – Joint Communication from the United States and Australia*, G/C/14, G/SG/N/12/USA/9, G/SG/N/12/AUS/2, 17 May 2002.

§ 8.07 Prohibited and actionable subsidies

[1] Overview

As discussed in § 5.09, the SCM Agreement provides a number of special or additional rules and procedures governing subsidy disputes. For the most part, SCM Agreement Article 4, dealing with prohibited subsidies, and Article 7, dealing with actionable subsidies, parallel comparable provisions in the DSU, but provide much shorter time limits for each stage of the dispute. The provisions relating to remedy, however, differ more significantly from their DSU counterparts.

Prohibited subsidies are those that are contingent upon export performance or upon the use of domestic over imported goods.[138] Actionable subsidies are those that, while not contingent on export or on the use of domestic over imported goods, cause "adverse effects to the interests of other Members."[139] Any subsidy, including so-called "domestic" subsidies, could be actionable.[140]

As discussed in § 7.08, SCM Article 4.7 requires panels finding that a measure is a prohibited subsidy "recommend that the subsidizing Member withdraw the subsidy without delay." It also directs the panel to define "without delay" by specifying in its recommendation the time within which the measure must be withdrawn. In the event that the subsidy is not withdrawn, Article 4.10 authorizes the complaining Member "to take appropriate countermeasures." Article 4.11 provides for arbitration under DSU Article 22.6 to "determine whether the countermeasures are appropriate." Footnotes at each use of the word "appropriate" state that, "This expression is not meant to allow countermeasures that are disproportionate in light of the fact that the subsidies dealt with under these provisions are prohibited."[141] The terms "withdraw," "countermeasure" and "appropriate" are not defined.

SCM Agreement Article 7.8 provides that, when the DSB adopts a report determining that a subsidy has resulted in adverse effects to the interests of another Member, the Member granting the subsidy "shall take appropriate steps to remove the adverse effects or shall withdraw the subsidy." Article 7.9 specifies that if those "appropriate steps" have not been taken within six months of adoption of the report, the complaining

[138] SCM Agreement, Article 3.1.
[139] SCM Agreement, Article 5.
[140] Part IV of the SCM Agreement temporarily made certain research, regional, and environmental subsidies non-actionable. This shelter expired 1 January 2000. SCM Agreement, Article 31.
[141] SCM Agreement, footnotes 9 and 10.

Member may "take countermeasures commensurate with the degree and nature of the adverse effects determined to exist."

[2] "Appropriate countermeasures"

The first Article 22.6 arbitration interpreting Article 4 of the SCM Agreement was *Brazil – Aircraft (Article 22.6 – Brazil)*. The term "countermeasures" was not at issue because Canada had requested authorization to take countermeasures in the form of suspension of concessions and other obligations under GATT 1994 and other agreements, and Brazil did not challenge this aspect of Canada's request.[142] The central issue concerned the meaning of "appropriate."

Canada did not request authorization corresponding to the level of nullification or impairment, but in the amount of the prohibited subsidy. Brazil agreed with the amount of the subsidy as the starting point of the analysis, but argued that it should be adjusted for various factors. In light of this agreement of the parties, the Arbitrators took the amount of the subsidy as the starting point of their analysis.[143] The Arbitrators rejected arguments for downward adjustment of that amount, concluding that, "when dealing with a prohibited export subsidy, an amount of countermeasures which corresponds to the total amount of the subsidy is 'appropriate.' "[144]

The Arbitrators said that footnotes 10 and 11 of Article 4, which specify that the term appropriate "is not meant to allow countermeasures that are disproportionate in light of the fact that the subsidies dealt with under these provisions are prohibited," were ambiguous.[145] They expressed the view, however, that "the reference to the fact that the subsidies dealt with are prohibited can most probably be considered more as an aggravating factor than a mitigating factor."[146] Accordingly, while the Arbitrators said they did not draw any firm conclusions as to the meaning of the footnotes, they reasoned that the footnotes "at least confirm that the term 'appropriate' in Articles 4.10 and 4.11 of the SCM Agreement should not be given the same meaning as the term 'equivalent' in Article 22 of the DSU."[147] In a footnote to that statement, they expressed the view that "the term 'appropriate,' read in the light of footnotes 9 and 10, may allow for more leeway than the word 'equivalent' in terms of assessing the appropriate level of countermeasures."[148]

[142] *Supra* note 53, ¶ 3.28. [143] *Id.* ¶ 3.27. [144] *Id.* ¶ 3.60. [145] *Id.* ¶ 3.51.
[146] *Id.* [147] *Id.* [148] *Id.* footnote 51.

The view that the reference in footnotes 10 and 11 to the fact that the subsidies involved are prohibited "can most probably be considered as an aggravating factor" is questionable. Certainly, subsidies contingent upon export or the use of domestic over imported goods are prohibited, but they are not any more prohibited than any other violation, such as denial of most-favored-nation treatment in violation of GATT Article I, imposition of tariffs above bound rates in violation of Article II, denial of national treatment in violation of Article III, or imposition of quotas in violation of Article XI. More likely, the use of the term "prohibited" for these subsidies is to distinguish them from those that are "actionable." These are subsidies that are not contingent on export or on the use of domestic over imported goods. They constitute a unique WTO obligation, one that depends not only on the granting of a subsidy, but on its impact on another Member: Article 5 of the SCM Agreement provides that no Member should provide subsidies that cause "adverse effects to the interests of other Members." Only if the subsidies do so, are they "actionable." Members are not required to demonstrate "adverse effects" to establish nullification or impairment under other provisions of WTO agreements. Indeed, they need have no "legal interest" or "substantial trade interest" at all.[149] On this reading, footnotes 10 and 11 serve to distinguish prohibited subsidies, which are prohibited no more nor no less than other violations, from actionable subsidies, which are, provided they cause no adverse effects, not prohibited and are, indeed, permissible.

The Arbitrators in *US – FSC (Article 22.6 – US)* found more certainty in the text of the footnotes than did the Arbitrators in *Brazil – Aircraft*. With specific reference to footnote 9 to Article 4.10, they said that the footnote "effectively clarifies" how the term "appropriate" is to be interpreted.[150] They saw the footnote as requiring them "to maintain a congruent relationship in countering the measure at issue so that the reaction is not excessive in light of the situation to which there is to be a response. But this does not require exact equivalence – the relationship to be respected is precisely that of 'proportion' rather than equivalence.' "[151]

The *US – FSC* Arbitrators agreed with their *Brazil – Aircraft* counterparts that the requirement of the footnote to consider proportionality in

[149] Appellate Body Report, *European Communities – Regime for the Importation, Sale and Distribution of Bananas*, WT/DS27/AB/R, adopted 25 September 1997, DSR 1997:II, 591, ¶ 132.

[150] Decision by the Arbitrator, *United States – Tax Treatment for "Foreign Sales Corporations" – Recourse to Arbitration by the United States under Article 22.6 of the DSU and Article 4.11 of the SCM Agreement*, WT/DS108/ARB, 30 August 2002, ¶ 5.16.

[151] *Id.* ¶ 5.18.

light of the fact that the subsidy is a prohibited subsidy "can only be reasonably construed to be [an] aggravating rather than a mitigating factor."[152] "Members are entitled to trade without other Members resorting to export subsidies," they said. "In our view, the . . . footnote directs that this in itself is a required consideration when it comes to assessing whether countermeasures are not disproportionate."[153]

The Arbitrators in *Canada – Aircraft Credits and Guarantees (Article 22.6 – Canada)* noted with approval the statement of the Arbitrators in *US – FSC* that countermeasures need to be adapted to the particular case at hand.[154] In that case, which involved a prohibited subsidy to finance the sale of aircraft, Brazil argued that the appropriate level of countermeasures would be the amount of the sale financed by the subsidy;[155] Canada argued that the appropriate measure was the amount of the subsidy itself.[156] While stating that, by its terms, Article 4.10 of the SCM Agreement does not exclude, *a priori*, recourse to either approach, the Arbitrators used the amount of the subsidy as the starting point but, because of the circumstances of the case, found it appropriate to increase the amount of authorized countermeasures by an additional 20 percent.

The factor that led the Arbitrators to this conclusion was Canada's statement that it did not intend to withdraw the subsidy.[157] In light of Canada's position, the Arbitrators "decided to adjust the level of countermeasures calculated on the basis of the total amount of the subsidy by an amount which we deem reasonably meaningful to cause Canada to reconsider its current position to maintain the subsidy at issue in breach of its obligations. We consequently adjust the level of countermeasures by an amount corresponding to 20 percent of the amount of subsidy as calculated."[158] The Arbitrators, accordingly, awarded Brazil the right to take countermeasures in an amount equal to 120 percent of the amount of the subsidy.[159] "Without such an adjustment," the Arbitrators said, "we would not be satisfied that an appropriate level of countermeasures had been established in this case."[160]

[3] Multiple complainants

The de-coupling of the amount of countermeasures from the nullification or impairment experienced by the complaining party raises the issue of multiple complainants. It is well established in GATT/WTO jurisprudence generally that a Member need not demonstrate any actual trade

[152] *Id.* ¶ 5.23. [153] *Id.* [154] *Supra* note 47, ¶ 3.92. [155] *Id.* ¶ 3.1. [156] *Id.* ¶ 3.2. [157] *Id.* ¶ 3.107. [158] *Id.* ¶ 3.121. [159] *Id.* [160] *Id.* ¶ 3.122.

loss in order to have standing to initiate dispute settlement.[161] Thus, arguably, all WTO Members could initiate dispute settlement against a single export subsidy and each could be authorized to take countermeasures in the amount of the subsidy, even if it did not experience nullification or impairment.

The Arbitrators in *Brazil – Aircraft* were aware of this possibility. In such a case, they said, "the arbitrator could allocate the amount of appropriate countermeasures among the complainants in proportion to their trade in the product concerned. The 'inducing' effect would most probably be very similar."[162]

In *US – FSC*, however, the Arbitrators saw the matter differently. The tax subsidy in that case benefited US exports to the territories of all WTO Members, not just the complainant EC. Nevertheless, the Arbitrators held that the EC was entitled to take countermeasures for the entire subsidy amount, including that amount granted on US exports other than to the EC. The obligation not to grant prohibited subsidies, they said, "is an *erga omnes* obligation owed in its entirety to each and every Member. It cannot be considered to be 'allocable' across the Membership."[163] If it were otherwise, the Arbitrators contended, the Member concerned would be only partially obliged to each Member, "which is manifestly inconsistent with an *erga omnes* obligation."[164] Therefore, the Arbitrators concluded, "the United States has breached its obligations to the European Communities in respect of all the money that it has expended, because such expenditure in breach – the expense incurred – is the very essence of the wrongful act."[165]

However, the Arbitrators in *US – FSC* went on to state that the fact that the EC was the sole complainant in the case seeking to take countermeasures was a factor in its analysis. "Had there been multiple complainants each seeking to take countermeasures in an amount equal to the value of the subsidy," they said, "this would certainly have been a consideration to take into account in evaluating whether such countermeasures might be considered to be not 'appropriate' in the circumstances."[166] The Arbitrators went on to note that "any hypothesis" of a future complainant "would give rise inevitably to a different situation."[167] They also said that

[161] Panel Report, *European Communities – Regime for the Importation, Sale and Distribution of Bananas – Complaint by the United States*, WT/DS27/R/USA, adopted 25 September 1997, as modified by the Appellate Body Report, WT/DS27/AB/R, DSR 1997:II, 943, ¶¶ 7.49 – 7.51.

[162] *Supra* note 53, ¶ 3.59. [163] *Supra* note 150, ¶ 6.10.

[164] *Id.* [165] *Id.* [166] *Id.* ¶ 6.27. [167] *Id.* ¶ 6.28.

they did not rule out, *a priori*, that, in a particular case, trade effects rather than the amount of the subsidy could "enter into consideration" as a relevant factor in determining the "appropriate" amount of countermeasures under Article 4.10 of the SCM Agreement.[168]

This question of possible multiple complainants was not directly addressed by the Arbitrators in *Canada – Aircraft Credits and Guarantees (Article 22.6 – Canada)*, but they did quote with agreement the statement of the Arbitrators in *US – FSC* that "countermeasures should be adapted to the particular case at hand."[169]

§ 8.08 Panel and Appellate Body implementation suggestions

[1] Overview

When a panel or the Appellate Body concludes that a measure is inconsistent with a covered agreement, Article 19 of the DSU directs the panel or Appellate Body simply to recommend that the Member concerned bring the measure into conformity with that agreement.[170] This is consistent with most prior GATT practice. The function of the recommendation, indeed the need for discretion when it comes to implementing a report by a WTO adjudicating body, was given by the Panel report in *US – Section 301 Trade Act*:

> The obligation on Members to bring their laws into conformity with WTO obligations is a fundamental feature of the system and, despite the fact that it affects the internal legal system of a State, has to be applied rigorously. At the same time, enforcement of this obligation must be done in the least intrusive way possible. The Member concerned must be allowed the maximum autonomy in ensuring such conformity and, if there is more than one lawful way to achieve this, should have the freedom to choose that way which suits it best.[171]

In addition, however, Article 19 also provides that both the panel and the Appellate Body may suggest ways in which their recommendations may be implemented. While this authority has been utilized a few times, panels and the Appellate Body have, for the most part, shown reluctance to suggest ways in which their recommendations could be implemented.

[168] *Id.* ¶ 6.33.
[169] *Supra* note 47, ¶ 3.92, quoting *US – FSC (Article 22.6 – US)*, *supra* note 150, ¶ 5.12.
[170] DSU Art. 19.1.
[171] Panel Report, *United States – Sections 301–310 of the Trade Act of 1974*, WT/DS152/R, adopted 27 January 2000, DSR 2000:II, 815, ¶ 7.102.

[2] Antidumping and countervailing duty cases

As noted in § 8.02, several GATT antidumping panels recommended not only that antidumping duty orders be revoked, but also that duties paid pursuant to those orders be refunded. In *Guatemala – Cement I*, the first antidumping dispute in the WTO, the complainant, Mexico, requested similar relief. Mexico asked that the Panel recommend both revocation of the measure and the refund of antidumping duties already collected.[172] The Panel expressed the view that, under Article 19.1, it was limited simply to making the recommendation that the Member concerned bring its actions or its measure into conformity and that, at most, it could merely suggest ways this could be done. It could not order specific action, such as the refund of duties.[173] In the circumstances of the case, the Panel decided to "suggest" that Guatemala revoke the measure, because "this is the only appropriate means of implementing our recommendation."[174]

While concluding that original panels do not have the authority to require refund of antidumping duties, the Panel in *Guatemala – Cement I* did not necessarily close the door on the possibility. It emphasized the distinction between a recommendation and the means by which that recommendation is implemented. If an antidumping recommendation is implemented without refund of duties, the Panel implied, this could be a proper question for a compliance panel under Article 21 of the DSU.[175] The Panel's ruling on this point was not reviewed by the Appellate Body, which reversed the Panel on other grounds.[176]

In *Argentina – Poultry*, the Panel stated that, "In light of the nature and extent of the violation in this case, we do not perceive how Argentina could properly implement our recommendation without revoking the anti-dumping measure at issue in this dispute."[177] Accordingly, the Panel suggested that Argentina repeal the resolution imposing definitive anti-dumping duties on poultry from Brazil.[178]

[172] Panel Report, *Guatemala – Anti-Dumping Investigation Regarding Portland Cement from Mexico*, WT/DS60/R, adopted 25 November 1998, as modified by the Appellate Body Report, WT/DS60/AB/R, DSR 1998:IX, 3797, ¶ 8.1.

[173] *Id.* ¶ 8.3. [174] *Id.* ¶ 8.6. [175] *Id.* ¶ 8.3.

[176] Appellate Body Report, *Guatemala – Anti-Dumping Investigation Regarding Portland Cement from Mexico*, WT/DS60/AB/R, adopted 25 November 1998, DSR 1998:IX, 3767.

[177] Panel Report, *Argentina – Definitive Anti-Dumping Duties on Poultry from Brazil*, WT/DS241/R, adopted 19 May 2003, ¶ 8.7.

[178] *Id.*

In *US – Stainless Steel*, Korea requested that the Panel suggest that the US revoke the antidumping order.[179] The Panel observed that, "Article 19.1 of the DSU allows but does not require a panel to make a suggestion where it deems it appropriate to do so."[180] It refused to make a suggestion, stating that revocation of the order would be only one way for the US to bring the measure into compliance.[181]

US – Lead and Bismuth II involved administrative practices of the United States with regard to countervailing duties on imports from companies that had been privatized after subsidies had been granted.[182] While the Panel found that the US practice violated the SCM Agreement, it declined the EC request that it "suggest that the United States amend its countervailing duty laws to recognize the principle that privatization at market price extinguishes subsidies."[183] The Panel reasoned that, since the EC had not identified any provision of US law that required the imposition of countervailing duties after privatization, it could not make such a suggestion.[184] Nevertheless, the Panel observed that the US had continued to apply the non-conforming methodology during the course of the dispute and said, "We would suggest that the United States take all appropriate steps, including a revision of its administrative practices, to prevent the aforementioned violation of Article 10 of the SCM Agreement from arising in the future."[185]

US – 1916 Act (Japan) did not involve an antidumping or countervailing measure, but the WTO-consistency of the Act itself.[186] Japan requested that the Panel recommend that the US repeal the act.[187] The Panel held that it could not make the requested recommendation, since its authority permitted it only to recommend that the measure be brought into compliance.[188] However, in light of its findings, the Panel observed, for the US to bring the law into conformity by amendment would

[179] Panel Report, *United States – Anti-Dumping Measures on Stainless Steel Plate in Coils and Stainless Steel Sheet and Strip from Korea*, WT/DS179/R, adopted 1 February 2001.

[180] *Id.* ¶ 7.8 [181] *Id.* ¶ 7.10.

[182] Panel Report, *United States – Imposition of Countervailing Duties on Certain Hot-Rolled Lead and Bismuth Carbon Steel Products Originating in the United Kingdom*, WT/DS138/R and Corr.2, adopted 7 June 2000, as upheld by the Appellate Body Report, WT/DS138/AB/R, DSR 2000:VI, 2631.

[183] *Id.* ¶ 8.2. [184] *Id.* [185] *Id.*

[186] Panel Report, *United States – Anti-Dumping Act of 1916 – Complaint by Japan*, WT/DS162/R and Add.1, adopted 26 September 2000, as upheld by the Appellate Body Report, WT/DS136/AB/R, WT/DS162/AB/R, DSR 2000:X, 4831.

[187] *Id.* ¶ 6.290. [188] *Id.* ¶ 6.291.

involve extensive changes that would eliminate some of its main features. Accordingly, the Panel said, "we suggest that one way for the United States to bring the 1916 Act into conformity with its WTO obligations would be to repeal the 1916 Act."[189]

Like *US – 1916 Act*, the dispute in *US – Offset Act (Byrd Amendment)* also involved the WTO-legality of the Act itself, and not an antidumping or countervailing measure. The Act provided that the proceeds of collected antidumping and countervailing duties would be paid to members of the domestic industry that supported the petition in the national trade remedy case. After concluding that this did not conform to WTO requirements, the Panel said, "we find it difficult to conceive of any method which would be more appropriate and/or effective than the repeal of the . . . measure."[190] Accordingly, the Panel suggested that the US bring the measure into conformity by repealing the Act.[191]

[3] Other WTO cases

While only a minority of panels outside of the antidumping and countervailing duty fields has made suggestions for implementation, the practice is not rare. The first instance occurred in *US – Underwear*, the fourth dispute brought to a panel.[192] There the Panel stated:

> We find that such compliance can best be achieved and further nullification and impairment of benefits accruing to Costa Rica under the [*Agreement on Textiles and Clothing*] best be avoided by prompt removal of the measure inconsistent with the obligations of the United States. We further suggest that the United States bring the measure challenged by Costa Rica into compliance with US obligations under the ATC by immediately withdrawing the restriction imposed by the measure.[193]

In *India – Patents (US)*, the United States requested that the Panel suggest to India that it implement in a manner similar to the way in

[189] *Id.* ¶ 6.292.
[190] Panel Report, *United States – Continued Dumping and Subsidy Offset Act of 2000*, WT/DS217/R, WT/DS234/R, adopted 27 January 20003, as modified by the Appellate Body Report, WT/DS217/AB/R, WT/DS234/AB/R, ¶ 8.6.
[191] *Id.*
[192] Panel Report, *United States – Restrictions on Imports of Cotton and Man-made Fibre Underwear*, WT/DS24/R, adopted 25 February 1997, as modified by the Appellate Body Report, WT/DS24/AB/R, DSR 1997:I, 31.
[193] *Id.* ¶ 8.3.

which Pakistan had implemented its obligations under the TRIPS Agreement to establish a mechanism to protect patent applications during a transition period.[194] The Panel declined, "since it would impair India's right to choose how to implement."[195] Nevertheless, the Panel noted that because India had failed to establish an appropriate mechanism, it would suggest that in implementing the recommendations and rulings of the DSB, "India should take into account the interests of those persons who would have filed patent applications had an appropriate mechanism been maintained."[196]

The Panel in *India – Quantitative Restrictions* suggested that the parties negotiate a phase-out period for the offending restrictions and, failing that, that the reasonable period of time be set in light of factors discussed by the Panel.[197]

As noted in § 7.07[8], the Article 21.5 compliance panel in *EC – Bananas III (Article 21.5 – Ecuador)* made suggestions as to implementation. In the Article 22.6 arbitration in that same case, Ecuador requested and received suggestions from the Arbitrators concerning the suspension of obligations under the TRIPS Agreement.[198] The Arbitrators reasoned that, while Article 19 of the DSU does not explicitly mention Article 22 arbitration proceedings, "there is nothing in the DSU that would preclude Arbitrators, acting pursuant to Article 22.6, from making suggestions on how to implement their decision."[199]

[4] Legal effect of implementation suggestions

The Panel in *Guatemala – Cement I* noted that suggestions are not part of the recommendations of the Panel or of the DSB if the report is adopted, "and are not binding on the affected Member."[200] However, should the Member concerned follow a suggestion of a Panel or the Appellate Body, it would seem that, *de facto*, its action would be found to be in compliance in any Article 21.5 review by that tribunal. Of course, the Appellate Body would not likely consider itself bound by a suggestion made by a panel

[194] Panel Report, *India – Patent Protection for Pharmaceutical and Agricultural Chemical Products – Complaint by the United States*, WT/DS50/R, adopted 16 January 1998, as modified by the Appellate Body Report, WT/DS50/AB/R, DSR 1998:I, 41, ¶ 7.65.

[195] *Id.* [196] *Id.* ¶ 8.2.

[197] Panel Report, *India – Quantitative Restrictions on Imports of Agricultural, Textile and Industrial Products*, WT/DS90/R, adopted 22 September 1999, as upheld by the Appellate Body Report, WT/DS90/AB/R, DSR 1999:V, 1799, ¶ 7.7.

[198] *Supra* note 17, ¶ 139. [199] *Id.* [200] *Supra* note 172, ¶ 8.2.

unless it had previously considered the suggestion in an appeal of the original panel report.[201]

§ 8.09 "Other situation" reports

The implementation of recommendations and rulings regarding "other situation" reports involving Article XXIII:1(c) of GATT are governed by the Montreal Rules.[202] The implications of the Montreal Rules for remedy in "other situation" disputes are not clear. If a developing country is involved, the Montreal Rules[203] provide that any action taken must conform to the provisions of paragraphs 21 and 23 of the 1979 Understanding Regarding Notification, Consultation, Dispute Settlement and Surveillance.[204] The implications of the 1979 Understanding for remedy are not clear. Given the dearth of cases under this provision during GATT's 47 years, and the retention, via the Montreal Rules, of GATT's positive consensus requirement, early clarification seems unlikely.

§ 8.10 Purpose of suspension of concessions

As the previous sections in this chapter indicate, the question of remedies in the WTO – the suspension of concessions or other obligations generally and countermeasures in the case of subsidies – is complex. Not surprisingly, it is an area of WTO dispute settlement that has attracted considerable scholarly comment and suggestions.[205]

[201] *See* generally, Robert E. Hudec, *Broadening the Scope of Remedies in WTO Dispute Settlement*, in Friedl Weiss (Ed) IMPROVING WTO DISPUTE SETTLEMENT PROCEDURES: ISSUES & LESSONS FROM THE PRACTICE OF OTHER INTERNATIONAL COURTS AND TRIBUNALS 369, 377 (Cameron May, 2000); Petros C. Mavroidis, *Remedies in the WTO Legal System: Between a Rock and a Hard Place*, 11 EUROPEAN JOURNAL OF INTERNATIONAL LAW 763, 784 (No. 4, December 2000).

[202] *Decision of 12 April 1989*, BISD 36S/61. *See* §§ 4.16 [4] and 7.09.

[203] Montreal Rules ¶ I.4, BISD 36S/61,67.

[204] BISD 26S/210, 214; *see* § 1.01 [5].

[205] *See, e.g.*, Joost Pauwelyn, *Enforcement and Countermeasures in the WTO: Rules are Rules – Toward a More Collective Approach*, 94 AMERICAN JOURNAL OF INTERNATIONAL LAW 335 (April 2000); Petros C. Mavroidis, *Remedies in the WTO Legal System: Between a Rock and a Hard Place, supra* note 201; Patricio Grané, *Remedies under WTO Law*, 4 JOURNAL OF INTERNATIONAL ECONOMIC LAW 755 (No. 4, December 2001); Chi Carmody, *Remedies and Conformity under the WTO Agreement*, 5 JOURNAL OF INTERNATIONAL ECONOMIC LAW 307 (No. 2, June 2002); Brendan P. McGivern, *Seeking Compliance with WTO Rulings: Theory, Practice, and Alternatives*, 36 INTERNATIONAL LAWYER 141 (No. 1, Spring 2002); Steve Charnovitz, *The WTO 's Problematic "Last Resort" Against*

In GATT, while the situation was not without ambiguity, the prevailing view was that remedies should "rebalance" the bargain between the parties. As noted in § 8.02, the closest municipal law analogue to the GATT system was that of partial recission of a contract, where partial non-performance by one party excuses equivalent non-performance by another, without vitiating the entire contract. A party's obligation to adhere to the provisions of the GATT was not always viewed with the same moral outlook that prevails in municipal contract law or in public international law generally, where the principle of *pacta sunt servanda* is fundamental. GATT, as a trade agreement, was looked upon under a more practical light. The rationale was well-stated by Kenneth Dam:

> [B]ecause of the economic nature of tariff concessions and the domestic political sensitivity inherently involved in trade issues, a system that made withdrawals of concessions impossible would tend to discourage the making of the concessions in the first place. It is better, for example, that 100 commitments should be made and that 10 should be withdrawn than that only 50 commitments should be made and that all of them should be kept.[206]

Whatever the merits of this view, it has not prevailed before WTO arbitrators.[207] Every Article 22.6 arbitration report, beginning with *Bananas III*, has stated that the purpose of suspension of concessions or other obligations, or countermeasures, is to "induce compliance" rather than to re-balance concessions.[208] Although the Arbitrators in *US – FSC* said that there "is nothing in [SCM Article 4.10] which suggests an entitlement to manifestly punitive measures,"[209] the Arbitrators in *Canada – Aircraft Credits and Guarantees*, as noted above, added 20 percent to the calculated amount of countermeasures to induce compliance after

Noncompliance, AUSSENWIRTSCHAFT, 57. Jahrgang – Heft IV, 409 (December 2002); Kym Anderson, *Peculiarities of Retaliation in WTO Dispute Settlement*, 1 WORLD TRADE REVIEW 123 (No. 2, July 2002); *see* also, three chapters in Kennedy & Southwick (Eds) THE POLITICAL ECONOMY OF INTERNATIONAL TRADE LAW: ESSAYS IN HONOR OF ROBERT E. HUDEC (Cambridge, 2002); Steve Charnovitz, *Should the Teeth Be Pulled? An Analysis of WTO Sanctions*; Gary N. Horlick, *Problems with the Compliance Structure of the WTO Dispute Resolution Process*; and David Palmeter & Stanimir A. Alexandrov, *"Inducing Compliance" in WTO Dispute Settlement.*

206 Kenneth W. Dam, THE GATT: LAW AND INTERNATIONAL ECONOMIC ORGANIZATION 80 (Chicago, 1970).

207 For an argument critical of the WTO's departure from GATT's "rebalancing" standard, *see*, Palmeter and Alexandrov, *supra* note 205.

208 *Supra* note 17, ¶ 6.3.

209 *Supra* note 150, ¶ 5.62.

Canada had said that it would not comply by withdrawing the prohibited subsidy.[210] It remains to be seen whether other arbitrators also will provide additional amounts in their awards in order to induce compliance, and whether, if they do, the practice will be confined to subsidy cases that are based on the amount of the subsidy, and not cases based on the amount of nullification or impairment.

[210] *Supra* note 47; *see* § 8.07 [2].

9

Conclusion

The World Trade Organization's Dispute Settlement Understanding represents, in the words of Celso Lafer, a former chairman of the Dispute Settlement Body, a "thickening of legality."[1] In the "symbiosis of diplomacy and litigation," the DSU represents a decided move of the GATT/WTO dispute settlement system away from diplomacy and toward litigation.[2]

But this move does not diminish the importance of diplomacy. Diplomacy and the negotiations that characterize it will, of necessity, remain central to any international organization composed of governments. Diplomacy, indeed, is the process by which international rules, including WTO rules, are established. Litigation is simply the application of those negotiated rules. The possibility of litigation and the foreseeability of outcomes based on agreed rules become part of the diplomatic process itself, factors that diplomats take into account in their dealings with one another.

A case may go forward because the outcome of the application of the rules to the facts of a particular dispute is not clear in advance. Or, it may go forward, even though the outcome is clear, because a government may wish to show a domestic constituency that it did all that it could, or because it may wish to show a parochial ministry the consequences of not considering international commitments before acting, or because it simply wants to "buy time" before making a change.

Often, however, the cases will be settled. A negotiated solution will be reached, even "on the court house steps." When this happens, it is a triumph both for diplomacy and for the rules-based litigation system that contributed to the outcome, if only by making the litigated outcome more or less apparent. And it has happened frequently in the WTO. In slightly

[1] Celso Lafer, The World Trade Organization Dispute Settlement System 11 (1996 Gilberto Amado Memorial Lecture, United Nations, 1996).

[2] The term is that of former World Court President Naendra Singh, quoted in Shabtai Rosenne, The World Court 259 (5th ed., Martinus Nijhoff, 1995).

more than eight years, through May 2003, 290 complaints had officially been notified to the WTO through requests for consultations.[3] Of these, 70 had resulted in adopted reports and 16 were before active panels, for a total of 86. Of the remainder, 40 had officially resulted in mutually agreed solutions, while 24 were termed "settled" or "inactive," for a total of 64.[4] Of the remaining 140, many clearly never will be brought before a panel and, if they are not the subject of formal, mutually agreed solutions, they eventually will be categorized as settled or inactive.

But, while negotiation and diplomacy remain paramount, the WTO now has an active legal system that certainly acts as a spur to negotiation. How far the WTO system has come from its diplomatic origins in GATT, how thick has become its layer of legality, can be seen by considering the reports issued by panels and the Appellate Body, described in this book, and comparing them to the report of the first dispute decided in GATT. That decision was made on 24 August 1948, well before the advent of panels or even working parties to deal with disputes.[5] In that first case, the Netherlands complained at a meeting of the CONTRACTING PARTIES that Cuba was applying a five percent consular tax to imports from some countries, but only a two percent tax to imports from others. The issue before the CONTRACTING PARTIES, therefore, was whether consular taxes were covered by the term "charges of any kind" in GATT Article I:1, dealing with most-favoured-nation treatment. The Chairman of the session ruled that they were:

> In response to a request for an interpretation of the phrase "charges of any kind" in paragraph 1 of Article I with respect to consular taxes, the Chairman ruled that such taxes would be covered by the phrase "charges of any kind."[6]

This single sentence constitutes the entirety of GATT's first dispute settlement "report." The process certainly was informal, but it was the seed from which the current system grew. True, the complaint at a meeting of the GATT CONTRACTING PARTIES, and the ensuing ruling by the chair, were not the result of "litigation" as that term normally is used. But if those events were not genuine litigation, they were not simple diplomacy either. In resolving that first dispute, the CONTRACTING PARTIES put

[3] *Update of WTO Dispute Settlement Cases*, WT/DS/OV/13, 1 May 2003.

[4] *Id.*

[5] *See* Robert E. Hudec, THE GATT LEGAL SYSTEM AND WORLD TRADE DIPLOMACY (2d ed., Butterworth, 1990).

[6] BISD II/12.

down GATT's first, thin layer of legality. The incremental addition of a multitude of layers over the years established today's rather remarkably thick system of legality as the basis for settling international commercial disputes.

Initially, GATT parties adapted Articles XXII and XXIII. Later, they added formality with the *Understanding on Notification, Consultation, Dispute Settlement and Surveillance* and its *Agreed Description of the Customary Practice of the GATT in the Field of Dispute Settlement* at the conclusion of the Tokyo Round.[7] Subsequent reaffirmations and the 1989 *Montreal Rules* preceded the negotiation of the DSU.[8] While the decisions to move from positive to negative consensus and to establish an Appellate Body were not part of this gradually thickening process, the decision to take these important steps was no doubt made far easier by confidence in the preceding system. The addition of the DSU, and its important thickening of legality, has resulted in the most active and most advanced legal system in the larger field of public international law.

[7] BISD 26S/210, 215. [8] *See* generally, § 1.01[5].

APPENDIX

Working procedures for the panel

1. In its proceedings the Panel shall follow the relevant provisions of the Dispute Settlement Understanding (DSU). In addition, the following working procedures shall apply.

2. The panel shall meet in closed session. The parties to the dispute, and interested third parties, shall be present at the meetings only when invited by the Panel to appear before it.

3. The deliberations of the Panel and the documents submitted to it shall be kept confidential. Nothing in the DSU shall preclude a party to a dispute from disclosing statements of its own positions to the public. Members shall treat as confidential information submitted by another Member to the Panel which that Member has designated as confidential. Where a party to a dispute submits a confidential version of its written submissions to the Panel, it shall also, upon request of a Member, provide a non-confidential summary of the information contained in its submissions that could be disclosed to the public.

4. Before the first substantive meeting of the Panel with the parties, the parties to the dispute shall transmit to the Panel written submissions in which they present the facts of the case and their arguments.

5. At its first substantive meeting with the parties, the Panel shall ask the party which has brought the complaint to present its case. Subsequently, and at the same meeting, the party against which the complaint has been brought shall be asked to present its point of view.

6. All third parties which have notified their interest in the dispute to the Dispute Settlement Body shall be invited in writing to present their views during a session of the first substantive meeting of the panel set aside for that purpose. All such third parties may be present during the entirety of this session.

7. Formal rebuttals shall be made at a second substantive meeting of the Panel. The party complained against shall have the right to take the floor

first to be followed by the complaining party. The parties shall submit, prior to that meeting, written rebuttals to the Panel.

8. The Panel may at any time put questions to the parties and ask them for explanations either in the course of a meeting with the parties or in writing.

9. The parties to the dispute and any third party invited to present its views shall make available to the Panel and the other party or parties a written version of their oral statements not later than the day after the oral statement is presented.

10. In the interest of full transparency, the presentations, rebuttals and statements referred to in paragraphs 5 to 8 shall be made in the presence of the parties. Moreover, each party's written submissions, including any comments on the descriptive part of the report and responses to questions put by the Panel, shall be made available to the other party or parties.

11. To facilitate the maintenance of the record of the dispute, and to maximize the clarity of submissions, in particular, the references to exhibits submitted by parties, it is suggested that parties sequentially number their exhibits throughout the course of the dispute.

12. The parties shall provide the Secretariat with executive summaries of the claims and arguments contained in their written submissions and oral presentations. These executive summaries will be used by the Secretariat only for the purpose of assisting the Secretariat in drafting a concise arguments section of the Panel report so as to facilitate timely translation and circulation of the Panel report to the Members. They shall not serve in any way as a substitute for the submissions of the parties. The summaries of the first written submission and rebuttal written submission shall be limited to 10 pages each, and the summaries of the oral statements at the meetings will be limited to 5 pages each. Third parties are requested to provide the Panel with executive summaries of their written submissions and oral presentations, of no more than 5 pages each. The executive summaries shall be submitted to the Secretariat within ten days of the original submission or oral statement concerned. Paragraph 17 shall be applied to the service of executive summaries.

13. A party shall submit any request for preliminary ruling not later than its first submission to the Panel. If the complaining party requests such a ruling, the respondent shall submit its response to the request in its first submission. If the respondent requests such a ruling, the complaining party shall submit its response to the request prior to the first substantive meeting of the Panel, at a time to be determined by the Panel in light of

the request. Exceptions to this procedure will be granted upon a showing of good cause.

14. Each party shall submit all factual evidence to the Panel no later than during the first substantive meeting, except with respect to evidence necessary for purposes of rebuttals or answers to questions. Exceptions to this procedure will be granted upon a showing of good cause. The other party shall be accorded a period of time for comment, as appropriate, on any new factual evidence submitted after the first substantive meeting.

15. The parties to the dispute have the right to determine the composition of their own delegations. The parties shall have the responsibility for all members of their delegations and shall ensure that all members of the delegation act in accordance with the rules of the DSU and the Working Procedures of this Panel, particularly in regard to confidentiality of the proceedings.

16. Following issuance of the interim report, the parties shall have two weeks to submit written requests to review precise aspects of the interim report and requests for a further meeting with the Panel. The right to request such a meeting must be exercised at that time. No later requests will be accepted. Following receipt of the written request for review, in cases where no further meeting with the Panel is requested, each party shall have one week to submit written comments on the other party's written request for review. Such comments shall be strictly limited to referencing the other party's written request for review.

17. The following procedures regarding service of documents will apply:

a. Each party and third party shall serve all of its written submissions, including the written versions of their oral statements and their answers to questions, as well as the executive summaries directly on all other parties, and on third parties as appropriate, and confirm that it has done so at the time it provides those submissions to the Secretariat.
b. The parties and third parties should provide their submissions to the Secretariat by *5:30 p.m.* on the deadlines established by the Panel, unless a different time is set by the Panel.
c. The parties and third parties shall provide the Secretariat with *nine paper copies* of each of their written submissions. Seven of these copies should be filed with Mr. . . (Office . . .). Two copies should be filed with the Secretary to the Panel. The final written versions of the parties' and third parties' oral statements shall be provided not later than *5.30 p.m.* of the day following the date of the presentation.

d. The parties and third parties shall provide electronic copies of all submissions to the Secretariat at the time they provide their submissions, if possible in a format compatible with that used by the Secretariat. If the electronic version is provided by e-mail, it should be addressed to DSRegistry@wto.org, and cc'd to. . and . . . . If a diskette is provided, it should be delivered to Mr. . . . .
e. The Panel will endeavour to provide the parties with an electronic version of the descriptive part, the interim report and the final report, as well as of other documents as appropriate. When the Panel transmits to the parties or third parties both paper and electronic versions of a document, the paper version shall constitute the official version for the purposes of the record of the dispute.

BIBLIOGRAPHY

Books

Brenner, Saul & Spaeth, Harold J., STARE INDECISIS: THE ALTERATION OF PRECEDENT ON THE SUPREME COURT (Cambridge, 1995).

Brownlie, Ian, PRINCIPLES OF PUBLIC INTERNATIONAL LAW (4th ed., Oxford, 1990).

Carter, Barry E. & Trimble, Philip R., INTERNATIONAL LAW (2d ed., Little Brown, 1994).

Chayes, Abram & Chayes, Antonia Handler, THE NEW SOVEREIGNTY: COMPLIANCE WITH INTERNATIONAL REGULATORY AGREEMENTS (Harvard, 1995).

Croome, John, RESHAPING THE WORLD TRADING SYSTEM: A HISTORY OF THE URUGUAY ROUND (World Trade Organization, 1995).

Dam, Kenneth W., THE GATT: LAW AND INTERNATIONAL ECONOMIC ORGANIZATION (Chicago, 1970).

Damrosch, Lori F., Henkin, Louis, Pugh, Richard, Schacter, Oscar, Schmidt, Hans, INTERNATIONAL LAW (2d ed., West, 2002).

David, Rene, FRENCH LAW: ITS STRUCTURE, SOURCES, AND METHODOLOGY (Michael Kindred, trans.) (Louisiana State University Press, 1972).

European Commission, REPORT ON UNITED STATES BARRIERS TO TRADE AND INVESTMENT (2002).

Evans, Malcolm (Ed), REMEDIES IN INTERNATIONAL LAW: THE INSTITUTIONAL DILEMMA (Hart, 1998).

Fitzmaurice, Gerald, THE LAW AND PROCEDURE OF THE INTERNATIONAL COURT OF JUSTICE (Cambridge, 1986).

Franck, Thomas, FAIRNESS IN INTERNATIONAL LAW AND INSTITUTIONS (Clarendon Press, 1995).

Gardner, Richard N., STERLING-DOLLAR DIPLOMACY IN CURRENT PERSPECTIVE: THE ORIGINS AND PROSPECTS OF OUR INTERNATIONAL ECONOMIC ORDER (Columbia Univ. Press ed., 1980).

Gaskin, Richard H., BURDENS OF PROOF IN MODERN DISCOURSE (Yale, 1992).

Gray, Christine, JUDICIAL REMEDIES IN INTERNATIONAL LAW (Oxford, 1990).

Hart, H. L. A., THE CONCEPT OF LAW (2d ed., Oxford, 1994).

Higgins, Rosalyn, PROBLEMS & PROCESS: INTERNATIONAL LAW AND HOW WE USE IT (Oxford, 1994).

Hoekman, Bernard & Kostecki, Michael, THE POLITICAL ECONOMY OF THE WORLD TRADING SYSTEM: FROM GATT TO THE WTO (Oxford, 1995).

Hudec, Robert E., ENFORCING INTERNATIONAL TRADE LAW: THE EVOLUTION OF THE MODERN GATT LEGAL SYSTEM (Butterworth, 1993).

Hudec, Robert E., THE GATT LEGAL SYSTEM AND WORLD TRADE DIPLOMACY (2d ed., Butterworth, 1990).

Hudec, Robert E., GATT AND THE DEVELOPING COUNTRIES (Trade Policy Research Centre, 1988).

International Law Commission, REPORT (United Nations, 2000).

Jackson, John H., THE WORLD TRADING SYSTEM (2d ed., MIT Press, 1997).

Jackson, John H., WORLD TRADE AND THE LAW OF GATT (Bobbs-Merrill, 1969).

Kazazi, Mojtaba, BURDEN OF PROOF AND RELATED ISSUES: A STUDY ON EVIDENCE BEFORE INTERNATIONAL TRIBUNALS (Kluwer, 1996).

Long, Oliver, LAW AND ITS LIMITATIONS IN THE GATT MULTILATERAL TRADE SYSTEM (Martinus Nijhoff, 1985).

MacCormick, Neil, LEGAL REASONING AND LEGAL THEORY (Oxford, 1978).

Matsushita, Mitsuo, 5 SELECTED GATT/WTO PANEL REPORTS: SUMMARIES AND COMMENTARIES (Fair Trade Center, Tokyo, 1999).

Messerlin, Patrick, LA NOUVELLE OMC (Dunod, 1995).

Montaigne, Michel de, THE COMPLETE ESSAYS OF MONTAIGNE (Donald M. Frame, Ed) (Stanford, 1965).

Oppenheim, Lassa, INTERNATIONAL LAW (Jennings & Watts, Eds) (9th ed., Longman, 1992).

Paemen, Hugo & Bensch, Alexandra, FROM THE GATT TO THE WTO: THE EUROPEAN COMMUNITY IN THE URUGUAY ROUND (Leuven University Press, 1995).

Preeg, Ernest H., TRADERS IN A BRAVE NEW WORLD: THE URUGUAY ROUND AND THE FUTURE OF THE INTERNATIONAL TRADING SYSTEM (Chicago, 1995).

Rosenne, Shabtai, THE WORLD COURT (5th ed., Martinus Nijhoff, 1995).

Sands, Phillipe, PRINCIPLES OF INTERNATIONAL ENVIRONMENTAL LAW (Manchester Univ. Press, 1995).

Schott, Jeffrey J., THE URUGUAY ROUND: AN ASSESSMENT (Institute for International Economics, 1994).

Shahabuddeen, Mohamed, PRECEDENT IN THE WORLD COURT (Grotius, Cambridge, 1996).

Shaw, Malcolm N., INTERNATIONAL LAW (Grotius, Cambridge, 1991).

Walker, David M., THE SCOTTISH LEGAL SYSTEM (W. Green & Son, 1981).

World Trade Organization, ANALYTICAL INDEX, GUIDE TO GATT LAW AND PRACTICE (1995).

Monographs

Bilder, Richard B., *The Fact/Law Distinction in International Adjudication*, in Richard Lillich (Ed) FACT-FINDING BEFORE INTERNATIONAL TRIBUNALS 95 (Transnational, 1991).

Charnovitz, Steve, *Should the Teeth Be Pulled? An Analysis of WTO Sanctions*, in Kennedy & Southwick (Eds) THE POLITICAL ECONOMY OF INTERNATIONAL TRADE LAW: ESSAYS IN HONOR OF ROBERT E. HUDEC 602 (Cambridge, 2002).

Davey, William J., *A Permanent Panel Body for WTO Dispute Settlement: Desirable or Practical?* in Kennedy & Southwick (Eds) THE POLITICAL ECONOMY OF INTERNATIONAL TRADE LAW: ESSAYS IN HONOR OF ROBERT E. HUDEC 496 (Cambridge, 2002).

Davey, William J., *WTO Dispute Settlement: Segregating the Useful Political Aspects and Avoiding "Over-Legalization,"* in Marco Bronckers & Reinhard Quick (Eds) NEW DIRECTIONS IN INTERNATIONAL ECONOMIC LAW: ESSAYS IN HONOR OF JOHN H. JACKSON 291 (Kluwer, 2000).

Horlick, Gary N., *Problems with the Compliance Structure of the WTO Dispute Resolution Process*, in Kennedy & Southwick (Eds) THE POLITICAL ECONOMY OF INTERNATIONAL TRADE LAW: ESSAYS IN HONOR OF ROBERT E. HUDEC 636 (Cambridge, 2002).

Hudec, Robert E., *Broadening the Scope of Remedies in WTO Dispute Settlement*, in Friedl Weiss (Ed) IMPROVING WTO DISPUTE SETTLEMENT PROCEDURES: ISSUES & LESSONS FROM THE PRACTICE OF OTHER INTERNATIONAL COURTS & TRIBUNALS 369 (Cameron May, 2000).

Hudec, Robert E., *The Role of the GATT Secretariat in the Evolution of the WTO Dispute Settlement Procedure*, in Jagdish Bhagwati & Mathias Hirsch (Eds) THE URUGUAY ROUND AND BEYOND: ESSAYS IN HONOUR OF ARTHUR DUNKEL 101 (Springer-Verlag, 1998).

Jansen, Bernhard, *Scope of Jurisdiction in GATT/WTO Dispute Settlement: Consultations and Panel Requests*, in Friedl Weiss (Ed) IMPROVING WTO DISPUTE SETTLEMENT PROCEDURES: ISSUES AND LESSONS FROM THE PRACTICE OF OTHER INTERNATIONAL COURTS AND TRIBUNALS 45 (Cameron May, 2001).

Lafer, Celso, THE WORLD TRADE ORGANIZATION DISPUTE SETTLEMENT SYSTEM (1996 Gilberto Amado Memorial Lecture, United Nations, 1996).

Mattoo, Aaditya & Mavroidis, Petros C., *Trade Environment and the WTO: How Real Is the Conflict?*, in Ernst-Ulrich Petersmann (Ed) INTERNATIONAL TRADE LAW AND THE GATT/WTO DISPUTE SETTLEMENT SYSTEM (Kluwer, 1997).

Mavroidis, Petros C., *Proposal for Reform of Article 22 of the DSU: Reconsidering the Sequencing Issue and Suspension of Concessions*, in E. U. Petersmann

(Ed) Preparing for the Doha Development Round 81 (European University Institute, Florence, 2002).

Mavroidis, Petros C., *Amicus Curiae Briefs before the WTO: Much Ado About Nothing*, in Armin von Bogdandy, Petros C. Mavroidis and Yves Meny (Eds) European Integration and International Co-ordination: Studies in Transnational Economic Law in Honour of Claus-Dieter Ehlermann (Kluwer, Leiden, 2002).

Palmeter, David & Alexandrov, Stanimir A., *"Inducing Compliance" in WTO Dispute Settlement*, in Kennedy & Southwick (Eds) The Political Economy of International Trade Law: Essays in Honor of Robert E. Hudec 646 (Cambridge, 2002).

Porges, Amelia, *Step by Step to an International Trade Court*, in Kennedy & Southwick (Eds) The Political Economy of International Trade Law: Essays in Honor of Robert E. Hudec 496 (Cambridge, 2002).

Shaw, Malcolm N., *A Practical Look at the International Court of Justice*, in Malcolm Evans (Ed) Remedies in International Law: The Institutional Dilemma 13 (Hart Publishing, Oxford, 1998).

Articles

Alexandrov, Stanimir A., *Non-Appearance before the International Court of Justice*, 33 Columbia Journal of Transnational Law 41 (1995).

Anderson, Kym, *Peculiarities of Retaliation in WTO Dispute Settlement*, 1 World Trade Review 123 (No. 2, July 2002).

Bartels, Lorand, *Applicable Law in WTO Dispute Settlement Proceedings*, 35 Journal of World Trade 499 (No. 3, June 2001).

Bourgeois, Jacques H. J., *Comment on a WTO Permanent Panel Body*, 6 Journal of International Economic Law 211 (No. 1, March 2003).

Carmody, Chi, *Remedies and Conformity under the WTO Agreement*, 5 Journal of International Economic Law 307 (No. 2, June 2002).

Cartland, Michael, *Comment on a WTO Permanent Panel Body*, 6 Journal of International Economic Law 211 (No. 1, March 2003).

Chang, Seung Wha, *Comment on a WTO Permanent Panel Body*, 6 Journal of International Economic Law 211 (No. 1, March 2003).

Charnovitz, Steve, *The WTO's Problematic "Last Resort" Against Noncompliance*, Aussenwirtschaft 57 (2002).

Cottier, Thomas, *The WTO Permanent Panel Body*, 6 Journal of International Economic Law 187 (No. 1, March 2003).

Croley, Steven P. & Jackson, John H., *WTO Dispute Procedures, Standard of Review, and Deference to National Governments*, 90 American Journal of International Law 193 (April 1996).

Davey, William J., *The Case for a Permanent Panel Body*, 6 JOURNAL OF INTERNATIONAL ECONOMIC LAW 177 (No. 1, March 2003).

Davey, William J., *Dispute Settlement in GATT*, 11 FORDHAM INTERNATIONAL LAW JOURNAL 51 (1987).

Ehlermann, Claus-Dieter, *Six Years on the Bench of the "World Trade Court" – Some Personal Experiences as a Member of the Appellate Body of the World Trade Organization*, 36 JOURNAL OF WORLD TRADE 605 (No. 4, August 2002).

Grané, Patricio, *Remedies under WTO Law*, 4 JOURNAL OF INTERNATIONAL ECONOMIC LAW 755 (No. 4, December 2001).

Howse, Robert, *Trade, Environment and the Role of NGOs*, 4 JOURNAL OF WORLD INTELLECTUAL PROPERTY 277 (No. 4, March 2001).

Lacarte, Julio, *Comment on a WTO Permanent Panel Body*, 6 JOURNAL OF INTERNATIONAL ECONOMIC LAW 211 (No. 1, March 2003).

Lennard, Michael, *Navigating by the Stars: Interpreting the WTO Agreements*, 5 JOURNAL OF INTERNATIONAL ECONOMIC LAW 17 (March 2002).

Long, Russell, *United States Law and the International Antidumping Code*, 3 INTERNATIONAL LAWYER 464 (1969).

Lugard, Maurits, *Scope of Appellate Review: Objective Assessment of the Facts and Issues of Law*, 1 JOURNAL OF INTERNATIONAL ECONOMIC LAW 323 (1998).

Marceau, Gabrielle, *A Call for Coherence in International Law: Praises for the Prohibition against "Clinical Isolation" in WTO Dispute Settlement*, 33 JOURNAL OF WORLD TRADE 87 (No. 5, October 1999).

Martha, Rutsel Silvestre J., *Presumptions and Burden of Proof in World Trade Law*, 14 JOURNAL OF INTERNATIONAL ARBITRATION 67 (No. 1, March 1997).

Martha, Rutsel Silvestre J., *World Trade Dispute Settlement and the Exhaustion of Local Remedies Rule*, 30 JOURNAL OF WORLD TRADE 107 (No. 4, August 1996).

Mavroidis, Petros C., *Remedies in the WTO Legal System: Between a Rock and a Hard Place*, 11 EUROPEAN JOURNAL OF INTERNATIONAL LAW 763 (No. 4, December 2000).

Mavroidis, Petros C., *Government Procurement Agreement: The Trondheim Case*, 49 AUSSENWIRTSCHAFT 77 (1993).

McGivern, Brendan P., *Seeking Compliance with WTO Rulings: Theory, Practice, and Alternatives*, 36 INTERNATIONAL LAWYER 141 (No. 1, Spring 2002).

Meagher, Niall P., *The Sound of Silence: Giving Meaning to Omissions in Provisions of the WTO Agreements*, 37 JOURNAL OF WORLD TRADE 417(No. 2, April 2003).

Monnier, Pierre, *The Time to Comply with an Adverse WTO Ruling*, 35 Journal of World Trade 825 (No. 5, October 2001).

Palmeter, David, *The WTO as a Legal System*, 24 FORDHAM INTERNATIONAL LAW JOURNAL 444 (November–December 2000).

Palmeter, David, *The WTO Appellate Body Needs Remand Authority*, 32 Journal of World Trade 51 (No. 1, February 1998).

Palmeter, David, *The WTO Appellate Body's First Decision*, 9 Leiden Journal of International Law 337 (1996).

Palmeter, David, *Section 337 and the WTO Agreements: Still in Violation?*, 20 World Competition No. 1 (September 1996).

Palmeter, David, *A Commentary on the WTO Anti-Dumping Code*, 30 Journal of World Trade 43 (No. 4, August 1996).

Pauwelyn, Joost, *The Role of Public International Law in the WTO: How Far Can We Go?*, 95 American Journal of International Law 535 (April 2001).

Pauwelyn, Joost, *Enforcement and Countermeasures in the WTO: Rules are Rules – Toward a More Collective Approach*, 94 American Journal of International Law 535 (April 2000).

Pauwelyn, Joost, *Evidence, Proof and Persuasion in WTO Dispute Settlement*, 1 Journal of International Economic Law 227 (1998).

Petersmann, Ernst-Ulrich, *The Dispute Settlement of the World Trade Organization and the Evolution of the GATT Dispute Settlement System Since 1948*, 31 Common Market Law Review 1157 (1994).

Petersmann, Ernst-Ulrich, *Dispute Settlement Proceedings in the Field of Antidumping Law*, 28 Common Market Law Review 69 (1991).

Quick, Reinhard, *Trade, Environment and the Role of NGOs*, 4 Journal of World Intellectual Property 281 (No. 4, March 2001).

Roessler, Frieder, *Comment on a WTO Permanent Panel Body*, 6 Journal of International Economic Law 211 (No. 1, March 2003).

Shoyer, Andrew W., *Panel Selection in WTO Proceedings*, 6 Journal of International Economic Law 203 (No. 1, March 2003).

Thomas, J. C., *The Need for Due Process in WTO Proceedings*, 31 Journal of World Trade 45 (No. 1, February 1997).

Trachtman, Joel P., *The Domain of WTO Dispute Settlement*, 40 Harvard International Law Journal 333 (Spring, 1999).

Valles, Cherise M. & McGivern, Brendan P., *The Right to Retaliate under the WTO Agreement: The "Sequencing" Problem*, 34 Journal of World Trade 63 (No. 2, 2000).

Wasescha, Luzius, *Comment on a WTO Permanent Panel Body*, 6 Journal of International Economic Law 211 (No. 1, March 2003).

Weiler, J. H. H., *The Rule of Lawyers and the Ethos of Diplomats: Reflections on the Internal and External Legitimacy of WTO Dispute Settlement*, 35 Journal of World Trade 191 (No. 2, April 2001).

Zonnekeyn, Geert A., *The Appellate Body's Communication on* Amicus Curiae *Briefs in the* Asbestos *Case*, 35 Journal of World Trade 553 (No. 3, June 2001).

INDEX